COMMUNION

COMMUNION

Contemporary Writers Reveal the Bible in Their Lives

EDITED AND INTRODUCED BY

David Rosenberg

ANCHOR BOOKS

New York   London   Toronto   Sydney   Auckland

AN ANCHOR BOOK
PUBLISHED BY DOUBLEDAY
a division of Bantam Doubleday Dell Publishing Group, Inc.
1540 Broadway, New York, New York 10036

ANCHOR BOOKS, DOUBLEDAY, and the portrayal of an anchor are trademarks of Doubleday,
a division of Bantam Doubleday Dell Publishing Group, Inc.

Book design by Jennifer Ann Daddio

The author gratefully acknowledges permission to reprint the following:

Pages 19, 533, 534, excerpts from ''Journey of the Magi'' and ''The Waste Land'' in *Collected Poems 1909–1962* by T. S. Eliot, copyright 1936 by Harcourt Brace & Company, copyright © 1963, 1964 by T. S. Eliot. Reprinted by permission of the publisher.

Page 28, excerpt from ''East Coker'' in *Four Quartets,* copyright 1943 by T. S. Eliot and renewed 1971 by Esme Valerie Eliot. Reprinted by permission of Harcourt Brace & Company.

Page 259, excerpt from ''Nothing Gold Can Stay'' by Robert Frost. Reprinted by permission of Henry Holt & Company, Inc.

Page 532, Ezra Pound, *The Cantos of Ezra Pound,* copyright 1934, 1938, 1948 by Ezra Pound. Reprinted by permission of New Directions Publishing Corp.

Page 503, from *The Changing Light at Sandover* by James Merrill, copyright © 1980, 1982 by James Merrill. Reprinted by permission of Alfred A. Knopf, Inc.

Library of Congress Cataloging-in-Publication Data

Communion: contemporary writers reveal the Bible in their lives /
edited and introduced by David Rosenberg.
p.   cm.
Includes bibliographical references.
1. Bible—Criticism, interpretation, etc.   2. Bible as literature.
3. Bible and literature.   4. Authors, American.   I. Rosenberg,
David, 1943–   .
BS511.2.C646   1996
220.6—dc20   95-31598
                                                              CIP

ISBN 0-385-47483-0
Copyright © 1996 by David Rosenberg

Acknowledgments

For assistance beyond the call, I wish to thank Lew Grimes, Roger Scholl, Papatya Bucak, John Morrone, Walter Brown, and my wife and partner, Rhonda.

Contents

Contents

Part Two

Contents

Part Three

Contents

Introduction: A New Revelation

D A V I D   R O S E N B E R G

Ten years ago I edited a book, *Congregation,* that has remained in print and become a classic in its field. Subtitled *Contemporary Writers Read the Jewish Bible,* it suggested a community of concern, although few of the authors—mostly novelists and poets of Jewish background—had written on the Bible before. How could these writers, from their various careers and backgrounds, share such a remarkably personal connection to a book that had barely figured in the work they were known for? This question, among others, provoked a wide range of appreciative reviews around the country which took the book's publisher by surprise. The publisher had not asked for a book that would break new ground in our culture, but rather for a reference work about the Bible that might be useful to students and others. The editor in chief hardly imagined the book would wind up being reviewed and bought by readers who had not thought about the Bible before.

I myself was not so much amazed as nervous on my publisher's behalf. Once I realized how the authors had taken to heart my suggestion that they write from their inner lives and personal experience, I knew the result would be far more unconventional than the kind of dictionary to the books of the Bible the publisher originally expected. I sensed it in the tremendous responsiveness from the authors, who called and wrote me often. "Do you think it's all right if I talk about my childhood?" several asked. I risked my editorial career by going beyond a perfunctory "yes" and instead encouraging as deep a personal involvement as the author would venture.

In the intervening years, *Congregation*'s way of reading inspired other editors to pursue the subject of writers and the Bible. I was glad to be consulted for Alfred Corn's *Incarnation* (1990) as well as Christina Büchmann's and Celina Spiegel's *Out of the Garden* (1994). Although the writers in *Congregation* had represented only themselves, something extraordinary united them. Their sensibilities as artists had been so long absent from the Bible as a *human* text that we had come to expect that the Bible belonged to an alliance of religious enthusiasts and authorities and academic experts. The human element that was there all along was suppressed, along with the knowledge that writers had authored the Bible's various books. It had become clear that it would take the sensibility of a writer today, a kind of peer across time, to remind us of the Bible's origins in a culture of dynamic writers.

Still, it's not a simple thing to persuade writers to peel away the layers of convention enveloping the Bible. But to start by finding their origins in history and their personal origins in families of various religious belief—this could challenge writers, I thought, to examine how their own voices developed. I began to conceive of a new book that would give these issues life by connecting the Christian tradition of spiritual autobiography to a "memoir of reading." I wanted to encourage a depth of personal reading that was actually a communion—by way of the text—between writers today and their biblical counterparts. In place of a wafer, we would confront the page as a link to the original sensibilities of the Bible's authors.

By convening a group of our leading imaginative writers of mostly Christian background, I had envisioned a book that would provide the basis for a new conversation about heritage, one that I hoped would be a revelation about the Bible in our time. The authors in *Communion* go back to their childhoods and compare the influence then and the influence now of this fundamental text in their lives and in our culture. Addressing both halves of the Bible, the Hebrew Bible and New Testament, Jewish and Christian, they reveal a truly Judeo-Christian Bible that has been turned inside out in our time, with the Hebrew Bible, or Old Testament, no longer being superseded by the New.

Why is it only now that many of our best writers are ready to face the Bible and their own counterparts among biblical poets, storytellers, biographers, and historians? Perhaps for the first time, writers are seeing themselves in the Bible. This vulnerability, so absent among scholars, allows a genuine bridge between two traditions and ways of reading, a Judeo-Christian communion of reading.

If the Bible seems stood on its head in many of these essays, the taboos broken are most likely to be ones against imagination. Every culture is made up of both fact and fiction. Our writers can help us confront the origins of our cultural creativity, as they reflect a clash of cultures in their essays, the Biblical and the American, as well as their childhood culture and the world of adulthood, and attempt to distinguish fact from fiction in each.

Go back, I encouraged the novelists and poets included in *Communion,* to your early experiences with the Bible, and explore the impact of specific books of the Hebrew Bible and the New Testament on your life. It's something all readers can do as well. When you contrast your early experiences to a rereading of the Bible today, I think you'll find a remarkable unfolding begins. In order to express how this process may continue to evolve in the future, I myself had to go back to my own struggle with origins, as it began early in my career as a writer.

One late night in the early 1970s I was making my way home down Second Avenue after a party for two poets who had read their work earlier that evening at St. Mark's Church. In those days in New York's East Village there was rarely any alcohol at such parties. Even the return to beer drinking was a year or two off. Instead, the host put out a table of juices and pot of Oriental teas. There was, however, plenty of grass—marijuana —and just inhaling the air in the crowded apartment would surely make anyone high.

The poets were colleagues of mine, as were most of the partygoers. We published in the same literary magazines. We served our art by holding any sort of job during the daytime while our nights were taken far more seriously, writing and talking poetry. At a typical after-reading party, the talk would move from the poems heard that night to the poems in our pockets. I distinctly remember having my navy pea coat's pockets jammed with folded, typewritten poems that crystalline winter night.

At 15th Street stood the shell of an Orthodox synagogue from the nineteenth century, its windows boarded up. I had passed it by day with no special regard, but now it beckoned in the empty street, the Hebrew letters engraved on its façade standing out among the street's commercial signage. Since I was walking as slowly and reflectively as my pious late grandfather, and this was a place he might have recognized, I stopped, or the words themselves stopped me, for I had noted there were more of them than common in a synagogue's name. I read the synagogue's otherworldly name and then these words: *Bet Midrasha*. I had not seen these words since childhood, it seemed to me, but their meaning effortlessly returned: House of Study. I could have passed the same words on a street in ancient Babylon; the feeling of facing my cultural exile was instantly clear to me.

I saw that I could read the words. I was studying them—or, more accurately perhaps, my soul was—and this lost building from another era had become my personal call to study. When I got home, I opened the Hebrew Bible to see if the words would remain transparent to me. I had not read Hebrew carefully since graduate school. As I read a psalm, I was amazed to see what the words meant, and how different they were from the English translation on the facing page. The psalm looked and read like a poem that could have been crammed in my jacket pocket, modern in punctuation, collagist, surreal in imagery, intensely personal. But the translation sounded impersonal and prayerlike, not at all like the vibrant original. I had *seen* what the words meant. That is, I read them with my own eyes as if they had been written yesterday, while the translation filtered it through a worn-out, institutional language. The English seemed less alive and less modern than the original on which it was based.

Without turning you into a professional poet and translator, as I have become, I believe the essays in *Communion* will provide a similar experience for you with regard to the Bible. Each author sees the Bible through his or her own eyes, unmediated by academic or religious theories. The fresh responses they evoke bring the text to life again, and that is because they have returned to the Bible through the familiar substance of their own lives.

The Bible is often the first *adult* text we confront in childhood; if not, it is probably the first ancient one. It offers a powerful sense of a communion with origins, with our historical as well as our personal childhoods. The Judeo-Christian tradition in particular offers this kind of bridge. What takes the place of an actual communion, metaphorically speaking, is the sacrament of reading and interpreting scriptures, so that communion with the Bible might be called the central sacrament. The act of reading itself becomes a confrontation with origins. In this sense, to commune with a text means to return to the wonder of childhood every time—and to find our way back every time over the bridge of experienced interpretation.

When we first became aware of the Bible as adults, it was layered over with religion, a book where the difficulties of the text were complicated by the theology and doxology of churches and denominations. There was the additional difficulty of Old and New Testaments, the Old a product of a Jewish culture to which Christianity itself was ambivalent. The fact that most of us may be less conflicted about reading Shakespeare than the Bible suggests how difficult it is to read the Bible as great literature, so appropriated has it become by contending aspects of our history and culture.

The Old Testament, as Christianity calls the Hebrew Bible, may make sense as a foundation for the New Testament, but the sense it makes avoids facing the loss of the Hebraic culture that produced it. Yet the culture that wrote the Jewish Bible is one with a long history of facing loss and remembering it. Why not reclaim it with all of its rich underpinnings? This is just what most authors in *Communion* suggest and appear to be doing as they reexplore and reclaim their own childhoods, embracing the whole of their lives and culture.

Communion may breathe life into a Judeo-Christian heritage forged from two seasoned traditions by putting reading back into the context of writers and writing. I knew that I was provoking a secular *Pilgrim's Progress,* asking for a maturity of reading and an exploration of personal growth in equal measure. If our heritage started with the narratives of writers, it continues with writers determined to search their experience and to unearth suppressed conflicts and hidden truths in our shared history.

The unmediated power of spoken words, in life as in dreams and movies, is what *Communion* helps to bring home, words that are artfully crafted to seem spoken directly to us. We feel as though they were spoken because the power of memory and art can recreate a world in which such speaking is possible. In the same way, the fountainhead of ancient writers and poets gave the Bible a sophisticated quality of spokenness: many of the authors imagined the reader hearing the words rather than reading them, passed down by an imaginative illusion of oral tradition rather than through scripture. This ancient irony echoes the modern literary convention of verisimilitude, lending psychological as well as social reality to fiction and poetry, something I learned in my own life as I reexamined my childhood.

As an adolescent poet in Detroit, I was not so much writing poetry as translating a memory of poetry, of how I heard the Psalms in childhood: a speaking to God, chanted gently as if God liked rhyme and lullaby—as if He were my parents' fathers and He was singing through them. I can remember standing no higher than my father's prayer shawl fringes, watching him sing the Hebrew psalms to himself in synagogue. I continue to think of poems as translations—even translations of a child's cries, just as the Bible's psalms will often cry out to mother and father, in between the murmuring and chanting.

Those cries of the inner child are a poet's proof that the unconscious is being heard. Poetry is often about rediscovering an original voice. This first voice remains within, never discarded but too often slowly growing anonymous, until we no longer hear ourselves in it. As a child sitting beside my father, did I want to know what the anonymous text meant? No, I just wanted to be next to my father, even if I began counting the lightbulbs in the chandeliers.

I was glad *he* was doing the praying, because I didn't want to. Yet as long as he participated, I felt part of the team, connected to invisible presences like Dad's father and mother, whose names were on a brass plate on the huge wall of the deceased, a tiny lightbulb beside each family name. I loved reading the names beside those lights; they satisfied my desire for connection, continuity. As I grew older and the biblical words grew plainer before my eyes, the texts themselves began to connect me to all the family names extending into the past.

Are the books of the Bible texts or are they voices? For I knew I had to discover the many human voices behind the liturgy: I had to hear the original poems, stories, and histories. The first voice I discovered in them was my own: had I written this psalm, I told myself as a young poet, I would have been deeply satisfied. Later, the voice within the text emerged, but only after I learned to distinguish the author's literary voice from what I imagined to be the author's intentions. I knew that if I failed to imagine them, I would miss a deep continuity preserved by great, ancient poetry. Today I can still put aside pretenses of progress in our world when I hear the personal voices of the past.

These ancient voices are echoed by the contemporary writers in *Communion*. But you can hear a living voice only if you are alive to the sensibilities of the authors. We can distinguish between the text of the Bible (the Bible as officialized by the religious authorities in the many centuries after the original authors) and the original writers themselves—for instance, those who lived and wrote within the dynamic court culture of the Solomonic period, or the author of the first Gospel from which later authors diverged. It's commonplace to think that the lives of the ancient authors are lost to us and we must respond strictly to an anonymous biblical text, but what holds us back from *speculation* about these authors, and in their full roles supported by modern knowledge? Wouldn't we do the same in reading Plato or Shakespeare if their works had been handed down anonymously?

What holds us back, even now, are the experts and authorities, those who were not imaginative writers themselves. Scholars often speculate about the scribes, interpreters, editors, and redactors of the text—in short, roles that reflect their *own* image—rather than the original writers. What creative writers have to offer in reading the Bible is something different: when they imagine the original writers, they help reveal within the text a voice—in fact, many voices. The new excitement about the Bible today is not over the text itself, but over the controversy of *text* and *voice*. By probing the origins and sources of their own voices, the authors in *Communion* give new authenticity to the experience of the Bible in our culture.

A well-known TV journalist recently explained to me that he wished to do a program about the relevance of the Bible. Could I suggest some writers for the program? I was not able to convince him that "relevance" is not what writers and creative people are looking for. To the contrary, the authors in *Communion* show that the influence of the Bible in their childhood presented a challenge of suppressed voices that had to be overcome. It is the growth of their own voices into literary artists that finally allows them to look back at their youth and see how the voices of the original authors went unpronounced. In place of mere relevance, these authors reclaim the text and give back to it a vitality that reminds us of the living, breathing biblical culture out of which it originated. Instead of illustrating their lives with the text, they illuminate the text with their lives. In what is a new development in our time, these writers respond to something behind the biblical text, sensing the disparate voices there, the various stories that reflect growth, wide-ranging perspective, and the ironies and wisdom of lived experience.

It is a misunderstanding of how writers work, both in biblical times and now, to assert that writers in some pious way engage "tradition." Writers work among living peers first. We cannot imagine a Shakespeare without a Marlowe, an Eliot without a Pound, or an eminent poet today like John Ashbery without an O'Hara. Nor can we imagine the biblical writers except in communication with *their* peers. If the gathering of writers in *Communion* can mirror the original biblical writers in their ambition, appetite for life, and playful (albeit serious) competition, it will be a landmark in American culture.

When it comes to traditions of reading the Bible, the emphasis, necessarily, ends up being on the vitality of the culture we inhabit. For most of us, that culture is not a parochial Christian or Jewish one, but a profoundly American one. In a new book of my own about two biblical authors, I note the tremendous influence of the relationship between David and his God upon Jesus and his Father. Since the Hebrew tradition is fundamental to the origins of the Bible, shouldn't a Christian reader embrace it without embarrassment? And aren't Jews also self-consciously ambivalent about Jesus and his disciples' Jewishness? I believe these concerns melt away before the essays in *Communion*. The writers care first for the vision, not the denomination. Defining a new tradition of reading, voice and text come together here to risk a renewed vulnerability as well as offer a personal testimony.

PART
ONE

Psalms

B R A D F O R D   M O R R O W

INTO THE DARK

I am on the road, dying. Wrapped in sheets and a thermal blanket, I am lying on my back, my knees up and arms at my sides. A woman holds my hand, my left hand. I don't know her, but my eyes are locked on her face. Walnut hair in waves frames an almond shape, pale with hazel eyes; the white blouse of a nurse, with buttons yellow as antique ivory; a strong upcountry woman younger a few years than her patient. Her hands broad, grip firm. She radiates natural compassion, and talks to me. Beyond the kind temper of her words I don't understand what she says. And I keep forgetting her name, however much I would like to remember. She is the last person I will ever see. This is what I have come to believe.

Chilled with fever, now a hundred and five, the infection in my belly has made me swollen like a barrel, and hard as an oak cask to the touch. No one can touch me, because of the severity of the pain. I do my best not to writhe. The Demerol does little to alleviate it, the antibiotics have failed to stem the tide of rot and venom. My white blood cell count has climbed above eighteen thousand toward twenty. My fingers and feet are frozen stiff, as if with frostbite. We are traveling very quickly in the ambulance on the road which is sometimes smooth, often not. When—if—we make it the hundred miles to the hospital in the city, they will open me up to find my sigmoid colon has ruptured, the breach no greater than a penny-nail head, so that in my peritoneum there exists a small, potent cesspool and my blood has become a river of filth. Peritonitis. I am jaundiced, my hands are yellow with hepatitis. For two days I have been septic, languishing in a small country hospital, misdiagnosed with classic acute diverticulitis. Would that it were, bad as that is.

I do not struggle to maintain consciousness; am terribly awake. This woman holding my hands is a nurse—I remember her name now—and yes, we are on the road in an ambulance. It is August and the high branches of maples and willows and ash, which I can see falling behind out the square windows, are lush auspicious green. I know this road well. The Hudson River is a few hundred yards to the east, rolling along at the base of sheer red cliffs.

My question is, Which goes into shock first, the liver or brain? And if I do survive will it be in a coma? My question is, Do the comatose dream? I must believe they do. And would a coma relieve me from this intimate torture? I doubt it would. My question is, Would these questions come to an end were I locked inside a coma?

The pain is difficult to pinpoint. That is, when they ask me, Where is the pain? I can answer with a wave of my hand over my middle, but it is now no longer the truth, no longer exact. The pain has grown toward completion. It embraces and envelops me so that it and I are becoming indistinguishable. Neither enemy nor perverse friend, the agony is me and none other. In my visual scape occasional corpuscle-shaped, fist-sized gray-black holes now and then float across the world inside the little silver room that journeys down the parkway. The nausea is persistent, and I am stiff as if rigor mortis had already set in. Bursts of quaking continue to surge through me from head down, or beginning in the shoulders and splitting outward into the arms. Each ripple, every seam and pothole, produces a thick searing sensation.

The driver has asked would I mind if he plays country music on the radio. I don't want to hear country music, but say nothing. Despite myself, I hearten to the singing, the Dobro, the classic country base line. Then, the music is forgotten. This dark room must be where the coma comes, is what I think, or thought.

Never learned to dance the fandango. Never read *Don Quixote,* failed to see the Parthenon, somehow never found time to visit my grandparents' graves in Blue Hill, Nebraska, and Decatur, Alabama. The unfinished work, the unsaid apologies, the unstated affections. Never had children, failed at marriage but not at the friendships. Here on the gibbet swung high, confessionless and solitary.

Thoughts, some clichéd and some not, cascade, then center again—a distinct passage, that manner of thought—what I might have done and didn't, what I should have said but hadn't, where I could have gone and never did—all these just ceased. Regret gone, I am back with the woman who sits beside me on a steel bench. The plastic bag hung on a corkscrew silver finger above jigs, drips into the vial that feeds the tube which snakes down to the needle in my forearm. Saline and Cipro. We pass under a stone bridge, pink granite and shiny gray. What a gentle, beautiful arch.

And then I am in a new sphere of reflection.

What is fascinating is that I am fascinated by what fascinates me, here in this—can it possibly be called?—predicament. What fascinates me is that all these bodily doings are the source of a kind of objective interest to me.

Is this evidence of mind-body duality? The mind is sharp and quick and has, I swear, withdrawn to the back of my skull, there in the lower right quadrant. That is where it has established itself. The body is going down as the imagination remains steadier than ever, and marvelously engaged. White noise impedes sometimes—the radio now bothers me and I think to ask the driver to turn it down, but then reconsider: maybe the music, which he loves, will help him get us there quicker—but for the most part, it is my imagination that may be keeping me alive now. And that fascination is, to me, fascinating.

Plato found that both pleasure and pain "arising in the soul are a kind of motion" and that an intermediate state between the two exists, which he termed "quietude." My imagination was operative, I believe, in this median realm, paradoxical as that might seem. It burst forth moment to moment, in agreement with a physical burst of agony, but generally held to quietude. It watched, as best it could, horrified and entranced. Because it harbored in quietude, language and imagery could move over its surface with fresh ease, and without my having to work at it. The imagery was dark and cast in a deep red the color of old rose hips. The words came, it seemed, in random ensembles, from memory. And it, my imagination, gathered these phrases like an herbalist rare, curative flora. I thought they were bits of verse from different books of the Bible, plaited with passages from hymns my mother taught me. But it had been so long since I read the Bible, I no longer could be sure even if they were biblical, let alone what book of the Bible they might be from. If they were debris from hymns I once sang in the children's choir, I couldn't remember which hymns were which. I had been away from the church for more than half my life. The sources were forgotten.

Still, like that herbalist, I collected the phrases against the prospect I might survive this journey. If so, it would be valuable to return to them in health and look at them in a stronger light. I wait and listen.

In Which Music Lifts like Firm Hands

The Lord was my shepherd, then the Lord was not. Once, I was made to lie beside still waters, guided perhaps with a staff veiled from my youthful eye, a rod and a staff that promised—in the perfect silence of fluid tranquility—something. Promised comfort, and promised peace. Peace, repose, serenity. Yet, my wars lay ahead of me, and peace was nothing that I might logically have yearned for back then. Of what use is repose to a wild boy growing up on the westernmost margin of high plains where the earth suddenly surges into mountains? I who could see the snow-hatted range of the Continental Divide from my bedroom window, who was far more likely to plunge into the slow, rich-brown irrigation canal near our house from a tire swing strung from a cottonwood, and make the cannonball splash as my friends howled and shrieked and raced back and forth on the dusty bank, than lie beside any still waters—what did I want with serenity, repose, peace? But yet the Lord was my shepherd, back then, and I was in the fold.

The family Bible lies opened on the kitchen table. My mother sits across the table from me as I recite. Wrote, rote; writ, rite. The words are learned by sound, as this is the only way I can hang on to them. Meaning seeps in later, or not at all. On the piano I can vault through Bach and Mozart, but these words are more slippery and difficult for me. The pure nonsense of naming the books of the Bible I find as easy as stringing together in memory consequent words such as those that make up a short psalm. Genesis, Exodus, Leviticus have the rhythm of Morse Code: dit-dah-dah, dit-dah-dah, dah-dit-dah-dah. Easy enough. But if there is meaning, already I want to remold, revise. The Lord is a shepherd, I push Him away. The Lord is your shepherd, have Him yourself. The tiniest verb changes everything, including the expression on my mother's face as she pours herself more coffee and urges me to try again.

She was the organist at the First Methodist Church. She also directed the choir. Too poor for baby-sitters, she brought me and my sister along with her to the church when she practiced. We played hide-and-seek in the sanctuary, raced the aisles between pews in endless games of tag, as the church reverberated with oratorios and hymns from the huge pipe organ. Massive ramparts of organ sound, the pedal bass so heavy it pommeled my bony chest, the carillon tinkling, the reedy oboesque and French horn notes made deliciously wavery through the speaker in the choir loft.

Religion was twofold for me. It was that swelling in my heart which I adored as I crouched in a dark niche on the altar, hiding from my sister— that swelling that was the natural response to my mother's music on the church organ. And it was that fought-for psalm that began with the words, *The Lord is my shepherd, I shall not want.*

Sermons were lost on me. I more clearly remember the scent of the Wrigley's Spearmint gum my grandfather was apt quietly to chew throughout the course of the service on Sunday mornings than any sermon. That, and my father's aftershave. Somehow, however, I got it into my head that I would grow up to be a preacher. This beanpole who survived Sunday mornings because of what that organ aroused in his narrow breast and little unto nothing else, a preacher? My early desire was eclipsed soon enough by the conviction I would grow up to compose religious music for the organ. In my head, in bed at night, I would improvise music for fantastic thousand-voiced choirs and impossible pipe organs. Violins, cellos, bassoons, timpani —the orchestras were vast, seated on hillsides, and responsive to the universal and unpredictable directions in which their mighty, if small, maker saw fit to take them.

Music *was* religion, in other words. And Psalm 23 became my whole and exclusive Bible, because it was music more than any other passage I read, its meanings almost (almost) secondary to its melody and measure. It has always been, like my impromptu, private cantatas and konzertes, subject to improvisational reshuffling. Even now, after glancing at the text, I see I have remodeled Psalm 23:2. *He maketh me to lie down in green pastures: he leadeth me beside the still waters,* it reads. And here I remembered it so clearly that He would have had me to walk with Him in green pastures and lie down beside still waters—the ponderous muddy waters of our dear canal.

THIRD MEDITATION

Words, then, from the old psalm streamed into my scalded consciousness and as I shored them against my ruin, my little personal apocalypse settling so naturally in on me, I recognized that "these fragments I have shored against my ruins" was itself a fragment. One learned later in life and not quite as basic, because shoring against one's ruin was an adult act and involved a strength and knowledge I sensed I might not have available to me. Shoring things, anything—timbers, the ideas of others—against one's ruin was work only accomplished by an able defender, wasn't it? If so, this was, for me, an absurdity. How might I be able to stave off catastrophe? There was no shoring against this ruin, I thought. I hardly knew where I was. Or what were my chances. Shantih, the peace which passeth all understanding.

This was me clambering outside the process of this death, which was what my body was experiencing that August evening, peritonitic, hepatitic, and gangrenous, the contents of my colon awash in me. I would find out some days later that I should not have survived.

But survival is another story. In the quiet chrysalis of the ambulance, the line from Eliot's *The Wasteland* helped define what was transpiring, while the other fragments were building materials borne into remembrance —and they were *borne,* very much so, special and somehow aloft. They were from the first book I ever read.

Yea though I walk through the valley of the shadow of death thy rod and thy staff they comfort me.

No, it was not prayer. Was it a deflection, a warding off, an inept vesper service conducted in helpless freefall? *I will fear no evil,* more words manifest as if by their own will, and though they didn't form themselves into prayer it would be untruthful to declare they didn't comfort me. There was a warmth and luxury of childhood carried with them, less psychic Dilaudid than the solace of familiarity and the reminder of times that were not like the present time, times that were so plentiful with the energy of simply being alive that the squalor, torture, flesh-sadness, the inarguable defeat of life by death was not so much as a fleck of a dark star on the horizon of possibility. Yahweh understood the power of language, and by giving Adam the task of naming all the beasts and plants on the earth, He gave Adam the opportunity of understanding this power. As I lay there dying, these few simple verses learned so early in my life came back charged with similar ineffable power. That is, their weight was irrationally meaningful, indeed they exceeded meaning.

As the words angled, pitched by, I was able to wonder at them. *The valley of the shadow of death,* now why not just the valley of death? What was the shadow of death? And in that wondering another fragment emerged, *leadeth me beside still waters,* which I placed in the geography of this reverie in the synclinal furrow of the valley.

He leadeth me beside the still waters. He restoreth my soul. All was better when the patient accepted his fate and gave up the critical enquiry and whatever regret would pool like so much worthless sludge, making the fragmentary remembrances darkened. *He restoreth my soul,* the chain of thoughts continued as if guided by their own imperatives. And, of course, I couldn't resist asking that question that had made religion all but impossible for me throughout the course of my life: Yes, all right, but what He? And where? And why?

So, what happened that summer afternoon was not an objective re-view of childhood passages from the book, a revered book, but a revival of remembered images prompted by an imagination that had become all but sure it was about to experience the death of the body that had always housed it. Or, through which it had garnered its knowledge. That is: the death of the hands that held the book in the first place; death of the eyes that read those lines and mouth that spoke the words. The pain was serious flame, a golden scorching ingot placed in my gut. With the psalm I hoped to lift the ingot away, wrest it in tendrils of word and phrase out of me.

Fourth Meditation

The shepherd psalm is not without human frailties and vice. King David is a biblical figure I cherish for the very reason he is so deliciously riven by mortal defect.

''Thou preparest a table before me in the presence of mine enemies,'' we read. As one scholar has noted, without comment: ''A petty ruler of the fourteenth century B.C. addressed the following request to the Pharaoh: 'May he give gifts to his servants while our enemies look on.' '' (El Amarna, 100: 33–35) Isn't it enough to be beloved of a powerful benefactor, and blessed with the various gifts such a Lord would lay upon your table? Must you pray for an envious audience of rivals to watch you eat, drink, and be merry?

Nor is there much largesse in the comfort that is conjured by the shepherd's rod, since the rod would be used to bash in the head of some hungry predator—a wolf or lioness who needs to feed her young, say— who has the bad judgment and rotten luck to come skulking around this particular flock. Better thee than me, poor starving wolf! Hardly the most selfless doctrine ever contrived by the ethicist or priest.

But still, self-sacrifice does not come easily, even to the most magnanimous. The spirit is willing but the flesh is weak, as Jesus well understood at Gethsemane. Indeed, all four evangelists concur that when it came time for Him to fulfill scripture and make His sacrifice, He did not go quietly into that good night, but let out a cry so anguished that even the centurion was moved to believe.

Just as the naming of the beasts of the field and fowl of the air was the first act of man (Genesis 2:19), perhaps a gradual loss of language is one of his last.

She told me her name, and I looked up at her, when we began to cross the bridge into the city and, as I say, I could not remember. The rigging and silver tower and the long graceful curve of the main suspension cables, lit now with white beams, the afternoon having drowned in evening dark, was visible out the windows in the back. I could not remember the name of the bridge. Words were being left behind, replaced by the visible. Words, which above all human inventions I had loved most, began to leave me. Adam had named the birds, and though I had worked hard to learn their names they were not with me anymore. Out the windows I saw a (seagull) drift through vertical cables of (the bridge), and was horrified to see I couldn't touch those simple, specific words. I saw faces and forms, hue and shading and movement, but the names that signed what they were, identified them, were shimmery and evanescent.

This is why the phrase *Yea, though I walk through the valley of the shadow of death* struck me with such power. The normal clamor in my head having abated, these earliest memorized words advanced with resonance and import that shook me with the thrill of discovery. It was as if I myself had invented the phrase. *My cup runneth over, for His name's sake*—what did that mean? because there was some One Named, named and therefore somehow comprehensible or kin, I was rich and even here in this difficulty there was abundance, something to be earned, or fulfilled.

But still, I wasn't so delirious that I claimed for myself full authorship of any of this. It was shared, but I couldn't tell with whom. These were sweet old Bible phrases, I thought, and more the pity I could never bring myself to accept any savior, take a leap of faith into the invisible arms that promised me that *surely goodness and mercy shall follow me all the days of my life.*

I will fear no evil, that comes next. And I didn't fear evil or death or much of anything, not even the ugly continuous pain, nor did I hope to make some deathbed covenant—ah, how American to die in a car—strike some deal, also so American, the usual business of "Please, God, I know I have not believed and know I could have done more and could have done better, please if you can see your way clear to letting me live through this I will, promise promise, cross my heart or hope to . . . I will do more and better in the future, will follow the rules and . . ."—no, that never happened. *I will fear no evil, for thou art with me,* and it would be dishonorable and a lie to claim that I felt altogether alone. As we crossed the bridge a thread of hope must have woven through some of these thoughts and staggered remembrances. After all, I was fighting for my life.

The river, the wide river, the murky light-lined river whose waters were never still, the river beside which I hoped not to lie, we crossed that river and made it to the hospital and within an hour I was anesthetized into oblivion while they opened me right from breastbone down to pubis, heart to loins, and saved me. All the way into the operating room I carried these jumbled fragments, like votive candles, like uncomprehended offerings against my ruin.

CHILDREN'S CORNER

For all the power words may have, they nevertheless are the most delicate thing in existence. We play with words, play hard and fast, exercising our ingenuity, imitating grandfather Adam as we name the world, miming grandmother Eve as we exercise our free will.

It is one of the best-known opening lines in all of literature: *The Lord is my shepherd; I shall not want.* And what do we do with it? As kids we thought we were terribly clever to expand upon the phrase, supplement, bowdler-ize.

> The Lord is my shepherd,
> I shall not want
> Him to make me lie down
> In dogshit to rot.

Another went,

> The Lord is my shepherd
> And I am his sheep,
> With his rod and his staff
> He beats me to sleep.

There were the locker room jokes about cups runnething over. There were pranks, were there not, that had to do with anointing someone's head with oil.

There are, without doubt, many versions more ingenious, sinful, and hilarious than those we esteemed after Sunday school or put into practice all the way through elementary to high school, cheerily blasphemous and, what is worse, painfully foolish.

The psalm survived these antics, just as it will survive each of us who took it up to play with as some toy.

SEVENTH MEDITATION: RETROSPECT

Rereading the Bible as an adult can be a complex, knotty experience. The text exfoliates as history, literature, myth, law, ethics, as well as religious discourse. And try as hard as one may, it is all but impossible to resist the temptations of cross reference, of stopping for a moment to speculate how various Bible stories have echoes and convergences throughout the vast caucus that is Western literature.

When Lot's wife looked back at Sodom and Gomorrah ablaze from brimstone and fire that God rained down from heaven, she disobeyed divine instruction—*Escape for thy life; look not behind thee*—and thus brought upon herself quick catastrophe. One can't help but be reminded of Orpheus and Eurydice; as Orpheus was turned to stone, for a while at least, after he failed to heed the gods' command not to look back at Eurydice until he had passed the valley of Avernus.

The Lord of the Old Testament is often a Lord of covenants and contracts, of apportionment and retribution. Though He doesn't suffer from the human vices that the gods of Ovid's *Metamorphoses* do—Yahweh would not be caught in flagrante delicto with some fair maiden, nor is he henpecked like lusty Jove—He does display a fondness for trials, some of them quite whimsical, at least on the surface. And we, adult readers having some store of complementary literatures, of Greek and Roman mythology, and of traditional fables, naturally make connections, however implausible they may sometimes be. The proviso, for instance, that God sets forth in Eden, that *Of every tree of the garden thou mayest freely eat: But of the tree of the knowledge of good and evil, thou shalt not eat of it,* resembles Bluebeard's. Both Eve and Bluebeard's wife are offered ignorance as the only alternative to disaster. The forbidden fruit and the forbidden door are one and the same. One could argue that Yahweh and Bluebeard both offer impossible choices and that their restrictions are meant to frame both territorial ascendancy of the overlord and the fact that knowledge is indeed power. Power won at a price, however: for, in both stories, it is the woman who is drawn by inquisitiveness to gain knowledge, while forfeiting security. Even the child who knows the fairy tale about Bluebeard doesn't cross-reference to Eve and the serpent in the Tree of Knowledge for comparison. The adult reader, on the other hand, cannot ignore such parallels. It is harder for the adult to read about the flood in Ovid, Gilgamesh, in the Popol Vuh and Hopi lore, and not be reminded of the flood in Noah's time.

There are other things that can draw the adult reader away just long enough to break the spell cast by the story. Seeing it as a maze of myths, and judging it thus. This breaks the concentration, so that the suspension of disbelief that even the most drab and coarse of novelists expects from his reader is not accorded Moses. Considering Eve and Bluebeard's wife, for instance, in the same interior colloquy, quite easily leads one to conclude that here are two equally cruel fables. Bluebeard's wife, inexperienced and virgin, and Eve, denied any childhood in which to grow and thus become experientially thoughtful, are miserably unmatched to the challenges set before them. And at least Bluebeard's wife is saved, by brothers in most versions of the fairy tale, by her intrepid mother in Angela Carter's feminist variation. Eve has no such luck, is put out into the cold along with her mate, whom she has known for all of a week. Judging the judge, in other words, becomes the delicate business of the secular adult reader.

Contemplation of moments where the divine text lapses into illogic or worse: this is not the most desirable approach, either, but it is difficult unto impossible for us to resist. Examples, there are many. Who among analytical Bible readers can abstain from recognizing the problem established by Moses' failure to provide for any origin of Abel's wife (not to mention the transgressive nature of incest in Christian thought—see Deuteronomy 27:22—contradicted by its common occurrence among the earliest generations depicted in the Old Testament). Genesis is so specific, detailed with begats and forested with family trees, that even believers must bridge the gap here: either there was an unnamed Eve prime, created in some separate act of God in order to circumvent the inevitability of incestuous second-generation marriage, or else Eve had a daughter who remains anonymous and was given by Adam the father as helpmeet to his murderous younger son. And what do we make of the famous contradictory accounts of Judas's death in Matthew 27:5 (commits suicide by hanging) and Acts 1:18 (in which Luke informs us that Judas Iscariot "purchased a field with the reward of iniquity; and falling headlong, he burst asunder in the midst, and all his bowels gushed out")? And what about these nine-hundred-year-old patriarchs walking the face of the young earth, and what of the maternity of century-old Sarah? Though, of course, in a world where serpents cajole, old women bear, and miracles are normative, men may die in more ways than one.

That Noah sends out a raven after the flood has abated, before he releases the dove that brings back the olive sprig—there are marvelous details one has forgotten, and these unsettle the reader and complicate in a fascinating way the experience of rereading as well. For an adult who is asked to return to a Bible that has stood on a shelf, the book is simultaneously fresh and timeworn. Thus the knottiness and complexity of the experience: it raises the very questions one found unanswerable so long ago and which proposed that it be shelved, for the interim, until maturity modified the questions, or somehow remedied the problems—like a mason points up cracks in crumbly concrete—that weakened the untenable answers to those questions.

Psalm 23 does not work this way, however. The valley of the shadow of death is, when one stands just there, in it, not much different from the valley of the shadow of death one imagined as a child reader, memorizing the psalm for Sunday school, haunted by it at night alone in bed. The comfort, plain and sweet, promised to the vulnerable child by the majestic, mysterious, benevolent shepherd of the psalm is attractive—no matter how resistant we can be—to the dying adult. But beyond the message, the language of the poem remains of the same surety. There are laws upheld in its construction, laws of wisdom and serenity, and yes of common sense as well. What this psalm offers the child it offers the adult in equal measure. Therein lies its genius.

"In my beginning is my end," Eliot once more rewords the Bible,

Now the light falls
Across an open field, leaving the deep lane
Shuttered with branches, dark in the afternoon
Where you lean against a bank while a van passes.

Life is music, death the pedal point. Life is the dance. Death the stamped earthen dance floor. The pedal point grounds the variation, the ground must be impressed. The shepherd psalm has been my C major scale, my Do-Re-Me. A place to begin, to move from the dominant to the next note, the D, or Re—king, beam of light, the dee of death—and thence up the scale until the octave is reached and repetition is possible. Bring us back to Do—the dough of food, the dew of drink, the do of accomplishment. Bring us back to the end which was again a new beginning for me. Back to the dark in that afternoon, where the van passed through the valley.

Numbers

J A Y N E   A N N E   P H I L L I P S

I am five or six one summer, and I go to Bible school at the Methodist church in my hometown. Later I won't remember much of what we do except the coloring: every day we color pictures of Jesus knocking on doors, turning water into wine, helping the lame to walk; the pictures have (unreadable, to us) Bible verses printed under them. I'll remember the church, how it feels to go there every day for four weeks, as though I have a job or a calling, how it begins to seem familiar, like my house. I've never been anywhere else: day care and kindergarten are still unheard of in West Virginia in 1958, and my family doesn't take vacations. I know I'll start school in the fall, and ride the school bus in from our rural road, but that seems a long way off. Bible school is my first alien sojourn and it takes place in what seems an intricate castle-fortress, a massive red-brick building with two vast stained-glass windows flanking either side of the sanctuary. Mothers walk their children through the wide-flung double doors and proceed down a staircase to the Sunday school rooms and the church basement. For real church we walk up another stairs through the Fellowship room to the sanctuary, a vaulted, massive room so large it holds three fanning curves of deep mahogany pews. I know the lower rooms well because my mother has begun teaching Nursery in the one on the right, the room with the toys. She will teach there for twenty-three years while her own children move on through older Sunday school, on through grade school and high school and college, marriages and divorces and bankruptcies, through all kinds of things—she will be here still, teaching the youngest children "Jesus Loves Me" while their parents attend Early Service.

Today is the last day of Bible school; we mount the stairs on a kind of field trip to the sanctuary, and we sit in the first broad row of pews. The empty sanctuary is as big as we imagine heaven to be: we file down the broad scarlet runway of the central aisle nearly to the chancel rail. I've already been to Communion with my mother and I know people kneel here in great long lines to drink their grape juice from tiny glasses like eyecups, and taste the strange flat wafers, little circular discs that vanish on the tongue. The minister came down from his carved throne to bless everyone with a drop of water. He kept saying, *"This wine is my blood which I shed for thee, take and drink this wine . . ."* The juice was blood and the wafer was bread and the bread was the body of Christ. I know Christ and Jesus are the same, that Jesus is the baby from Christmas, that he grew up and was nailed to the cross. My mother says the cross was in the plan, that it was meant to happen. My older brother, who is eight, says the nails were big as spikes and they went right through Jesus' hands and feet, and that's why there are crosses everywhere in church, even on the front of the minister's robe. The choir wear plain dark red robes and they stand arrayed in lines three deep behind and above the minister in their special loft, and behind them rise the impossibly vast pipes of the organ, each one golden, tongued with a slit.

Numbers

Today the organist is here to play for us and talk about how the organ works. I've worn my best dress for the last day; I sit up straighter and try to keep my crinoline slip from rattling when I move. The organist launches full volume into what she plays during the offering and we feel the music as an avalanche in the empty, echoing sanctuary; the vibration inside us penetrates to the depths of our bones and seems to shake the pew. I know the words: *Christ the Lord is risen today.* That's why it was all right that he got nailed to a cross: later he came back to life. Most of the kids don't know there are words and have never heard the organ. They immediately cover their ears with their hands and howl, and it takes the teacher a while to calm them down. Then she tells us the story of "Jesus and the Children" while we watch noon light stream through the stained-glass panels of the big window above and to our right. There Jesus sits in his scarlet robe and long brown hair, with children gathered near him like angels; there is an indistinct garden all around them, pale green and lavender and pink. "Jesus' helpers thought he was too busy and important to bother with children," the teacher says, "and they sent the children away. But listen to what Jesus said to them: *"Suffer the little children to come unto me, and forbid them not, for of such is the kingdom of God."* The boys near me are getting restless; they lean on one another, the better to lean on me. I plant my patent-leather shoes firmly against the pew in front of us and refuse to be moved. I smell the dusty, boy smell of them and wonder what it means—*suffer* the children. Why should it hurt to come to Jesus? I know: because of what happened to him. For a strange moment I see, in my mind, the crowd below him, all of them in gownlike clothes, looking up in the hot dusty air, and the smell of the boys near me is the smell of that old dust, like trampled flowers drying into smoke. The air is an odd color, luminous and coppery, bronzed almost, and darkening. I hear him breathing; I know I'm in his mind, inside a warmth that is floating and viscous, suffused. I don't have time to be scared, it just happens, and when I come back to myself I glow with the roll and dark float of it, tingling in the shape of my limbs.

The boys are laughing. They've pulled away from me and sit giggling, watching me. I look up at the massive image in stained glass but I can't see. The light has fallen directly into my eyes, directly onto me, like a searchlight; that's why the boys are laughing. Motes of dust float sleepily near my face and I peer through them at the teacher, who suddenly stops talking and looks at me. I realize I haven't heard her voice; I heard something else, a murmurous swell of sound and voices and heavy air, a hymnlike confluence threaded with panic and resignation, as though all the time between now and then was trapped in a shell pressed to my ear. The teacher claps her hands and we're all getting up and filing out. We're out of the sanctuary, off the soft carpeting and on the landing of the broad stairs, which is covered in linoleum, like someone's back hallway. The boy behind me jostles close and whispers, ''Look, it's still there.'' I don't look but I know he means the light is still there, pouring down in one piece.

Downstairs in our basement room there's a party, Coca-Cola, sugar cookies in the shapes of doves, Oreos, and taffy. The teachers organize three whirling circles of Drop-the-Handkerchief, and as we all run frantically chasing each other in our slick-soled shoes the concrete ceiling seems to get lower and lower. Colors flash past me in a whirling continuum underscored with sounds I remember from upstairs, confused, songlike murmurs, and weeping. I walk out of the circle, my vision furry-edged, feeling for a wall to stand against, and I walk right into the teacher. She's knelt in front of me, her hair all blowing back, her face brightly lit. She's moving toward me in the faraway air but she will never reach me, ever. ''What's wrong, hon?'' she says, ''You're not feeling well, are you?'' I say something back in the cadence of speech, but the words aren't words at all and come out confused. ''Never mind,'' she says, ''I've already phoned your mother. She'll be here very soon.'' Suddenly the boys from upstairs jostle into us with their full cups of ice chips and Coke, one of them trips, and the ice and sticky syrup hit me full in the face. I'm so hot and flushed that the cold shock feels like deliverance. I taste the sweetness on my lips and then I fall forward, slowly and luxuriantly, for what seems a long time, though I hear voices sliding past me. *This is my body . . . take and eat this bread . . . a very high-strung child . . . no, too much candy is all . . . honestly, they've ruined this dress . . . get me a wet cloth,* and when I wake up they're pulling my arms out of my sleeves as the other children mill around, cacophonous and released, and my mother is bending over me, wiping my face until I'm cold. I tell her I fell asleep. "No," she says, "you got sick, you fainted, we'll get you some air." She folds the organdy dress she'd ironed so carefully into a small paper bag and puts it in her purse, then she lifts me up a long way and holds me. We make our way up the stairs through an adult crowd pulsing downward, and we're standing on the broad front steps of the church in bright sunlight. Other classes have all ended, there's a huge, loud crowd. I feel naked and weightless in my slip and panties, amazed my mother has undressed me in front of everyone, she who insists on straight bows and starched pinafores for church. I am floating in my mother's arms above the crowd and the air blows a dark thrill through me, as though what happened in the sanctuary cracked me open and the thrill exists in that deep, narrow space. Here in the noontime summer there is a brooding shadow above and around us all. I close my eyes.

I go to church throughout my childhood, sometimes reluctantly, but my mother has such control over us that we dress up each Sunday and sit quietly in a row, my brothers and I, listening to the adult sermon. My father, of course, will have none of it; my mother says wryly that he'd never *darken the door* of a church. When I'm ten the new minister comes, and I'm aware this is a big occurrence among my mother and her friends. They were *devastated* to lose the last one, but she heads the committee to welcome the new man and his family. His name is Reverend Snow, and I realize now he was relatively young, maybe in his mid-thirties. He is trim and tall, with a square face and dark-rimmed glasses; his black hair, slicked back, always looks wet. He's not cold, like his name; he is ruddy and moist and *enthusiastic* (my mother's word); it's as though the dew of perspiration across his brow and nose when he preaches is part of his enthusiasm, the way the scent of aftershave corresponds to the constant shadow on his cheeks. He knows he has a hard act to follow, replacing the kindly professorial man who ran things at the biggest church in town for twenty years, dealing with devastation in the hearts of so many. There is much devastation and there are many churches: the Central Methodists, the EUBs and the Presbyterians, the Central and Southern Baptists, the Lutherans, the Episcopalians, who are practically Catholic, and the Catholic church itself, down by the car dealership on the edge of town. Further out there are other, numerous sects and fellowships up the dirt roads of the hollows, but the doctors and lawyers and dentists of the town, the professors who teach at the local Methodist college, all seem to come here. There are no psychiatrists in our town, no marriage counselors, no (what would later be called) hospice services. There are divorce courts and lawyers and AA meetings, but those are public, and it falls to the ministers to provide what counsel there is concerning death, concerning the business of getting through the day. My mother has told me that once, years ago, she asked my father to go and talk to the minister with her, but of course he wouldn't, he said, *I don't have a problem,* you *have a problem,* you *go and talk to the minister.* Reverend Snow has a secretary to book his appointments: he meets with the men of the church about running the church and he meets with the women about everything else. After services, some of the men and women line up to shake his hand, and I do this with my mother every Sunday, habitually, almost unthinkingly, while my brothers run outside to jostle each other impatiently on the steps. Sometimes she's talking to this or that person and I line up by myself. Today, as I pass the table where they're laid out on a tray, I pick up a palm-sized booklet called *The Upper Room.* I've seen these little pamphlets at home, collections of day-by-day meditations and Bible verses, distributed every month. I know the upper room is where the Last Supper took place, and there on the cover is Jesus with the disciples, behind the long table draped in scarlet. I glance through the pages idly as I move along in line, but I'm thinking about "The Report of the Spies," the presentation I had to give in Sunday school. The disciples all look like spies on the cover of *The Upper Room,* leaning and conversing, talking behind their hands. One of them will betray Jesus with a kiss, the way boys betray girls in Sunday school, kissing the backs of their hands noisily when the girls get up to talk. They do this with me, especially, but they stopped today, immediately, when Reverend Snow came in. He drops in on the classes sometimes, making the rounds, and it seems to be him, too, behind all these presentations—church homework, my brothers call it, and they make no pretense of cooperating. But I find the language of the Bible soporific and odd, with God a mean dad in Numbers, unhappy with the spies. *How long shall I bear with this evil congregation, which murmur against me?* he asks Moses, and he lets only Caleb and Joshua, *who followed him fully,* into the land; he says all the others *shall fall in this wilderness,* and he tells them their hapless children *shall wander . . . forty years, and bear your whoredoms.* I look "whoredom" up in the dictionary but can only find "whore." I know about sex, but the concept is complicated: *bear* as in *give birth, whoredom* as in *kingdom.* Does it mean the children grow up in the wilderness and give birth to girl children who have sex for pay? After all, in forty years, they *would* grow up, moving in a pack like wolves, lost all their lives. And what about boy children born in the wilderness; could boys be whores? How would they do that, and who with?

I don't mention all this in my report. I just say how the Israelites were told by God to displace the sons of giants in the land of milk and honey, how Moses sent his men to *spy out the land of Canaan . . . And see the land, and whether it be fat or lean . . . from the wilderness of Zin unto Rehob,* forty days of grapes and pomegranates. They came back to tell Moses the people were strong, and the cities walled and very great, and they made an evil report to discourage the Jews: *And there we saw the giants, the sons of Anak, which come of the giants, and we were in our own sight as grasshoppers, and so we were in their sight.* They lied or they exaggerated the bad odds because they didn't want to fight and lose, and that's why God was angry.

The boys shuffle in their seats. Fight and lose?

"And what do you make of it?" Reverend Snow asks me. "That is, what's your impression of this passage?"

"Well," I say, "he tells the spies to take the land away from the people who built the walls and cities, and whether they're giants or not, that doesn't seem right, does it?" Looking at Reverend Snow, I imagine snow blowing across the deserts of Egypt, across the moving shadows of wandering children. "I mean, I know the Israelites were slaves and have nowhere to live, but God tells them to take . . ."

"You bring up an interesting point," says Reverend Snow, "and that is the matter of the chosen people. God does make judgments and demands of those who follow him. He is the champion and savior of those who follow him, over those who do not. He tells those who have questioned him that they will fall before their enemies *because ye are turned away from the Lord, therefore the Lord will not be with you.*"

"So because they are chosen," I say, "they will have the land."

"Yes," he says softly, "and from that land, they will spread God's word throughout the world." He stands up and looks around the room at all of us. "It's not easy to be chosen. It's not like winning a contest and getting a prize. It's more like seeing what others don't yet see."

Lost all their lives, I think.

"Holding a live treasure others don't recognize can be a burden," he goes on, "having to protect it and nurture it and explain it, teach it to others." He looks at his watch and nods at me. "Good job, all of you." After he leaves the boys erupt in a frenzy of noises and we all join in, relieved. Now, in line, I look around for my mother. I already intuit that she knows about burdens, carrying her weekday lesson plans and graded first-grade workbooks and writing tablets all carefully corrected in red pencil, the loops of the Bs and Ks and Ps made rounder for kids to trace, carrying paper bags of our outgrown winter clothes to the poorest ones, the ones with no coats or gloves. On Sundays she carries books of Bible stories to read to the nursery kids and an art project in a box, all the pieces cut out to be assembled. When I think about what my father carries I just see him crossing the street in his heavy stride, broad-shouldered, nearly hulking in his winter jacket and felt hat, his head down. I think about *The Upper Room*, voices behind hands, the *murmurings against me,* and suddenly I'm at the front of the line and Reverend Snow has grasped my hand.

"Every Sunday since I've come to this church," he is saying, "this wonderful little girl has come to shake my hand." He bends down and kisses my forehead, and when he touches me with his mouth a wash of electric feeling pulses through me. I step back in surprise and confusion and discover my mother behind me, her hands on my shoulders. I feel myself contained in her hands and sense she is pleased at this recognition of me, but I stand quite still, aware of feeling more than any of them intends. *Neither fear ye the people of the land,* said the words of Numbers, *for they* are *bread for us: their defence is departed from them.* A shudder of wakefulness moves in my chest, secretive and dense. I tilt my head back to look up, up above all our heads at the oculus in the center of the ceiling. There in its round window of chartreuse glass is painted one clear eye, like a mirror, I know, like a spy.

Genesis (Rebecca) and Luke

V　A　L　E　R　I　E　　　S　A　Y　E　R　S

I.

I was born and raised in coastal South
Carolina, where Protestants knew the Bible, chapter and verse, and
Catholics told stories. It wasn't that we didn't memorize, the way
Baptist children did—only that we memorized catechism, not scripture. And it wasn't that we didn't study the word of God systematically, the way Jewish children did—only that we were more likely to
embellish, to dramatize.

On Thursday afternoons, we Catholic children, who went to
public school like everybody else in town, gathered in a big old house
on the river that had been transformed into a parish center, the
bedrooms and sitting rooms and porch reconfigured for our catechism
lessons. The setting, with its fireplaces and its ancient footed bathtubs,

was so uninstitutional that we might have been gathering for a session of ghost stories told by a dotty aunt rather than for Bible stories told by the mission sisters.

The sisters prodded us on a slow march through the *Baltimore Catechism* drills—*What are the seven deadly sins? Think now, what's that called when you laze around on your bed all day reading comic books?*—and then we settled down to the stories. I see a nun holding up a large stiff card with a colored illustration of the woman taken in adultery, but I'm not sure if I am dreaming. The figures in that bland desert landscape are clothed in rich dark reds and greens; the face of the woman is at once shameful and apologetic. The men, hefting stones big as boulders, appear anxious to crush her flat. Iconography is so central to the Catholic tradition and to Catholic vision that I believe I eventually came to think in colored illustrations, and I may well have supplied this picture, and the large stiff card on which it is printed, in my imagination.

I know, however, that I am not dreaming the nuns imported from New York to tell us our Bible stories. Southerners are supposed to be the storytellers, but the nuns from the North were quick studies, extending the narrative, improvising dialogue, pointing out motivation. They liked to mix in the lives of the saints with Bible stories: Maria Goretti, battling off her rapist, was prompted by Mary Magdalene at Christ's feet. Time was fluid, sex pervasive. Sister paused, in the middle of a story, lips pursed, calculating how she might phrase the next sentence. *He wanted to . . . violate her.* Mystery was an old friend, more familiar than biology.

It was in that old white house, the river breeze floating in, the nuns in habit gesturing dramatically, that I pictured the Bible's cast of characters, vibrant as the movie stars who played them and lighted in the same distancing glow. The men, always in leading roles, had the earnest look that comes with a beard. The women were harder to define. The Bible is filled with concubines and women lurking on the edges of a scene: listening, waiting, interceding. We Catholics had Mary as our central vision of womanly purity, of course, but statuary of Mary—arms outstretched, foot crushing the serpent—suggested her silence, her balance, her resolve, her acceptance. To a girl attracted, simultaneously, to rebellion and obedience, Mary was a comfort and a consolation, but she was difficult to read and harder to emulate.

Then there was Rebecca, conniver.

Again I see, or imagine, a stiff, colored card. The scene shows Isaac seated, old and gnarly, eyes squinted, as Jacob approaches to steal away his brother's blessing. Whether the illustration was one a nun held high for a catechism class or one my imagination supplied, I am certain that the story we learned in that old white house focused on a father and two brothers, on smooth Jacob clothing himself in animal skins to masquerade as hairy Esau, on Isaac's horror when he learns of the deception. The story was not about Rebecca.

As a child, my first response was dismay at the injustice of it all. Jacob, having tricked his father, keeps the blessing. He emerges from the scene triumphant and goes on, like those bearded movie stars embarking on their manly adventures, to wrestle with an angel. Perhaps the theme of sibling rivalry was too close to home to hold much fascination. My second and, as it developed, my lasting response centered on the wife and mother who does not appear within the frame of this illustration. What sort of woman sets her husband and her sons up this way? It is Rebecca, after all, who conceives the plot in the first place, Rebecca who decides that Jacob should dress as Esau, Rebecca who talks her younger son into betraying her firstborn. Rebecca, spy in the shadows. Old temptress, Eve's daughter. I gave her a face: an aging beauty, a thousand bitter lines radiating from her mouth. She must have carried herself with grace. She must have still been beautiful—in her younger son's eyes, at any rate. I don't suppose I knew the word *seductive,* but those were seductive lines I used to draw my picture of her. She must have hoarded slights for years, packed her resentments tight in a small bombshell and passed them on to her son. It would not have even occurred to him to light the fuse were it not for his mother. This was a woman who spoke in a hushed voice and smiled a conspirator's smile.

Years later, starting a novel, the name *Rebecca* came to me. The naming of fictional characters is as weighty as the naming of children, as far as I'm concerned, and *Rebecca* took me by surprise. I had conceived a comic novel about three women whose husbands and lover leave them and about their efforts to haul the men back in. The title, *How I Got Him Back,* came first: I wanted to play with the notions of retrieval and revenge, and I meant for the novel to eventually work itself round to one of the characters retrieving religious faith *(Him* as Christ, with a capital H). The name Rebecca suggested a flood of childhood associations: beauty, bitterness, resentment, betrayal. Conniving. I opened the pages of Genesis to read her story again and remembered Rebecca as a young woman at the well, where Abraham's servant, sent to find a wife for Isaac, first sees her.

Rebecca was, in the New American Catholic version I would have read as a child, "a young woman undefiled" and "very beautiful." (The nuns stressed physical beauty, and so did the illustrated cards they held. My heart never failed to sink. These biblical women looked as wistful and docile as Miss America finalists holding each other's hands while one by one they were eliminated from the competition. I suspect that the connection between Rebecca in Genesis and Miss Alabama in her white evening gown is not that much of a stretch for any woman raised in the fifties and sixties, regardless of her religious background.)

In any case, Rebecca is not only beautiful but good: she is chosen when she offers water to Abraham's servant and to his camels. I see the well where they stand. It is identical, in my childhood imagination, to the one where Jesus also asks a woman for water: the well as the bustling center of society, women dipping for water, men hovering nearby. The girls and the women are set loose from their dark dwellings to gossip and jostle and live in the world for a brief moment. Then they will fill their buckets and return with their burdens. The women guard this most basic necessity of life. For Rebecca, the well is the chance to demonstrate her grace. She will go to her husband with dignity and great generosity of spirit. What happens, then, in the intervening years to turn her against her older son and to plot with her favorite for Isaac's blessing?

When she is pregnant, Rebecca feels Jacob and Esau battling within her (in *How I Got Him Back,* Rebecca Perdue's twins are called Jack and Ethan; they also do battle before birth). Yahweh tells Rebecca that two nations are battling within her, that the elder will serve the younger. Is she then following Yahweh's word when she favors her younger son? If that is her motivation, it is soon clouded over with her own very human brand of domestic intrigue.

Esau is an outdoorsman, hairy and ruddy; in David Rosenberg's lovely translation, "they named him Esau, ruffian." The Bible, as always, is absolutely clear about the nasty business of parental favoritism: Isaac favors Esau, Rebecca loves Jacob. Jacob is quiet and keeps to the tents; his mother can control him if he stays close by. And Jacob, who clutched his brother's heel at birth, can control Esau in turn. When an exhausted Esau asks his brother for a mouthful of stew, Jacob sells it to him for the price of his birthright.

Rebecca's deviousness has not yet come into play. She is not even present at Jacob's early moment of capitalist inspiration, when Esau dismisses his birthright, nor is she the only parent doing the favoring. She is only one of four schemers in the family power struggle now, but when her sons pass into manhood she will step forward from the family group and take charge.

Years pass, years in which we must assume that the struggle continues. Rebecca is still beautiful: Isaac tells the men that she is his sister so they will not kill him for her. Esau marries two wives who cause his parents unhappiness. When Isaac is old, his sight failing, his death approaching, he calls Esau to hunt and prepare a meal for him, so that he may give his elder son his blessing.

But Rebecca is eavesdropping, and it is she who tells Jacob to disguise himself as Esau to trick his father. It is her scheme. She goads her son on, prepared to robe him in animal skins so he will be hairy like his brother. She is willing to deceive the old man who has been her husband these long years in order to assure Jacob's ascendancy. Jacob protests that his father will see through the disguise, that he will bring a curse on himself instead of a blessing, but Rebecca's resolve is only strengthened. ''Let the curse fall on me,'' she says. She dresses Jacob in Esau's clothing and the skin of kids, and sends him in to his father with the savory food she has prepared.

And then Rebecca leaves the scene. She is not, as I have said, in the illustration. The picture is only of Isaac and Esau learning together of the deception, Esau weeping bitterly. Isaac tells him that he will live by his sword and serve his brother. Esau resolves to kill Jacob as soon as his father dies. Rebecca reappears briefly, when she learns of the murder plot, to send Jacob away from his brother's wrath, and says to Isaac: ''I am disgusted with life because of the Hethite women: if Jacob should marry a Hethite woman like these, a native of the land, what would life mean to me?''

In those words Rebecca reveals the intervening years of her life: the bitterness she feels toward her elder son's daughters, the jockeying for Jacob's place. *I am disgusted with life.* The generous young woman at the well has turned brother murderously against brother and has tricked the old man her husband has become. *Let the curse fall on me.*

Imagining the claustrophobia of those tents where Rebecca passed her days—her years—I gave her namesake, the character Rebecca Perdue, a cloying atmosphere as well. Rebecca Perdue lives in a subdevelopment in her own desert tent, with bland beige carpeting and an island for her kitchen. Rebecca Perdue also sees her life defined by her husband and her sons; she also favors one son shamelessly; she also has slid from generosity of spirit to manipulation without even knowing she is on the slide. But Rebecca Perdue, fictional character, has her own story (and daughters, through whom she might see a reflection of her early grace). The story of Rebecca, wife of Isaac, mother of Jacob and Esau, must be supplied largely through imagination.

And yet, even with so little of her story told, she is a strong character, this biblical Rebecca. She has stayed with me from childhood, a vision of domestic ambition. Her sons will embrace and make peace, but not for years to come and not until they are far from her tent. And what of her old age? What of *Let the curse fall on me?*

I see her strong to the end. There is resolve in the Rebecca who offers a servant water, who leaves her family to find Isaac in the desert, who schemes to trick Isaac. What must their last days together be like: the deceived old man companion to the aging, beautiful, resolute woman whose sons have finally left home? Where does Rebecca direct her ambitions in her old age, now that she can no longer go out with a bucket, and mingle with the world, and offer it what she has?

Rebecca was not my first character borrowed from the Bible. Early on, my adolescent poetry was filled with references to the sisters Mary and Martha, from Luke's gospel. The story is simple: Jesus visits a village, where a woman named Martha welcomes him to her house. Her sister Mary sits at Jesus' feet to hear him speak. Martha, meanwhile, is busy serving and finally, in frustration, complains to Jesus that her sister is giving her no help. Jesus answers that "only one thing is needful. Mary has chosen the best part, and it will not be taken away from her."

I cannot say how often, over the course of a dozen years of religious education, I heard nuns tell the story of Mary and Martha, but I can certainly remember how clearly they conveyed its centrality to their understanding of the gospels. The story was told with a strange affection I only now recognize as vindication. I was quite shocked to learn later that the whole incident in Luke comprises just five verses. The versions the sisters told us seemed, in my childhood, to rank with the sorrowful, joyful, and glorious mysteries of the Rosary: the most significant events of Christ's life, seen through the eyes of his mother. No wonder this story of another Mary and her sister, Martha, seemed equally significant. Here were not one but two female perspectives.

As the nuns embellished the story, I was able to picture Martha knocking herself out with the housekeeping and serving. I am quite sure I saw her vacuuming (with an ancient Mideast Hoover?), my own chore. I must have pictured, too, the mindless physical pleasures of cleaning, the exhilaration when a small plot of chaotic territory is reclaimed to order, the drudgery of the same work done day after day. I remember distinctly the nuns' sympathy for Martha when she approaches Christ with her tremulous complaint: *I am doing all the work.* We were all on Martha's side, all we females in the class. How many times had we seen our mothers stoop to pick dark male socks off the floor? How many dishes had we washed while brothers in another room sat in front of the television and watched the game?

When the nuns had Jesus tell Martha to *relax,* to take it easy and follow her sister's example, to sit at his feet, I am sure they rolled their eyes for dramatic effect. Just like a man. Exactly how does he think the meal will appear on the table?

But at this point, the nuns, having established their solidarity with overworked housebound women, switched gears. Look what Jesus is doing, they said. He gives Martha permission. (Here the rebellious among us might have protested silently: to sit *at his feet?* But we were too late. The sisters were already picking up speed.) He gives her permission, they said, to take part in the discussion, to have opinions and ideas, to take a break from her toiling, to share with men the thoughts men think.

I remember one youngish nun, eyes ablaze. Clearly, the story of Mary and Martha gave her permission to lead a life of the mind, a life of the spirit, and all fired up, she gave us girls the same permission. I can remember the childhood process of moving past indignation on Martha's part to slow realization of Christ's subversiveness. Still, to a preadolescent girl, full of herself, not yet buttoning her own lip, the notion that women were entitled to sit with men in conversation hardly seemed revolutionary.

And yet the nuns who repeated the story made the two sisters central to my own understanding of women's work, of women's imaginative lives. My writing filled up with Marys and Marthas. In those young poems of mine, Mary was the dreamy intellectual, Martha the practical bustling sister who dealt with dirt and waste and childbirth. If the sibling rivalry of Jacob and Esau, focused on birthrights and blessings, did not hold me, the sibling rivalry of a talker and a cleaner engaged me completely. I was already quite naturally obsessed with sisters and their roles: I had five sisters of my own, and I was of a generation and a place whose girls graduated from high school or, if they were ambitious, college, and tied aprons on immediately thereafter. I not only accepted the notion that I would do the same, I embraced it, and I suspected that for all my gradual understanding of Jesus' words to Mary, I would likely be the Martha hollering out from the bathroom that there were wet towels on the floor and somebody had better come help me pick them up.

My first novel (mercifully, it molders unpublished in a basement box) was called *My Sister Has Left Me,* from Martha's entreaty to Christ: "My sister has left me to serve alone," she says. "Tell her therefore to help me." I named my two sisters Norah and Martha: Norah is the serious, quasi-intellectual sister; Martha is boy-crazy, crazy enough to sleep with her sister's lover. The theme of rivalrous sisters is older than Mary and Martha, of course (I think of Jacob's wives, Rachel and Leah)—but the task I gave Norah in that first novel went beyond forgiving her sister for her treachery. The task is to forgive her sister for *who she is:* a young woman not at all interested in intellectual matters, but rather in mucking about with people, getting to know them, sexually and otherwise. In this way the sisters strangely mix up Mary and Martha: the intellectual sister is withdrawn from the world, the practical sister needs to be in the company of others. Certainly the novel's theme of the need for male approval originates in the story of Mary and Martha. They are not able to mediate their own dispute, but need Jesus to verify which role is important. But, the nuns implied in catechism class, having established the important role, Christ gives Mary and Martha permission to think it through, to mull it over, to discuss it in company. He gives them permission to engage each other in a way that transcends their workaday roles, their daily obligations. Later they will break bread: the first communion is talk.

I see again the young beautiful Rachel at the well: she is only performing a household duty, after all, but she is out in the world, communing with it. She is useful, purposeful, generous, in these days before she retreats into her tent and her intrigues. She has a sense of what she is obliged to give others.

I see Mary at Christ's feet, yearning for a life beyond the domestic.

I see too the nuns come down from New York to teach us Southerners in our Protestant town our Bible stories. They frightened me a little, not because they were the cruel nuns of off-Broadway (our nuns were softies who let us get away with murder), but because they seemed otherworldly with their scrubbed faces, their obscured hair, their hidden bodies. Surely they had toilets to brush, too, in another life: they taught us that all physical labor is dignified, if it is done with dignity, and I believe that to this day—sometimes I even believe it about intellectual labor.

But meanwhile, in the old white house where the nuns left the world of the convent for the larger world, their habits floated out in the breeze right past the world of the domestic. They floated into the life of the mind, into the life of the spirit.

Ezekiel

J   A   M   E   S   C   A   R   R   O   L   L

Catholics called it Our Lady of Perpetual Help, but to the Jews and Protestants who also took turns worshiping there, it was just the chapel. Mary's statue and the crucifix were mostly kept behind blue curtains—Air Force blue, the color of the carpeting, and of the needlepoint kneelers, and of the pew cushions. The little white church with its poking steeple and clear glass Palladian windows could have been the pride of any New England Main Street, but it was the base chapel at Bolling Air Force Base on the north bank of the Potomac River in Washington, D.C. A block to one side, hangars loomed above it, and up the hill, on the other, a Georgian mansion, the Officers' Club, dwarfed the small church, a reminder of what really mattered here.

On a Saturday in February of 1969 more than two hundred people filed into the chapel. The statue of Mary and the wretched crucifix were on display. The paraphernalia of a Roman Catholic liturgy were laid out on the side table and altar—the cruets, the covered chalice, the beeswax candles, the oversized red missal—which the chaplain's assistant would spell "ile." The congregation consisted, among others, of Air Force officers, some in uniform—that blue again—since this event had the character of an official function. A number of them were generals, having come down from Generals Row, the ridge road along the upper slope of the base, beyond the club, where the vice chief, the inspector general, and members of the Air Staff lived. These were the chair-borne commanders of Rolling Thunder, an air war which by then had dropped more bomb tonnage on a peninsula in Asia than the Army Air Corps ever dropped on Germany.

The generals and their wives, easing down the blue carpet of the center aisle, looked for their host and hostess, and found them already seated in the front pew, waiting. They were Lt. General and Mrs. Joseph F. Carroll: Joe and Mary. He was the Founding Director of the Defense Intelligence Agency, the man in charge of counting the enemy and picking targets in Vietnam. Today he wore civvies, a trim blue suit—navy, not Air Force. But with his steely hair, fixed gaze, and erect posture, he looked like what he was. She, a staunch, chin-high Catholic woman, was nearly in possession of a lifelong Irish dream; she was a newly minted mother of a priest. But there was worry in her fingers as beads fed through them. Her lips were moving.

A bell rang. The airman at the Hammond organ began to play, and a seminary choir overcame the thin pipe music with a song. The people stood, joining in with a set of coughs that moved through the chapel like a wind sent to rough up the chipper happiness of the seminarians. A line of altar boys entered from the sacristy in the rear, ambling into the center aisle, leading a procession of a dozen priests wearing stoles and albs, a pair of candle-bearers, a thurifer, the surpliced master of ceremonies, and, last of all, the newly ordained priest come to celebrate his first mass and preach his first anointed sermon. That new priest, with his primly folded hands and his close haircut and his polished black wing tips, was me.

A few minutes later, the Air Force Chief of Chaplains, Maj. Gen. Edward Chess, by church rank a monsignor, whom I had known since he'd accompanied Cardinal Spellman to our quarters for a Christmas visit at a base in Germany years before, stood at the microphone to introduce me. "In a day when our society is so disjointed," he said to his fellow generals, "it is a great joy to know that Father Carroll is on our side."

Say what? On whose side?

I was celebrating my first mass here, as tradition required, because it was my parents' parish—not mine. True, as a student, I had served as an altar boy in this chapel nearly a decade before. My brother Brian had been married at the sister chapel across the Maryland hills at Andrews Air Force Base. A rotation of Air Force chaplains had been welcomed into our family like bachelor uncles. When I had myself entered the seminary after a year at Georgetown University—where I was named Outstanding Air Force ROTC Cadet—it had been with the specific intention of becoming an Air Force chaplain myself. General Chess had been my spiritual director.

But on their side?

When had that unambiguous phrase ceased to describe my position? Perhaps beginning on a Tuesday in November of 1965, when, directly below my father's third-floor window at the Pentagon, a thirty-two-year-old Quaker named Norman Morrison had set himself on fire. It took a couple of years, but by October 15, 1967, I took up a position of my own on roughly the same spot below my father's window. No self-immolator, I only chanted antiwar slogans—but I dared do even that only because fifty thousand others stood chanting with me. I was sure it would never occur to my father that I was out there, and I was careful not to isolate myself from the throng. He never saw me.

As a seminarian I had embraced as an ideal Jesuit Daniel Berrigan, priest and poet. Only months before my ordination, he and his brother led the infamous raid on the draft board offices in Catonsville, Maryland. On their side? By comparison to the Berrigan witness, my anonymous participation in Washington's massive antiwar demonstrations was the height of timidity. In secret I had taken the stainless-steel model B-52 bomber that was my prize for that ROTC award out to a ravine behind the seminary, and I had hurled it, the napalm machine, into a fetid swamp. I remember its gleaming arc as my version of the gods dispelling in mid-air, their annihilation, not ours, as Wallace Stevens had it, "yet it left us feeling that in a measure, we, too, had been annihilated." Shame, hate, permanent shock at photos of little slant-eyed people with melted chins and no eyelids and charred blue skin and fused fingers which had given new meaning to the old word "hit," as in "hit of napalm." I had dreams about the war, about flying airplanes in it—but my puerile fantasy had become a nightmare. Once I dreamed of crashing a jet plane into my parents' house on Generals Row. But it was all a secret, and not just from them. When Gen. Curtis LeMay, a 1968 vice presidential candidate, had put, only a few months before, the most savage warmongering on display, I could not square my shame with the near-worship I had felt for him as our next-door neighbor at Bolling in the early sixties. That was a secret too. I dreaded the thought that my fellow protesters might learn who my neighbors were, much less my father. In public, standing alone, neither to the left nor to the right, had I ever declared myself on the war.

And now? What to my father surely seemed a proper obeisance had become to me the secret cowardice of a *magnum silentium*. He had reason to take absolutely for granted the reliable decorum of my first priestly performance. But my mother, with her worrying fingers, had reason to be anxious, for she had learned never to trust the arrival of a dream, even if she could not imagine, quite, how it might shatter.

Despite my clergy draft exemption, or because of it, mounting the tidy pulpit of that pristine war-church felt exactly like conscription. "On their side?" The chief chaplain's words had hit me like a draft notice, and I felt naked as any inductee before my well-clothed brothers, friends, and neighbors; before a few of my fellow seminarians, hardly peaceniks; before beaming chaplains and generals; before my parents; before—here, finally, was the deepest feeling—the one-man congregation of my father. I could no more look at him than God.

I remember looking at the other bright, uplifted faces. I remember the ridged wood of the lectern edges inside my clutching fingers. I remember the blue of the carpet, the draperies, and those uniforms. And I remember the text it was my sacred calling then to proclaim:

"The hand of Yahweh was laid on me, and he carried me away and set me down in the middle of a valley, a valley full of bones. He made me walk up and down among them. There were vast quantities of these bones on the ground the whole length of the valley; and they were quite dried up."

A mystical vision? The prophet Ezekiel in an epileptic trance? Yet news accounts not many weeks before had described exactly such a scene in the valley below a besieged hilltop called Khesanh. Ten thousand men had been killed in a matter of weeks, and that carnage was in my mind when I, violating the order of the liturgical cycle, chose that reading as the starting point of my first proclamation as a priest—which was my first mistake.

Dry bones? Even before, in subsequent verses, Ezekiel went on to make the meaning of the symbol explicit—"These bones are the whole house of Israel . . . saying our hope has gone, we are as good as dead . . ."—the metaphor rang in the air above that blue-trimmed room, a double-edged image of rebuke, cutting both ways, toward the literal Asian valleys of the dead, and toward the realm of crushed hopes about which some of us had never dared to speak.

"Can these bones live?" I asked in my excursus, repeating Ezekiel's refrain. "Dried and burned by time," I said, "and by desert wind, by the sun and most of all"—I paused, knowing the offense it would be to use a word that tied the image to the real; the one word I must never use in this church, never use with them—"by napalm."

It was as specific as I dared get—or as I needed to. No one but opponents of the war referred to the indiscriminately dropped gelatinous gasoline that adheres to flesh and smolders indefinitely, turning death into torture or leaving wounds impossible to treat. Napalm embodied the perversion of the Air Force, how "Up we go into the wild blue yonder" had become the screeches of children. There was a sick silence in the chapel which only deepened when I repeated, "Can these bones live?" Only now the meaning was, "Can they live after what you have done?"

That was not a real question, of course, about the million Vietnamese whose bones the men in front of me had already scorched, or the thirty thousand Americans who had fallen by then. They were dead, dead, dead. And even a timid, metaphoric evocation of their corpses seemed, in that setting, an act of impudence. "Can these bones live?" I realized at that point in my sermon that I had unconsciously clenched my fist, and raised it. All Power to the People! Hell, No: We Won't Go! Ho, Ho, Ho Chi Minh! NLF Is Gonna Win! *My* fist upraised, as if *I* were Tommie Smith or John Carlos on the medal stand in Mexico City, as if *I* were Bobby Seale. I recall my stupefaction, and now imagine my eyes going to that uplifted arm, draped in the ample folds of my first chasuble. "Can these bones live?"

I answered with Ezekiel's affirmation of the power of Yahweh, the great wind breathing life into the fallen multitude; an image of the resurrection hope central to the faith of Christians. I reached for the spirit of uplift with which I had been trained to end sermons, and perhaps I thought I'd found it. Yes, we can live and love each other, and be on the same side, no matter what. "Peace," as LeMay's SAC motto had it, "is our profession"—yours, perhaps I said, as well as mine. None of us is evil. God loves us all. Who am I to judge? Coming from one who'd just spit the word napalm at them, what crap this must have been to those generals. Amen, Alleluia, Risen indeed.

Can these bones live? In fact, the answer to the question that day was no. Below the blue surfaces, we all knew it. In my mind now I look down at my parents, stiff in the front pew, my mother staring at the rosary beads in her lap, my father stupefied like me, meeting my eyes. He must have known that I had chosen this text. He must have known exactly what it meant: bones? Vietnam? To ask the question was to answer it. My fist was clenched in my father's face. "Prophesy over these bones!" Yahweh commanded. And, coward that I was, I did.

In the Catholic Church to which I was born the theology of the priesthood affirmed that the effect on a man—always a man—of the sacrament of Orders was an "ontological change," a transformation at the deepest level of one's essence and existence. It is an absurdly anachronistic notion, I would say now, but that morning I was living proof of it. My ordination the day before by His Eminence Terence Cardinal Cooke in New York—himself the Military Vicar, the warriors' godfather—had given me an authority I never felt before, and in my first sermon as a priest, it prompted me to break the great rule, as we defined it then, of the separation of church and state, claiming an expertise not only about an abstract moral theology, but about its most specific application; an expertise that my father, for one, had never granted me. "I was not ordained for this," I would have said, sensing the wound that my timid reference had opened in him, "But I can't help it."

After my first mass, there was a reception at the Officers' Club, and I was far from the only one who noticed when my father's fellow generals did not show up. They had no need to pretend, apparently, that my affirming peroration had undone the damage of my impudent reference to the war. My father himself stood stiffly beside me in the boycotted reception line. Looking at it from his side, as I was conditioned promptly to do, I saw that his presence next to me displayed a rather larger portion of parental loyalty than I deserved. I had by then already begun to see what I had done in referring to Vietnam not only as an act of smug self-indulgence, but, conversely, as yet more proof—because I had not, say, refused to offer the Kiss of Peace in that company—of my cowardice. "These bones," I saw too late, were also the whole house of our relationship, and, no, they would not live.

The most dramatic symbol of the ordination ceremony comes when the candidates prostrate themselves on the cold stone floor of the sanctuary. The choir and congregation sing the litany of saints above them, but the *ordinandi* themselves enact the roles of those who have died. Died to the world, is the idea; died to the flesh and the devil. Their bones litter the place before the altar.

"Prophesy over these bones. Say 'Dry bones, I am now going to make the breath enter you, and you will live. I shall put sinews on you. I shall cover you with skin, and give you breath and you will live. And you will learn that I am Yahweh."

While the strains of the litany rose and fell above me the day before my first sermon, I lay on the floor with my face in the crook of my arm. The dry bones were the house of my own soul.

"I prophesied as he had ordered me, and the breath entered the bones. They came to life again, and stood up on their feet."

As I did, without knowing it until later. There were two lasting effects of the sermon I gave on February 23, 1969. The first, and most painful, was the breach it caused between me and my father. For more than two years I had feared that if I dared even to hint at my rejection of the war, however unheroically, if I hinted at my not being "on his side" in the home-front war against armies led by the Berrigans or even Bobby Seale, he would neither understand nor forgive me. In prospect, to a young man, such a consequence is fearsome, but abstractly so. I anticipated my father's reaction accurately, but I never imagined, first, how debilitating to him would be—not my rejection, but all that it symbolized; nor, second, how depressing to me would be our lifelong alienation.

The second effect of that sermon was its manifestation of the kind of priest I had become. Alas, the wrong kind. Wrong for the country—both Berrigans would soon be in jail. And wrong for the Church. Pope John had famously opened the windows to let the wind in. I didn't know it at ordination, but Church renewal had already failed a few months before with the anti-birth control encyclical *Humanae Vitae*. Pope John's wind moved across the valley of dry bones, but did not enter them. I think now that my fate as one who, a short five years later, would violate his solemn vow and leave the priesthood was sealed in that inadvertently clenched fist of mine. The strident question—Can these bones live?—found an answer in Jesus' savage words, "Let the dead bury the dead."

Today, when I read Ezekiel 31:1–14, it is as one who has long since forgotten the trick of tacking uplift onto the end of sermons. To have survived not merely the pain of a father's disapproval, which I foresaw, but the catastrophe of our permanently broken relationship, which I simply could not have imagined, changes the meaning of those dry bones utterly— my meaning, not Ezekiel's. At last I realize what a misreading it was not to see that Ezekiel himself was being bitterly ironic—not uplifting—in the question he put, as well as in the answer he proposed. Ezekiel would be the last to be surprised by the way the death valleys of Vietnam have opened into those of Salvador, Somalia, Haiti, Bosnia, and Rwanda. The bone-littered valleys of *fin-de-siècle* American cities justify the defiant question as much as Khesanh ever did. Notwithstanding the prophet's vision and Yahweh's promise of the wondrous breath, and its power to enflesh bones and reknit sinews and quicken aspiration, it seems to me now that Ezekiel's readiness to apply an accurate image to the real condition of the "whole house of Israel" is what is precious here. No wonder I cannot remember how, in that sermon, I described the prospect of our bones coming alive. What I had no way of knowing yet is that the coming to life is in the telling the truth.

A certain kind of Christian mind inevitably sees the unity between the potent images of Israel's story and the patterns in the life of Jesus. For some, it is impossible not to hear the question Can these bones live? as a version of what pierced Jesus asked on the cross; of what his friends asked at the tomb. At the words, "Yahweh says, 'I am now going to make the breath enter you, and you will live,'" how quickly certain Christian eyes fill in a church-school picture of the stone rolled back on Easter morn. What Jesus never did himself, his followers have been doing ever since— exempting him from the laws of history, the laws of time, according to one of which even his bones have long since crumbled unto dust. St. Paul is famously cited for saying our faith is "foolishness" without the resurrection, but a piety of the resurrection that bypasses the harsh, hope-destroying fact of the crucifixion—bones forever marked with nails—may console us in our lesser suffering, but it does nothing when what we lose is everything. In speaking of the resurrection, some preachers—I was one— are like the chaplain's assistants of my youth, hiding the wretched bones of the real crucifix behind blue curtains.

I read Ezekiel now not as a priest, but as a writer; not as a son, but as a father; not as one denouncing the failures of others, but as one who failed. I accept the bitterness of these verses as of their essence. Instead of providing cheap uplift, the promise that the bones will breathe again, that the house of Israel shall be "settled on its own soil" manifests the present alienation as our true and lasting condition. The Wallace Stevens passage long ago evoked by my discarded stainless-steel B-52 concludes that the mid-air annihilation of the gods "left us feeling dispossessed, and alone in solitude, like children without parents, in a home that seemed deserted." If we dream of a saving reversal, it is to know more fully that such reversals, in our dispensation, do not happen. And that knowledge itself, the opposite of denial, is the sign of our redemption. Whether or not there are benches with their names on them in a garden of the resurrection has no importance for those whose bodies have been—or are being—dismembered. The more mundane horrors of a life like mine—after all, I was lucky, war being what it is, that all I lost was my dad—nevertheless open on the same dark valley. No one asks of strewn bones how they got there.

My faith now is rooted in a writer's imagination, centered on the lived, but also literary experience that the way out of tragedy is through tragedy. Fulfillment and catharsis, joy and redemption are the effects of tragic drama. The movement from pity, which we feel as observers of suffering, to fear, which we feel upon learning that *we* must suffer, approximates the movement from guilt to forgiveness. Words on paper describe the worst things that can happen to a human being, and because the words do so beautifully and truthfully, readers not only survive, but are ennobled. Not only consolation becomes possible, but also hope. "The imagination," in Coleridge's great statement, "is the repetition in human beings of the creative I AM of God." Here is an uplift on which we can depend. The tragic imagination opens onto the religious: if God comes to us, it is in *this* state, not in the restored innocence—youthful body—of a shallow Christian eschatology in which the tragic present is forgotten.

During the Nixon administration, William Rogers defended the team ethic of the Vietnam War by saying, "There gets to be a point where the question is: whose side are you on? Now, I am the Secretary of State of the United States, and I'm on our side."

Because of accidents of my personal history, I associate the forcing of that question with an Air Force chaplain's remark, and Ezekiel's vision of the dry bones. For me, the image of the death-littered valley has always overwhelmed the image of a promised restoration, those bones up and dancing. Even in the era when I could rhetorically evoke the magical breath of God, I did so dutifully. I was too innocent to know it, but my cherished version of the Good News was too thin, too devoid of irony, and too cheaply won to sustain me as a preacher—much less to carry the weight of what was coming. The death-littered valleys of Vietnam—within weeks of my first mass we would learn of the one at My Lai—changed the way I thought of my family, of my nation, of my faith, and of myself. Ultimately, of course, it was all a lesson in mortality: my parents died, although not before my infant daughter did. And now I know, as privileged twenty-six-year-old American men never do, that my bones, too, will be scorched, and the breath will leave my body forever. Far more devastatingly, I know already that I will die as my father did—a failure; the failure I was already when I wounded him with a sermon that was not cruel enough. And why shouldn't this soul be sorrowful?

Yet from here, precisely in this am I seized, not by some falcon-Yahweh who lifts me up, but by the story. I am a writer, no priest: I believe that to be made in God's image is to do this—arrange memory and transform experience according to the structure of narrative. The story is what saves us, beginning in this case with Ezekiel, coming down through valleys and a blue curtain to Jesus, my only God, whose fate was, and remains the same as my father's, mine, and everyone's. Telling his story, in my tradition, is what makes him really present. And that is why this soul, also, can rejoice.

Genesis and Matthew

J   O   H   N   B   A   R   T   H

1.

Bereshith—in Hebrew, the first word of
the first verse of the first chapter of the first book of the Bible—says it
more aptly than does the usual English translation, "In the beginning." Both expressions are adverbial, and their sense is inarguably
the same: *Bereshith* means, indeed, "in the beginning,"[1] its first sylla-
ble corresponding to the English preposition. But if, as John's subsequent gospel affirms (1:1), "In the beginning was the word," then
any form-conscious writer of a creation story will prefer that beginning word to be the word *Beginning*. The text of Genesis (called, in
Hebrew, *Bereshith),* especially its opening chapters, is virtually proto-
Postmodernist in its deployment of what art critics call "significant
form"—the form a metaphor for the content, or form and content

reciprocally emblematical—and the original Hebrew begins the story best: *beginningly.*[2]

In the "Near Eastern" stacks of my university's library, once the distinguished haunt of William Foxwell Albright's Oriental Seminary, there is half an alcove of scholarly commentary, in a babel of languages, on the text of Genesis; enough to frighten any self-respecting fictionist back to his/her trade. Of all this (except for Sacks's excellent treatise aforenoted) I remain programmatically innocent. No professional storyteller, however, especially of the Postmodernist or romantic-formalist persuasion, can fail on rereading this seminal narrative to be struck by two circumstances, no doubt commonplaces among Bible scholars: (1) that the structure of Genesis, particularly of its opening chapter, is self-reflexive, self-similar, even self-demonstrative; and (2) that its narrative procedure echoes, prefigures, or metaphorizes some aspects of current cosmogonical theory.

• Taking, like an artless translator, second things first: As everybody knows, according to the generally accepted Big Bang hypothesis (as opposed to various currently disfavored "steady state" hypotheses), our physical universe in one sense came into existence "all at once"—at the moment dubbed by astrophysicists "Planck Time" (10^{-43} seconds after T-Zero), prior to which the concept *time* is virtually as unintelligible as are physical processes at the infinitely high temperature of the original "naked singularity." Exquisite scientific reasoning from known physical laws and processes has made possible a remarkably precise scenario/timetable for the universe's subsequent expansion and differentiation, through its radical metamorphoses in later fractions of that first second,[3] to the formation of galaxies and solar systems over subsequent billions of years and the evolution of life on Earth—including if not culminating in the day-before-yesterday development of human consciousness and intelligences capable of such rigorous formulations as the Big Bang hypothesis in all its scientific/mathematical splendor. In two other senses, however, the astrophysical creation story ongoes still:

• The observable universe continues the "creative" expansion and exfoliation more or less implicit in its first instant (in the language of complexity physics, or chaos theory, its processes are "sensitively dependent on initial conditions," more particularly on certain aboriginal inhomogeneities crucial to the uneven distribution of matter into galactic clusters, superclusters, and superclusteral "superstrings")—a continuation whose own continuation apparently depends on the as-yet imprecisely known amount and distribution of "dark matter" out there. Moreover,

• The intelligence capable of observing, experimenting, reasoning, theorizing, and reporting on these astrophysical matters likewise continues to evolve, refine itself, and build upon its accumulated knowledge, toward the point where the question of the universe's ultimate denouement (infinite expansion, apocalyptic Big Crunch, whatever) will in all likelihood prove answerable, perhaps also the question whether the extraordinary intelligence that can conceive and successfully address such questions is confined to a few *Homo sapiens* on planet Earth or is after all less parochial than that.

In the astrophysical beginning, in short, were the seeds of several beginnings-within-beginnings: the beginning of spacetime, the beginning of matter, of radiant energy, and of galaxy formation, down (or up) to the beginnings of life, of human consciousness, of rational inquiry, of scientific reasoning and experiment, and of contemporary cosmological speculation capable even of some empirical verification of these several beginnings.

Analogously, Genesis 1:1—"In the beginning, God created heaven and earth"[4]—in one sense says it all. And then the next four verses (i.e., Day One: the creation of light, its division from darkness, their naming as Day and Night, and, coincidentally, the initiation of time) sort of say it all again; and then the remaining twenty-six verses of Chapter 1 (the ensuing five days of creation, echoing on a larger scale and with more particulars the first five verses, themselves an expansion of 1:1) sort of say it all *again*. Whereafter, Chapter 2 (following God's three-verse rest on Day Seven) proceeds to say it all yet again—"This is the generations of the sky and the earth in their creation on the day in which God made the earth and the sky," etc.—replaying the same creation-riffs in so different a key that some scholars take it to be another tune altogether (Sacks, pp. 18ff.). In either case, what's undeniable is that each successive expansion *is* an expansion, both in textual space, like the universe's expansion of physical space (not, strictly speaking, *in* physical space, since at any moment its expanding space is all the space there is), and also in particularity, differentiation, multiplicity. From mere sky and earth in 1:1, we have evolved by 2:23 a cosmos replete with heavenly bodies in motion, speciated life on Earth, and sexually differentiated human beings endowed with language and intelligence, though not yet with upper-case Knowledge and its attendant hazards.

The rest, as they say, is history:[5] the rest of Genesis (creation + fall, flood, and bondage); the rest of the Pentateuch (Genesis + Exodus through Deuteronomy); the rest of the Hebrew Bible (Pentateuch + prophets and "writings"); the rest of the canonical Christian Bible (Hebrew Bible + New Testament)—all implicit in the beginning, *bereshith*. Indeed, one might call the opening verse of Genesis the macrobang from which evolve not only the Jewish and Christian sacred texts but the centuries of commentary thereupon: an evolution no more "finished" than that of the physical universe, as biblical scholarship and archaeology expand our knowledge and understanding of the texts. Witness, for example, the recent scholarly catfights over publication of the Dead Sea Scrolls, and the expectable deluge of associated books and papers now that the text is readily available.

As a creator myself, of word-worlds, I'm admiringly envious—not so much of the universe's genesis, which is beyond my agnostic ken, as of Genesis's genesis; less of divine Creation than of this artfully created creation story.

Did I ever actually *believe* any of it? The six-day cosmogony, Adam and Eve and the serpent, and for that matter the text as God's word and the a priori existence of its divine author? In the sluggishly Christian but essentially secular household of my small-town boyhood, one dutifully attended the neighborhood Methodist Sunday school as a child and then, as an adolescent, the Friday evening Junior Christian Endeavor, as well as "joining church" round about puberty time. I did all that, in the same mainly unprotesting spirit in which I attended Cambridge (Maryland) public schools: It was what one did. But the air of our house, while not openly skeptical, was in no way suffused with religious belief; God, the afterlife, the authority of biblical texts—such matters never entered our table talk. The first time I heard the Genesis story questioned on scientific grounds (God knows where, in that venue), whatever notional assent I'd given it as a literal account slipped lightly away forever, as did by high school days any notion of its divine authorship. Later, in university years and the beginnings of my own authorhood, I would come to appreciate metaphor and to respect the power and profundity of great myths, the biblical creation myth included—but that's another story.

As for the one told in the book of Genesis: Bravo! What a splendid beginning!

2.

For believing Christians, Act Two of the creation drama is mankind's vicarious redemption by the Messiah from Man's original sin and fall from grace in Act One.[6] I shall now audaciously rush in where no angel would presume to tread and draw another analogy with contemporary theoretical physics, as I understand that vertiginous discipline.

Werner Heisenberg's celebrated Uncertainty Principle and Erwin Schrödinger's quantum-mechanical wave-function equations, taken together, declare in effect that the position of an electron, say, is "merely" a field of probabilities until we observe it, whereupon its "wave function collapses" and it may be said to *have* a position. Extrapolating from these axioms of quantum physics, some later theoreticians have maintained that in a sense, at least, such observation may be said to be not only uninnocent (i.e., not non-disturbing) but downright causative: We didn't observe Electron X to be at Point A because that happens to be where it was; that's where it was *because we made the observation,* prior to which its position was no one particular point but a probability field. On the microlevels of particle physics and the macrolevels of astrophysics, such counterintuitive *bizarries* are in rigorous conformity with empirical observation; quantum physics has been an extraordinarily successful scientific theory, with formidable predictive power. The Anthropic Principle, which comes in several flavors,[7] carries these extrapolations to startling lengths: Had our universe not happened to develop precisely within a number of very critical parameters (as could just as possibly and much more probably have been the case), there would have been no evolution of planetary systems, of life, and of intelligences capable of measuring (never "innocently") and theorizing upon those critical parameters. Depending on whether you take your Anthropic Principle in its diluted or its industrial-strength versions, the universe may thus be said to have evolved precisely such that astrophysicists can exist to understand its evolution, or it may be said to exist as we observe it to exist at least in part because we make those (never nondisturbing) observations. As John Wheeler succinctly puts it, "The observer is as essential to the creation of the universe as the universe is to the creation of the observer."

Without rigorous amplification, at least, this smacks of teleology, not to say tautology, as even some proponents of the principle agree

(Wheeler declares that he wholeheartedly believes in his Participatory Anthropic Principle "every February 29th"). It also echoes, in my ears anyhow, the "Christian-dramatic" view that the universe was created as the theater of mankind's fall and messianic redemption. In this view, while the Old Testament implies and validates the New, the New reciprocally completes and validates the Old (more to come on this reciprocity). Every playwright and novel-plotter knows that while the events of Act Two will appear to the audience/reader to have been necessitated by the events of Act One, it is reciprocally true that the events of Act One may be said to have been necessitated by the requirements of Act Two. To Chekhov's aforenoted injunction I would add that many a scriptwriter has been obliged to go back and hang a pistol on the wall in the story's beginning because it turns out to be needed for firing at or near the story's end.[8] Do physicists observe the universe to be such-and-so because its evolution has narrowly permitted the existence of physicists, or vice versa? Was the Messiah's coming necessary because of Original Sin, or was Original Sin (in Catholic tradition, *felix culpa,* Man's "happy fault") necessary for the Messiah's coming?

Either way, it all begins in the beginning, dramaturgically speaking, prefigured in Adam and Eve's tasting the forbidden fruit of knowledge—including self-knowledge, the original causative, uninnocent observation:

> And the eyes of them both were opened, and they
> knew that they were naked; and they sewed fig leaves
> together, and made themselves girdles. . . .

And they likewise stitched together, in their subsequent/consequent generations, everything from scripture and scriptural commentary to quantum physics and the Anthropic Principle—all implicit, though not predictable, *bereshith.*

Not predictable? So says chaos theory of the exfoliation of any complex system, such as the weather or the evolution of life on earth, "sensitively dependent on initial conditions"—small differences among which (Eve eats the apple; Eve doesn't eat the apple; Eve eats, but Adam doesn't; they both do) rather quickly generate large differences in outcome.[9] But such paradoxes of postlapsarian self-consciousness as the Anthropic Principle permit us to muse on some other modes of "reciprocal validation," which I'll approach via a brief detour from scriptural into secular literary classics.

Virgil's *Aeneid* is more aware of itself as a monumental epic poem than are its great predecessors and models, Homer's *Iliad* and *Odyssey*. Just as the poem's story line traces the triumphant Roman empire back to wandering refugees from fallen Troy (and thus settles historical scores with Homer's Greeks), so the Roman poet programmatically combines in Aeneas's adventures an Odyssey and an Iliad, respectfully going one-on-one with the master, so to speak, in episode after episode, as if to say "Anything you Greeks did, we Romans can imitate, equal, and perhaps exceed." Politically and militarily there are winners and losers in such competitions; in art, one does better to speak not of victors and vanquished but of inspiration and reciprocal enrichment. Readers who know both Homer and Virgil find their enjoyment of each enhanced by its prefiguration or reorchestration of the other. Whether or not, as Jorge Luis Borges declares, "Every great writer creates his own precursors" (a sort of literary Anthropic Principle), great artists unquestionably enrich and revalidate their precursors, as well as conversely.[10]

In analogous wise, the Christian New Testament is much aware of itself—or at least its compilers and commentators have been thus aware of it—as following, perhaps as "completing," the Hebrew Bible. To this lay and respectfully agnostic reader, that awareness is most intriguing in what I think of as the Jesus Paradox. Indeed, at a point some decades past in my novelizing career, this paradox virtually possessed my imagination, although I came to it not from any particular preoccupation with the Bible but via a more general preoccupation with the myth of the wandering hero—Joseph Campbell's "hero with a thousand faces"—as it appears in virtually all ages and cultures. The résumés of such mythic figures are famously similar: Lord Raglan's early study *The Hero* lists twenty-two items more or less common to their CVs, from "(1) The hero's mother is a royal virgin," to "(22) He has one or more holy sepulchres," and proceeds to measure against this template a fair assortment of candidates, from Oedipus to Robin Hood, giving each a score.

Fascinated, in the 1960s, with three novels under my authorial belt, I set myself the following thought-experiment: Imagine a candidate for or aspirant to mythic-herohood who happens to *know the script,* so to speak, as Virgil knew Homer's epics and as Dante knew both Virgil's and Homer's, and who takes it as his project to attain mythic-herohood by following that script to the letter: by repeating or imitating in detail the curriculum vitae or typical career moves of his eminent predecessors. Those precursors, let us imagine, unself-consciously did what they did, as we imagine the bardic Homer unself-consciously composing, evolving, or refining his brace of epics; our man, however, does what he does *because he knows that that's what mythic heroes do.* He is, in a word, uninnocent. I then imagined (and got gratifying fictive mileage from) two exemplary, perhaps cautionary, case studies: the minor Greek mythic hero Bellerophon and the tragicomic protagonist of my novel-then-in-progress, *Giles Goat-Boy.*

In Case 1, per my reorchestration of the myth, Perseus's envious cousin Bellerophon conscientiously and meticulously imitates the pattern of mythic-herohood as embodied by his celebrated relative and becomes, not the mythic hero he aspires to be, but a perfect imitation of a mythic hero, which is of course not the same thing at all. He has completed the curricular requirements, as it were, but that circumstance no more makes him a bona fide mythic hero than completing the requirements for an M.A. makes one a true master of the arts. Similarly (to reapproach our subject), one . might imagine a Jim Jones or David Koresh who takes himself to be not only divinely inspired but in some sense the son of God, and who also happens to know the Old Testament prophecies; in order to validate himself as the Messiah, he sees to it that whatever that script calls for—''whatever the part requires,'' as proverbial starlets say—he does, perhaps including even death by immolation or poisoned Kool-Aid. He has followed, more or less to the letter, the messianic curriculum, but . . .

Case 2 is altogether more problematical and interesting: Suppose our candidate to be not merely an aspiring mythic hero or one more entertainer of messianic delusions, but a bona fide young Aeneas or, in fact, the long-prophesied Messiah. He understands what he must do[11]—here is the monster to be slain, as aforewarned; here is the prophesied kingdom to be established or reclaimed; here approaches the foretold dark consummation, etc.—and he does it, not in this case because that is what aspiring mythic heroes or messiahs are expected to do in order to qualify, but because he is in very truth a mythic hero or the Messiah. In short, while the template or the prophecies validate him, he likewise validates them. To get right down to it: Among Jesus' contemporaries, the fellow's claim to messiahship might be buttressed by his doing what Isaiah and company predicted that the Messiah will do; to believing Christians, however, it is at least equally Isaiah's claim to prophethood that is buttressed by Jesus' fulfillment of the prophecies.

That reciprocal or coaxial validation—for Christians, the very crux (pardon the metaphor) of that between the Old and New Testaments—is the paradox of the Jesus Paradox, to which I shall return after pointing out that its secular analog applies not only to ''later-arriving'' mythic heroes like Bellerophon and Aeneas but to later-epic authors like Virgil, not to mention us Postmodernists. As aforesuggested, by writing an *Aeneid* that combines an *Odyssey* with an *Iliad,* Virgil gives the impression of wanting to outdo the Homer of whom he is the self-conscious heir and to whom his Latin epic is also a homage, just as Augustan Rome is at once the cultural heir and the political master of classical Greece. You want to be a great epic poet? Here are your models. Virgil follows them—programmatically but not slavishly—and because he happens to *be* a great epic poet, his *Aeneid* turns out to be not a monumental Case 1 imitation of the great model, but a great epic poem. Thirteen centuries later, Dante compounds the stunt, taking as his literal and figurative guide not "unself-conscious" Homer but self-conscious (and Homer-conscious) Virgil, and not only scripts *himself* into the wandering-hero role but orchestrates his own welcome, as aforefootnoted, into the company of the immortals—in a Limbo, moreover, where they must ineluctably remain but from which he will proceed through Purgatory to Paradise. Talk about chutzpah! Happening to *be* a great poet, however, Dante brings the thing off—and we now return to the Jesus Paradox.

Of the gospeleers, the most "Virgilian" in this respect is Matthew, in whose account of Jesus' career just about *everything* goes literally by the book:

• The Annunciation (1:22, 23): "All this took place to fulfill what the Lord had spoken by the prophet: 'Behold, a virgin shall conceive [etc.].' "[12]

• The family's flight into Egypt (2:15): "This was to fulfill what the Lord had spoken of by the prophet, 'Out of Egypt have I called my son.' "

• Their subsequent residency in Nazareth (2:23): "And [Joseph] went and dwelt in a city called Nazareth, that what was spoken by the prophet might be fulfilled, 'He shall be called a Nazarene.' "

• Jesus' later move to Galilee (4:12–14): ". . . he withdrew into Galilee . . . that what was spoken by the prophet Isaiah might be fulfilled. . . ."

• His "confidential" healing of the sick and the lame (12:15–21): ". . . many followed him, and he healed them all, and ordered them not to make him known. This was to fulfill what was spoken by the prophet Isaiah: '[The Messiah] will not wrangle or cry aloud, nor will anyone hear his voice in the streets. . . .' "

And so on and on. It is from the master himself, one guesses, that the apostle borrows this operative formulation: from Jesus' flat-out declaration in the Sermon on the Mount, as Matthew reports it (5:17)— " '. . . I have come not to abolish [the law and the prophets] but to fulfill them' "—to his reminding those of his followers indignant to the point of violence at his arrest and impending judgment (26:53, 54): " 'Do you think that I cannot appeal to my Father, and he will at once send me more than twelve legions of angels? But how then should the scriptures be fulfilled, that [what's about to happen] must be so?' " For this reader, the climactic such moment comes at the Last Supper, when, facing the prospect of his "death foretold," Jesus declares (25:24), "The Son of man goes as it is written of him." Even nonbelievers may feel a *frisson* at that remark: the hero's calm acceptance of his hard fate. He has, in effect, no choice: If upon his agonized later prayer the bitter cup really *were* rescripted to pass from him, then either he or the sacred original script would be falsified.

Self-conscious, uninnocent mythic herohood; historically aware and prescient messiahship—they are not callings for the faint of heart.

In real, nonscripted life, of course, the distinction between Case 1 and Case 2 heroes and saviors is often notoriously less clear, at least as perceivable from "outside," than it is in these thought experiments.[13] God knows whether the Nazarene from Galilee was the Messiah, although every

Christian ipso facto believes him to have been, and it is only on the hypothesis of his *having* been that the Jesus Paradox is energized. He knows by heart the excruciating script; per the poignant paradox, however, he isn't *acting,* but reciprocally validating to the end what has validated him— from the beginning.

NOTES

1. More precisely, I'm told, it means "In the beginning *of."* Its deployment sans object in Genesis 1:1 is linguistically odd enough so that disagreement among biblical commentators begins, appropriately, with this initial word of scripture. See e.g., Robert D. Sacks, *A Commentary on the Book of Genesis* (Lewiston/Queenston/Lampeter: Mellen Press, 1990), pp. 2–3.

2. In fact, some such English adverb as *Beginningly* or *Originally* would be the formal-metaphoric equivalent of *Bereshith.* But *beginningly,* alas, is an overself-conscious coinage, and *originally* is both forceless and inexact, implying some subsequent re-creation, as in "Originally the story began here, but later . . ." etc. An analogous problem faces English translators of Marcel Proust's *À la recherche du temps perdu:* That monumental novel about time opens with the word *Longtemps,* famously rendered and vitiated by C. K. Scott Moncrieff as "For a long time," which moves the key word to fourth place. The poet Richard Howard's version makes an ingenious restoration: "Time was . . ." (in the sense "There was a time when . . .").

3. E.g., separation of the four elemental forces, prodigious inflation, reciprocal but not quite equal annihilation of subatomic particles and antiparticles, "quark confinement," and the commencement of nucleosynthesis, all within the initial second of Planck Time.

4. Some commentators judiciously prefer "the *sky* and the earth," inasmuch as the theological connotations of *heaven* play no part in this part of the creation story. See Sacks, p. 4.

5. A history which itself rebegins in Chapter 5—"This is the book of the generations of Man," etc. —with its recapitulation of Man's creation on Day Six of Chapter 1 and again in Verse 7 of Chapter 3.

6. Act Three—when, as Chekhov reminds us, all the pistols hung on the wall in Act One must be duly fired—will not be addressed in this essay: Armageddon, Judgment Day, the end of the created world in the Big Crunch of Apocalypse.

7. Notably the Weak, the Strong, and the Participatory, more or less advocated by such distinguished physicists as, respectively, Brandon Carter, Stephen Hawking, and John A. Wheeler.

8. My literary comrade-in-arms Joseph Heller declares that he begins his novels by writing their last chapter first, after which he invents a sequence of events that necessitates that ending.

9. Concerning biological evolution, for example, as well as human history, Stephen Jay Gould remarks, "History can be explained, with satisfying rigor if evidence be adequate, after a sequence of events unfolds, but it cannot be predicted with any precision beforehand" ("The Evolution of Life on Earth," *Scientific American,* October 1994).

10. E.g., Dante's out-Virgiling of Virgil in Canto IV of the *Inferno,* where he writes of himself being saluted in Limbo by the shades of both Homer and Virgil (not to mention Horace, Ovid, and Lucan), who welcome him as their peer.

11. Aeneas sometimes strays from destiny's path, as in his Carthaginian interlude with Queen Dido (Virgil's dutiful remake of Odysseus's long tryst with Calypso), but Mother Venus soon enough corrects his course.

12. A passage that never fails to remind me, profanely but respectfully, of Yeats's awed question in *Leda and the Swan:* "A shudder in the loins engenders there / The broken wall, the burning roof and tower / And Agamemnon dead. . . . / Did she put on his knowledge with his power . . . ?" On Matthew's evidence, the son, if not the mother, did.

13. As instanced by Virgil and Dante, the vocation of artisthood bears some analogy to those of mythic-herohood and messiahship—conspicuously so for the Romantics and the great early Modernists, with their characteristic conception of the artist as hero (one recalls James Joyce's Stephen Dedalus, originally named Stephen Hero, vowing to "forge, in the smithy of my soul, the uncreated conscience of my race"), more modestly so even for Postmoderns. In at least some cases, the present author's included, one's apprentice sense of calling may be far from clear even to oneself, and the "Jesus Paradox" may take on difficult additional dimensions, though seldom with such high stakes as attend the callings of mythic heroes and messiahs. One may be uncertain of both one's vocation and one's talent for it, or confident of one of those but not the other, or confident of both but mistaken, or *doubtful* of both but mistaken, or correct on one or both counts. In the happiest case, one comes to have reasonable faith in both calling and gift and at least some "objective" confirmation that that faith is not altogether misplaced. But "real, nonscripted life" is slippery terrain, in which templates and prophecies are ill-defined, elastic, arguable, and verdicts are forever subject to reversal. One crosses one's fingers, invokes one's muse, and does one's best.

Jonah and Gospels

C A T H E R I N E   T E X I E R

I grew up outside Paris, a French Cath-
olic schoolgirl raised by a devout grandmother who came from Ven-
dée, one of the most fiercely religious provinces of France. It was an
identity that ran deep. I was not just baptized but *vouée au bleu et au
blanc,* which means that for years all my clothes had to be baby blue
and white in honor of the Virgin Mary, and I wore her medal around
my neck. As if that was not enough, I was given Mary's name, plus
the names of four saints, including my first name, Catherine.

In spite of the separation of church and state, French life in the
fifties marched to the tune of the Catholic calendar. Mass on Sunday,
fish on Friday, Lent, Easter Monday, Pentecost, Assumption, Christmas, Epiphany, and every saint's day in between.

Being Catholic meant reciting one *Notre Père* and one *Salut Marie*
every night, and countless more after Confession, the hard wooden

church bench biting against my bare knees, the flames of the white candles jumping around in the dark, steps echoing on the marble floor, dim light filtering through the stained-glass windows. It meant going to Lourdes in pilgrimage for my thirteenth birthday. It meant catechism, Première Communion, Communion Solemnelle. It meant pictures of Jesus crucified, blood dripping from the crown of thorns, and statues of the Virgin Mary with her blue and gold veil, and Nativity scenes at Christmas, and the little white host coming out of the *ciboire* for the communion, tasting bland on the tongue, stuck against the palate until it slowly, slowly melted—you were not supposed to touch it with your teeth. It meant the smell of incense and wax and the shuffle of the choirboys, and the purple and the gold and the sign of the cross.

But it sure didn't mean the Bible.

The Bible was for the Jews and the Protestants, the enemies of Christ and the Heretics. It reeked of sulphur and cold rationalism. It was used by people so puritanical that they eschewed the mysteries and the pomp and the drama of the sacraments for a scholarly life, looking for God between the words. How could God be in a book, since he was hovering above us in the sky in the dazzling light?

We had our missal, our mass book, and what the missal referred to was basically the Gospels and the Apostles' Acts and Epistles, with a few sprinklings from the Old Testament. I don't know if anyone around me had ever owned or held a Bible. I doubt that the curé had one to prepare his sermons. He was known to carry a *bréviaire*. Only at catechism class were we told about the different sections that formed the Bible. But we never saw the book. All we had was our missal, and it is a book of liturgy, a book of rituals, which is not at all the same thing.

I found my old missal back in my mother's house in the South of France. The cover was green leatherette, the leaves tissue-thin, a type of paper that we—ironically—call *papier bible* in French, with the edge still gilded, and when I cracked it open, *images pieuses* floated out from between the pages. They were pictures my friends and I had exchanged at our communion, mostly reproductions of famous religious paintings: Mary holding Baby Jesus, Rembrandt's Emmaus Pilgrims, a Fra Angelico.

This was what I grew up with: the gilded images, the stories, the life of Jesus, the parables, mostly segments of the New Testament cut up and rearranged following the Catholic calendar. As I turned the thin pages, I recognized them, laid out in twin columns—one side in Latin (translated from the original Greek), the other in French: the three Wise Men, the Canaan Wedding, the Healing of the Paralytic, the Merchants in the Temple, the Prodigal Son, all marching forward to culminate in the Stations of the Cross, the Crucifixion, the Resurrection.

The Old Testament stories were more obscure, wild, in the order of the Greek myths: Job and Lot and Abraham and Moses and Noah and Jonah and Jahweh himself were not that distinguishable from Zeus and Hera and Apollo, except they gave off a more somber odor, darkly moralistic and punitive, not as playful. In any case they figured only as background, rumblings announcing "the triumph of Christ and the Church" (quote from my missal).

To open the Bible now, for the first time, is to tread on twice-foreign territory: not only is it the Book of the Heretics, but this particular one that I am holding in my hands, the Oxford Annotated Bible, is in English, the language of the Heretics. So what a surprise to see how familiar it all is. The stories again: Genesis, Noah's ark; the teachings; the Ten Commandments; the parables, each replaying an older theme like a jazz motif.

Jonah, for instance, is one character that I associate with Pinocchio because of his sojourn in the belly of the whale. Didn't Walt Disney make a musical out of Jonah's adventures? But no, Jonah is a prophet, with a whole book to himself. Nineveh and its sinful inhabitants also ring a bell. A quick check in my missal reveals the story of a memorable forty-day fast, forerunner of our Lent, but not a word about Jonah's adventures at sea.

The Book of Jonah, it turns out, is only two and half pages long, a mere blip of a short story compared to the epic Genesis or Exodus. And yet it's packed with enough drama and details to carry a novella, even a novel.

God asks Jonah to preach to Nineveh, the wicked city. Nineveh's wickedness, as I discover by reading the subsequent Book of Nahum, is to have been a "bloody city/all full of lies and booty" where horsemen charge and stumble over dead bodies, "who betrays nations with her / harlotries, / and people with her charms." Sounds like another Gotham.

Understandably overwhelmed by the task, Jonah refuses to give in to God's will. He flees, boards a boat headed for Tarshish, a port in southern Spain, as far away from Israel as you could get in those days traveling by boat. Angry at Jonah's rebellion, God punishes him by unleashing a terrifying storm. Jonah plays dead and hides in the hold. But the ship's sailors cast lots to find out who is responsible for the elements' fury and should be sacrificed.

This whole episode reminds me of the old popular French song *"Le Petit Navire,"* in which a ship sailing across the Mediterranean is stranded without food. The sailors cast lots among themselves to find out who will be eaten. The lot falls on the youngest sailor, who is about to be sacrificed when a school of fish miraculously appears in the waters surrounding the ship, solving the sailors' predicament.

Jonah should be so lucky. Designated by lot, he asks to be tossed overboard. Satisfied, God appeases the sea, but he won't let Jonah off the hook. He sends a great fish (no mention of a whale) to swallow him whole. After a dramatic change of heart, Jonah gives in to the Lord and is spat out, alive, on the shore in order to accomplish his mission.

Whether you believe that God is a deity, Jonah's conscience, or his superior self, God is depicted as almighty and unrelenting. Jonah resists his calling, and as a result is thrown into a series of trials, culminating in his rebirth as a superior human being. What Jonah wants is to live a peaceful and undemanding life. He doesn't want any pressure. He wants to hang out. Sleep. Hide. But his conscience (God) won't leave him alone.

What happens to Jonah in the belly of the beast, we'll never know. The psalm that interrupts the narration is an after-the-fact prayer. One presumes that out of terror, Jonah made a bargain with the Lord: save me and I will answer your call. Or he may have undergone a true rebirth as "the waters closed in over [him]" and accepted his calling. The sojourn "into the deep, / into the heart of the seas" allows Jonah to find his true self through the most horrendous trial, and give up the "vain idols." Now Jonah doesn't run away anymore, he faces his mission, his vocation.

Being sucked into a fish gullet big enough to hold an adult body and rocked by the movements of the deep sea is an irresistible metaphor for a return to the womb. It is the ultimate, terrifying regression that is necessary to be reborn into a higher, wiser consciousness. Isn't it the very experience that some New Age practitioners are looking for when they undergo a "rebirthing"?

The story of being swallowed by a beast is a common myth. There is a Zulu story in which two children and their mother are swallowed by an elephant. Osiris is thrown in the Nile into a sarcophagus by his brother Set and then returns from the dead. Joseph Campbell believed that the image of the belly of the whale symbolizes the passage of a magical threshold into a sphere of rebirth. In order to attain a higher consciousness, a creature must first undergo a kind of death before being reborn. It is an act of self-annihilation. The ego to which the hero clings has to be let go in order to reach a higher consciousness. Then he will return to the normal world transfigured, ready to teach the lesson he has learned.

But isn't that the very path that Jesus himself will follow in the New Testament: self-sacrifice to save the human race; death and burial; rebirth as the son of God? A. N. Wilson, in *Jesus, A Life,* tells of rites of initiation in which catechumen were wrapped in grave-clothes and then "reborn" to their faith. In fact, the myth has survived to this day, with Elvis still routinely spotted coming back from the dead.

It is a powerful image, a pagan story of annihilation and rebirth to explain major rites of passage.

But the story of Jonah doesn't end here. A moralistic ending seems tacked onto it, and I am not sure how to read it. At first glance, I'd say the second part of the Book of Jonah is much less satisfying, from a narrative standpoint, than the first. The dramatic tension fizzles out. So, the conversion of the Ninevites is an unmitigated success. No sooner have they heard of Jonah's prophecy than they cover themselves with sackcloth and proclaim a fast, to be followed by all, from the King to the lowest of the flock. And God forgives them.

All's well that ends well. But that's *not* all.

Jonah, who turns out to have clung to some of his ego after all, in spite of his dramatic experience, is really angry at God's clemency. How can God pity the wicked, while he himself has had to endure inhuman trials just for having run away from the Lord? This is a theme that runs all through the New Testament as well: Jesus' mercy for the worst sinners (the whores, the tax collectors, all the low-life of Israel) who used to irritate the Pharisees mightily. I can understand Jonah's anger. All the Ninevites have to do is repent. But Jonah, whose only sin is to have run away from God's calling, seems to be held to a higher standard. Now there is definitely a sense that not everybody's fate is equal. Equal in the love of God maybe, but some have a higher calling. So Jonah, once again, grumbles. Once again he wants to die rather than deal with his conflicting emotions. It's as if nothing has happened to him. The sojourn in the belly of the fish? All but forgotten. "Do you do well to be angry?" God asks him like a stern father. Jonah doesn't answer, he storms out of the city in a funk and sits by himself, like a sulky teenager, nursing his anger.

This is beginning to sound ridiculous, maybe even intentionally funny. And it goes on, the story rising to a fevered pitch.

Now God is beside himself with divine fury. He makes a plant grow to give Jonah shade, and then creates a worm that will eat the plant so that it withers, and so on. Jonah gets angrier and angrier. The obvious point of the story is to give a lesson to Jonah: you pitied the plant, why shouldn't I pity the Ninevites? But when Jonah says: "I do well to be angry, angry enough to die," he is not pitying the plant at all, he is sorry for himself because he has now lost the shade of the plant and the sun is beating down so hard (we are in the desert) that he is faint. So the concluding lesson, which makes the case of universal love for all creatures, is lost on Jonah and, as a result, on us readers.

But is it the concluding lesson? As a twentieth-century, nonscholar reader, I have an undeniable reverence for the words written hundreds of years ago. It is hard to imagine any playfulness between the lines, any double-entendre. I might question God's intentions, but I might not question the narrator's intentions as I would those of a contemporary author. And yet . . . there is something of a comedy routine in the silly games God plays with Jonah. What if the Book of Jonah was played for farce, as a two-character satire? Jonah, the recalcitrant prophet, running away from the Lord, and God, like a bad Genie out of the bottle, pursuing Jonah with his magic powers, now appointing the great fish, now a plant, now a worm, now the wind, until he corners the poor prophet and bludgeons him over the head with his morality lesson.

What if this was meant to be funny? What if, God forbid, this was a parody? We, postmodern readers, tend to forget that we didn't invent irony. And there is a good reason for our ignorance: the more ancient the manuscript, the harder it is to pick its allusions and cultural references, so that any level of narration beyond the surface of the text may be lost on us.

On first reading, I'd say that the final trials that God puts Jonah through do not have the resonance of a powerful symbol of initiation or deepening of consciousness. They read like tricks masterminded by the storyteller to shoehorn his denouement or moral.

But if we look at them in a satirical light, then the Book of Jonah ends on a very funny, irreverent note.

The commentaries extoll the Book of Jonah for its teachings about mercy and forgiveness. The theme of universal love, which will be developed later on by Jesus, is clearly an essential ingredient of the Judeo-Christian religions, the bedrock of a modern sense of morality and fate. Yet for me, and this is true whether the Book of Jonah is to be read straight or as a satire, its power comes from the presence of the ancient myth, the unforgettable image of Jonah trapped in the big fish and then reborn on dry land.

Reading the Gospels in the text for the first time, I am fascinated to see the Old Testament themes reenter the stage with different actors. Again, pagan myths appear, entwined with moral preachings. But the Gospels have the advantage of telling one unified story, in which Jesus' life and his teachings are one, culminating in this most dramatic of mythical events: the Resurrection, the ultimate Rebirth. It is, story-wise, an unbeatable ending.

Still, there's an awful lot of preaching and moralizing till you get to the bloody fireworks (the crown of thorns, the blood, the nails, the vinegar, the empty grave)!

I am not coming to the New Testament with an open mind and a sense of wonderment. I have an ax to grind, it turns out. Which surprises me. I haven't been a practicing Catholic for thirty years—I thought I had buried that part of me on the other side of the Atlantic—and yet a fresh rage leaps from me to the page.

What I really want to know—this is beginning to feel like an old wound that I rub with salt—is this: do Jesus' teachings, as reported by the Apostles (who had their own agenda and may not have been the most reliable witnesses) really urge masochism, self-sacrifice, and martyrdom?

There. I said it. The gnawing question. The dark heart of the Catholic religion.

Not the question of sex, lust, masturbation, extramarital affairs, and whatnot. No matter what Jesus said or not, sex is not a true issue in

Catholic France. The culture is just too permissive to allow religion to stand in the way. In any case, these were not the issues that tortured me. Rather, it was this one, and it preempted the question of sex by a long shot: how good did I have to be? How much was I supposed to sacrifice myself? Should I emulate the saints (St. Catherine, Virgin Martyr, comes to mind)? Did I have to annihilate every one of my desires?

In my old missal, each parable or fragment of parable is framed like a religious painting on the wall of a church: surrounded by alleluias, songs, commentaries, prayers that have mysterious names like *graduel, trait, collecte, secrète*. With the exception of the Passion and the Crucifixion, which are recounted at length, most parables are edited down and quoted out of their original New Testament contexts, and set like gold nuggets to fit into the Catholic ritual and dogma.

In the New Testament, the parables are strung back to back, sandwiched between the Sermon on the Mount and the Last Supper, and every one of them, at first glance, seems to praise the weak and the meek—just as I remember—to probe into the hearts in order to expose the flimsiest sinful thought, to harp about the hypocrites who follow the rules but deep in their hearts are more sinful than the sinners, to urge the turning of the other cheek.

And yet, as I read them more closely, their message is not so clear and it is more complex when taken in its historical context. Jesus is not talking to us, twentieth-century neurotics, post-Freud heirs of the repressed Victorian times. He is talking to Pharisees, themselves surrounded by pagan Romans in full decadence and moral breakdown. The Pharisees were a sect of very virtuous Jews who obeyed the laws (including strict dietary laws and laws pertaining to the respect of the Sabbath) to the letter, and a lot of Jesus' teachings seem to do battle with a more legalistic view of religion. Over and over in his parables Jesus stresses purity of heart and faith against simple obedience to the laws. Jesus appears in fact very rebellious against the authorities (''A disciple is not above his teacher, nor a servant above his master." [Matthew 10:24]), and although he professes respect for the Ten Commandments of the Old Testament, he often puts a spin on them that makes his message at times ambiguous, at times anarchic if not downright nihilistic.

Certainly Jesus is not all peace and love: "Do not think that I have come to bring peace on earth; I have not come to bring peace, but a sword. For I have come to set a man against his father, and a daughter against her mother, and a daughter-in-law against her mother-in-law; and a man's foes will be those of his own household. He who loves father or mother more than me is not worthy of me." (Matthew 10:34–37) What ever happened to "Honor thy father and mother"?

The Parable of the Publican (Luke 18:9–14) is morally unsettling to say the least. The pharisee goes to Temple and congratulates himself on his righteousness, whereas the tax collector (considered the lowest of the low by the Jews) dares not lift his eyes to heaven and beats his breast in repentance for all his sins. "I tell you," Jesus says, "this man went down to his house justified rather than the other."

Now I am feeling the confusion again, and the hopeless rage. Is Jesus chastising the pharisee for his arrogance? Or is he saying that virtue doesn't count? You're better off sinning and then repenting, that's what he is saying. God prefers the sinner who throws himself at his mercy.

The ambiguity is here, in the text, either badly reported by Luke, or never fully explained. No wonder I could never get it right. No wonder the lives of the saints were so appealing in their absolute abnegation. Since showing off your virtue was no good, being virtuous was not much better, and faith was an unfathomable affair, there was only one true path to salvation, the very path Jesus himself had followed (and many martyr-saints after him): self-sacrifice and repression of your innermost desire to atone for everybody's sin and your own (and doing it in secret, to boot!).

Parable after parable ring the same note. In the Lost Sheep (Luke 15:3–7), the shepherd abandons his whole herd to go after the lost sheep and rejoices when he finds it. "I tell you, there will be more joy in heaven over one sinner who repents than over ninety-nine righteous persons who need no repentance." In the Prodigal Son (Luke 15:11–32), the younger son leaves with his share of his father's property and squanders all his money "in loose living." Tired of being poor and eating with the swine, he remembers that he could live more comfortably at his father's place, so he decides to go back home and make amends. His father's reaction? Kill the fat calf and throw a party. The older son is angry: "Lo, these many years I have served you, and I never disobeyed your command, yet you never gave me a kid, that I make merry with my friends." And the father says: "Son, you are always with me, and all that is mine is yours. It was fitting to make merry and be glad, for this your brother was dead, and is alive; he was lost, and is found."

Another parable underscores Jesus' disregard for hard work and justice. A bunch of laborers (Matthew 20:1–16) arrive at dawn to toil in a vineyard and agree to be paid one denarius by the owner of the land. But the owner promises the same payment to other laborers who arrive later, including a group who arrive at the eleventh hour, and end up working only one hour. To the anger of the laborers, the owner answers: "Am I not allowed to do what I choose with what belongs to me? Or do you begrudge my generosity? So the last will be first, and the first last."

There's no reward in any of these parables for good work or for doing good. What matters is God's power to do as he pleases, without any sense of what we would call justice, and a willingness to reward the least worthy. So why bother? Why bother following an ethic of good living when Jesus tells us that it doesn't matter, that what matters is to trust God and his erratic behavior?

But if you replace the idea of God by that of fate, then the parables take on another meaning. They may be an attempt to justify man's basic inequality in life and to appease his/her anger at the inequality of fate.

The Parable of the Talents (Matthew 25:14–30) brings an interesting twist to this idea. A master going on a journey entrusts his property to his servants: "to one he gave five talents [a talent is a sum of money], to another two, to another one, to each according to his ability." When the master comes back, he praises the servants who have invested their talents and made a profit. "Well done, good and faithful servant . . . enter into the joy of your master," he tells them. But the third servant only hid the talent in the ground and gives it back, untouched, to his master. Probably out of guilt, he turns against his master, accusing him of being greedy and dishonest and explains that he had been scared to invest the talent (and presumably risk bad investments). "You wicked and slothful servant!" the master answers. "Then you ought to have invested my money with the bankers, and at my coming I should have received what was my own with interest." So the master takes away the talent from the servant, gives it to the one who made the most money, and "[casts] the worthless servant into the outer darkness."

What a severe punishment for a servant who really did nothing wrong, at least according to conventional morals—he didn't waste his money on harlots like the Prodigal Son, nor did he sin like the tax collector, nor did he show arrogance and hypocrisy like the Pharisee! What did he do, then? He failed to develop the talent his master had bestowed upon him. He buried it out of fear. He wasted his gift. He put his light under the bushel. That, for Jesus, was the worst offense.

If you understand talent not just as money, but in its derived meaning of natural ability, or "gift committed to one's trust to use and improve" (Webster's definition), the Parable of the Talents takes on a much more revealing meaning. It becomes an encouragement to self-realization and risk-taking. And that doesn't square at all with the idea of self-sacrifice and turn the other cheek.

There is something morally rebellious in these parables, something that borders on nihilism. You can imagine Jesus, the angry young man, rebelling against the Law of the Father, challenging the do-gooders and cautious Pharisees who followed the old Jewish Law to the letter and measured each one of their actions relative to the reward they would bring. What Jesus is saying is truly revolutionary: Follow your calling in life (even if it means turning against your parents). Take your chances. Forget about being good; you can't buy your way through life with good behavior. It won't get you anywhere. Make your mistakes (sins) and when you know better you'll repent. Have mercy. Trust God (fate), have faith and cultivate your talents.

This is a credo that sounds thrillingly modern and Western, very far from the pious ethic of self-abnegation I was taught. To the Pharisees and the Romans, it must have seemed incredibly threatening. No wonder Jesus was crucified.

Yet, in the end, what Jesus said is swept away by the power of his own myth. He would have been relegated, just another prophet preaching in the desert, if the Apostles had not made a hero out of him, sending him on the classic, mythic journey of self-sacrifice and rebirth. Crucifixion and Resurrection.

I have come full circle. I feel that I have moved away from the text of the Bible and back to the pagan rites and the mysteries which are a good part of the Catholic religion. I don't believe a religion can exist without the myths that sustain and inspire it. Words can be bent, they can be interpreted, they can be manipulated. Of course, the Bible is full of myths. But here I am going to show myself a true Catholic, after all. A book, to me, just doesn't have the same power on the imagination as the reenactment of that ancient ritual: sacrifice and redemption. How far is the Eucharist from the sacrificial lamb, decapitated, dripping blood on the shrine? The pagan drama of the ritual is what allows us to transcend our humanity, to reach back to our primitive origins, to feel the *frisson* of the sacred.

Genesis (Hagar)

BHARATI MUKHERJEE

I was born into a practicing Hindu family of the Brahmin caste in an unself-consciously insular neighborhood in Calcutta, India, and so didn't happen upon the Book of Genesis until a writer-friend, Max Apple, invited me to join a seminar at the Jewish Theological Seminary in Manhattan in the late eighties. Though my mother, who had been married off in her mid-teens into a family more orthodox Hindu than her own, encouraged me to respect all religions, neither she nor I had any bookish knowledge of the scriptures and traditions of Sikhs and Muslims, let alone of Jews and Christians.

The only Muslim I saw in my early childhood was an itinerant holy man. He passed through our neighborhood irregularly. He always announced himself with the shout "The Ridder of Troubles has come to rid you of your troubles!" while flailing the air with a long, thick whisk of horsehair. This holy man of Islam did not ever actually enter our homes. In the still caste-conscious Calcutta of the forties, there must have existed between us a complicitous understanding about boundaries. The whisk-wielder stood on one side of the rusty iron little gate, the almsgiver on the other. We children peeked at him from behind the capacious back of an older cousin or aunt as she dropped into his grimy gunnysack a cupful of rice or pulses. In thanks for the alms, ''The Ridder of Troubles'' waved his whisk over our bowed heads and chanted blessings in a language we didn't understand. His unfamiliar clothes, his animal-hair prop, his alien language, all made him more terrifying, more special, than the Bengali-speaking panhandlers in shabby dhotis or saris who worked our comfortable neighborhood. ''Otherization'' as a guilt-inducing concept hadn't yet breached our innocence's ramparts.

There were no Christian residents on our block. Christians, we knew, came in two varieties: they were either the hated Europe-born colonials and their Anglo-Indian (mixed race) aides who brutalized Bengali freedom-fighters; or they were the former low-caste Hindu-born converts who had defected from (but whom we didn't allow to escape) the hierarchy of the caste system.

I sighted my first Christian—he appeared in the shape of a blustery Anglo-Indian police officer—when I was four or five years old. These were the last years of the British Raj, and all Bengalis were buoyant with rage and audacious hope, and when the funeral processions of martyred imperialism-resisters, some no older than twelve, galvanized even shy, pliant housewives like my two grandmothers to rush to their front gates and howl, ''Shame! Shame!'' in the face of all lackeys of colonials. One dawn, I woke up to find that our house had been surrounded by baton-twirling policemen, and to hear the suety-faced officer yell, in the Anglo-Indian patois of poor English and poorer Hindi, that he had come to arrest one of my many young uncles for freedom-fighting activity. Communal memory has alchemized my personal experience. Over and over again, I replay a visual: a huge-eyed child watching from under a bed as the tallest, burliest man she has ever seen is spiritedly ejected by her petite, widowed, paternal grandmother.

The small Jewish community of Calcutta intersected my life very early, because my father's partner in a pharmaceutical company he had started up soon after getting back from his doctoral and postdoctoral studies in pre-World War II England and Germany was an Iraqi Jew. This partner was a self-made man of much mystery and some charm. All we knew for certain about him was that he had come to Calcutta as a stowaway on a cargo vessel, and that he had survived his first year in our city hawking ties at crowded intersections. He was a light-skinned man, considered a sahib or European in those years just before and just after Independence. He did not ever come to our house. We visited him, instead, for rare Sunday lunches in his flat in Chowringhee, the European quarter of the city. Before these visits, my two sisters and I were made to assiduously practice eating with knife and fork instead of with fingers and to rehearse a brief set of questions and answers in English, a language we rarely heard at home. Q: What is your name? A: My name is Bharati. Q: How do you do? A: How do you. Q: How are you? A: I am well, thank you.

I realize now that all the non-Indian guests at these Sunday dinners were Jewish refugees from the Middle East, guests with names like Ezra, Judah, and Saul.

About hostilities between Muslims and Hindus, we had paranoia-adumbrated stories dating back centuries to the time of Mughal emperors like Jehangir and Aurangzeb; and, in 1946, we also had my father's first-hand experience of violence during the Hindu-Muslim riots.

This is our family story about the bloody pre-Partition riots when politicians exploited visceral fear and religious fanaticism. In this story, the Hindu is the victim, the Muslim the assailant, and the Jew (meaning my father's partner) the quick-thinking huckster-hero. Our pharmaceutical factory was located at the time in a Muslim part of town, because some of the drugs being manufactured required beef-extract, offensive to cow-revering

Hindus. One weekday noon in that ugly season of riots, the factory was overrun by a mob of neighborhood toughs brandishing knives, staves, metal pipes, and homemade bombs. Three Hindu factory hands were slain before they could race their way into the secured-section of the building. More workers might have been killed or maimed if the Jewish partner hadn't clambered to the rooftop and stalled or bemused the mob by pleading, "Jews and Muslims are bhai-bhai, brother-brother! Our religions share the same homeland! So do me, your brother, this favor. Don't harm these Hindus while they are under my protection!" The besieged were eventually rescued that evening by units from the city's special riot-management squad.

Soon after I turned eight, my father took my mother, sisters, and me to Europe for a period of about three years. We spent most of that time in London, Liverpool, and Basel, sites of large pharmaceutical companies where my father advanced laboratory research and his partner negotiated collaborative efforts for the future manufacturing of drugs at our Calcutta plant. The Protestant schools I attended in England and Switzerland should have provided me with my first exposure to Judeo-Christian theology, but they didn't. Out of consideration for my Hindu sensibility, the headmistresses insisted on excusing me from the morning assembly, which included the recitation of prayers.

The Irish nuns who ran the clubby, private school for young women that my parents enrolled me in when we came home to Calcutta, however, guiltlessly included Religious Knowledge [of Christianity] and Scripture and Moral [according to the Pope] Science in its short list of mandatory courses. The fifties was an exhilarating decade of cultural identity–construction for Indian nationals; it must have been a desperate dig-your-heels-in decade for the Galway expatriates. Missionaries continued to run the elite schools favored by socially prominent families (almost all of whom were non-Christian), but academic year by academic year, they lost to non-Christian parents and to nationalist India's education-reformers their battle to influence students' minds and morals. To competitive Hindu schoolchildren focused on the medals and books to be awarded on Prize Day every December, acing tests in Religious Knowledge and Scripture, seemed no less urgent than acing them in Geometry, General Science, European History, French Language and Literature, and Elocution (which was my particular favorite course and which required me to recite from memory entire Shakespearean plays in Elizabethan English as well as Christian psalms). In my Hindu-dominated class of twenty at the convent school, there were three Anglo-Indian Catholics, one Indian Catholic, one Eastern Orthodox Czech, and one Shiite Muslim Iranian. I speculate now that there had to have been a scattering of Jewish students in the school, children of visiting foreign experts, but I don't know what coping strategy they invented to resist the Anglo-Indian students' unthinking equating of Pharisee with Jew.

The Galway nuns did not actually prescribe any text of continuous narrative titled the Holy Bible. They worked through biblical material at an eccentric pace, dispensing with the Old Testament (by way of an illustrated text of abbreviated legends) in a couple of years of elementary school, then lavishing all the years of middle school and high school on the Gospels according to Mark, Matthew, and Luke, the Acts of the Apostles, and *The Life of the Savior,* which came in easy-to-clutch discrete texts that we had to learn by heart on pain of detention and the archaic turns of phrases of which we were required to emulate as well as admire. Until I stayed in my first motel in the United States, I had never actually seen a copy of the Bible. Because I skipped a couple of grades when I started the convent school in Calcutta where placement was according to ability rather than age as it had been in Europe, I missed the nuns' guided tour of the Old Testament altogether.

Looking back, I am thankful that I came to the Book of Genesis as an adult unburdened by childhood memories of missionary bias.

In the late eighties, around the time that my second book of stories, *The Middleman and Other Stories,* came out, Max Apple invited my husband,

Clark Blaise, and me to join the one-Wednesday-a month discussions on the Book of Genesis over free dinner at the Jewish Theological Seminary on the Upper West Side of Manhattan. I accepted for a deplorably wrong reason: nostalgia for the exotic Jewish cuisine I had tasted at the Judah family's in Calcutta.

I didn't expect to enjoy the required reading as I did the Hindu religious epic poems, such as *The Mahābhārata* and *The Rāmāyaṇa*. The Hindu epics humanized spiritual abstractions by presenting them through a huge cast of flashy characters, which included gods, shape-changing de-mons, militarist monkeys, gullible damsels and their good-hearted but shortsighted protectors equipped with sci-fi weapons, and by embroiling that cast in a mega-plotted Marquezian soap opera. *The Rāmāyaṇa* and *The Mahābhārata* were fun reading that suckered the waffler or the nonbeliever into salvation-facilitating conduct through their storytelling powers. Having grown up in a religion that seeks to erase the binaries (for instance, sacred/ profane, religion/art, good/evil) familiarly accepted by Christianity, and instead, to define salvation as the clearing up of a vision opaque with misplaced emotion, I accepted without the least confusion contrarinesses of Fate's workings and moral ambiguities in heroic mortals. The nuns of my Calcutta girlhood had unsubtly implied that the Catholics had a lock on salvation. They had presented the New Testament to us not as a metaphorized narrative for moral deportment but as an unadorned, absolu-tist religious document. Their unstated message was that if—compared to the flamboyant suspensefulness of the Hindu epics and Puranic tales we read on our own at home or to the willful meanness of Greek deities in the Sophocles, Racine, and Milton plays we studied in our postcolonial curricu-lum in school—the New Testament seemed to us too solemnly didactic, then we should conclude that solemnity was synonymous with spiritual sophistication. I finished high school shortly after my fifteenth birthday, and though I went on to a Calcutta University–affiliated women's college run by the same order of Irish nuns in the same leafy compound, I was no longer required to take courses on biblical knowledge. My teenage imagination extended the New Testament's no-frills didacticism to the Hebrew Bible as well. Though as an Honors-level English Literature major I was thankful for the nuns making accessible to me scriptural references in my favorite allusive poet, Gerard Manley Hopkins, I couldn't muscle up enough curiosity in the Bible as literature to read it for pleasure.

That's why when I first encountered the Book of Genesis—in Everett Fox's translation, *In the Beginning*—as an adult in Manhattan, I was totally unprepared for its narrative playfulness. I found myself responding to Abraham as a resourceful protagonist wandering through obstacle-studded adventures rather than as a patriarch charged with a specific divine mission in a sober instrument of moral instruction. Being outside the Judeo-Christian pale, I felt guiltlessly free to improvise the context for my reading of Yahweh's transactions with Abraham and to my (oh well, eccentric) understanding of the pentagonal connection between Yahweh, story-author, English-language translator, protagonist, and reader. In the city of my birth, I'd glided through Christian scriptures with the dispassionate ease of the seasoned test-taker; now in Manhattan, the borough where I felt I most belonged, I could stalk the Book of Genesis equipped with the questioning curiosity of the adult writer and the scarred soul of the nonwhite, "naturalized" American novice culture-renovator.

As a minority woman who, over thirty-odd years, has had to battle the sometimes conscious, frequently unconscious, racism of European-American editors and administrators, I couldn't (even if I'd wanted to) isolate my persona as politicized citizen from my personae as impassioned woman and as storyteller. It is this "fused" rather than "compartmentalized" consciousness, as well as an obsessive fascination with the fragility of patriarchal power, that I bring to bear on Abraham's and Sarah's feisty domestic negotiations. I savor the writerly strategies that tease suspensefulness out of material the outcome of which must remain familiar. I admire the authorial hand that transforms agents of a divine mission into psychologically complex, vulnerable men and women who roll with the punches of their exceptional lot. I fret over the sexual politics in Abraham's household. I want to disrupt the omniscient reasonableness of the *grand récit*. I long to let the sharp-tongued, skeptical Sarah recount in her own vigorous words the physical and emotional toll that a sudden old-age pregnancy must have taken on her. I daydream of Hagar the bondswoman seizing more space in the text to vent her frustrations. And the culture critic in me marshals frail intuitive powers to detect the subtle accommodations that contemporary American translators make to appease "political correctness" patrols in our rights-conscious era.

The King James Version, The New Revised Standard Version, David Rosenberg's translation in *The Book of J,* a manuscript copy of Robert Alter's rendering of the Hagar episodes pile up. Once upon a time in Calcutta the sonorous euphony and archaic spelling of the King James Version had seemed most natural for the getting across of the holiness of the official religion of the busted British Raj. At first in New York, the rhetorical ordinariness and accessibility of the American-language translations had shocked me. Where was the stateliness of syntax? I couldn't visualize myself in Elocution Class at Loreto House, waiting for Mother Joseph Michael to give me the nod so that I could pitch my voice to the last row of the cavernous Assembly Hall auditorium and launch into the Americanized verses with the oratorial intensity and precise enunciation that I'd always thought scripture required. But, as a catalyst text, provoking me to think about and to argue over social and philosophical issues, the American translations worked much better, because they were the eclectic acquisitions of a willful adulthood.

I make no apology for my compulsive pursuit of Abraham. What can be more natural than for me—an emigrant of, and immigrant in, three continents—to be fixated on a protagonist who survives the trauma of repeated unhousements and rehousements?

> Now there was a famine in the land. So Abram
> went down to Egypt to reside there as an alien, for the
> famine was severe in the land.
>
> *(HOLY BIBLE, THE NEW REVISED STANDARD VERSION, 12:10)*

Abram came into Egypt, a starving alien; he left Egypt a very rich man at the Pharaoh's expense.

The story of Abraham may be the story of the fulfillment of the covenant, but the story of Abram—the man he was before he was renamed by Yahweh—is surely the archetypal story of the economic refugee who is forced to make his fortune in a country he will never accept as his new "homeland." When I first read of Abram's sojourn in Egypt, I was living in an ungentrified Upper West Side neighborhood east of Broadway. Our annual "block party" was organized by Dominican residents of rent-controlled flats and by small businessmen who operated storefront travel agencies that catered to Spanish-speaking aliens. Our corner laundry was managed by a Peruvian family of Chinese origin, and the gyro take-out place next to the laundry was staffed by Bangladeshi bachelors. My building's janitor and doormen, with whom I talked in the patois of body-language, had just arrived as political refugees from Poland. I can't imagine anyone on our block not considering Abram's decision to misrepresent his marital status to border guards as he slipped into Pharaoh's land of plenty with his starving entourage one very smart move.

> When he was about to enter Egypt, he said to his
> wife, Sarai, "I know that you are a woman beautiful in
> appearance; and when the Egyptians see you, they will

say, 'This is his wife'; then they will kill me, but they will let you live. Say you are my sister, so that it may go well with me because of you, and that my life may be spared on your account.''

(THE NEW REVISED STANDARD VERSION, 12:11—13)

Of course, I know that tradition expects me to process Abram's "scheme" as his self-surrender to divine will. But what's so wrong with wanting to spare oneself nasty torture and/or execution while doing Yahweh's work? What most intrigues me in this verse, though, is the psychological and emotional conflicts that must have preceded Abram's decision. As a male who believes in the moral and social rightness of patriarchal hierarchy, how he must have suffered when he had to relinquish control of his wife's honor to another male. That that male was a scorned foreigner, and as king his social superior in Egypt, must have deepened Abram's torment. Having been brought up in an inflexibly patriarchal culture that fetishes protection of virgin daughters' chastity and wife's honor, and having had my adolescent imagination inflamed by Bengali-language tragedies in which chaste Hindu heroines are cast out by their own families because they have had the misfortune of being held up by Muslim pirates, I can't help projecting onto Abram my troubled Hindu understanding of the pain of emasculation. There's so much more I want to know, but the text tantalizingly withholds. Did Abram ever doubt Yahweh's benevolent guarantee to run interference? Did he torture himself with specious visions of Sarai succumbing to the rich and exotic monarch's temptation? And what's being offered through Abram's stratagem as the model of moral conduct? As a woman who has had to cope with continuous cultural erosions and accretions, I want to find in Abram's lie support for two qualities I value: resilience and adaptiveness. Knowledge of moral correctness is visceral, but moral integrity manifests itself in protean ways. Inflexible adherence to form may turn out to be the unacknowledged vice of the narcissist and the vain. If the author of Genesis had fashioned the George Washington and the cherry tree apocrypha, would the future founding father have sloughed the blame off on someone else?

I came of age, intellectually, in the post-Women's Movement United States. All the same, I cannot view Sarai as being "objectified"—a favorite word on campuses these days—by either Pharaoh or by Abram. She both anticipates and transcends the female hero of popular feminist fiction in America. Not for her the woe and rage of our victimology-obsessed culture. This housewife is mad as in "angry," not mad as in "neurotic." When threatened, she chooses to take preemptive action rather than to mope. In Egypt she deploys her physical beauty as weapon against Pharaoh, establishing herself as her husband's scrappy co-warrior and not his put-upon chattel.

It's the representation of Egyptians as a uniformly debauched people that dismays me. If the Egypt episode of Genesis were being composed by a contemporary American woman writer on her laptop, could she get away with dismissing all Egyptians as crudely sex-crazed consumers? She might also have to put a new spin on her portraits of Pharaoh and Avimelekh, to bring out their naïveté, to play down their sensuality, to make the reader wince with grudging pity for rich, privileged fellows who can't protect themselves from being duped by a foreign transient.

Pharaoh commits a crime, is punished, and pays a fine. But how are we, living in a self-consciously multicultural democracy, to classify a crime that does not violate the official religious laws and criminal codes of the kingdom? The American author of the nineties might reclassify Pharaoh's crime as ignorance of the religious and cultural sensitivities of minority communities in his land.

It is, of course, Hagar's story that haunts me. Hagar floats into my nightmares on work-toughened feet, and shrieks for a fairer representation of the disempowered and the abused. I urge Hagar not to take Sarai's afflicting of her too personally. But she rattles the bars of complacent aestheticism. She demands recognition as more than utilitarian plot device necessary for providing Abram with a not quite acceptable firstborn, whose banishment enables the progeny's bifurcation. What does plot have to do with how she *feels* when she is marginalized and humiliated? It's time to give her more space, to invest her with the resonance worthy of a sensual, sentient human.

So let me start by clearing up some clutter about Canaanite Hagar's position in Israelite Abram's household. Robert Alter and the New Revised Standard Version translate her job-description as "Egyptian slave-girl." Louis Ginzberg's *Legends of the Bible* avoids "slave" and settles on "Egyptian bondwoman," making it easier for us to picture Abram as supervising indentured laborers rather than owning slaves. But a male boss who treats his female worker as his economic property and legitimizes the converting of her womb into a production site without seeking her consent makes for an ambivalent hero these days. Both Everett Fox and David Rosenberg *(The Book of J)*, in their more recent translations, address our potential ambivalence by redescribing Hagar as "maid," elevating her status to that of an "employee." I wouldn't be surprised if a future American translation completed this sanitization by passing her off as a "domestic." Over dinner at Chez Panisse in Berkeley, Greil Marcus, the rock critic, offered me a fresh and attractive perspective on the household relations. "Hey, think of Abraham as a cult leader," he suggested. "Think of Hagar as part of his 'family.'" Okay. If only I didn't suspect this cult leader of being something of a closet imperialist!

Yahweh seals the covenant with a promise of vast real estate for Abram's descendants. The patriarch's seed will own the lands of the Kenites, Kenizzites, Kadmonites, Hittites, Canaanites, Girgashites, Jebusites. No sons, no expansion of territorial holdings. Sarai's barrenness suddenly balloons from domestic tragedy to economic catastrophe. And the author finds herself in the tricky situation of having to come up with a credible solution for Sarai's gynecological deficit without Sarai losing the reader's sympathy. Time to trot out Hagar, "the other woman." Sarai initiates Hagar's bedroom assignation with Abram. "Go into my slave-girl," she instructs her husband, "it may be that I shall obtain children by her." (Genesis, 16:2, The New Revised Standard Version) But "obtain children" may be a coy and misleading translation. As Robert Alter points out in his commentary on this verse, the Hebrew word *"ibbaneh"* of the original implies the bearing of *sons* rather than of children. Obtaining daughters means no increasing of land holdings. We don't get Hagar's reaction to Sarai's plan of farming out her womb. Those of us who have experienced class prejudice and colonialism can be forgiven for reading into this omission the sad, silenced issues of disenfranchisement.

Physically Hagar must have been young, healthy, ripe, an ideal child-bearer. Was she also beautiful? Sexy? We can't be sure that Abram gave Sarai his guarantee that there would be no emotional involvement, that he would bed Hagar down as though she were a toy facilitator of procreation. Everett Fox and Robert Alter weight their translation of *"ishah"* as having wifely respect. The boss and the maid come together; the maid becomes pregnant. This unequal distribution of fecundity destroys all preexisting relations between them. Hagar, now the carrier of the boss's child, assumes the self-respecting deportment of a "person." Postmenopausal Sarai feels threatened as a woman. And the author amuses herself by presciently anticipating some of our rent-a-womb era's emotional (if not legal) confusions.

Once the plot has bulldozed obstacles to the birth of Abram's first-born, narrative art dictates that Sarai complain of Hagar's arrogance. If barren Sarai has imagined Hagar's slighting of her, her pain and her bitter defensiveness as a childless woman in a fertility-celebrating culture become endearingly believable. If the insult is real, Hagar is practicing dissent.

Wife warring with concubine can mean only domestic unpleasantness for the husband. The author has to spring Abram from this mess without scuffing his masculine and moral prowess and without dimming his heroic wattage. If this were hyperfiction, I'd try out options more dramatic than letting Abram reclassify "class revolt" as a "women's problem." I would want a rowdier quarrel between aggrieved wife and embarrassed husband. And I would definitely want Hagar to confront Abram about how he really feels about her and why he doesn't stop his wife from battering and banishing her.

Abram and Sarai grow in spiritual stature and merit being renamed Abraham and Sarah by Yaweh, but flawless characters are hard to write up as mesmerizing. Sarah as a jealous woman with fragile ego provides better show than Sarah the idealized miracle-recipient. Sarah may be blessed with eventual fructification, but she must needle herself with the real or false memory of Hagar's emotional intimacy with her husband. A violent out-burst is more riveting to readers than pontifications. Sarah must scold, beat, drive out the Canaanite servant and her part-Canaanite, part-Israelite son.

But what if . . . just what if Hagar were to stride out of the slave-owners' reach of her own volition and hurl herself into her own heroic adventures on uncharted narrative terrain?

Ruth

C   L   A   R   K   B   L   A   I   S   E

Once upon a time, Naomi had a husband, Elimelech, and two sons, Chilion and Mahlon . . . They left Bethlehem—we do not know why, the Bible is silent—to settle in Moab where they became prosperous farmers. The sons married Moabite women, Orpah and Ruth, whose histories we can only guess at. Elimelech died, and soon after, the sons died, leaving Naomi the head of a widowed house in a foreign land with alien daughters-in-law. She decided to return to Bethlehem. Ruth and Orpah elected to go with her. So begins the Book of Ruth.

We know nothing of the reasons for the men's deaths—violent or natural, sudden or prolonged—or how to interpret their character. The Bible is silent. We don't even know which of Naomi's sons Ruth had married. The men are of the named but undifferentiated populations of the Bible, false specifics.

Whose story is this? It's called the Book of Ruth but if this were fiction we'd cry "Indirection! Irony!" Ruth is not the energy source. Her perceptions and actions do not drive the plot. She is passive throughout, and except for one inspired moment when she pledges loyalty to Naomi and to Naomi's God and people, she is the victim or beneficiary of her mother-in-law's manipulation. A modern reader might conclude that this is Ruth's story only if passivity and assimilation are the ultimate morals.

And yet, *and yet,* like a bygone movie star with a special gift or claim on our affections, Ruth is an enduring icon. Of all the women in the Bible, she is one of the very few—a Catholic woman of my acquaintance swears she's the *only* one—to lead a normal life, to act on normal desires, to be tested by familiar temptations not as a nun or as a whore. Desirable, docile, loyal, she represents a collection of virtues that God himself anoints with favor. She becomes the founding mother of Israel's greatest line of kings, great-grandmother of David.

We can also see, through Ruth, the Bible as a men's club. God speaks directly to men no matter how base and brutal they may be. He does not speak to women, no matter what their virtue and devotion. Naomi may well be responding to promptings from God in deciding to return to Bethlehem, but a man would be instructed, "Go ye back to the land of thy birth" (with intricate and inscrutable instructions about the number and nature of sacrifices to be made along the way), while Naomi's decision is undignified by commandment. She can only say to her countrymen, "Do not call me Naomi. Call me Mara [the bitter one], for the Lord has dealt bitterly with me." Women are spoken to by men, by older women, and by society, all of whom they must obey.

Why did they leave Moab? Under what conditions will they be treated in Israel—or in Moab, if they remain? The Bible is silent. Moabites were not dissimilar to Israelites, a Semitic people, Edsels of the family tree, ancient apostates excluded from the Covenant. In Hollywood terms (which the story strongly invites), Ruth comes across as an Irish Catholic maid in a rich Protestant family. Bridget.

The Book of Ruth can be read as the simplest in the Bible, almost a piece of fluff, an obvious primer of virtue. Ruth—in the Doris Day role— is a pert, young (mid-twenties, if she married as a teenager, mid-forties according to legends; the Bible doesn't say) childless widow who follows her mother-in-law—in the Rosalind Russell role—out of Moab and back to Bethlehem. Can a more appealing, more deserving creature than Ruth be imagined?

It's a strange configuration, Naomi and Ruth, mother-in-law and daughter-in-law; the relationship lends itself more to jokes than piety. (I can't think of another devoted daughter-in-law story anywhere, in any culture.) Why would a normal daughter-in-law, freed by her husband's death from further contact or subservience to his mother and her people (who disdain her), choose to remain in her power? There are only three answers: she's a good, docile person, obviously grateful for Naomi's love and protection; she's an ambitious person, out to regain her lands and status at any cost in a time and place that does not honor women's claims; she's compelled by a higher force. Sunday School piety, revisionist feminism, Jewish mysticism.

To finish the plot summary: Orpah and Ruth decide to go with Naomi back to Israel, declaring their love and their loyalty. But this is the Bible, still ruled by God; love of a person is not enough. A few miles outside of town Naomi tries to dissuade them. Orpah—in the practical, unsentimental Eve Arden role—thinks it over and goes back to Moab. (According to legend, Orpah went back to Moab and became a harlot. Eventually she settled down and had four sons, one of whom was the giant Goliath.) Orpah is one of the *sparträgers* of the Bible; she may love Naomi but she cannot make the second vow, which is far more important, that of religious conversion. But *what* an elegant plot twist: Orpah is merely human, doing the expected thing. She makes a reasonable decision. It is her role to tell us that Ruth is not reasonable. Ruth is somehow inspired. Orpah's defection sets up Ruth's great line: *"Whither thou goest, I will go; and where thou lodgest, I will lodge; thy people shall be my people, and thy God my God."*

It's Ruth's triumphant moment. Whatever possessed her to make such an extravagant promise, one of the most far-reaching, all-encompassing, uncompromising statements in the Bible? Is it a spur-of-the-moment thing, what we used to call a conversion experience? (The Bible is big on roadside conversions, Saul to Paul.) But it's also mysterious—hadn't she converted before marriage? Or is this a reconversion, all the more sincere for its passion of the moment borne on a lonely road to a mother-in-law and not her husband?

Once back in Bethlehem, Naomi is dependent on Ruth's labor for subsistence. Conversion has brought no obvious benefit. A wealthy relative, Boaz, allows Ruth a place in the fields "gleaning" (she owns that verb). She is little more than a field hand stooped in the alien corn. We don't know how Ruth responds to widowhood—no "Mara" for her—or to her new God and people, or to the coarsened labor in the fields. The Bible is silent. Boaz instructs his hired hands to lay off leering and fondling. (We can almost hear his thoughts: "Who *is* that new girl?") Before too long Naomi sees a way out of her predicament.

Naomi instructs Ruth to go to the threshing floor one night and lie down next to Boaz. When he awakes, he finds her asleep at his feet. Soon, he wants to marry her, but there's a catch, many catches, in fact. Tob, a male relative older than Boaz, should marry her and retire the debt on Naomi's lands. Boaz tricks Tob (this plot twist is worthy of Faulkner) by claiming he must pay for Ruth's share as well, effectively doubling the price. (The legends are even more convoluted. In them, Boaz cites the historic exclusion of Moabites from the Covenant as a reason for shunning Ruth, knowing full well that the exclusion was binding only on males, and that Tob was too bluntly pious to question it.) When Tob backs out, Boaz purchases the land and announces their marriage.

Ruth then has a son by him, Obed, who becomes the grandfather of David. (In the commentaries, the eighty-year-old Boaz dies the day after the marriage.) A radiantly happy ending, then—lands restored, money distributed, marriage, motherhood, and even an honored widowhood—worthy of Hollywood at its corniest.

Ruth can be seen as a *shiksa,* an attractive and available outsider, or as one of the Bible's great upwardly mobile *au pairs.* A contemporary reader could recast Ruth as a multicultural, immigrant hero, an icon of assimilation. In most traditional societies widowhood, unlike widowerhood, is a terminal condition holding out no prospects for remarriage, yet for this story to achieve its ending, whether it be sentimental, ironic, or religious, she must remarry.

For the pious Christian, her abject servitude to Naomi and Boaz is rewarded with marriage, wealth, and motherhood. God is testing her new faith and finds it holding steady. A feminist interpretation could argue the opposite side: in a culture that confers no inheritance on women, desertion of her people, sexual subservience to an old man, and backbreaking labor are familiar and unexceptional prices for the recovery of her dignity. (We know from Margaret Atwood's *The Handmaid's Tale* the murderous uses male chauvinism has for biblical howlers such as the tale of poor, docile Ruth.) To religious Jews, the story of Ruth is the working out of a plan rooted in scripture. The men of the family have died so that Naomi would be forced to return. The marriages of Ruth and Orpah were barren (the dogs that didn't bark), an indication of God's disfavor. In crude plot terms, Ruth's first husband must die so that a different seed shall quicken her womb. The conversion of Ruth the Moabite to the God of Israel, and to the Jewish people, is rewarded through motherhood in the lineage of kings.

There are, in fact, dozens of novels and a few hundred Hollywood stories suggested by Ruth. Along with Ovid's *Metamorphoses,* it's one of the great god/human epics, humans becoming gods, gods envying humans: French underground widow nursing wounded parachutist; Swedish or Irish maid learning (all too well) American ways and ending up marrying the priggish son of the host family; frontier widow holding farm and family together; a nun submerging her womanly desires because of some unspeakable guilt in the past; impoverished but provident daughter of shiftless parents; unjustly convicted prisoner; schoolmarm, librarian, slave girl; orphan; any celibate beauty thrust into a situation not of her making, requiring resourcefulness, courage, and a certain sexless solitude to survive. She is to be reconquered by a show of greater courage, greater patience, greater understanding. The Bible, of course, outdoes Hollywood. In being reconquered she becomes the matriarch.

I had an aunt named Ruth . . . the prettiest and most talented of my mother's four then living sisters, our only blonde. In 1947, at the age of thirty-two she died from congenital kidney disease. Her saintly doctor-husband, John McMurtchy, whose arrival in her life had been considered providential, couldn't save her. (Many years later, after a second marriage and children, he committed suicide.)

I was only seven, but I was affected by my mother's grief ("Ruthie, Ruthie, no, no!" I remember her running from the mailbox to our trailer with the torn letter in her hand), even from a continent away. We were living in Florida and Ruth had died in British Columbia. Letters traveled faster than people in those years; even if we could have afforded it, primitive air service would have made my mother's attendance at the funeral

impossible. In my Canadian-in-America family, Moab—mysteriously similar to Israel but somehow lesser by most accounts, outside God's grace, and
now extinct—appealed to me. We were Moabites, indefinably different
from our neighbors, living in Israel. I always read "Canaan" as Canada.

My mother's name was Anne, her remaining sisters were Kay, Lil,
and Mary. Edith had died in childhood. I mention these plain-Jane names
only to suggest a hint of exoticism in Ruth. She was, as my mother variously said, "in the Bible," or "from the Bible." She was beautiful, talented, tragic, and in the Bible; the combination of my Ruth and the Bible's
Ruth echoed in my head for years. The scene of Ruth's declaration of love
for Naomi, her people, and her God was a full-page painting in my illustrated Bible. Ruth of course was blond and beautiful; Naomi, dark and
rebeccoid. In that semiotic confusion I was spared the simpler interpretations of Ruth. I cut right to the heart of Ruth's fascination. I saw her as
Ingrid Bergman and Veronica Lake, but subconsciously I saw her dead and
Canadian, a perfected form of my mother.

Ruth's death was a sign to my mother, I realize now, of her irrevoca-
ble captivity in America and permanent estrangement from her country and
people. Ruthie's was the first contemporaneous death in her family, and the
first of any kind in mine. My mother was forty-four that year. Today, in my
Iowa City house, I'm ten years older than my mother was and have four of
Ruth's sunny Florida and California watercolors (as do my cousins in Win-
nipeg and Ottawa) and all ten of her somber, death-driven British Columbia charcoals.

Even before I read the Bible, I was prepared to like Ruth, to sympa-
thize with her, to fear for her, and to see the simple rituals of her life as a
kind of heroic defiance of fatal odds. Ruth was family before she was Bible,
but "Ruth," unlike Sarah and Leah, Jezebel and Rahab, Naomi and
Hepzibah, is one of the biblical names that seems unestranged, contemporary and ethno-neutral. (But not plain, like my aunts, or like the stars of the

New Testament, Peter, Paul, and Mary—or *Timothy,* for Christ's sake.) A name for all seasons and all peoples, a story to appeal on some level to every reader.

Years pass. I marry into an Indian family . . . and I come to know something about families in traditional societies, especially about the relationship between husband's mothers and son's wives. They hate each other. Through India—admittedly its relevance to the Middle East is tenuous at best—I come to know about family devotion, oppression, and resentment. (In modern India, oppression is often pushed to dowry murder. That's extreme, but it wouldn't happen if there were not murderous hostilities already built into the traditional roles.) Feeling such loyalty to a mother-in-law, after her husband's death, when she's a foreigner? It's unthinkable.

If I were a clever author, or a teacher out to make a provocative point, wouldn't I choose an improbable situation to carry it? *Imagine* (as difficult as it may be) *a devoted daughter-in-law who follows her mother-in-law back to Ma's country, converting to Ma's god in the bargain* . . . and I can imagine the smiles in the audience turning to consternation as the story continues without a punch line. What? He's *serious!*

Ruth, the character, animates a level of collective story-making. Her docility and helplessness, her passionate loyalty, her early marital mishap, humble origin (although the legend has her and Orpah as daughters of a Moabite king—the Bible is silent), her ability to transform herself as need demands, her *eruption* from obscurity and servitude to a position of honor and acclaim is one of the great metamorphoses, or (in modern terms) role-reversals in the Bible, or drama or moviemaking. Transformation is the driving force of fiction and of drama and of moviemaking; Ruth (or someone like her) is like an undercoat, the first layer of most male romantic fiction. In Ruth, a man can honor (or court) wife, lover, daughter, and mother.

⁑

The Book of Ruth is one of the shapeliest tales of the Bible, in many ways a surprisingly modern fiction. Modern in the sense that its meanings are disputable, its characters almost pure dualities. Naomi is cunning and wicked; she is kind and bountiful. Ruth is a quick-study lapdog, helpless and loyal; she is steadfast and noble, an outsider learning the role of matriarch. Boaz is opportunist and deliverer. Are Israelites to Moabites occupiers and exploiters, or messengers and exemplars?

All those opposites point to a greater unifying principle. Ruth is a teachable fiction; Ruth is an approachable character. Through this brief, tender, lyrical story, much of the Bible's obscure, or even frightening, vision is suggested. God's plan unfolds on a level of divine disinterest. This is what it means to be "Chosen"; you take the good with the bad. Bitterness is not permitted. Every now and then, a human voice like Ruth's breaks through and gets God's attention.

The Hebrew Bible is a great chronicle, the origin of all our "big" fictions. How did we get here, why are we here, how should we live? Does anyone care, is it for a higher purpose, is that all there is? The characters are vivid, their lives are plotted, and a force invisible to all is working behind the scenes. They behave with purpose, with clarity. They know precisely what is expected of them at all times, because they are part of a tribal consciousness ruled by faith. *Except for Ruth. Ruth doesn't have a clue.* Ruth sleepwalks except for her one great moment, her eternal declaration.

Even with all that clarity of purpose, however, with all the assurances that God is directing the play, nothing is given outright. God demands sacrifices, He demands love, He commands respect, even if He has promised the results in advance. For example, to borrow from an adjacent story to Ruth, the Book of Joshua, there was never a question that Jericho would *not* fall to Joshua—it's been promised—yet Joshua's soldiers still must carry stones, they must march and trumpet in the prescribed manner, and must arrange to save everyone in the family of Rahab the Harlot for the service she rendered in hiding the army spies.

(In fact, the mini-story of Rahab the Harlot becomes as important as the recounting of the great military triumph. Her service to the Israelite spies, inspired by fear of the Jewish God and anecdotal memory of the Red Sea's parting, outweighs the slaughter of thousands of so-called innocents. They are not "innocent." They follow false gods. They are enemies of God's people; they are abominations.)

The story of Ruth is a parable about the testing of faith—Naomi's; Job's retold. (Women cannot be tested as harshly as men because their souls are not as valuable.) It's also about the rewards of virtue—Ruth's; Mary's foretold. Pious Christians are right to see Ruth as a *figura* of Mary, but that's all they want to see, and there's a lot they deliberately ignore.

The Book of Ruth is also about establishing dynasties and destroying false gods. It is an unembarrassed theocratic vision of nation-building. Ever since the expulsion of Adam and Eve, God had been searching for one good man and one good woman to found a nation, and it doesn't matter how many imperfect men and women are slaughtered in the process. Much of the Hebrew Bible is a record of God's ongoing wrath and disappointment, fallout from the original expulsion. Ruth's dedication to Naomi and to Naomi's people, like Rahab's demonstration of faith, are mild reversals of human failure that earn more than just a hearing. Ruth's formula ("thy people, thy God") brings Moab and Israel together. Her promise of faith and duty lifts her people to God. Preserving the soul of the faithful but unvirtuous Rahab the Harlot balanced out the destruction of her people. Faith is the way to virtue, not the other way around.

It's a Christian concept to cite the rejoicing in heaven over the saving of a single sinner, but here, perhaps, we see an equivalent, in tribal, not individual terms. The winning of an alien Moabite soul restores a tribe that had been lost since the time of Lot. The barrenness of Ruth's earlier marriage had been a judgment against her; her pronouncement of love and of faith not only brings her fertility, but a blessing that endures. She founds a race that will slay giants.

Revelation

M A R Y   G A I T S K I L L

I did not have a religious upbringing and I count that a good thing; almost everyone I know who has had one appears to have suffered for it. I know there are exceptions, but when I think of "religious upbringing," I think of the two little girls I once walked home with in the fourth grade who, on hearing that I didn't believe that Jesus was the Son of God, began screaming, "There's a sin on your soul! You're going to hell!" I think of my friend who, as a kid, was repeatedly exorcised in her mother's fundamentalist church and who still has nightmares about it at forty-five. I think of a thirteen-year-old boy I recently met who told me he believes that God will punish his sexually active classmates by giving them AIDS. I think of watching *The Exorcist* in theaters and seeing adult moviegoers jump up and stumble toward the exits, retching and/or weeping with fear.

My mother, to her credit, told me that "God is love" and that there is no hell. But I don't think I quite believed her. Even though I have very little conscious religious anxiety, since childhood, I periodically have had dreams that suggest otherwise; dreams of hooded monks carrying huge, grim crosses in processions meant to end in someone's death by fire, drowning, or quartering. Of endless liturgies by faceless choirs to faceless parishioners in cavernous dark churches. Of trials, condemnations, sacrifices, and torture. I have no idea where this stuff comes from. Horror movies and creeping cultural fear are obvious sources, but my unconscious has taken these images in with such kinetic intensity and conviction that mere suggestion doesn't seem to be the culprit. When I wake from these dreams, it is with terror.

When I was twenty-one, I became a born-again Christian. It was a random and desperate choice; I had dropped out of high school and left home at sixteen, and while I'd had some fun, by twenty-one, things were looking squalid and stupid. My boyfriend had dumped me and I was living in a rooming house and selling hideous rodium jewelry on the street in Toronto, which is where the "Jesus freaks" approached me. I had been solicited by these people before and usually gave them short shrift, but on that particular evening I was at a low ebb. They told me that if I let Jesus into my heart right there, even if I just said the words, that everything would be okay. I said, all right, I'll try it. They praised God and moved on.

Even though my conversion was pretty desultory, I decided to pray that night. I had never seriously prayed before, and all my pent-up desperation and fear made it an act of furious psychic propulsion that lasted almost an hour. It was a very private experience that I would find hard to describe; suffice to say that I felt I was being listened to. I started going to a bleak church that had night services and free meals, and was attended heavily by street people and kids with a feverish, dislocated look in their eyes. And, for the first time, I started reading the Bible. For me, it was like running into a brick wall.

I was used to reading, but most of it was pretty trashy. Even when it wasn't, the supple, sometimes convoluted play of modern language entered my mind like radio music—then, of course, there was the actual radio music, the traffic noise, the continual onrush of strangers through the streets I worked, the slower shifting movements of friends, lovers, alliances, the jabber of electricity and neon in the night. All of which kept my mind and nervous system in a whipsawed condition from which it was difficult to relate to the Bible. "The earth was without form and void; and darkness was on the face of the deep. And the Spirit of God was hovering over the face of the waters. Then God said let there be light and there was light." I couldn't even appreciate the beauty of the words. The phrases seemed like big dumb swatches of form imposed on something swift-moving and endlessly changeable. The form was mute, huge, and absolutely immobile. It made me feel I was being smothered. One clergyman after another would quote from it so intensely, as if its big majestic opaqueness was meaningful in and of itself, and I would try to at least feel the meaning if I couldn't comprehend it. But all I felt was that persistent sense of truncation, the intimation of something enormous and inchoate trying to squeeze through the static form of written words.

This feeling became most intense when I read the Revelation. The Revelation is the most cinematic and surreal part of the Bible—it's a little like a horror movie, which is probably why it was relatively easy for me to take in. It certainly confirmed my free-floating fear. It seemed terribly real to me; I would walk out into the streets, amid the big buildings in which commerce ground forward, and I would feel the violence, the lies, the fornication, and so on pitching and heaving under the semblance of order. The air would crackle with the unacknowledged brutality of human life, and I would feel acutely all the small, stupid betrayals and lies I committed every day, both against myself and others. The angels with their seven stars and their lamp stands, the beast with his seven heads and ten horns—the static imagery was terrifying and senseless to me, and yet all the more convincing for it. I could imagine angels and beasts looming all about us, invisible because of our willful stupidity, our refusal to see the consequences of our actions, our little petty vanities. Their stars and lamp stands and horns seemed like peculiar abstractions on the page, but, I feared, when the horses came down, with their fire and teeth and snake tails, their reality would be all too clear. I lay in my bed and prayed, trying to convince myself of God's love, but, in the face of such mayhem, my prayers seemed a rag in a typhoon.

Besides, I couldn't help but think it was a little harsh. Locusts, malignant sores, scorpions, fire, men "gnawing their tongues" with pain—I knew people were horrible, but even in my youth I could also see that most people did the best they could. Even as angry and fearful and disappointed as I was, I knew I wouldn't torture people in such a way, and I didn't see how I could be more compassionate than God. I was moved when I read, in First Corinthians 13: "Love suffers long and is kind; love does not envy; love does not parade itself, is not puffed up; does not behave rudely, does not seek its own, is not provoked, thinks no evil, does not rejoice in iniquity, but rejoices in truth; bears all things, believes all things, hopes all things, endures all things. Love never fails." But I also remember thinking that, well, yes, and love is not pathologically cruel, either.

The fury of Revelation sometimes made my compassion feel weak and mealy-mouthed, but my reservations were not only humanitarian. I was more perturbed by what to me was the mechanical quality, not just of Revelation, but of the whole Bible. You had to worship God in exactly a certain way, according to certain prescriptions—and Revelation hinted that the rules set out in, say, the Ten Commandments, were only one tiny piece of a vast schema in which human ambivalence was not a factor.

I had a dream which was not about the Bible but which embodied my consternation about it. In the dream I lived in a house with several other people. We could not get out of the house and our relationships with each other had been preordained, regardless of feeling. Our actions were controlled by masters whom we never saw. One day a man came to visit us, ostensibly for lunch. He was very polite and even friendly, and we were also friendly with him. But it was understood that he was one of the people who controlled us, and the atmosphere was one of pure dread. During lunch, when one of the men of the house suddenly attacked and killed one of the household cats, we knew it was because our visitor had somehow made him do it. I couldn't hide my horror completely and our visitor looked at me a moment and then said, referring to the mangled body of the cat, "That's what I'm going to do to you one day." I understood him to mean that he was going to rape me, and I said, "But I'm married," not because it mattered to me, but because I knew that the only thing that mattered to him was his laws. Then I became too angry to go along with this and I added, "Even though I don't respect my husband." Very threateningly—after all, it's part of the law that we love our spouses—the visitor asked, "Do you have sex with your husband?" I answered yes, and it was clear from my tone that I did so only in order to obey the law. "That's good," said the visitor, "because your husband is a very intelligent man." This was a strange moment because there was such a sense of approval for the fact of my husband's intelligence, but it had nothing to do with the man he was; rather the approval was all for an idea of an intelligent man and a dutiful wife paying him the homage of sex. The hellish thing was, it was true. Even though I didn't love my dream husband, I considered him intelligent. And so I said, "Yes, he is very intelligent." I said it for complicated reasons. Partly to please the visitor, whom I was afraid of, but more to make some emotional contact with him by invoking a concept he had codified as law, and making him see that I respected intelligence too. The way he looked at me when I said this was also complicated. It was a look of respect for my miserable loyalty to my husband, for my detached admiration for his mind. It was a look that appreciated my humanity, but would only give it a tiny space to breathe, a look a torturer might give a victim who had just expressed a sentiment the torturer considered noble, but that would not prevent torture from taking place.

This prison-house seemed to me our human state, the circumstances of our birth into families not of our choosing, and our inability to free ourselves from psychological patterns learned before we can decide for ourselves. The visitor seemed like the God in the Bible who is kind only as long as you adhere to the rules, and who will sometimes decide to punish you anyway. God doesn't afflict Job because of anything Job has done, but because he wants to prove a point to Satan. When, for example, the angel in Revelation criticizes the church of Pergamos for having members who "hold the doctrine of the Nicolaitanes, which thing I hate," we as readers aren't required to know what this doctrine is or why God hates it or what we might think of it if we knew what it was—that is all irrelevant. And on a larger scale, all our complicated feelings and conflicted impulses about, say, sex are irrelevant. If it's outside marriage it's bad, period.

My conversion lasted only about six months. I was still calling myself a Christian when I took a GED and returned to Michigan to attend community college, but I gradually let it go. I began to write seriously for the first time in my life and I used my passion in telling stories instead of saying prayers.

Twenty years later, I am sympathetic with my first assessment; to me, the Bible still has a mechanical quality, a refusal to brook complexity that feels brutal and violent. There has been a change, however. When I look at Revelation now, it still seems frightening and impenetrable, and it still suggests a fearful, inexorable order that is unknowable by us, in which our earthly concerns matter very little. However, it no longer reads to me like a chronicle of arbitrarily inflicted cruelty. It reads like a terrible abstract of how we violate ourselves and others and thus bring down endless suffering on earth. When I read "And they blasphemed God of heaven because of their pain and their sores, and did not repent of their deeds," I think of myself and dozens of other people I've known or know who blaspheme life itself by failing to have the courage to be honest and kind. And how we then rage around and lash out because we hurt. When I read "fornication," I no longer read it as a description of sex outside marriage: I read it as sex done in a state of psychic disintegration, with no awareness of one's self or one's partner, let alone any sense of honor or even real playfulness. I still don't know what to make of the doctrine of the Nicolaitanes, among other things, but I'm now inclined to read it as a writer's primitive attempt to give form to his moral urgency, to create a structure that could contain and give ballast to the most desperate human confusion.

I'm not sure how to account for this change. I think it mainly has to do with gradually maturing and becoming more deeply aware of my own mechanicalness and my own stringent limitations in giving form to immense complexity—something writers understand very well. It probably has to do with my admittedly dim understanding of how apparently absolute statements can contain an enormous array of meaning and nuance without losing their essential truth. And it has to do with my expanded ability to accept my own fear, and to forgive myself for my own mechanical responses to things I don't understand. In the past, my compassion felt inadequate in the face of Revelation because my compassion was small— perhaps immature is a better word—and conditional. I could not accept what I read there because it did not fit my idea of how life should be, even though I could feel the truth of it in my psyche. Now I recognize, with pain, a genuine description of how hellish life can be, and how even God can't help us because we won't allow it. Paradoxically, I find that the more you accept the pain and fear inherent in human experience, the greater your compassion can become, until finally it is no longer merely your compassion but a small part of the greater love epitomized in the Bible as Jesus.

To me, these realizations don't mean I have arrived at a point of any real knowledge; they are simply interesting as small markers of my development. I imagine that twenty years from now, when I read the Revelation I will once again see it the same, yet differently. I am looking forward to it.

Genesis (Jacob) and Luke

J A M E S   M C C O U R T

Jacob the Trick

Jacob was one of the many stories read out by exuberant nuns, my primary school teachers (given to notions of angels and of dreaming) and a great favorite of Sisters Timothy and Thomasina (seventh and eighth grade), who between them decided that since though always there I was seldom present ("three sheets to the wind" was the phrase) I was likely to turn writer.

All Catholic families then were (happily) alike. All Protestant families were (unhappily) different, perhaps because of their *reading* and *interpretation* of the Bible. They seemed to advertise an aura of Close Encounter with The Lord in the Garden (a maneuver we might attempt *meditatively* in the first sorrowful mystery of the rosary but, having the Eucharist, not otherwise ambitiously pursue). Old Testament plots and New Testament "fulfillments" of them were read at Sunday Mass, as pretexts for homiletics. (Called "chapters" in the earlier Church, their praxis was identical to that of segments of low-budget thriller serials —also called *chapters*—given us at Saturday matinees, along with Movietone News, westerns, and biblical epics. We got our goods, worldly and heavenly, on the installment plan. My problem was that in the cliff-hanger serials the hero always got away—*got away with it*—whereas I must be arrested, mocked, scourged, spat upon, and crucified with Christ to be redeemed.)

Perhaps because they'd often told me truth was stranger than fiction and always to keep away from strangers, I tended to opt for fable, and so finally opening the Bible looked on it as escapist fiction and read it compan-ionably, aided by Hollywood (which furnished if not exactly exegesis, then surely eroticism, and exegesis without Eros is bread without salt). Catholics left real Bible interpretation (Old and New Testaments respectively) to the Jews and to the American College in Rome. (The chief mystery of the Jews was that as God's chosen people, they hadn't chosen to become Christian. Clearly a manifestation, the more liberal theology of the fifties suggested, of the difference between the Will of God and the wishes, even wish-fulfill-ment fantasies, of The Second Person of the Blessed Trinity in His human nature.)

Finally I became as intellectually anti-Protestant as I am culturally philo-Semitic (although I'm somehow drawn to Southern Baptists, particu-larly in high office). If you were Irish Catholic and wanted a career other than one in the metropolitan clergy, it was necessary to assimilate to something else, and given a choice between the dowdy, self-appointed American elect and the worldly (clothes, show business), cultured (book publishing, music), liberal, and sexually tolerant *mishpuccah* of New York Jewry. . . . (A purely imaginative exercise. I'd have made a weak Jew surely, given to capricious readings of the Torah, *a virtue that is no virtue* as the exegete Rashi insists, rather than to the conscientious study of Mishnah and the Talmud. I settled for the cultivation of Yiddish idioms and that gorgeous, and a little tasteless, sense of humor, for no New Yorker who writes about New York and neglects them can be on the qui vive.)

These predilections were the product of anxiety in the face of assimilation to the WASP ascendancy. Their like had accounted for the simultaneous enlistment in various underworld and civic brigades that made nineteenth-century American Irish both the most blatantly criminal *element* in New York life and the majority on metropolitan police forces (and was later manifested in the flirtation of the Kennedys with both the Sicilian mafia and Hoover's FBI). It created untoward resistance in me to the intentions of the Framers, the Movers and the Shakers, and excluded me from the enthusiasm of my fellow educated Americans for the Authorized Version (the very idea of a Father *which art* in heaven!). We read the Douay-Rheims Bible. Also for Milton (we were thoroughly Spencerian, in full, gorgeous, perhaps a little tasteless sacramental and ceremonial panoply) and for Emerson.

I was an estranged boy, yet Jacob's oneness with Israel spoke to my singular identification with America. It is the peculiar affectation of those born as I was on the Fourth of July that they can become something of another stripe (as it turns out, sadly for the Catholic, always the result of self-inflicted—and therefore by definition *protestant*—lash marks). Hawthorne, born on the Fourth of July, wrote of being branded.

The Bible was the Word of God. That word was passed along, and like that the *exact wording* of the written form was of far lesser consequence than the *understood intent* of a man who had given you his word: no gentleman *required* it as part of the agreement. It was to De Mille and Nicholas Ray and not to Milton we turned for elaboration: to *Samson and Delilah* and to *King of Kings.* (In *Samson and Delilah,* male sexual prowess and the ability to bring the house down met its match in Woman, especially when Rise Stevens sang Delilah at the Met, outdoing Hedy Lamarr as a biblical wanton hands down. Being struck blind was allegory: it was perhaps wise to turn a blind eye to Woman. In *King of Kings* we all met our match in Jeffrey Hunter's Jesus.)

The Bible was not sincere. (As Oscar Wilde pointed out, sincerity is the hallmark of bad poetry, and the Bible is great poetry. Moreover, it takes only the merest glance at the *Oxford Dictionary of English Etymology* [ed. C. T. Onions] to understand that if the Bible were sincere, it would require no exegesis, no hermeneutics. No John the Divine breaking the seven seals to get at the big ending.) The notion that the Bible is sincere was born in some long, wet chilly Northern European Protestant winter and unhappily exported to America, where it devolves into fundamentalism. To think that the Bible is sincere is finally impudent: it argues for a *reciprocal* God whose outpouring of favors *procures* love, and as two great writers on dulcet resignation, St. Teresa of Avila and Baruch Spinoza understood, to love God is the supreme *command* (as health is the primary duty) of life. They who do so with all their hearts have no such impertinence as to *expect* to be loved by God in return.

Not sincere, and yet God's word (and two senses of *word* were operative under the rubric of the Logos: this sense of bond or promise—"He's as good as his word"—and the sense of "What's the good word?" as in the *on dit,* the noise). Therefore the Voice of God in the Bible is the Voice of the Trickster. It addresses the devout (particularly the devout in uniform, in canonical or clerical dress) in much the same way and delivers much the same message as that vouchsafed Cary Grant (in the uniform of the Salvation Army) by the salvific American genius Mae West: "You can be had." The great promise of the Old Testament can be summed up in one line: every valley shall be exalted; and that of the New in another: the last shall be first. What can this be but God saying: *if* you take to this idea—this will be that—the opposite will obtain; then only a little thought (as the Wizard of Oz assured the Scarecrow) will yield the notion that in what you call the afterlife, every *existent* will be *non*existent . . . and this means you. The

East of course has touted this famously relaxing ambiguity for nearly three millennia.

Jacob the Trickster, the third member of the Jewish Trinity of Patriarchs (since we always thought in trinitarian terms), was the one aligned with our Holy Spirit. (Abraham was so clearly the Father and Isaac the Son who was both sacrificed and spared, that Jacob had to be the mysterious third, who proceeded from the love between the father and the son, for even though the Old Testament was full of all those strong women, we still imagined patrilineally.) Jacob's consorting with angels in his dream signals an identification. Jacob is an angel, a good boy (not as to his purity—the thief of the birthright is in a sullied existential position—but as to *aesthetics:* he broadcasts the message).

Consider Rebecca. The mother of the queer son always tries to enlist the son against the father. She correctly sees the son as her chief rival in the world (which may be why God put straight men in charge of politics and war, and women and queer men in charge of fashion and manners. And why, when the two camps join forces, as in fifteenth-century Florence, sixteenth-century Spain, Elizabethan England, the France of Louis Quatorze, Hollywood in the 1930s and 1940s, and New York in the 1950s and 1960s, renaissances occur.).

Rebecca encourages Jacob to put on some older male hair, the exterior of the firstborn, to beguile (seduce) his father Isaac (who was in my queer reading himself the near victim of *his* father's terror in reaction to homosexual attraction, saved only by the angel of the Lord). Jacob's deception is tantamount to donning a wig, becoming a transvestite (or transsexual), and having his way with the father (old and blind to the truth: the way queer boys in anguish see their fathers always. Whether or not they, the fathers, are good to them or bad to them, they, the queer sons, are conditioned to take the old man for a ride.). Jacob is therefore both the Trickster and the Trick himself, a smart operator, a *smoothie*. A lustrous preadolescent boy of angelic countenance (without body hair). There is no way he can become Israel until he butches up his act (be a man, go out and kill something. The mother will cook it: men slay, women cook up the results.). And if he wants to do that he has to imitate his brother, and, by doing so, supplant him—or kill him.

Jacob's mother helps him pose as a man (cooking up and dressing the event). Jacob wears not only a goat skin, but Esau's dirty old clothes: the old goat's sense of the smell of his own favorite kid delivers the kicker erotic charge. (There is nothing more effective in certain situations, every hustler knows, than cheap scent. For me it is as telling as a boxer skipping rope. Jacob was like that cheap scent, that boxer. I'm reminded of the late Glenway's advice to a cadet, and how the older homosexual addressing the younger would habitually say, "Now listen to your mother." Westcott advised, "It's best not to fight, but if you have to, if you feel you must, then for pity sake, fight dirty.")

This ability of the mother to act as Fixer, to rearrange the dictates of any order (a bow to the capricious power of Nature) is carried into Christianity in the radical veneration of the Mother of God in Mediterranean countries and in Ireland, where it is accepted that to get to Him you go through her, the Mediatrix of all grace. Jesus of Nazareth's first miracle, changing the water into wine at the marriage feast of Cana, was done at the express request of Mary, over His objection that His time had not yet come. She said in effect, "I'll be the judge of that."

The mother of the queer son is ambivalent as she dispatches him. Saying, with Rebecca, "My son, any curse would be mine. My voice guides you—only follow," she is confident the husband-father will be charmed by him, but also torn between the fear that he, *fructus ventris,* will succeed, displacing her and rendering the role of woman ancillary to the parthenogenic rule of celibate men (the story of Jesus Christ), and that he will fail, arousing the wrath of the father, and be rejected. (The same story, ending in the naked outcry *Eli, Eli, lama sabachthani!*)

I also detect in Esau and Jacob an echo of the Dioscuri. Although Jasper Griffin, in a recent issue of the *New York Review of Books,* assures readers that the Hellenic Greeks, whose manners Jews adopted after the Babylonian exile, were "cheerfully ignorant" of Hebrew literature, there is surely a resemblance between the older Greek story of the twins, one mortal, one immortal, and that of Esau and Jacob. As surely as Esau is ordinary, mortal, and (perhaps therefore) susceptible to being tricked, so Jacob, by virtue of tricking, wrestling with God, and becoming Israel itself, achieves what for the Jews is the only acceptable immortality: memorial fame, attached, not as for the Romans (and for our time) to violence and publicity and glamour, but to fecundity and stability and guile. It has often been pointed out that the chief glory of Greek expression is its celebration of the fleeting moment (the one-time life) and in the Democratic Age Greece comes into its glory, but all along there has been the other lurking thing: the mortal *and* immortal self (or strain of self, or strain of self-similarity; the latest version: DNA). The Hebrews, in their foundation (Jacob/Israel) had, it seems to me, a grip on the immortal self (the same grip characteristic of the maritime Celts, who had no literature before Church Latin gave Irish an alphabet, but an epic oral tradition as old as the Phoenicians and still operative in the west of Ireland).

Myself the second son, I seem to have tricked my way through childhood on a curious alternation of savage hysteria and winsome ways, then crashed, spending an uncomfortable if eventful year of my adolescence as a bullied boy, adopting for the siege a manic-depressive defense. It was in that time, in Jackson Heights, that I began to pine after memories of Jacob, Oz, and latency, and to replace peer rejection with replays of the "special and invisible friend" stage fantasies of one's guardian angel's friends (guardian angels were dogma). Later still, in Identity Crisis (aged twenty-eight), I came to view Jacob as the first analysand, his pillow as the first analytical couch, his vision the first exercise in free-association, his wrestling the first against the death instinct. ("But Jacob's cunning," writes Harold Bloom, "is the defense of a survivor, and while it guarantees the continuation of his long life, it does not protect him from suffering.") Analysis replaces the imaginary angelic friend with whom one wrestled gaily in the assurance of no resentment, and finally, as with Jacob and his angel, in pursuit of the kindly blessing. (Analysis, popularly supposed a wrestling with demons, actually reveals the difference between one's angels and one's demons to be chiefly one of dress-up: the engagement, the embrace, the agon is what matters. According to psychoanalysis, *neurotic* suffering can be replaced with ordinary unhappiness: the Tragic Sense of Life by day; camp sensibility by night.)

Hence although aperçus, epiphanies, and orgasms came one upon another in sequence (and sequins), trotting up and down night ladders, they had a uniform resemblance, like Ziegfeld girls on that spotlit stairway to paradise. I realized this was what was called aestheticism, something in those days to be tempered with a diet of red meat: political commitment . . . social concern . . . but I was hooked. Jacob was the Great Aesthete and Judaism the type of the lost "original" religion for which I'd been greatly longing.

THE GOOD THIEF

Unnamed in the gospel, he was called by the Church St. Dismas and a special emphasis was put upon him, as it was upon all exemplars of the grace of conversion. We prayed to him, as I recall, for benignity, a virtue akin to humility (we prayed for that to the publican in the same evangelist's Parable of the Publican and the Pharisee) but more guilelessly energetic.

> *And there were two other malefactors led with him to*
> *be put to death . . .*
>
> (*LUKE* 23:32)

*And one of the malefactors which were hanged railed
on him, saying, If thou be the Christ save thyself and us.*

*But the other answering rebuked him, saying, Dost
thou not fear God, seeing thou art in the same condemnation?*

*And we indeed justly; for we receive the due reward of
our deeds: but this man has done nothing amiss.*

*And he said unto Jesus, Lord remember me when thou
comest into thy kingdom.*

*And Jesus said unto him, Verily I say unto thee this day
shalt thou be with me in Paradise.*

(*LUKE 23:39–43*)

The story in this form is unique to Luke the physician (and psycholo-
gist, the Chekhov of the gospelers). In Matthew and Mark, both thieves rail
at Jesus along with the chief priests, the Pharisees, and the rabble. Luke
calls them, unspecifically, *malefactors,* and John simply records *two others,* but
John, uniquely present as the Beloved Disciple was, it may be presumed,
too enrapt by the stunning glamour of Jesus' direct address to him in the
matter of the care of Mary the Mother (John 20:25–27) to attend to a
competitive discourse. And after all, "Look after this, will you, dear?" and
then (the God/man turning to not-so-much-as-a-disciple-never-
mind-a-minion-but-only-the-nearest-mouth-full-of-kind words, and directing) *"You come with me"* constitutes the kind of erotic contretemps one
would hardly either brave or record with feelings of unmixed delight.

But what about the grace of benignity? It was deemed, as I've said,
more dynamic, more *candid* than humility (a stance that often seems ravenous with studied deserving) by those aligned with the virtue of simplicity
(and at root with the idea of salvation through Faith, evidenced by a
demure, *stricken* quality cognate to the meekness that would inherit the
earth).

My grace is sufficient for you, my power is made perfect in weakness.

(2 CORINTHIANS 12:9)

Nuns had it sometimes, and those downtrodden (or never prosperous) unaccountably good secular Americans (glamorized on the screen from Tol'able David through John Doe right down to Forrest Gump), players often represented as equipped dealing with less than full decks or rolling incompletely dotted dice, who make the Game of Life's winners seem commonplace and mean. The underlying sense: purely good works are categorically impossible in a fallen nature and would in any case add nothing to God's estimation of a soul, an estimation undeceived, radically severe, and infinitely merciful.

I came to an understanding of the intrapsychic melodrama the story of the two thieves represents. All three of the crucified on Calvary are Christ, who, suffering unto death is confronted with two reactive personae, and must first abide the negative before embracing the positive. For what is the bad thief's railing but the mirroring, the doubling of Jesus' own *Eli, Eli, lama sabachthani* (Matthew 27:46; Mark 15:34), while the resignation of self in the good thief is the doubling of "Father, into thy hands I commend my spirit." The moral lesson, a reiteration of the Redeemer's own dictum, "Unless you become like little children," is not to expect the fulfillment of motive (the kingdom of heaven) before helplessness, infantile wailing, and even the failure of recognition (an undoing parallel to the formation from helplessness through rage to some sense of functional autonomy in the first part of life) has been undergone. The anomaly that it is self-referring man's fate to negotiate successive stages of maturation (storing up treasure) only to fall backward through them again before the apocalypse of the distinguished thing, is *the* unanswered question. As Chekhov, ending his last, greatest play said, "If only we knew."

Gospels

M A R I L Y N N E   R O B I N S O N

One Easter I went with my grandfather to a small Presbyterian church in northern Idaho, where I heard a sermon on the discrepancies in the gospel accounts of the resurrection. I was a young child with neither the habit nor the expectation of understanding, as the word is normally used, most of what went on around me. Yet I remember that sermon, and I believe in some degree I took its meaning.

As an older child in another church and town, on no special occasion, I heard the Eighth Psalm read, and kept for myself a few words from it, because they heartened certain intuitions of mine—"When I consider thy heavens, the work of thy fingers, the moon and the stars . . . What is man, that thou art mindful of him? and the son of man, that thou visitest him? For thou hast made him a little lower than the angels . . .'' I quote the King James Version because those were the words I heard and remembered. The thought never entered my mind that the language could be taken to exclude me, perhaps because my experience of it was the religious one, of words in some exceptional sense addressed precisely to me.

I can imagine myself that primal Easter, restive at my grandfather's elbow, pushing my nickels and dimes of collection money into the tips of my gloves to make toad fingers, struggling with the urge to swing my legs, memorably forbidden to remove my hat, aware that I should not sigh. In those days boredom for me was a misery and a passion, and anticipation a pleasure so sharp I could not tell it from dread. So of course I hated holidays. For these and other reasons my entire experience of being in the world was slightly galled and antagonized. Quotidian events, dawn and evening for example, I found almost unbearable. I remember exasperating the kindly intentions of elders with moodiness and weepiness I could not explain. I do not remember childhood as happy but as filled and overfilled with an intensity of experience that made happiness a matter of little interest. I can only imagine that other versions of me, realer than the poor present self forever being discarded in their favor, larger than I and impatient with my immaturity and my awkwardness, simply wanted out. Metamorphosis is an unsentimental business, and I was a long time in the thick of it, knees scraped, clothes awry, nerves strained and wearied.

I doubt I concealed my restlessness, or much of it, and I doubt my grandfather knew the hour was anything but tedium for me. He would not have known, because no one knew, that I was becoming a pious child, seriously eager to hear whatever I might be told. What this meant precisely, and why it was true, I can only speculate. But it seems to me I felt God as a presence before I had a name for him, and long before I knew words like faith or belief. I was aware to the point of alarm of a vast energy of intention, all around me, barely restrained, and I thought everyone else must be aware of it. For that reason I found the majestic terrains of my childhood, to which my ancestors had brought their ornate Victorian appreciation at daunting cost in life and limb, very disturbing, and I averted my gaze as I could from all those luminist splendors. I was coaxed to admire, and I would not, admiration seeming so poor a thing in the circumstances. Only in church did I hear experience like mine acknowledged, in all those strange narratives, read and expounded and for all that opaque as figures of angels painted on gold.

This is of course to employ language a child would never use. Then again, I describe experience outside the constraints of understanding that asserted themselves in me as I grew into this strange culture and century, and which oblige me to use language as little mine as mine is the language of that child. I describe the distantly remembered emotions of a girl long vanished—I am sure if I met her on the street I would not recognize her. In another time and place she and I might have grown up together, and she would have been able to speak for herself. Asked if I romanticize or exaggerate the world she saw and felt, she would reply, She does not touch the hem of it.

All the old writers on the subject remark that in every age and nation people have had the idea of a god of some sort. So my archaic self might have been nothing other than a latter-day pagan whose intuitions were not altogether at odds with, as it happened, Presbyterianism, and so were simply polished to that shape. Or it might have been that I was a mystic by vocation and, despite Presbyterianism, suffered atrophy of my gift in a life where I found little use for it. For all I know I am a mystic now, and simply too close to the phenomenon to have a clear view of it. In any case I began as a pagan and have ended as one, though only in the sense that I have never felt secure in the possession of the ideas and loyalties that are dearest to me. I am a Saxon in a basilica, refusing to admire so that anyone can see me, thrown back on impassivity as my only notion of decorum. I am surely wrong if I blame history for this sense I have of tenuous claim, wrong to invoke the notion of blame at all. Interloper though I may be, I enjoy the thief's privilege of pleasure in the simple preciousness of things that are not my own. I enjoy it far too much to attempt to regularize my situation. In my childhood when the presence of God seemed everywhere and I seemed to myself a mote of exception, improbable as a flaw in the sun, the very sweetness of the experience lay in that stinging thought—not me, not like me, not mine.

By the standards of my generation, all my life I have gone to church with a kind of persistence, as I do to this day. Once recently I found myself traveling all night to be home in time for church, and it occurred to me to consider in what spirit or out of what need I would do such a thing. My tradition does not encourage the idea that God would find any merit in it. I go to church for my own gratification, which is intense, though it had never occurred to me before to try to describe it to myself.

The essence of it, certainly, is the Bible, toward which I do not feel in any degree proprietary, with which after long and sometimes assiduous attention I am not familiar. I believe the entire hypertrophic bookishness of my life arose directly out of my exposure, among modest Protestant solemnities of music and flowers, to the language of Scripture. Therefore I know many other books very well and I flatter myself that I understand them— even books by people like Augustine and Calvin. But I do not understand the Bible. I study theology as one would watch a solar eclipse in a shadow. In church, the devout old custom persists of merely repeating verses, one or another luminous fragment, a hymn before and a hymn afterward. By grace of my abiding ignorance, it is always new to me. I am never not instructed.

I have shifted allegiances the doctrinal and demographic inch that separates Presbyterians from Congregationalists, but for all purposes I am where I ought to be, as sociologists calculate, and I should feel right at home. I will concede only that the sensation of exclusion is more poignant to me in these precincts than in others, being after all these years so very familiar. The people around me every Sunday are as reserved and attentive as I am, like very respectful guests, in a church they own, sustain, and entirely govern.

From time to time on the strength of the text the minister will conclude something brave and absolute—You *must* forgive, or, If you think you have anything because you deserve it, you have forgotten the grace of God, or, No history or prospect of failure can excuse you from the obligation to try to do good. These are moments that do not occur in other settings, and I am so far unregenerate that they never cease to impress me deeply. And it touches me that this honorable art of preaching is carried forward when there is so little regard for it among us now. But the most persuasive and forthright explication is still theology. For me, at least, the text itself always remains almost entirely elusive. So I must come back to hear it again; in the old phrase, to have it opened for me again.

The four Gospels do not agree in their accounts of the discovery of the empty tomb on the morning of the resurrection. The sermon I heard with my grandfather established that fact with the forensic concern for textual detail some ministers reserve for grand occasions. This would account for the great restlessness which, as I recall, nearly overthrew my better self.

As it happens, Matthew reports that, apparently ''with Mary Magdalene and the other Mary'' watching, ''behold, there was a great earthquake: for the angel of the lord descended from heaven, and came and rolled back the stone from the door, and sat upon it. His countenance was like lightning, and his raiment white as snow: And for fear of him the keepers did shake, and became as dead men. And the angel answered and said unto the women, Fear not ye: for I know that ye seek Jesus, which was crucified. He is not here: for he is risen, as he said. Come, see the place where the Lord lay.''

In Mark's account ''Mary Magdalene and Mary the mother of James, and Salome'' came to the tomb at the rising of the sun with spices to anoint the body. ''And they said among themselves, Who shall roll us the stone away from the door of the sepulchre? And when they looked, they saw that the stone was rolled away: for it was very great. And entering into the sepulchre, they saw a young man sitting on the right side, clothed in a long white garment; and they were affrighted. And he saith unto them, Be not affrighted: Ye seek Jesus of Nazareth, which was crucified: he is risen; he is not here: behold the place where they laid him.''

According to Luke, women who had come with Jesus from Galilee prepared spices and ointments and came to the tomb to find the stone rolled back. ''And they entered in, and found not the body of the Lord Jesus. And it came to pass, as they were much perplexed thereabout, behold, two men stood next to them in shining garments: And as they were afraid, and bowed down their faces to the earth, they said unto them, Why seek ye the living among the dead?'' The disciples with whom, unrecognized, Jesus walks to Emmaus, tell him the women described ''a vision of angels.''

In the Gospel of John, Mary Magdalene goes to the tomb early in the morning, sees the stone rolled back, and runs to tell the disciples that the body of Jesus has been removed. Peter and another disciple, presumably John himself, run to the sepulcher, and Simon Peter ''went into the sepulchre, and seeth the linen clothes lie, and the napkin, that was about his head, not lying with the linen clothes, but wrapped together in a place by itself . . . But Mary stood at the sepulchre weeping: and as she wept, she stooped down, and looked into the sepulchre, and seeth two angels in white sitting, the one at the head and the other at the feet, where the body of Jesus had lain. And they say unto her, Woman, why weepest thou?''

The minister who drew my attention to this mystery, a plump old man in a white vestment as I remember him, must have asked how it came about or what it could mean that this essential moment was described differently in every report of it. What I recall of the sermon would have been offered as an answer to that question. He dwelt on the other figures at the tomb, not the women or the disciples but the figures described as angels in three accounts and in one as a young man in a long white garment. He asked what it would mean if all the descriptions were in fact of one or two young men, followers of Jesus who had simply stayed the night by the tomb or arrived there before the women in the morning. Or if the one young man was in fact an angel. The Bible, he said, was full of proof that angels could pass for men, which must certainly mean that men could pass for angels. He concluded that, insofar as a young man is seen under the aspect of joy and kindness and holiness, he is properly seen as an angel, because that is a vision of his immortal nature. And that insofar as the joy and kindness and holiness of angels are addressed to human beings, angels are like us and at one with us, at their most beautiful when they express attributes most beautiful in us. That such a confusion could have occurred is central to the meaning of the resurrection, because it reminds us what we are. Amen, he said, having blessed my life with a lovely thing to ponder.

The families of both my parents settled and established themselves in the northern mountains, where there is a special sweetness in the light and grace in the vegetation, and as well a particular tenderness in the contact of light and vegetation. We used to hunt for wild strawberries in places in the woods where there had once been fires. These meadows, which for decades or centuries would hardly have felt more sunlight than the floor of the sea, were avid for it. Because of the altitude, or the damp, or the kind of grass that grew in such places, they were radiant, smoldering, gold with transparency, accepting light altogether. Thousands of florets for which I would never learn names, so tiny even a child had to kneel to see them at all, squandered intricacy and opulence on avid little bees, the bees cherished, the flowers cherished, the light cherished, visibly, audibly, palpably.

John Calvin says that when a seed falls into the ground it is cherished there, by which he means that everything the seed contains by way of expectation is foreseen and honored. One might as well say the earth invades the seed, seizes it as occasion to compose itself in some brief shape. Groundwater in a sleeve of tissue, flaunting improbable fragrances and iridescences as the things of this strange world are so inclined to do. So a thriving place is full of intention, a sufficiency awaiting expectation, teasing hope beyond itself.

To find in the sober woods these little Orients of delectation was like hearing a tale of opulent grace poured out on modest need or of a miracle astonishing despair, a parable brilliant with strangeness, cryptic with wisdom, disturbing as a tender intention full of the frightening mercy of foreknowledge. God will wipe away all tears, the dead will rise, meant to me then, Little girl, you will mourn and you will die. Perhaps that was some great part of the difference I felt between the world and myself, that while it was a thousand ways true that it knew me as I could not know myself—my old relatives remembered people with my voice or my eyes and how they lived and how their lives ended—I hoarded the notion of this singular self in this singular moment, as if such things could exist, and shrugged away intention and anticipation and cherishing, knowing they meant that even I never was my own.

I knew my grandfather for many years, but I am not sure I ever knew him well. He seemed stern to me and I was very shy of him. I had heard sad stories about him as a boy and a young man, and when I was with him I always thought of them, and I was cautious, as if the injuries might still be tender.

It may be that I knew my grandfather very well *because* I thought of him as a boy and a young man, and explained his silence to myself in such terms. My memory of him allows me to interpret the dignity of his shrinking height and stooping back as an effort of composure of the kind people make when the shock of cruelty is still new to them, when resignation is still a novel labor. I interpret the memory of his polished shoes and his habit of gardening in his oldest suit and his worst necktie as evidence that I sensed in him diligent pride in the face of sadness not otherwise to be borne. Perhaps he himself could not have told me how near the truth I was.

His gardening was uncanny. The flourishing he set in motion brought admirers from other counties. I remember once following him down a row of irises, not sure whether I was invited, whether the irises were being shown to me. He would hold one blossom and another in the tips of his fingers, at arm's length, and tilt his face up and back to look at them. It was an old man's method of scrutiny, but to me it seemed as if he were revealing prodigy or sleight, the way a magician opens his hand to reveal a dove. I looked carefully at every blossom he appeared to commend to me, noting how they were made of cell and capillary, whisker and freckle, frail skin tented on white bone, and how they were chill to the touch, and how they curled on themselves like smoke, and how, till the life was wrung out of it, each one accomplished a small grandeur of form.

In those mountains there is a great constant silence surrounding any brief local silence and one is always aware of it. When I was a child it seemed to me sometimes it might be emptiness that would tease my soul out of my body, with some intention too huge even to notice my fragile flesh. I knew that the mountains and the lakes and the woods brought people's lives to disastrous conclusions, often too frightening to repeat in the hearing of children. There were people whose loss could hardly be borne no matter the years that passed, and whose names were spoken rarely, and then softly, with rue and grief—Steven and Lewis and the precious Virgie, a woman or girl I have mourned my whole life in the absence of all particulars, just for the way they said her name. I lived so as to be missed with bitterness, and I learned to be good at the things they praised, preparing and refining their regret. I poured myself into the vessel of their memories, which are mine now. I save all those people in myself by regretting the loss of them in the very way they taught me.

Oddly, perhaps, in the circumstances, no one so far as I remember ever spoke to me of heaven. Certainly no one ever spoke to me of hell. Though absentmindedly they sometimes murmured hymns to themselves, among my kindred religion was rarely mentioned. I believe I ascribed this fact to the power of it, since it was characteristic of them to be silent about things that in any way moved them. It never occurred to me to wonder if they were devout, nor have I any great reason to wonder, looking back. Religion was simply among the burdened silences I pondered and glossed, feeling no need to inquire, assuming an intimacy with the thoughts of those around me which may well have been entirely real.

Among my family, my training in the right conduct of life seemed to assume that left to myself I would rather not break a commandment, and to bend its coercive energies to improving my grammar. The patient old women who taught me Presbyterianism taught in parables. God spoke to Moses from a burning bush, Pharaoh dreamed a dream of famine, Jesus said, "Take up your bed and walk." We drew or colored pictures of these events, which were, I think, never explained to us. No intrusion on the strangeness of these tales was ever made. It was as if some old relative had walked me down to the lake knowing an imperious whim of heaven had made it a sea of gold and glass, and had said, "This is a fine evening," and walked me home again. I am convinced it was all this reticence, in effect this esotericism, that enthralled me.

Surely it is not true to say that the gospel stories were written in the hope that they would be believed, rather that, by the time they were written down, they were the cherished possession of the early church and had taken forms many had already found to be persuasive, and also beautiful and moving. It seems wrong to suggest that in their accounts of the resurrection the intent of the writers is to persuade their readers and hearers of the truth of an incredible event, simply because there is so much evidence that resurrection would not have been considered incredible. The prophet Elijah had brought a child back from the dead. He himself ascended into heaven without dying, and his return was awaited in Jesus' time. John the Baptist was believed to be Elijah. Jesus was believed to be Elijah. Herod thought Jesus was John the Baptist back from the dead. Jesus restored to life Lazarus and the temple official's daughter. Before the resurrection of Lazarus, his sister Martha dutifully misinterprets Jesus' assurance that he will live again to refer to a general resurrection of the dead. The Sadducees are described as those "who do not believe in the resurrection," a phrase which surely implies that the idea was abroad independently of Jesus. At the moment Jesus died graves are said to have opened and the dead to have walked in the streets.

In the world the gospels describe there seems to be no skepticism about miracles as such, only about the authenticity or origins of particular miracles. Indeed, where in the premodern world would one find such skepticism? The restoration of the dead to life is not only anticipated but reported, with, if anything, less astonishment than the healing of those born blind or lame.

It seems to me that the intent of the gospel writers is not to make the resurrection seem somehow plausible or credible—this could hardly be done without diminishing its impressiveness as miracle—but instead to heighten its singularity, when, as event, it would seem by no means unexampled. I believe it is usual to say that the resurrection established who Jesus was and what his presence meant. Perhaps it is truer to say the opposite, that who Jesus was established what his resurrection meant, that he seized upon a narrative familiar or even pervasive and wholly transformed it.

When, in the Gospel of John, weeping Mary Magdalene stoops to look into the tomb and sees the angels, they ask her, "Woman, why weepest thou?" The text creates the dreamy impression that the two angels speak together. Then she turns and sees a man standing behind her, Jesus, whom she mistakes for a gardener. He speaks the same words as the angels did, "Woman, why weepest thou?" and he asks, "Whom seekest thou?" Does he see and hear the angels too? Or does he know her thoughts? Or was it his voice she heard in the first place? Mary herself would not have known. Jesus seems to be teasing her toward delight and recognition, ready to enjoy her surprise, in something like the ordinary manner of a friend. The narrative asserts that he is a figure of unutterable holiness, only pausing to speak to Mary before he ascends to heaven, yet it is his very ordinariness that disguises him from her. Splendor is very well for youths and angels, but when Jesus takes up again for a little while the life he had wept to leave, it is the life of a plain man.

If Jesus was not a messiah after the manner of David, neither was he a spiritual leader after the manner of Elijah, though his resurrection, if it were not insistently interpreted in the light of his life and teaching, might well have encouraged that association, which was clearly very available to his followers. The great difference is simply embrace. Elijah's ascent expressed God's love toward him. Jesus' resurrection expressed God's love toward humankind. Jesus tells Mary, "Go to my brethren, and say unto them, I ascend unto my Father, and your Father; and to my God, and your God.''

This moment is surely full of implication. Imagine Jesus as an ordinary man, the sort to fall prey to the penalty of crucifixion, by means of which Roman law terrified the humble by depriving offenders of their dignity together with their lives. Then if, after his ordeal, Jesus had gathered around himself just the composure of an ordinary man, so that he could be mistaken for someone going about his work, that would seem like miracle and grandeur, that would be an astonishing beauty. It seems to me that the narrative, in its most dazzling vision of holiness, commends to us beauty of an altogether higher order than spectacle, that being mere commonplace, ineffable humanity.

''What is man that thou art mindful of him?'' A question is more spacious than a statement, far better suited to expressing wonder. The method of the Psalmist is exuberant. He offers the heavens to our consideration, than which nothing vaster can be imagined, then diminishes them in relation to God by describing them as the work, not of his will or even of his hands, but of his fingers. There is a wonderful implication that the great moon and the innumerable stars are astonishing not for the vastnesses they fill so sparsely and illuminate so slightly, but because God should delight in making anything so small and fine as the heavens and their adornments, every way exceeding them as he does. I have always imagined the trace of a gesture of conjuration or display left in the clouds of stars curling on themselves like smoke.

The strategy of the Psalmist is to close the infinite distance between God and humankind by confounding all notions of scale. If the great heavens are the work of God's fingers, what is small and mortal man? The poem answers its own question this way: Man is *crowned* with honor and glory. He is in a singular sense what God has made him, because of the dignity God has conferred upon him, splendor of a higher order, like that of angels. The Hebrew Scriptures everywhere concede: yes foolish, yes guilty, yes weak, yes sad and bewildered. Yes, resistant to cherishing and rebellious against expectation. And yes, forever insecure at best in his vaunted dominion over creation. Then how is this dignity manifest? Surely in that God is mindful of man, in that he "visits" him—this is after all the major assertion of the whole literature. "What is man?" is asked in awe—that God should be intrigued or enchanted by him, or loyal to him. Any sufficient answer would go some way toward answering "What is God?" I think anxieties about anthropomorphism are substantially inappropriate in a tradition whose main work has been to assert and ponder human theomorphism.

When, in the Gospel of John, Jesus says to Mary Magdalene, "Woman, why weepest thou?" he is using, so scholarship tells me, a term of great respect and deference. Elsewhere he addresses his mother as "woman." I know of no other historical moment in which this word is an honorific. Of course Jesus, however he is understood, whatever powers are ascribed to him, could only use the words he found ready for use, and this must mean that over generations the culture in which he was to live his life had been preparing a certain improbable consensus about the meaning of this one word, which, in the narrative, is the first one he speaks in the new world of his restored life.

How much speculation should detail such as this be asked to bear? It is as true of these old texts as it is of anything that we do not really know what they are. I would suggest their peculiarities reflect problems of art, more than they do discrepant memory or uncertain transmission. I would suggest that they attempt to preserve a sense of Jesus' presence, that they are evocation and portraiture first of all, meant to achieve likeness rather than precision, in the manner of art. The Old Testament is full of characterization, of great Moses, especially. But in those narratives the nature of the hero and the nature of God are separate mysteries, the second vastly overshadowing the first. In the Jesus narratives they are the same mystery, so attention dwells on him in a manner entirely unique in Scripture.

The agreement among the varying accounts is profound, more strikingly so because they differ in their particulars. For example, in all the varying accounts of his encounters with his followers after the resurrection, Jesus is concealed from them by his ordinariness—as, for that matter, he had been in life. In every instance he is among them on terms of friendship, once even making a fire and cooking supper for them. If, let us say, memories were transposed to provide eloquent detail, or even if some details were invented, it would be in the service of creating a likeness, not a history, and discrepancies would matter not at all.

To say that literal representation is different from portraiture is to make a distinction like this: Jesus, even in the interval before his ascent into heaven, did in fact address a woman with courtesy and deference. Or, it would have been *like* Jesus, even in the interval before his ascent into heaven, to address a woman with courtesy and deference. A statement of the second kind could easily be truer, and is certainly more meaningful, than a statement of the first kind.

How to describe the powerful old life of Scripture? As a pious child, Jesus must at some time have heard the words, "What is man, that thou art mindful of him?" and also the psalm that begins, "My God, my God, why hast thou forsaken me?" These narratives seize their occasion. They flourished in the perception and memory of those near Jesus, and in the stories they told about him. They were clearly in his mind. More is meant by prophecy, and more by fulfillment, than that narratives shape and recur. But without them there would be neither prophecy nor fulfillment.

"Woman," Jesus, when he had lived and died, said or would have

said, using a word perhaps not used so gently since Adam was a gardener—
"Woman, why weepest thou?" Mary Magdalene could hear this as the
question of a kindly stranger, but it means in fact, there is no more cause
for weeping. It means, perhaps, God will wipe away all tears. "Who
seekest thou?" a question of the same kind, means, she need not look
farther. To Jesus, or to the writer whose account renders what he took to
be implicit in the moment, these questions might be wider altogether, full
of awe. How did sorrow enter the world? What would be the nature of
comfort or of restitution? The scene we are given answers its own questions, and does not answer them at all. Here is Jesus, by great miracle an
ordinary man, except that he carries in his body the marks of mortal injury.
From whatever cosmic grandeur the moment claims for him, he speaks to
the friend of his humanity with joy and kindness but also with deference,
honoring her. When Mary looks at Jesus, knowing who he is, what does
she see? A more amazing question—when Jesus looks at Mary, and whenever he has looked at her, what does *he* see? We are told that, in the days
before death and sorrow, God walked of an evening in the garden he had
made, that he saw his likeness in the gardeners, that he spoke with them.
What can these strange stories mean? After so much time and event and so
much revelation, the mystery is only compounded.

So I have spent my life watching, not to see beyond the world, merely to
see, great mystery, what is plainly before my eyes. I think the concept of
transcendence is based on a misreading of creation. With all respect to
heaven, the scene of miracle is here, among us. The eternal as an idea is
much less preposterous than time, and this very fact should seize our
attention. In certain contexts the improbable is called the miraculous.

What is eternal must always be complete, if my understanding is
correct. So it is possible to imagine that time was created in order that
there might be narrative—event, sequence and causation, ignorance and

error, retribution, atonement. A word, a phrase, a story falls on rich or stony ground and flourishes as it can, possibility in a sleeve of limitation. Certainly time is the occasion for our strangely mixed nature, in every moment differently compounded, so that often we surprise ourselves, and always scarcely know ourselves, and exist in relation to experience, if we attend to it and if its plainness does not disguise it from us, as if we were visited by revelation.

Job

R I C H A R D   B A U S C H

I was thirteen or fourteen years old be-
fore I understood that the gospels that were read on Sunday at Mass
were taken from the New Testament, and that the *Gradual,* the *Introit,*
and the *Lesson,* were all taken from the Old Testament. I'd become
extremely interested in salvation, like almost everyone else at that
time—Sputnik had just been launched; the Russians not only had the
Bomb, they had something circling the earth on the margins of space,
something that for all we knew was spying on us. The end of the
world was always about to drop in our laps, and the monolithic
Communist conspiracy was in full swing; they were getting in everywhere (I remember associating the word *communism* with the phrase
communicative disease).

Moreover, as youthful members of the one and only Apostolic

Roman Catholic Church, we were always being exposed to dire pictures of the other side of salvation—what happens when you don't get to heaven. I remember one depicting the souls tumbling into hell. They looked like a lot of very frightened people, most of them women. We heard their shrieks, and the roar of the flames. A murmuring recorded voice said, "Listen to the screams of the damned, as they fall into the pit." It was a slide show. A moment later, the little dull bell dinged, the machine made its small cranking sound, and the image was pushed aside for another: someone's idea of the glorious throne of God.

In some important ways, it was a different church, then—the one that existed before John XXIII and Vatican II.

The only piece of the Old Testament that I knew was the Ten Commandments, of course, which we were forced to recite in the religion classes we attended on weekends. Confraternity of Christian Doctrine. Instruction for Catholic children who were forced by circumstances to attend public schools. We learned the catechism, too, of course. *Who made you? God made me. Why did God make you? He made me to know, serve and love him with my whole heart and my whole mind and my whole body.*

But I don't recall that much time was spent on the Commandments as such. We recited them. *Thou shalt not kill,* of course. *Thou shalt not steal. Thou shalt not bear false witness. Thou shalt not take the name of the Lord Thy God in vain. Thou shalt not have false Gods. Thou shalt honor thy father and thy mother.* They were words. We loved our parents, all six of us did, and of course we were not likely to begin worshiping golden calves in the desert. At Belt Junior High School there were few inducements to murder or slander. It was easy enough not to steal, since nobody had anything much to begin with.

But mostly, it seemed to me the priests and nuns when they talked about sin were talking about sins of the flesh. One priest, Father X, let's call him, never hesitated to strike the back of the neck of someone who displeased him, and when there was a real infraction among the altar boys, he had a little thing he called "the belt line." It was a gauntlet of forty boys facing each other in two lines of twenty, each with his belt out and held like a whip; the offender had to run between the two lines, and take the beating, a whack from either side, twenty times, until he came out of the gauntlet on the other end. The stupid, brutal, unchristian nature of this never seemed to occur to Father X—though he had radar when it came to the use of filthy language (his phrase), and he had a lot to say about the sinful way the girls dressed in summer, the condemned filth in movies and books.

When, at that very tender and raw and innocently passionate age, I discovered what all young boys discover about their bodies, I was completely unprepared for it. In the first blush of the moment, I thought I'd made the find of the century, and wanted to tell everyone I knew. I didn't, though. Since what I had discovered was after all a privy act, and since the possibility had struck through me that I might in fact have been the last person to discover a thing everyone else already knew.

I decided to keep my eyes and ears open, on the chance that someone, an adult, might say something which would reveal the real case to me. When, in the following two weeks no one did, I consulted the family Bible —the book where all the marriages and births and deaths were recorded, the one that sat on the living room table in my Grandmother Roddy's big old house in the Brookland section of Washington, D.C., and looked again at those Ten Commandments I'd been made to memorize. Since I did not know what *covet* meant, and hadn't yet reached the stage of knowing that every word of biblical texture carries weight and force in the collective mind of the whole country I live in, I settled on the word *adultery*. I had heard the word used in one of Father X's sermons about the sinful sex lives of certain Hollywood stars, who flaunted their immorality before the public. This was 1958 remember, when the Legion of Decency was rating

motion pictures, and much of the world's greatest literature was proscribed.

Adultery. It was a mortal sin. I remembered with a sinking heart that
this was what the priest had said, and now it dawned on me that the
commandment must serve as a blanket for all sexual activity outside of the
Holy Matrimony Father X was talking about. So I hurried to confession, at
the first opportunity, and when the sliding wood panel opened in that dark
little space, I murmured into the small square screen with the shadowed
profile in it, "Forgive me, Father, for I have sinned. My last confession was
two weeks ago. I lied to my mother three times about the dishes. I said
unkind things to my sisters four times. I disobeyed my mother once. I took
the Lord's name in vain five times. And—and I committed adultery twenty
or thirty times, Father. I lost count."

The priest, not Father X but a kindly man named Father McManus,
gave forth what I thought was a cough.

I waited.

"And who did you—was there a partner?"

"You can do it with partners?" I said, a little too loud.

There was another coughing spell.

"How old are you, son?"

I told him.

"There was no one else involved?"

"No, sir."

"Then that's not adultery."

"It's not a *sin?*" I couldn't keep the joyousness out of my voice.

"Oh yes—it's a very big sin. The sin of self-abuse. And if you die
with it on your soul you'll go straight to hell, just as if you had committed
the—uh—" He coughed again. "The adultery."

"Yes, Father," I said.

And he gave me penance, and I went out into the world the Bible had
made, or that generations of people had made out of the Bible.

Like most young writers who are as yet unknown to themselves, I read widely and indiscriminately as a young man, and when I finally came to read *the* book, I found that in it were many of the prayers and psalms I had liked most in the Mass when I was a child. I read the book now not out of any religious sense, but as literature, or I should say *because of* literature. So much of what I was then reading seemed to be permeated by it—from Tolstoy's deeply Christian searchings, through Faulkner's Bible-haunted Southerners, to Melville's Scripture-sounding whale story *(And I only have escaped alone to tell thee)*—that I started searching out the sources of these allusory figures and shapes I was encountering.

One of the first such journeys brought me to the Book of Job because I had liked Robert Frost's *Masque of Reason* in which God speaks to Job. I went to the Book of Job, because I wanted to know the poem better, and reading the biblical text (King James, of course), I discovered meanings that had been part of my existence long before. For instance, all my young life, I had heard how this or that member of my large family, in this or that trying circumstance, had the "patience of Job." I had never understood the sense of the phrase as it was meant. Not exactly. And again, long ago in my earliest schooling, when for two years I *had* been in Catholic school, there had been a phrase on the wall above the scarred blackboard in Sister Mary Margaret's rundown classroom, large block letters I had stared at and wondered at, even then, for their seemingly abject faith: "Though He slay me, yet will I trust in Him."

There was also the allusion, in Frost's poem, to the famous opening passage of the Gospel of John, which I had heard so many times at Mass: *In the beginning was the word, and the word was with God, and the word was God. The same was in the beginning with God. All things were made by Him, and without Him was made nothing that was made: in Him was life, and the life was the light of men; and the light shineth in darkness, and the darkness did not comprehend it.*

Of course, when I came to read Job I discovered that the context of those words—"though He slay me, yet will I trust in Him,"—was anger, not abject faith. That Job is in fact seeking an explanation for his suffering when he says these words, and that the true sense of the line is, to put it roughly, "I don't care if He kills me, I demand that He explain!"

Well, God—or Yahweh—explains, all right. And the voice speaking out of the whirlwind is a good deal less reasonable than the one Frost gives to Him. *Doth the eagle mount up at thy command, and make her nest on high? . . . Canst thou draw out leviathan with a hook?*

When I was twenty-two, and thought I was a poet, I traveled with four young women to Montgomery, Alabama. We were a rock 'n' roll band, and we were to spend a week down there. This was the summer of 1967. We drove down in a light gold '62 Caddie with a trailer hitched to the back bumper, and at a gas station somewhere between the Mississippi line and Montgomery, I had a sort of blind fit over something I'll have to take some trouble to explain. We were coming from Iowa, and though I had grown up in Virginia, I had not been privy to the kind of systematic discrimination that was then prevalent in the South. It is probable that my very good and moderate parents had kept me from this, Virginia being Virginia. In any case, we had driven all night and after sunrise we stopped at this Standard Oil station, and everyone got out to use the rest rooms. We had been talking about the Book of Job for hundreds of miles. I was coming to know that what I would write about, more and more, was the problem of pain, of the suffering of good and decent people who don't seem to deserve it. I had a Bible that had been given to me by some man hanging around a train station across from one of the places we had stayed at traveling across the Midwest to Iowa. We were all imbued with the sort of excitement in ideas and in the world's strangeness that people that age are—or used to be, anyhow—prone to. We pulled into this gas station and piled out of the car, talking about the travail of innocent people. We crossed the hot asphalt lot in the early morning sun, and I was the first to see that there were three bathrooms, marked MEN, WOMEN, and COLORED. The first two were designated with painted black letters on closed doors; the third was simply an open, dirty doorway, with plastic letters affixed to the crossbeam. I stopped, and the others stopped. They looked at me: four young women I had known for a period of years, ranging in age from twenty-four to seventeen. They were my friends. We loved each other and were idealistic and hopeful about the future (after all, there were so many like us out there, surely we would transform the face of the world); we were filled with the fervor of protest songs, and poems I'd written about the injustice of racism, the cruelty of war. I looked at the gas station emblem—Standard Oil, the headquarters of which I knew were in New Jersey—and I had an image, suddenly, of this Northern company cynically agreeing to build a gas station with three rest rooms. Something drifted loose inside me. It may have been that I had this friendly audience, though I don't think so: we knew each other so well, I wasn't likely to impress them, or change anything about their feeling for me at the time. It may have been the grogginess of being on the road all night. And it also may have been what it certainly felt like: righteous indignation. I did not have the patience of Job, but something Job-like flamed up in me, in any case. I went to the open doorway, jumped up and hung on the plastic sign, and bent it down far enough to stand and pull on it until it came loose—it did so with a cracking noise that echoed—and then I threw it, sailed it off into the farm field beyond that end of the lot. My young friends approved, though they were concerned about our safety—one of them went off into the field and retrieved the sign, so she could take it home with her. She put it into the trunk of the Caddie, then rejoined us. We stood there. We might've been people waiting for some indication of life in a ghost town. There wasn't even any traffic.

"Justice," one of my friends said, smiling at me. Her name was Faith, and she was the drummer in the band. "We're prob'ly in someone's sights right now." She turned and looked about her.

The quiet was eerie.

"Either there's nobody here, or any second we're gonna hear the shot."

A moment later, the proprietor walked out from the side of the building and asked in a normal tone of voice if he could help us. He was evidently not aware of what had just taken place.

"No," the twenty-four-year-old said. Her name was Charlotte. "We wondered why you wouldn't build *four* bathrooms if you really wanted things to be separate but equal."

The man was wiry, blond, not much older than we were. He looked at us, and then he looked at the license plate on the front of the gold Caddie. "You all fixin' to cause trouble around here?" he said.

"No," Charlotte said. "We were just wondering."

"I don't want no trouble," he said.

"No trouble," Charlotte's sister, Christine, told him. "It just isn't equal, like you people say. You know."

"Don't you think it's unfair?" the rhythm guitarist, Mary, said. She had been the one who went and brought the sign back and put it in the trunk of the car. She stood there with her hands in the back pockets of her jeans and waited for him to answer.

"Well, you know," he told us, shifting a little to one side, "this separation stuff, I never give hit much thought." He looked off toward the field. Then he spit a little and wiped his mouth.

"Does it seem fair to you?" Mary asked him.

He spit again. "Don't really know what's fair."

"It's not only not fair," Charlotte said to him. "It's not legal."

"Well," he said, spitting again and wiping his mouth with the back of his hand. "You all want gas er not?"

"Do you own this place?" I asked him.

"Nope."

"If you did, you'd—you wouldn't—" I couldn't finish the thought.

He was our age. He was of us, if that makes any sense; I knew he listened to at least some of the same music, and that he had seen some of the same movies. I needed to hear from him that he was not part of the system he was in. But I didn't have the words. He was staring off, his mouth working slightly. He shook his head a little, spit and wiped his mouth once more. "I ain't got all day, folks."

"You don't really believe in segregation," I said. You used the word, then. It was a position people took. It was a word as loaded as the phrase "pro-choice" is now.

He seemed to pull into himself. "Hit's in the Bible."

"Where?" I said.

He shrugged. "Hit's there. I done heard it read out on Sundee."

I was beginning to worry that he'd notice that his sign was gone. He stood there spitting and wiping his mouth.

"Look, you all want gas er not?"

We said no, and got back into the car, and rode away with his sign. He was a boy who went to church on Sunday, and possessed all the virtues valued most in the place where he lived: hard-working, independent-minded, industrious, loyal to his family and friends, helpful, serious, good-natured, kind, generous. Bigoted.

And I went out into the world the Bible had made, or that generations of people had made out of the Bible.

I am almost fifty now. The question of salvation is still unanswered, of course, and I have stood in winds and demanded answers that I did not get. I am only mildly facetious in asserting this. I have taught young adults who are completely ignorant of the Bible, though every day they swim in intellectual waters that spring from it. This is a weirdly secular time—in the midst of so much public religious fervor—so close to the brink of the next millennium and whatever *that* will hold: deliverance, some unifying struggle, undreamed of catastrophes. Gains in the society where I make my home have been eroded, and there is a new separatism afoot in the land; a fragmentation of groups, all clamoring to embrace abstractions about each other and about all the other groups. Without meaning to seem pompous about it, I will say that I have come to believe that the *stories* we tell—now more than ever in our history—have a much deeper worldly and spiritual significance than merely to entertain. Now it seems to me that the importance of what we do, insistently and continually writing about individuals, telling the stories of individuals, cannot be understated. When I try to write a story I want to speak with the tongues of angels, and when I feel as though something is speaking *through* me—every writer knows this feeling, no matter what he chooses to call it—I prefer to think it is something greater than I, that seeks always to make manifest the value of individual *being,* the worth of the solitary self in its struggle to find salvation. And that it is what I have in life to do, now, to help stem the tide of tribal hatreds and suspicions through which we are all always moving.

Without being presumptuous (after all, my "muse" could be a minor clerk in the hall of angels who is being punished for too refined an interest in American football), I believe that the few, great stories which come near enough to the heart of Truth always achieve this process of making the individual life palpable, that they always fly in the face of those who would objectify and make an abstraction out of whole groups of people, and that they do so mysteriously, ineffably, in ways almost impossible to describe or define, exactly as with the stories of the Bible. Job's story speaks down through the ages because it is one man's struggle with his God. Like that great story, great writing seeks grace, and partakes of sanctity. *He who has ears to hear, let him hear.*

Epistle to the Hebrews

L A U R A   F U R M A N

As an adolescent, I drifted around in the Bible—an edition my father kept on his bookshelf, the size of a picture book with large type for easy reading—and I was lost, happily, in the language of the Psalms and the Song of Solomon, not worrying about understanding the text. I didn't read the Bible or anything else to gain understanding. Most often I read to lose myself. I stuck to the Old Testament, for the most part, in my biblical grazing. I had a hard time with the New Testament, except for Revelation, which was as poetically hypnotic as anyone could want. The rest of the New Testament seemed too businesslike to dream over, as if all its stories were burdened by messages addressed to me personally so that I might make a decision.

Though neither of my parents was religious, there was never any question about their identification as Jews or mine. My father at-

tended synagogue on the High Holy Days. My mother, as far as I can remember, never went to temple. When I was ten or so, I requested that I be allowed to go to the religious school that met on Sunday and was part of the Reform Congregation Shaare Tefila on Eighty-first between Columbus and Amsterdam. I was motivated not so much by an interest in God as by an admiration for the Gerbis, who also attended the temple and whose daughters went to the religious school. The Gerbis were linked to the part of being Jewish I counted as most important: Dr. Gerbi had escaped fascist Italy and completed his medical school in the United States. Everything about their lives—especially the heavy silver menorah and ceremonial cups that stood year-round on the side table in their dining room—spoke to me of the European Jews who had not managed to escape. The spiritual aspects of Judaism were less important and accessible to me than the feeling that the dead millions were counting on me not to forget them.

I and my Judaism came from a particular time and place—the Upper West Side of Manhattan in the 1950s, less than a decade after the end of the Holocaust. I was born in 1945 in America. I grew up knowing that had I been born in another place a year earlier, I wouldn't have survived, nor my parents and my sisters, all because we were Jewish. The time and place of my birth didn't cost me my life or make me an accidental martyr. Identification with Judaism seemed to me a necessary act of loyalty. Hence my attendance at religious school and at temple some Friday nights and Saturday mornings, and also my resistance to reading the New Testament and to the evidence of Christianity around me.

My elementary school, P.S. 75, was on West End Avenue and to reach it I walked or took a crosstown bus west along Ninety-sixth Street. Many times, then, more times than I could count, at Amsterdam Avenue—across from the majestic, columned Dime Bank where my class deposited its weekly dimes to teach us thrift—I passed a Franciscan church called Holy Name of Jesus. Outside the church was an enormous stone statue of Jesus or Mary, hands out in welcome, sculptured robes to the floor, a hooded head. (I didn't know who it was. Parochial and ignorant, I learned the story of the Immaculate Conception for the first time in high school from an Episcopalian friend.)

Often the doors of Holy Name were open, I suppose because the times of my coming and going from school coincided with Mass. There was not a time when I looked into the church through the open doors that I didn't feel afraid. When I walked past I tried not to turn my head and look inside, as if a look at the statues and the ornament-laden altar and pews in the candle-lit darkness would cause me to be sucked inside and changed forever.

My only contact with the Catholic Church was watching Pat O'Brien and Bing Crosby movies on TV. There was no mystery to that Catholicism, only a cloying sweetness and a misty frame around the edges of the black-and-white images. My reaction to the movies confused me. I was swayed by the sentimentality and the absolute quality of the belief demonstrated and rewarded in such flatfooted ways. The emotional timbre of movie Catholicism was in synch with the voice of Joe McCarthy over the radio during the hearings of the House Un-American Activities Committee and Frank Sinatra singing "The House I Live In" for a school film on the virtues of the Melting Pot. This was my world and it was not. I was exposed to a version of it, but I was not part of it. The ideal Christ—I could understand and admire the Sermon on the Mount—seemed a different fellow altogether from the one whose Church blamed the Jews for Christ's death, thereby institutionalizing anti-Semitism.

Whatever I was actually told about the Jewish religion in the school that I attended for about five years—continuing after my mother died when I was thirteen, through to my confirmation—I retained my own version of Judaism, a nonmystical allegiance to the Jews that did not require belief in God or heaven, but only an ethical sense of fairness and charity that has proved difficult enough. Though I said Kaddish for my mother, I did not believe she was in heaven or that I would ever see her again. The whole point was that I wouldn't see her again, and the truth of this fact was reinforced in a hundred ways every day. I derived comfort from the school and the temple after she died because they represented a continuation of my routine, not because they reassured me that she was happy in heaven or that we would be together again. Also my attendance was a way to get out of the house and away from my father and sisters whose misery matched mine.

When recently I read St. Paul the Apostle's Epistle to the Hebrews, I felt the familiar resentment and distance, but my altered circumstance challenged me: I am a woman of forty-nine, not a child any longer, and I am married to a man who was raised and educated as a Catholic. Reading and reacting in the old way is a luxury I can't afford.

The Epistle's opening argument is simple: Jesus Christ is at the right hand of God, the Chosen Son who is better than the angels. (Hebrews 1:4) Though the Jewish high priests must make sacrifice of goats and bulls every year, Christ's sacrifice of himself was made once and suffices for all time. His blood, shed for all mankind, is more powerful than the blood of goats or bulls (Hebrews 9:12–14): "For it is not possible that the blood of bulls and of goats should take away sins." (Hebrews 10:4)

It is an oddly economical argument about a religious practice. I responded to the quantitative and qualitative belittling of Judaism in the Epistle with an irrational swell of resentment, for when did I last see a rabbi sacrificing a goat?—and then I caught myself. Why should this inflame me any more than a reading of a text about the carving of designs on flesh by West Africans or the provision of food and treasure for the dead by ancient Egyptians? The answer is that I don't live among West African animists or pharaonic Egyptians. I live in a predominately Christian country, and half of the extended family in which I'm raising my son is Christian. In reading Epistle to the Hebrews, I came to understand news that I found less than welcome: in my insistence on my own identity as a Jew there's an active hostility to Christianity and in that there is also a lack of understanding.

When I left my neighborhood I entered the world of Christians. Not only are some of my best friends Christians but I am a different person. I have many fewer sure opinions about how other people should behave than I did as an adolescent. I can't thrive without attempting to understand others, be they beloved others or strangers to me.

Reading on, I see that there is more to the Epistle to the Hebrews than exhortations to conversion. It is a moving articulation of faith and wonder at the sacrificial gift of Christ. It is the urgent testimony of one who believes and cannot understand why others do not; its undertones of aggression and astonishment at the resistance of the beloved audience to "a new and living way, which he hath consecrated for us, through the vail, that is to say, his flesh" (10:20), are like those of a parent who cannot understand why a child resists good advice. Such parents may be wrongheaded, but they are not necessarily malicious. Most moving perhaps of all, and most surprising, is Paul's amazement at the constant miracle of God's gift to mankind, of putting his own Son into mortal flesh to live as a human being and to suffer an unjust end. Paul has faith like a rock and much of the Epistle is unappealingly grounded, yet he puts into words most powerfully the ephemeral: what it is to have faith. Toward the end of the Epistle he says, "Faith is the substance of things hoped for, the evidence of things not seen." Faith is a paradox, holding opposites in the same place. I was intrigued by Paul's formulation, which made me wish for faith, not in Jesus but in something. Yet I was unable to understand what Paul meant until a series of events that took place over a year and a half, starting with a funeral.

One September night, I was in a church, a Catholic church, for the funeral of a man I'd never met, a sea captain married to a woman who made her living organizing other people's offices and lives. He was Irish and romantic, and Lynn was the burnished product of a trailer-park childhood in California. They sounded like the luckiest of middle-aged couples, but

Michael had become ill on their long airplane journey from one life in the Far East to another in Austin, and he died when a blood clot formed after an emergency appendectomy.

Years before, when Lynn was living with a man my husband worked with, a group of office friends had traveled to Galveston for a weekend at a borrowed beach house. Come Sunday morning Lynn and I were the only ones awake. She seemed crisp and clean to me—not only then but always —and when she told me of her chaotic childhood the immediate feeling I had for her was respect. I don't know if Lynn was a practicing Catholic then. I didn't know if she was Catholic at all. My husband and many of our friends had been raised Catholic, and I would have predicted then that their relationship with the Church would remain as mine has with my Reform Jewish background: testy and distant but still related. The funeral was in a church across from the university where I teach in Austin. I'd been to two weddings there. In former days, the groom in one wedding and the bride in another had shared with my husband a large collection of Pope memorabilia: Pope postcards, Pope soap on a rope, newspaper clippings about Pope lawn sprinklers to commemorate His Holiness's visit to San Antonio, the papal figure bestowing blessings all around as the sprinkler turned.

Times had changed. At one of the weddings, I read Genesis 2:18–24. I felt honored to be chosen by the bride and groom to read, and I was nervous at speaking before a large group of people. The pulpit where I stood rose above the large nave, which was punctuated on its outer walls by the Stations of the Cross. The wedding guests and families nearly filled the pews. Behind me was the altar and a large wooden crucifix, the figure of Christ curved along the rigid upright.

" 'And the Lord God said, It is not good for the man to be alone. I will provide a partner for him,' " clear past the beautiful " 'bone of my bones and flesh of my flesh,' " to " 'That is why a man leaves his father and mother and is united to his wife and the two become one flesh.' " My voice rang out loud and clear, and the words sounded so true, shocking, and primitive that I felt like a messenger from a past I didn't know. When I was seated back with the congregation and my heart stopped beating so hard, I listened to the other readings. They sounded quieter, less harsh and real. It occurred to me that I, a Jew, had been reading from the Old Testament to a company of Christians, people of the New Testament. I didn't feel like an outcast, just alone.

My husband stopped believing in God in his early adolescence. He continued going to Catholic schools and received a good education in comparative religion, but even more so in Church history. He probably cannot recite all the popes from memory but he can narrate with great clarity the twists and turns of theological rules and customs. The Barna family is mostly believing and practicing, and family weddings and funerals take place in a Catholic church. When my mother-in-law visits us for the weekend, she most often goes to Mass but sometimes invokes a rule that "We're allowed when we travel not to go to Mass." The first time she said this I couldn't imagine whom she meant when she said "we," and who was doing the allowing. I live in a Christian, mostly Protestant, place and I am inured to the Protestant way where dispensations and excuses are internal and individual, resembling, in this way, the Reform Judaism in which I was raised.

At first it was difficult for me to attend church with the Barna family. Before my marriage, I had considered myself a tolerant person, the kind of amateur anthropologist people with liberal arts educations tend to be, able to look at the customs of others with respect and interest, unthreatened by religious or cultural differences, and certainly not seized by superstitious fear. But it made me uncomfortable to be inside a Catholic church, especially one that was not a work of art and didn't contain works of art (where my presence would have been sanctioned by my pursuit of cultural education), just an ordinary church in a working-class neighborhood, a relatively unadorned space that existed to serve the congregation in their quotidian religious lives and to house their ceremonies through birth, marriage, and death. In the family churches there was no intellectual force to be reckoned with, no rabbinical deliberation of meaning, no Graham Greene-esque struggles with Faith. The priest at one family wedding inveighed against the *New York Times*. The priest at my brother-in-law's funeral said the words of the Mass, but nothing particular that had to do with Chris and his brief life. I was left cold by the ceremonies. I didn't know the prayers or the songs. I didn't know what came next. If the ceremonies felt hollow to me, so did my presence in church. I was there out of duty and respect for my parents-in-law and the Barna family. I thought of a friend's father who drove to a church miles from home to attend the shortest Mass in the city. But still he went.

The funeral service for Michael was Catholic, but it was Catholic with a difference, led not by the white-haired priest who sat in the sanctuary but by a compelling, slightly theatrical dark-haired woman in her thirties, whose assumption was that we all had come to the ceremony to be healed, and that as we shared in the grief and the memories, our presence would help Lynn. She seemed to be trying with her body and her voice to convince us of something. The possibility she held out to each of us was spiritual therapy, peace of mind, and her implication was that if we went along with the sentiments and the words, something good might happen. She told us the stories that had been told in the days since Michael's death, very personal stories about the love Lynn and Michael felt for each other and the detailed plans and wishes they had recorded in a book about their future.

The ceremony was full of feeling and good intentions, talky and personal. The lectors were close friends of Michael's and Lynn's, and their demeanor bore witness to their shock and sorrow. I became sadder as the service went on, more sorry than ever that I'd never met Michael and terribly sorry for Lynn. But the leader's theatricality put me off and I asserted, against my sadness, my own discomfort, as I might have at any solution being foisted on me—psychological or religious. There was an assumption of sameness in the leader's address—we are all friends, we all feel the same, we are all equally stricken, and, more, that we are in agreement about what happens to us after death. I wanted, and felt childish for wanting, to assert my real differences: I knew Lynn and not Michael, I was a Jew and not a Christian, I did not believe in heaven. I wondered if in my internal emphasis on difference I wasn't avoiding thanking God that I was not a widow as Lynn was, but the thought of the terrible possibilities available in life was unavoidable. Meanwhile, the emphasis on the Resurrection skewed the ceremony toward the living: Michael was in heaven; it was the living widow, family, friends, who were left grieving for his sudden death and his permanent absence.

At Barna family events there was an absence of theatricality in church, in that there was no attempt to reach out to or to sway the audience/congregation. It was assumed that everyone in church knew what to do and would do it without any fuss or even much display of emotion. The Resurrection was spoken of without heat, accepted as unquestioned belief, another stop on the train, and I didn't give much thought to the concept. But at Michael's funeral, perhaps because of the leader's outreaching style of delivery and my resistance to it, I was struck by the thought that my friends in the church might really believe—not metaphorically but literally—in life after death, might really believe that Michael had gone on, as they would in their turn, to a final rest and a better place. The clichés of death took on new meaning. I had not considered that belief in such a thing was really possible. I had assumed that though words might be said and prayers memorized and uttered, that it was the repetition and the words that were comforting because actual belief was impossible. I tried to rationalize and understand the belief: wherever the dead man's soul was, it was not with us any longer, and it might as well be called "in heaven" if heaven is the release from human life. This might have been a way for me to understand but it was a distortion of their belief, and it felt inadequate and lame.

The old priest rose to perform communion, always for me the great divide. A little dumpy and stooped, he might have officiated at my niece's wedding or my brother-in-law's funeral. He was a figure from another time, another Church. I listened closely to the words of the Gospel: *This is my body which is given for you: this do in remembrance of me . . . this cup is the new testament in my blood, which is shed for you.* Goats and bulls, the blood of Christ: the ancient basis for the religion was being acted out before me. I watched as most of the congregation approached the Sacrament.

At the same moment at Barna family occasions in church I'd always felt the most alienated. If the ceremonies had seemed without mystery, it was plenty strange to watch as people I was related to by time, custom, and marriage lined up to receive a wafer I had never tasted and never would, to sip at a chalice held by someone else. Does the wine actually turn into the blood of Christ? If the wafer becomes the flesh of Christ, why eat it? Paul's paradox of faith was being enacted and I didn't understand it.

After the ceremony was over, I stayed long enough to speak to Lynn and to Michael's relatives who had traveled from Ireland for the funeral, then I left the gathering in the church social hall. I had a forty-five-minute ride ahead of me and all the way home I puzzled over heaven and Communion, troubled as I had never been before by my lack of understanding of what it was to believe in both concepts. When I got home I asked my husband what Catholics really believe, not just educated liberal Catholics but all of them. How could anyone possibly believe in heaven, flesh eating, blood drinking? He tried explaining the ancient origins of the ritual ingestion of the god, the sacrifice of the king, but that wasn't what I was getting at. What puzzled me—and the vehemence of my reaction to the funeral surprised me—was individual belief. My husband couldn't answer my question because he didn't believe, and I hesitated to ask my returned-Catholic friends who did. "How can you believe that?" may be an unanswerable question, and not just about the Communion wine and bread. Such belief, like love between married people, may be inexplicable, and, within the bounds of polite friendship, unquestionable also.

In the summer after Michael's funeral, my husband, our son, and I went to stay with friends at a family house, a falling-down plain brick rectangle on a cliff over Copano Bay that was filled with old furniture, books, photographs, and souvenirs, as if it had been theirs forever. Actually, most of the furnishings came from the real family house in a nearby city. The beach house had been bought by our friend's aunt, filled and furnished, but used only for occasional weekends and holidays. In winter the whooping cranes land on the lawn, mostly unobserved, I suspect. Our friends' son was just about our son's age, and the two boys were active and wild, inside the house and out. They ran in circles on the flat green lawn that ended in a sudden slope down to the bay. While the children played, we adults got slower and slower with the heat, humidity, and general torpor of the flat South Texas landscape. For dinner one night we ate a giant pot of corn, sausage, crab, and shrimp, all cooked together with crab boil. The adults were laid even lower by the feast, and the boys grew more active, their last burst before sleep. Our son grabbed a heavy cane from a basket of canes, umbrellas, and parasols next to the table, and began to play with it.

"Be careful! That's Will's great-grandfather's walking-stick," our friend said, so forcefully that we all looked at the unremarkable cane as if it *were* Will's great-grandfather. Once my son relinquished the cane and returned it to its place, our friend spoke of how much she'd loved her grandfather, of family complications after his death, and how much her son had loved his great-grandfather. We embarked from the table to wash dishes, move our sons toward sleep, and then we adults talked about birds, little boys, and architecture until we were yawning too much even to pretend to converse.

I woke at three in the morning and wandered with a book into the living room, hoping to lure myself back into sleep. Instead, I settled into a comfortable chair from which I could see the sun rise in a few hours, and I thought about the walking-stick and the moment the night before when a dead man unknown to half of the people in the room had been invoked, brought back, and loved for a few minutes before the bustle of the present took over. In talking about him, our friend had reenacted her regard for him when he was alive. Where was he, I wondered, and understood for the first time what it might be like to believe in heaven. He was dead, Lynn's husband Michael was dead, and why not say they were in heaven? Faith in heaven might mean that a fate as unfair and arbitrary-seeming as Michael's might be not just be borne but accepted. If this was not precisely Paul's paradox of the substance of hope, it was close to it.

I thought of young Will, who would probably forget as he grew up, if he hadn't already, his much loved great-grandfather, though he would remember the stories his mother told and would surely remember the love, however complicated, in the family for the dead man. I thought of the family my husband and I form with our son. The love in our family is, like all relations of love, a hope that is transformed into substance each day by our actions.

In the church where Michael's funeral was held were many people who were shocked and frightened that a young man could be struck down so quickly. For the first time I understood what the act of Communion might mean to the grieving. It is an act of wishful transformation, wine into blood, wafer into flesh, making the generous and forgiving Christ part of one's own body. The ingestion of the god is the incorporation of faith, and "Faith is the substance of things hoped for, the evidence of things not seen." To an unbeliever Communion might look like whistling a happy tune, but to one who even hopes to believe it is an affirmative act that transforms fear and anxiety into faith. In the absence of faith—not only religious faith but any faith in the workings-out of each life—there is anxiety, and a dismal, untransforming present.

On the Texas coast there is no subtle, quiet period after dawn; once the sun is up it is bright and hot enough to be noon. The others in the house awoke. Another day began. What I came to was not a complete understanding of Communion or of Paul's Epistle to the Hebrews, a letter I will reread like other, more personal letters that I revisit from time to time, but it was all I wanted. I was able to imagine what my friends and family were doing when they received Communion, and this work of my imagination was communion for me.

Daniel

MAUREEN HOWARD

Do Way

The Bible lived next door in my grandmother's house. It was set on a recessed shelf with the Catholic Encyclopedia (tooled leather) and old city directories. The room with these books, the only books in that big, well-set-up house, was somewhat sacrosanct and referred to as the office. My grandfather's working life was long over, but the office—after his crippling stroke and after his death—lived on as a comforting fiction that prosperity was not a thing of the past, that we partook of the commercial life of our city which was the culture, even the dominant faith of that city. I do not remember the Bible, the *Do Way,* as I called it, ever being read. It was placed properly at a distance, for it was a forbidden book.

Is forbidden too strong a word? Proscribed, considered off-bounds for secular Catholics, the stories, poems, advice, rules, and regulations set forth in Holy Writ being too difficult for us to pursue without pastoral guidance. The last thing I aim to do in recalling my childhood deprived of Bible is to take yet another easy swipe at the paternalistic Catholic Church in its American version. That paternalism has come to a fine pass which may bring schisms, which may in turn bring ruin or salvation to the Church in the next century, but as a child I was pleased to be under the protection of the Holy Father and the parish Father. Like any kid, I liked being among the chosen and always being right. I went to the right church, the right movies, the right parochial school. I read the right books and early on, I suppose about the time I figured out it was the Douay version of the Bible in the office, I understood it was not so much wrong as it was unnecessary to read the sacred text.

Was Douay the translator or the publisher? I never asked the foolish question and I am not scandalized now by the incurious child who took in the French place name without a clue or a care to its meaning. The Bible was read for me, or rather culled, by the designated and, I presumed, heavenly authority who set down the ritual of the Mass. Aside from the gospels and epistles, there are few biblical passages acknowledged in the Ordinary of the Mass which I followed in my Missal. The Ordinary is that framework which directs the sequence of ritual that is ordinarily used in the daily Mass; but on any feast day, or in the Proper of the Time or of the Saints which make up the liturgical year, I'd been reading the Bible all along —Psalms, for instance. Pick a day, any ordinary day, let's say, Thursday after the first Sunday in Lent:

Gradual: Psalm 16. Keep me, O Lord, as the apple of my eye; protect me under the shadow of thy wings. Let my judgment come forth from thy countenance; let thy eyes behold the things that are equitable.

Or the Offertory: Psalm 33. The angel of the Lord shall encamp round about them that fear him, and shall deliver them: taste and see that the Lord is sweet.

Or the Introit for Ember Wednesday in Whitsunday Week: Psalm 67. O God, when thou wentest forth before thy people, when thou didst march through the wilderness, alleluia, the earth shook; the heavens also dropped, alleluia, alleluia, etc.

Yes, like Molière's gentleman, I had been silently speaking that which I could not name all along. Reading my Missal, I mouthed to myself the English words, knowing in some untutored way that this poetry should be heard. I may not have had the Bible firsthand, but the rhythms and the elevated tone of Biblespeak were in my ear as well as Latin. The priest reeled off Latin before a raised altar, often with his back turned, performing the next office that moved us on to the central rite, the consecration of the Host and the taking of Communion, which made up the Sacrifice of the Mass, of God become man in Christ, of Christ's death, which was *our* salvation. Why, with such dramatic liturgy, would we need the Bible? The Missal, being a translation of the New Missale Romanum according to the Sacred Congregation of Rites, took the Bible's place with authority, that authority quite literally reenforced by the imprimatur on the flip side of the title page. And how fitting for that good schoolgirl, Maureen, that the provincial, the Censor Librorum, and the archbishop who assured the "absolute correctness" of my treasured Missal were all Irishmen. Naturally, I would have found the imprimatur on the Douay Version of the Bible had I cared to look.

I did not care to look for I was an obedient and pious child. You may wonder why I was familiar with odd days of Advent and Lent. Because of this posturing piety which came over me as a preadolescent, a last-ditch effort to be worthy, pure, inviolate as in those psalmlike litanies to Mary— a somewhat degraded poetry, but how would I have known?

ALTERNATE TEXTS

Stories in the Bible, even the extraction of stories from the gospels, could not instruct like the *Baltimore Catechism*.

> Who made the world?
> God made the world.
> Why did God make you?
> God made me to know, love and serve Him in this
>   world and to be happy with Him in the next.

This was *ur* instruction, if instruction is taken to mean implant, not impart, information. The questions did not beg answers, they begot them. The catechism was anti-Bible; its blue paper cover might look ephemeral but its words, including each rhetorical question, were to be memorized forever; no need for the substantial black cover of Holy Writ with those tales which might produce wonder; no need to wonder.

"You don't know the Bible!" This scolding from my brother's wife. She was raised Presbyterian and senses my defensive ignorance. Sometimes I feel like a Bible-less child, but it's not quite true. We had stories, never called Bible Stories (that has the ring of something passed out to Methodist or Baptist kids), but we had Adam and Eve, Moses, Noah, Jacob and his brothers, Isaac—all that was suitable and morally instructive in the Old Testament. We were told these stories by the good sisters or we read them in a weekly paper designed for Catholic schools. Moses, absolutely, for how else would we come upon the Ten Commandments, which must be committed to memory. That the story of Moses' birth (Exodus 2) recording Pharaoh's terrible edict to slay all male infants, Jews, prefigured that of Herod's order (Matthew 13) and the flight into Egypt, was never noted, though it would have fit nicely into our teachers' agenda. That agenda, as I see it now, was to use the Old Testament as a guarded warm-up for the

New. The New Testament we surely had, not from the text of the Douay itself, but from the seasonal liturgy, from the observance of the Advent and Lenten calendars, from Christmas and Easter. We had the New Testament because it can be read as a biography of Jesus.

Matthew, Mark, Luke, and John did not bless the bed that I slept on. Saints all, we knew their names, but not their writing as separate gospels which can be obscure and contradictory, for the New Testament was organized in my Missal to tell a consistent narrative. Matthew and Luke, therefore, are called upon to relate the Passion, for they wrote it in detail. I did not note this growing up and it was not noted for me, that the editors (what a secular word) of the liturgy of the Mass I was raised on were brilliant anthologists. Thematic anthologists to be sure, for they assembled the texts according to the concerns of the day. Thus, a Lenten Mass, daily not Sunday, quotes both Exodus and Kings from the Old Testament, passages in which Moses and Elias in their stories spend forty days and forty nights sustained by the Lord. I got on to this system of converging multiple texts and have never got off. I worry my students with the question: "What are your themes?" I worry myself to death writing against the doctrine of continuous narrative, investigating themes that incorporate multiple texts. It is a presumption to write and a transgression to savor versions of fact as though they are fictions, fictions as though they are facts, as though I yearn to be on the Index, that list of truly forbidden books, with great sinners like Boccaccio and Voltaire. But the Index is no more.

Yes, I read the Epistles, the Pauline Epistles to the Corinthians so often used in the liturgy as though we were, despite our smug certainties, as much in need of instruction as newly converted Galatians or fringe sects in Corinth. I memorized long passages, for even in third-, fourth-hand translation, Paul's drop-dead rhythms were enchanting. And I will say this of my Bible-deprived youth, his cadences somehow got in my thick Mick head as did the metrical flair of the Gospel According to St. John, drumming the catechismal patter out of my head.

But the *Lives of the Saints!* The dour Douay was hardly tempting when we had so many grand tales of spiritual triumph, tales of sin and conversion, of mortal pain and the ultimate sacrifice for the ultimate gain. The favorites back then were Blessed Catherine Tegawitha (Native American) and Blessed Martin de Porres (mulatto Peruvian), both bucking for sainthood; and St. Thérèse of Lisieux, a dedicated sufferer who had passed to her reward but a few decades earlier. I took the stories of these lives, and those of Francis of Assisi, Catherine of Alexandria, to be literally true. They were awfully good stories told again and again, more user-friendly than the Douay, stories of exemplary lives that children could get hold of, perhaps even emulate in acts of great sacrifice and humility performed in a godless, industrial Connecticut. To this day I love reading the *Lives of the Saints* in any version, those true legends which need not be true.

In the Lion's Den

The introduction to the Catholic Missal of my youth informs me that the prayer said after the offering of the chalice, *In spiritu humilitatis,* etc. ("In a humble spirit"), are words from the "three children in the fiery furnace, who offered themselves to God as a pleasing sacrifice." (Daniel 3:39–40) I was not encouraged to read their story in the Bible, but took it on faith, so to speak, that the story was true and that those children were saved as I would be saved if *In spiritu humilitatis,* etc., for that very brief passage in the Mass leads to the mystery of the Incarnation, the Sacrifice, and so to possible redemption. It is shameful that I never cared to know more about those kids, that I swept their dramatic trial by fire so easily into my observance of ritual, but absolutely humiliating that as a child who read obsessively, I was not eager to get it all—the fiery furnace! But I had accepted half-told tales and this snippet was not only partial but cleaned up.

Daniel is a wild, apocalyptic book, a dreamy book full of terrifying dreams. I read it now with great pleasure, unsure if I understand this difficult visionary work but amazed at the powerful stories, cruel tests put to Jews who will not turn against the scriptures of their faith. Put to Daniel and his friends, young men: nowhere, save in the old Missal, are they described as children. Shadrach, Meshach, and Abednego cannot be children for Nebuchadnezzar allots them provinces to tend after they survive the fire, the fire he has heated seven times hotter than usual. There is vengeance in Daniel. The men who threw Daniel's young friends in the furnace are consumed by the flames and the King decrees that "Any people, nation or language that speaks against the God of Shadrach, Meshach, and Abednego shall be torn limb from limb, and their houses laid in ruins; for there is no other god who is able to deliver in this way." (Daniel 3:29)

I hope that I have some little understanding of the spectacle of the Catholic Mass, even reverence for its spectacular dramatic structure. I have no complaint as to the brevity of *In spiritu humilitatis* or any biblical bit taken out of context. Still, I am happy to have got hold of the unexpurgated fiery furnace; of the Book of Daniel entire, with its harsh trials and even harsher punishments for the nonbeliever. The tough stories of the Old Testament, which were softened for me as a child, might have prepared me more thoroughly to receive the predicted wonders and the comforting stories of the New as it was presented to us without the fierce imagery of Revelation. I would like to have known, not only that Daniel came unharmed from the lion's den, but that those who had accused him were cast in with the lions —they and their children and their wives. I like to think I might have understood the full text in 1944, the date inscribed in my Missal.

Daunty and the Afterlife

I am uncomfortable limiting my biblical past to early childhood, to scenes in which I stumble across the school platform, wings flapping, and announce to Mary Elizabeth Morton, a flaming redhead with eye shadow and breasts, "Unto you a child will be born"; or to tattle on the nun who told us The Kyrie in the Mass was said in Greek because, in his great mercy, Christ loved Greeks, too. The anecdotal sets me back to relishing innocence even as I laugh at the child's blind acceptance. These childlike tales will no longer do, not for me, and I do not believe such confusions will sustain the vast hordes of "children" in Asia, Africa, South America. But in the Church we were to remain children: "Unless ye become as a little child . . ."

What a shock, then, to first enter as a grown girl, the chapel at Smith College, the so-called chapel, for it looked like a public hall, bare of any vulgar religious iconography. I understood, for my mother attended this college, visited museums, subscribed to *Art News,* that the plaster saints and stations of the cross I'd left behind were dreadful, but I had never stepped inside a Protestant or nondenominational chapel in my life. I thought this place with clear glass windows cold, cold beyond spare. I did not sing those hymns. I did not say those prayers. I had no recourse but to listen to the beautiful readings from their Bible. Yet I could not tell you what I believed in then, certainly not the show I had made of religion in my childhood. The Bible as Literature was taught by Mary Ellen Chase—King James, of course, a *belle lettriste* approach. How I wish I had the nerve, the independence of mind, to take that course. I ran to the alternate texts, to Chaucer, to Daunty as Joyce calls him in *Finnegans Wake.* If I remember correctly, I read *The Divine Comedy* through five times. I read not for class to be graded, believing that the great poem kept me in some way a Catholic, an intellectual Catholic, a brand of belief I had not tried. Daunty got it all, the system that I dare not live without was all there, the specific sins and their punishments, the imaginary landscape of the real journey to hell which was—ah, political as well as spiritual.

Yes, political, like the politics that made the Puritans strip their meeting houses of distracting idolatry. Political—Dante in exile, the poem suppressed. I fell through the rabbit hole. The rules were all changed and I was on my own. I read and wrote on the Grail Legends, continuing my search for the transforming text, the one text that would dispel my disdain of the bingo games, Father's patronizing sermons, the embarrassing, less classy Douay Bible. In my scholarly fumblings, I found so many sources, variants upon variants, fragments which the writers were attempting to shape into some order, to form a continuous narrative having to do with the cup Christ blessed at the Last Supper, which was a Seder. I drew the conclusion that the Grail Legends, the best of these romances, Wolfram von Eschenbach and Chrétien de Troyes, were attempting to become novels, a naive argument which came from the fact that I was writing while saturated with nineteenth-century novels—Eliot, Dickens, Hardy—delightful, en-riching, bourgeois.

I wanted to write novels, though I would never have confessed it, and thought in those days that if I were to go home to the bookshelf, that almost hidden shelf in the office, I would take the city directories as my guide with their revelations of getting and spending, of failure and success, of property and class, of Yankee and Irish, and the newer immigrant population. It would be years before I realized I needed all the alternate texts—the fast, often lurid story lines of the many saints with their miracles and conver-sions; the pop appeal of "real" images with flesh-colored faces and bright biblical garments suggesting too much; the spare chapel at Smith suggesting too little; the high poetry (vulgate) of *The Divine Comedy* and the varying sources of romance to demonstrate a lost point about brains and belief; the discontinuous narrative of the suspect King James as well as the Jerusalem and the one and only Bible which, as a child, I never read. I have no sacred book, yet there remain many hard sayings, the difficult passages to construe daily. Though faith is admittedly something you cannot figure.

The Douay? Oh, that's the Rhemes and Douay Version (1601), a translation of the Bible pretty much as it was done up in the Vulgate Latin by St. Jerome (early fifth Century C.E.), patron of librarians and students. The

Catholics who translated it into their native English had taken refuge in Reims, but that's Elizabethan politics. Where the Protestant Bibles say "maiden," for instance, the Douay insists on "virgin." St. Jerome was rather down on women and marriage, a knotty problem in the religious politics of his day, which surely connects, these centuries later, to the religious and political impasse within the Catholic Church of our day. As a child, I knew only the sweet story of the lion who came to Jerome with a thorn in his paw and our saint removed it. He is often pictured with this tame and grateful creature, hunched over his work, scribbling away. It is a nice, though insufficient story.

Genesis, Jeremiah, & Gospels

R O B E R T   F L Y N N

As a child I didn't read comic books. They were available but they were pale compared to the stories from the Bible. The best stories were in the Jewish Bible we called the Old Testament. David and Goliath. Samson killing Philistines with the jawbone of an ass. There was nothing in comic books that could match the story of a Levite and his concubine who spent a night in Gibeah.

I read those stories from the authentic King James Baptist Bible that proved that God and Shakespeare spoke the same language. In fact, God sounded a lot like Shakespeare. And so did Jeremiah and Jesus. No one else, except a couple of Marine drill sergeants, came close to sounding like God.

The King James Bible is still my favorite translation to read if I don't have to understand it or read it aloud. I hear echoes of King James in Patrick Henry's "liberty or death" speech, William B.

Travis's last message from the Alamo "to the People of Texas and All Americans in The World," Lincoln's Gettysburg Address, Martin Luther King's "I have a dream." They couldn't match the signification of God, but real men always sound a little profuse when they speak.

My childhood heroes were from that Bible: Abraham, Isaac, Joseph, King David, Samson, Sam Houston, Robert E. Lee, Stonewall Jackson. Well, some of those weren't from the Bible but it took me a while to separate them.

Few Texas children of my day would have been surprised to discover that the heroes of the Jewish Bible had been Texans. They seemed peculiarly Texan, although perhaps born in Tennessee or Virginia. Maybe it was their outsized virtues and vices. The Hebrew kings could have used some generals like Sam Houston, Robert E. Lee, Nathan Bedford Forrest, or Stonewall Jackson. James Bowie, William B. Travis, and Davy Crockett would have been at home during the sieges of Jerusalem but probably would have chosen different deaths at Masada.

The patriarchs, judges, prophets, even the kings of the Jewish Bible seemed Texan, or at least Southern. They were our heroes, our history, our mythology, almost our family. They were close to our lives. Rural folks, a lot of them, shepherds, cattle owners. My father was what was genteelly known as a farmer-stockman. We raised crops and livestock. Some days I worked in the field and some days I worked with animals. How could I not identify with Hebrew heroes? How could not any Southern boy? I herded sheep and cattle and saw myself as an ancient Hebrew writing psalms. I worked the fields with one eye searching the horizon for Philistines. Like the Hebrews we were surrounded by trouble but overshadowed by a watchful, if demanding, God.

Adam and Eve, with Eve getting the blame for everything, was a Southern story. Cain and Abel was certainly a Southern story, although I think most Southern folks preferred Cain. The feuding of Isaac and Ishmael was as serious and long-lasting as any Southern feud. The sibling rivalry between Jacob and Esau was something that I and most Southern boys understood in our bones, although I suspect most of us preferred Esau. Jacob was too much a Yankee trader. God does not always pick the right side. Joseph and King David could have been charismatic Southern politicians with the kind of devoted followers that Robert E. Lee had and Lincoln didn't.

Samson and Delilah was the quintessential Southern story. The strong, softhearted, and weak-willed hero pitted against the delicate but steely flower of Southern maidenhood who wins first his heart and then his head.

King Saul was a Southern story. Saul was almost a Jefferson Davis. The tall, humorless, egoistic, deluded hero promoted to power he was unable to harness, who understood neither God nor his people, neither the present nor the future. I saw a tragic grandeur in King Saul watching a virile young man upstaging him, a songster who, as yet, knew nothing of defeat and despair. No matter if Saul killed a thousand, David killed ten thousand. No matter if Lee killed a thousand, Grant had ten thousand more.

An old order was ending, a new one beginning: a major theme in Southern literature. Saul's meeting with the witch of Endor, seeking his departed glory in the spirit of the dead prophet Samuel, reverberated in Nathan Bedford Forrest pledging as Grand Wizard of the Ku Klux Klan to protect Southern whites from indignities and to defend the Constitution of the United States.

Southerners read Israel's and/or Judah's history as our own. Ministers, and sometimes teachers, compared the South to fallen Israel that would be redeemed. We were God's chosen people. Our forefathers had fought a holy war and had lost because God was punishing us for our sins. (Slavery and racism were not among them.)

Southern boys, even those on frontiers like West Texas, breathed the glories of the Lost Cause and the noble giants who fought not for slavery but for principle, for honor, for home. The North had been driven mad with liberty, when what was needed was authority. The Confederacy was the emblem of virtue, morality, and religious principle. Never mind that my paternal grandparents were from the North. That was probably true of half those in my hometown. The Noble South was a concept, an ideal, a myth that rarely collided with reality.

I attended the burial of my maternal great-grandfather, a Confederate veteran. My childhood, and that of many other Southern children, was touched by fallen heroes beset by demons, clinging to the tattered remains of their glory, their chivalric code of Christian virtue and military honor. As one Confederate veteran wrote for his epitaph, "An unreconstructed Johnnie, who never repented, who fought for what he knew to be right from '61 to '65 and received one Mexican dollar for two years' service. Belonged to the Ku Klux Klan, a deacon in the Baptist Church and a Master Mason for forty years." That man could have been in Jerusalem throwing stones at Jeremiah.

Jeremiah was the true Southern hero. Jeremiah tried to save Jerusalem from Babylon but failed. Jeremiah could have been under siege in Atlanta with Sherman's troops ravaging the countryside, or maybe even in the Alamo.

The book of Jeremiah begins like a Southern story. "Did you hear what Jeremiah said, Hilkiah's boy? those folks from Anathoth? Benjamin County?" The upward inflection not directed at the reader's doubt but her memory. "You know, old Jeremiah from over Anathoth way."

Jeremiah sounds like a Southern boy. "Before I formed thee in the belly I knew thee; and before thou camest forth out of the womb I sanctified thee, and I ordained thee a prophet unto the nations." (Jeremiah 1:5) And Jeremiah said, "Who me? You talking to me? I'm just a kid. I'm not one of them rarified folks. Well, okay, if you're sure you want me to."

Jeremiah even preached the kinds of sermons I heard almost every Sunday, in almost the same language. "Wherefore I will yet plead with you, saith the Lord, and with your children's children will I plead. For pass over the isles of Chittim and see; and send unto Kedar and consider diligently, and see if there be such a thing. Hath a nation changed their gods, which are yet no gods? but my people have changed their glory for that which doth not profit. Be astonished, O ye heavens, at this, and be horribly afraid, be ye very desolate, saith the Lord. For my people have committed two evils; they have forsaken me the fountain of living waters, and hewed them out cisterns, broken cisterns, that can hold no water." (Jeremiah 2:9–13)

We heard the prophets' cries for a return to the living waters of the past as moral guides for our own land. In my youth, in country churches in the South, preachers still advocated the virtues of the Confederacy: a hierarchical social order just as in heaven, a benevolent paternalism of man over woman, minister over church, white over black, and non-European immigrants and God over all; and a moralistic, nonmaterialistic society. That nobility was being abandoned, preachers said, and we children were embracing the commerce and materialism of the evil North that had intro-duced its false god Mammon in our conquered but holy land.

We Southerners were heirs to an unquestioned moral superiority but my generation was in danger of abandoning the true moral standard to lust after materialism and worldliness. Sermons were illustrated with stories of Robert E. Lee, who chose to be a poorly paid educator rather than seeking financial or political gain from the glorious sacrifices of his men. Ministers compared Lee's temptations to Christ's temptations; Lee rejected money, power, and fame to fight for right. "Simplicity, hardihood, self-sacrifice," our preachers thundered. General Kirby Smith died deeply in debt shortly after rejecting a financial offer to lend his name to a lottery. "Better to be ennobled by poverty," we were taught, "than to be corrupted by Yankees and their gold."

Preachers also preached against other uniquely Northern sins imposed on a demoralized and impoverished people. Demon Rum, distilled in the

North to corrupt the South. Preachers quoted our saint, Stonewall Jackson. "I am more afraid of King Alcohol than of all the bullets of the enemy." My friends and I eschewed alcohol in our make-believe battles where we sank bayonets in Sherman, and especially in that sot Ulysses Grant.

Carpetbaggers had sneaked gambling into the poverty-ridden South, but it would be a sin to gamble in the land of men of honor and integrity like Robert E. Lee and Stonewall Jackson. Wealth was to be feared, if not despised. Southerners did not flaunt wealth, they quietly used it in the service of God and in open-hearted hospitality. That hospitality did not extend to former slaves or immigrants with foreign religions that Yankees had thrust upon us. "The south above any other section represents Anglo-Saxon, native-born America," claimed Episcopal Bishop Theodore DuBose Bratton. "The preservation of the American government is in the hands of the South, because Southern blood is purely American." The Philistines lived among us but mostly they lived in the evil cities and worked in factories, enslaved by the lust of the eye.

There was something else that made Jeremiah especially appealing to me. Jeremiah was a failure, and I had certainly failed at everything that mattered. I wanted to be a star on the football field and I was almost never on the field, barely on the team. I wanted to be a star so I could be humble. You can't be humble if you're not a star; you're just someone who has nothing to be proud of.

I was a cavalier student, with a splendid disdain for the grubby competition for grades. The girl I really liked preferred a boy who cussed when I had given up cussing and chewing tobacco so God would be on my side. God has never had much luck with women.

Jeremiah was also extremely unpopular. I wasn't extremely unpopular or even unpopular. I was elected class president one year, and class favorite, and one year I was runner-up for Sweetheart of the Future Homemakers of America, local branch. I just wasn't as popular as I wanted to be, as popular as my charm and good looks deserved, and I liked to imagine it was because I, like Jeremiah, was set apart to be unloved by God's call. There was something romantic about being disliked because one was especially truthful, noble, faithful, and forthright.

There was another reason that I was drawn to Jeremiah, a reason I didn't tell anyone. I wanted to write the words that would save my country, that would mend its ways, heal its spirit, and make it grand and noble the way it, or at least the Confederacy, had once been. To do that, I needed credentials. No one listened to me. I needed God to validate me so folks would recognize that I was born in the castle, that I was authentic, that I had something to say.

God failed me, just as he failed Jeremiah. Jeremiah was unable to establish the authenticity of his voice. The rulers and the people preferred the prophets who made happy talk and cried ''peace'' when there was no peace. ''A wonderful and horrible thing is committed in the land; the prophets prophesy falsely, and the priests bear rule by their means; and my people love to have it so: and what will ye do in the end thereof?'' (Jeremiah 5:30, 31)

Jeremiah was commanded not to have a wife and family as a living metaphor and warning of the destruction to come. He was censored by the king, who threw Jeremiah's book in the fire. He was mocked, called a traitor, and thrown into a cistern to die. God's words were such a burden that Jeremiah wanted to stop prophesying.

''O Lord, thou hast deceived me, and I was deceived: thou art stronger than I, and hast prevailed: I am in derision daily, every one mocketh me. For since I spake, I cried out, I cried violence and spoil; because the word of the Lord was made a reproach unto me, and a derision, daily. Then I said, I will not make mention of him, nor speak any more in his name. But his word was in mine heart as a burning fire shut up in my bones, and I was weary with forbearing, and I could not stay.'' (Jeremiah 20: 7–9)

I thought I could handle the scorn that went with an unpopular message, the frustration of not being heard, of being misunderstood, of being censored. Maybe even being thrown into a cistern. But I could already tell that not having a wife was going to be a problem.

In time I realized that Jeremiah wasn't a Southern hero after all. The South had no Jeremiah. "For among my people are found wicked men: they lay wait, as he that setteth snares; they set a trap, they catch men. As a cage is full of birds, so are their houses full of deceit: therefore they are become great, and waxen rich. They are waxen fat, they shine: yea, they overpass the deeds of the wicked: they judge not the cause, the cause of the fatherless, yet they prosper; and the right of the needy do they not judge. Shall I not visit for these things? saith the Lord: shall not my soul be avenged on such a nation as this?" (Jeremiah 5:26–29)

Sam Houston preached against the evil of secession. Sam, not notoriously pious, lost all the credit he had earned at San Jacinto and as first president of the Republic of Texas supporting the Union. If it hadn't been for San Jacinto, he very well might have been hanged by less heroic Southerners.

And from those who were supposed to be the moral and spiritual leaders? Not silence; that might have been understood. Methodists, Baptists, and Presbyterians in the South seceded from their Northern brethren even before the states did in order to begin the creation of a civil religion that defended slavery by citing biblical examples of it and interpreting a passage in Genesis to doom blacks to eternal servitude. There was no judgment of slavery and racism by the Christian love ethic. No one recalled the words of Jeremiah: "Woe unto him that buildeth his house by unrighteousness, and his chambers by wrong; that useth his neighbor's service without wages, and giveth him not for his work . . ." (Jeremiah 22:13)

Southern culture, they preached, was the high-water mark of civilization and Northern industrialization was sinful and inhumane. The Southern cause was a holy one, and when the war began, battle victories were seen as God's blessing. Defeats were God's punishment for sin. G. W. Anderson wrote, "As the Israelites at every stop were wont to set up the tabernacle and offer sacrifices to the God of battles, so at every stop Confederates would arrange at once for religious worship—their sacrifices the souls of brave men, who might fall in battle the next day, offering themselves to God by faith." The war was a baptism of blood through which the Confederacy would find redemption.

No one cried, "Therefore thus saith the Lord; Ye have not hearkened unto me, in proclaiming liberty, every one to his brother, and every man to his neighbor: behold, I proclaim a liberty for you, saith the Lord, to the sword, to the pestilence and to the famine . . ." (Jeremiah 34:17)

Identifying the South as God's chosen people left little room for self-criticism. Defeat in war and occupation by enemy troops did not threaten that self-identity but strengthened the South's identification with fallen Israel. After the war, religious and moral leaders did not attack the evils of Southern culture that had led to defeat. In ensuing years they did not attack white supremacy, the oppression of labor, of the weak and the poor. They did not demand rights for women, blacks, and other minorities. They sought to preserve the status quo using the defeated warriors as saints in the civil religion.

The South was devoid of a Jeremiah until Martin Luther King called us out of our slavery to the false god, the Golden Confederacy. When his voice was stilled, a thousand other voices took up the cry. "Return, thou backsliding Israel, saith the Lord; and I will not cause mine anger to fall upon you: for I am merciful, saith the Lord, and I will not keep anger for ever." (Jeremiah 3:12)

After I spent some time in the Marines I began to see Jeremiah in a new light. Southern Christianity closely linked military and religious values. The romantic South loved the cavalier, Robert E. Lee. The moralistic South identified with the puritan, Stonewall Jackson. They were both role models of Christian manhood.

Sometimes, it seemed to me the Confederates had won the war. The

Southern ideal of rugged individualism for white men and family values for blacks, women, and other unfortunates had swept the land. Military honor and Christian virtue, or at least Judeo/Christian virtue, dominated America. Spiritual leaders from the North joined their Southern brethren in singing praises for military and economic aggrandizement. Episcopal minister and Confederate veteran Randolph McKim saw World War I as "a Crusade. The greatest in history—the holiest. It is in the profoundest sense a Holy War." He saw little room for debate about the issue. "If the pacifists' theory be correct how could Robert E. Lee have been such a saint as he was?"

To be an American Christian male, especially a good American Christian male, one had to serve in his country's military. I enlisted in the Marines during Korea, seeing it as much a religious as a military duty. Thousands of others from all over the country raced to the flag and cross during Vietnam, Desert Storm, and briefer, lesser wars to make sacrifice to Mammon and to Mars. The American military-industrial complex had become the religious-military-industrial complex.

Today Americans are obsessed with celebrity, popularity, being loved, being successful. We have difficulty identifying with Jeremiah, who was a failure, a pariah. We are flag-waving patriots, quick to ascribe God's name to commercial, political, military adventuring. Jeremiah was not loyal to civil or religious authority. He condemned priests and prophets whose loyalty was to the crown rather than the truth. Like other prophets, Jeremiah compared Israel's apostasy to adultery and described her as "A wild ass used to the wilderness, that snuffeth up the wind at her pleasure; in her occasion who can turn her away? all they that seek her will not weary themselves; in her month they shall find her." (Jeremiah 2:24)

He was branded a traitor and was beaten and imprisoned. Political leaders called for his death because he demoralized the people in time of war.

"Therefore the princes said unto the king, We beseech thee, let this man be put to death: for thus he weakeneth the hands of the men of war that remain in this city, and the hands of all the people, in speaking such words unto them: for this man seeketh not the welfare of this people, but the hurt.'' (Jeremiah 38:4) That has a contemporary ring to it, doesn't it?

Despite his faithfulness to the truth, the siege of Jerusalem was temporarily lifted and Jeremiah was mocked and the false prophets were celebrated for their pleasing words. Despite the wrongheadedness of his people, Jeremiah remained in the city to share their fate. He wept over the destruction to come, and while the beloved city burned, the destroyer, Nebuchadnezzar, offered Jeremiah a reward for his usefulness to the enemy. Jeremiah, who had tried to save Jerusalem. Imagine Jeb Stuart being offered a medal by Lincoln for his service to the Union.

Jeremiah remained with his people, and when they fled to Egypt he went with them, and was appalled at how quickly they embraced heathen gods. After that, Jeremiah is lost in the mist of tradition, but certainly he died as unloved and as unpopular as he lived. Despite the tragedy and despair in his own life and in all he saw around him, Jeremiah proclaimed hope. ''But this shall be the covenant that I will make with the house of Israel; After those days, saith the Lord, I will put my law in their inward parts, and write it in their hearts; and will be their God, and they shall be my people. And they shall teach no more every man his neighbor, and every man his brother, saying, Know the Lord: for they shall all know me, from the least of them unto the greatest of them, saith the Lord: for I will forgive their iniquity, and I will remember their sin no more.'' (Jeremiah 31:33, 34)

I didn't have a childhood hero from what we called the New Testament. I preferred the Jewish Bible, which was also my Bible. The stories were better. The New Testament had nothing to compare with Shadrach, Meshach, and Abednego in the fiery furnace, Daniel in a den of lions, Samson killing a lion, David killing Goliath and a lot of other people. Feeding five thousand wasn't nearly as interesting. Feeding the hungry has never been as much fun as slaying the wicked. Not as rewarding either.

Where were the stories of fathers and sons? Of Abraham offering Isaac to God? Of Isaac blessing Jacob rather than his favorite, Esau. David weeping for Absalom. Jesus told stories about a father welcoming a prodigal son and a father having two sons, one who says he will obey but doesn't and one who says he won't but does. Preachers and Sunday School teachers pointed out that the father in the parables was God, not a human parent.

Where were the stories of friendship closer than brothers such as David and Jonathan? Where were the stories of sibling rivalry such as Cain and Abel? Jacob and Esau? Joseph and his brothers who sold him into slavery? Jesus' disciples John and James and Peter and Andrew did seek to be the greatest in the new kingdom, but they competed as much with the other disciples as with their brothers.

I didn't like the idea of Jeremiah not getting married. That seemed altogether too much just to make a point; but where were the great love stories in the New Testament? Jesus spoke of two bodies becoming one flesh in a mystical union. Ministers, when they spoke of sex at all, spoke of it as communion. I had dimly recognized sex as the articulation of the sacred and profane, the spiritual and the temporal, the love of God and the love of woman, the intimacy of religious worship and the intimacy of physical adoration. I didn't know how, but I wanted to find out.

I needed answers about love and sex and I didn't want to learn from schoolmates who were as puzzled as I was, or ministers who didn't think much about it, or from my parents who didn't know much about it. I sought insight into life where I had always sought it—in stories. Particularly Bible stories, such as Samson and Delilah, Abraham and Sarah, Isaac and Rebekah, Jacob waiting fourteen years for Rachel, Joseph fleeing Potiphar's wife, Samson pursuing Delilah, David seeing Bathsheba at her bath, Solomon and his thousand wives and concubines. Where were the great love stories of the New Testament? There was Jesus, but Jesus loved everyone, even more than Solomon loved.

Jesus said two bodies could become one flesh. Where were the examples? Jesus was an example of perfection and he never thought about sex. Judas was an example of failure and he didn't seem to think about sex either. Peter was bumbling enough to be a reasonable role model and he was married, too. He had a mother-in-law and perhaps children. However, the Christian writers give us no scenes of Peter explaining to his wife, or his mother-in-law, that he needed to spend more time with his male friends or that he must be about his business even if it meant being away from home for long periods of time. Paul seemed austere and ambitious to a fault. Not many Christians would want him for a husband or father.

My church didn't say sex was bad or evil, only that it was special and should be saved for a special person and a special relationship. I wanted to remain pure, but not forever. I wanted sex to be special, but I needed help for the thoughts that didn't seem special, the desire for someone who wasn't special. The lust for everyone or anyone or all of the opposite sex.

For an adolescent grappling with sex and love, in comparison to the Jewish Bible, the New Testament seemed sexless, almost bloodless. I couldn't look to Mary and Joseph. Mary married Joseph but she didn't make love to him. At least not in the pages of the Bible. This was a role model Christian women seemed to have taken to heart. Or maybe Joseph didn't make love to Mary. Either way, there was a problem for a Christian adolescent in love with love or at least infatuated with his hormones.

I was a Protestant who didn't revere Mary as a virgin, or regard her as one in the long run. The Christian Bible referred to her other children. "Mother of God" seemed blasphemous to me. God was the Mother of God, the Mother and Father of us all. When I was a child, Luke's account of the birth of Jesus seemed right. As an adult writer, I prefer John's ethereal, austere account but not all the time. John is Bach, Luke Beethoven, and when I read either, I think, "Yes, that's the way I would have written it, if I could.'' To question whether or not Mary was a virgin at the time seems not only trivial but rude and puerile.

Mary was good enough for God and his purpose; she's good enough for me. But as an adolescent, I would have been comforted to know that Joseph sported with Mary, watched her bathe with fascination, or worked fourteen years to get her. I might have been willing to wait fourteen years for my own Rachel.

Both the Bible and tradition presented Mary as a mother, not a wife. I knew of no pictures of Mary kissing Joseph awake, sitting beside him while he worked, or putting the kids outside so she and Joseph might have an afternoon to themselves to restore body and soul to their marriage. Tradition pictured Mary as the eternally young, porcelain-pale, adoring mother, untouched by work, worry, or doubt. It was a portrait I could not identify with.

My favorite story of Mary was when she and her other children tried to rescue Jesus from himself, his mission, because people said he had gone mad. That was a mother I could identify with. ''Don't climb too high, son. Don't jump too far. Don't attract attention to yourself.''

I would have liked to have such stories about Mary as a wife. Mary and her children telling Joseph, ''We want you to come home.'' Mary telling Joseph, ''Put down the hammer and saw and talk to me.'' Mary looking at Joseph the way she is pictured looking at Jesus.

Joseph seemed to have loved Mary, at least to have had compassion for her, but Mary's love seemed to be reserved for Jesus. Could a woman be both mother and wife? Don't go to the Christian Bible to find out. Paul admonished wives to be submissive to their husbands. Did Paul ever meet Mary? Was Mary submissive to Joseph? All in all, I, and I think most Christian boys, would have preferred Rachel for a wife and maybe for a mother.

I would like to have had one good family role model in the New Testament to show how to handle Potiphar's daughters, Delilahs wanting both your heart and your head, working for one girl and getting another, seeing Bathsheba sunbathing next door.

Like Jeremiah, Jesus didn't marry. If sex wasn't sinful why couldn't there be one story about Jesus loving some girl or even woman? It would have been useful to me for Jesus to have married. To have demonstrated how to deal with the birth of unwanted children, loss of a job, separation, the death of a beloved child, love turned to indifference, work that was more important than family. Most of my heroes left wife and children to discover a new world, or trade route, or business partner, or to conquer the enemy, defend the empire, or take help, healing, and Hebrews to the heathen.

I didn't want to read Casanova or Henry Miller. I wanted to read a Bible story about a Christian as pure as Joseph, as playful as Abraham, who finds a wife like Bathsheba, and with her, discovers all the pleasures of Solomon. Instead of instructive stories, I got instructions. All in all, Paul thought celibacy was best but it was better to marry than to burn.

I was burning but I was caught between Scylla and Charybdis. Jesus said anyone who divorced his wife and married another committed adultery. If I got married, I had better wait until I was smart enough not to make a mistake. On the other hand, Jesus said, anyone who looked at a woman to lust after her committed adultery with her. That made an adulterer of me and every teenage boy who sat in church having Jimmy Carter thoughts about the women in the choir.

Jesus' statement about looking at a woman with lust was a body blow. I was astonished that Jesus knew me that well; I was stricken that I was denied the pleasure and given the pain. Life was not fair. I didn't have my cake or eat it and I still had to do the dishes. I struggled with that guilt for a long time; I couldn't not look. And when I looked, I lusted.

As an adult reader, the Jewish Bible seems to me a book of failures: man's bent to fail, God's intent to redeem. The Christian Bible is a book of failure, redemption, and coming to terms with redemption that looks like failure. The redeemed didn't act much different than the unredeemed. They only pretended to be sexless.

The writers of the Jewish Bible knew more of desperation. There is nothing in the New Testament to equal Job demanding that God justify his ways. Isaiah and Jeremiah knew despair despite their faith that the nation would be resurrected. There isn't that kind of brooding in the New Testament although Jesus does weep over Jerusalem. The Christian Bible has a kind of determined cheerfulness, even in those epistles expecting the imminent end of the world, even in the apocalypse, even in the gospels when the writers knew the crucifixion was coming; they knew the end of the story.

It's like trying to write about the Alamo today. Writers can't convey the shock and horror of the Alamo because they know about San Jacinto. If there had been no San Jacinto, the crucifixion might have some of the despair of Job. Like the Alamo, there is grandeur in the cross rather than gloom.

Jeremiah's most urgent messages were written in poetry. Today, we think of poetry as trivial, esoteric, or decorative. The important messages, we believe, are written in deadly serious governmentese, technoise, law-blab or academalarky. We memorize the Thou Shalt Nots and engrave them on our walls.

Jesus' words on divorce came in one of those familiar question-and-answer episodes that are like verbal wrestling. There is little poetry here and Jesus' statement that remarriage was adultery seems harsh even today. I still have the same wife, but it seems unfair to place such a penalty on someone who might have made an honest, youthful mistake. It seemed harsh to the disciples who said, "It is good not to marry." And Jesus said, "All men cannot receive this saying, save they to whom it is given." (Matthew 19:11)

Jesus was holding up an ideal and the ideal was equality in marriage. The question had been, "Is it lawful for a man to put away his wife for every cause? And he answered and said unto them, Have ye not read, that he which made them at the beginning made them male and female. And he said, For this cause shall a man leave father and mother, and shall cleave to his wife: and they twain shall be one flesh?'' (Matthew 19:3–5)

Jesus takes the high view of creation. Woman was not an afterthought, not a spare rib, not created for the sake of man, but an equal. Man's hardness of heart had made them unequal, but that's not the way God made them. The ideal was the spiritual union of two physically different-but-equal bodies that lasted unto the grave.

Jesus' statement on lusting comes in a compilation of poetry commonly known as the Sermon on the Mount that begins with the beatitudes. ''Blessed are the poor in spirit: for theirs is the kingdom of heaven.'' ''Blessed are the meek: for they shall inherit the earth.'' ''Blessed are the peacemakers: for they shall be called the children of God.'' And it ends, ''And it came to pass, when Jesus had ended these sayings, the people were astonished at his doctrine.''

That bit of understatement must have caused a few chuckles over the years, following as it did what Christians prefer to believe is Eastern exaggeration. ''And if any man will sue thee at the law, and take away thy coat, let him have thy cloak also.'' ''But when thou prayest, enter into thy closet.'' ''Take therefore no thought for tomorrow.'' ''And everyone that heareth these sayings of mine, and doeth them not, shall be likened unto a foolish man, which built his house upon the sand.''

Christians have spent two thousand years revering Jesus' Sermon on the Mount and rationalizing his meaning. Perhaps Monty Python rationalized best in *The Life of Brian*. Blessed are the cheesemakers refers to the makers of all dairy products.

Jesus said, ''Ye have heard that it was said by them of old time, Thou shalt not commit adultery: But I say unto you, That whosoever looketh on a woman to lust after her hath committed adultery with her already in his heart. And if thy right eye offend thee, pluck it out, and cast it from thee: for it is profitable for thee that one of thy members should perish, and not that thy whole body should be cast into hell.'' (Matthew 5: 27–29)

Even allowing for Eastern exaggeration, that statement seems a denial of human nature. How else do men look at women? But that's the heart of it. That's the root of women's complaint. That's the politically criminal ''lookism.'' Seeing women as things to be used and possessed. Any man who reduces a woman to a sex object, a thing for his pleasure, is guilty of adultery. Her worth is not restricted or equal to her usefulness to a man. She has worth to herself.

Understanding that resolved one of my adolescent mysteries. I had lusted after my female classmates when they were not around, I had devised stratagems for their seduction when I was alone, but when I was with one of them, I was as courtly as Robert E. Lee. I desired them, but I desired them as women to be loved, not things to be used or possessed. At least, that's my memory.

After one out-of-town football game, the team and the pep squad girls were allowed to mix on the buses for the return home. When I got off the bus, some of the girls thanked me for being ''so nice.'' That wasn't what I wanted either. Why couldn't I be a dangerous sexual being who was also intelligent and under control?

The Christian Bible replaced laws that people were scarcely able to keep with ideals that no one could match. Redemption looked like failure because the redeemed could not measure up to Jesus' ideal, ''By this shall all men know that ye are my disciples, if ye have love one to another'' or to Paul's, ''There is neither Jew nor Greek, there is neither bond nor free, there is neither male nor female: for ye are all one in Christ Jesus.''

Failure can be understood. What cannot be understood is denial. As Southern churches denied freedom to black Christians in the name of God, churches all over the world have denied equality to Christian women in the name of God.

Love is an act. As a noun love is good for nothing but a song. And it doesn't matter whether the song is about women, country, or God. Looking at a woman to lust after her is not an act of love. Neither is setting a trap for men. Using a neighbor's service without wages, not proclaiming liberty to your neighbor, not judging the cause of the fatherless. It is not an act of love to God or country to cry "peace" when there is no peace or "justice" when there is no justice. Or to speak pleasing words to gain the favor of rulers or the fame of the crowd.

To look upon a woman and seek to use her person for your pleasure is to commit adultery in your heart. To look upon your country and to lust after its privileges to reserve them to yourself is to commit sedition in your heart. To look upon your religion and to lust after its power to force conformity to your will is to commit blasphemy.

When I read the Bible today I am astonished at how captive our religions have become to our culture. More than captives; they are turn-coats. The dominant voice in the land is not the plea for the cause of the fatherless and the right of the needy but the shrill call of the false prophets to worship at the altars of Mammon and Mars. From George Custer to George Patton our heroes are not peacemakers whose lives are characterized by love but are stained with vainglory and blood. From Jean Lafitte to John D. Rockefeller to Henry du Pont to Howard Hughes our patriots are not poor in spirit but reek of ambition and pride. Our prophets are not reviled for righteousness' sake because they lust after the favor of the crowd.

Our churches pray for the hungry and lobby for power and privilege for themselves. From "conquer we must when our cause it is just" to "Oh, the Yankee boys for fighting are the dandy O!" to "He is trampling out the vintage where the grapes of wrath are stored" to "like a mighty army moves the Church of God" to "praise the Lord and pass the ammunition," our anthems praise our self-righteous hate. We have found God and he is us.

Genesis (Esau)

L E S   S T A N D I F O R D

I grew up in the 1950s in Cambridge, Ohio, a small town on the northern downslope of Appalachia's reef. It was a mining and manufacturing center, a place with a bar on every other corner and just as many churches hopscotched in between. Though mining and manufacturing had already taken their early body blows and the sprawling potteries and glass factories that had put the place on the map were going quietly about their dying, we still had the RCA plant, and Ecko Kitchenware, and Champion Spark Plug, and the marvelously euphonic Vanadium Corporation of America, and any number of mom and pop-ish factories springing up to stamp out parts in an odd new substance called plastic.

We also had a boundless faith in the future, so vital that we had been named, in the early days of that exercise in boosterism, an "All American City." Scott Fitzgerald would have given us very high marks on the "Possibility" index. I was a bright and industrious student and more than one of my teachers assured me that I would be President one day. Despite the fact that my assembly-line working mother and my truck-driving father were a few notches below the Kennedys in wherewithal, if not sophistication, I recall taking this not so much for praise as for casual prognostication, as in: "The way that boy eats, he'll turn out big as a house," etc.

I am not sure of all the reasons why we felt such simpleminded certainty, but feel it we did, and of all that I have taken from that far-distant home, that essentially formless but relentlessly Christian upbringing, my loving parents, those earnest teachers, elders, and friends, nothing has marked me like that indefatigable, ineradicable, romantic readiness, that Gatsby-esque capacity for hope.

I was reminded of this legacy not so long ago, as I nursed a drink in a nondescript bar in a small central Florida town ("Don't miss the Phosphate Museum while you're here"), killing time until I was due in a bookstore, the next in a series of exercises in ignominy and humility devised by my publisher and euphemistically referred to as "the author tour." While such tours, my publicist assured me, had become *de rigueur* for authors, it had been something of a surprise to me to learn that it was not over once one had (a) written a book and (b) found a publisher for it. One needed to (c) hit the road to spread the word about said book, appearing and signing, interviewing and reading wherever one could.

Though it was explained to me that the opportunity to "tour" was something of a plum; and though I did not especially dread the prospect of going out to press the flesh, I had begun to understand the pitfalls. For one, there was never any real guarantee there would be much flesh to press along the way. (Clerk, shouting into the empty recesses of small-town bookstore: "Hey, Edna. Guy says he's here to sign his books. You know anything about that?) And ego-deflation aside, the exercise had begun to seem a bit cynical, even a bit at odds with why I had chosen writing (as opposed to public speaking) as a means of communication in the first place. (Visions of me behind a card table in a striped apron, pile of books on one side, Veg-o-matic and garden vegetables arrayed on the other . . . "We're going to slice and dice in just a minute, folks, but first, let me tell you about this marvelous book.") Wasn't the work to speak for itself, in the best of possible worlds?

But I had no business complaining, I reminded myself. I was lucky to have the opportunity, wasn't I? And in any case, I had gone along.

This final thought led to a pause, a quiet moment in a quiet place, and I glanced up at the bar's television screen just as Dan Rather's image faded and an incomprehensible pollster's statistic claimed his place: "Will the future be better?" someone had asked the American Public. A whopping eighteen percent of us had ventured to think so.

Eighteen percent? The former President-to-be was moved to call for another drink, a little lighter on the vermouth this time, thank you. Could the citizenry of Cambridge, Ohio, have been included in this poll? Sure, I had witnessed a half-century's worth of the sad twists in the world's ever-accelerating tragedy, along with everybody else . . . but eighteen percent? I could hear Fitzgerald calling from the grave for a recount.

I took the fresh drink from the guy behind the bar and thought of asking him what he thought, but then I took another look at the grim expression on his face and forgot about it. Eighteen percent. I hit the drink and stared into the dying ice cubes as if they were tea leaves.

Several fingers of gin and a few jukebox country songs later, I had moved myself to at least consider the opposition's viewpoint. Another drink and I could even formulate their outraged prose. Who the hell were we, we smug, vacuous, Rotarian-minded lightweights, anyway? What on earth had possessed us to dismiss Vietnam, the shadow of the mushroom cloud, enduring poverty, obdurate racism, escalating unemployment and homelessness, the million treaties proffered by dwarfish, flat-eyed men in Washington and snatched back from us all? Dear God, here I was a veteran of the author tours, and I was still identifying with the mindless eighteen percent?

More drink, I thought, at the same time remembering a conversation, a dozen years before, with a group of German students in a biergarten in Heidelberg. At least it began as a conversation. About possibility. Or rather the lack of a sense thereof, at least as I had experienced it among the students of the Rhineland. Possibility, one fairly snarled back at me. You Americans. Live a lifetime within short-range-missile shot of Russia, my respondent told me, see how you feel about possibility then.

I remembered the sneer on his face, the escalating tenor of our polite debate, the ease with which it tipped over into close-quarters combat, the two of us rolling over and over on a beer-soaked floor until a bouncer lifted us apart, one in each hand. Some ambassador of hopefulness, I had been, working the territories in more or less the same fashion as the Crusaders. And then, sitting on a bar stool in the shadow of the shuttered phosphate museum and thinking of Crusaders, of possibility's battered image, I remembered Vacation Bible School.

Though it seems odd to me now, some manifestation of faith more appropriate to a memoir out of Dixie, it did not seem so to me then: scarcely had classes ended for the summer at Glass Plant Elementary School than several of its paid-for-and-maintained-by-the-taxpayers classrooms were commandeered by a tall, mild-mannered missionary and his equally pleasant, moon-faced wife, the couple having swept in from who knows where to instruct those of us sent along by our summer-stunned parents in the finer points of an ecumenical, fundamentalist Christianity. I seem to remember coming home from school clutching a mimeographed flyer announcing this seminar, and though I don't remember any theological debate about it, I am sure that, given the prospects for a child's diversion in Cambridge of the 1950s, my mother and I were equally enthusiastic in signing me up for two free weeks out of the house.

I don't remember very much about the actual proceedings at Vacation

Bible School either, though I am sure things went along much as they did in Sunday School at the Methodist church I more-or-less regularly attended: the usual mind-numbing rehash of parables and stories deemed worthy and instructive for children, exhortations to live out all week what we professed on the Sabbath, reminders to bring our mislaid child-scaled tithing envelopes in next week, etc. But VBS had one feature that I will never forget, it being one of the first undeniably real signs that what those kindly aunts and neighbors said about me becoming president might just be true. For in addition to whatever else we did in those weeks, we read a heck of a lot of the Holy Bible. And we did not just read, we memorized, and for this memorization, we were rewarded, in the form of an intricately worked out series of colored coupons and cards, varying in color, weight, texture, and complexity of congratulatory text, these to be presented as one committed ever more staggering quantities of biblical verse to memory.

I did this very well, far outstripping my peers, ascending so rapidly up the ladder of spiritual mnemonics that Brother Bill and his wife Jane (as we will call them) took me aside somewhere toward the end of week two to inform me that a meeting with my parents would be necessary. For a minute, I was concerned that they'd found out who was responsible for breaking into the school the previous weekend and leading a gleeful rampage of graffiti writing and minor vandalism in and out of the classrooms, the principal's office, and, especially, the girls' bathroom, where someone had defecated in the middle of the floor . . . but, as it turned out, I had nothing to worry about.

Once my parents were summoned, Brother Bill explained that he and Jane, in all their nomadic years, had never run across a fifth-grader who had remembered so much in so short a time. The fact that I had about as much understanding as a macaw of what I could spout by rote did not seem to matter. The fact was that if the coupons I had collected could have been redeemed for heavenly dinnerware, then I was moving in on the Holy Chalice itself. And what this meant was, Pastor Bill and his wife Jane wanted to take me away with them: I would be a kind of acolyte, an object lesson, an inspiration for other Vacation Bible Schoolers the length and breadth of the land, or at least as much of it as the two of them could canvas in a summer season. And they promised to have me back home in time for the start of school that fall.

While I am sure that it was as much a flattery and a temptation for my parents as it was for me (my mind aswirl with visions of the girls' bathrooms in such exotic and far-flung cities as Coshocton, Chillicothe, Ravenna, Painesville, and Portsmouth), we had to turn Bill and Jane down. For one thing, my parents had the appropriate suspicions any hill folk have of flatlanders, no matter how spiritual a game they might talk. They were not about to turn over their eleven-year-old son to a couple of strangers, even holy strangers. And as for me, I was a mama's boy of the first water. Though I might manage a night's sleepover at a friend's house down the street, the notion of being *away from home* for an entire summer was absurd, as incomprehensible as it was magnificent.

Bill and Jane were sad, but finally accepting, and we parted with assurances that we'd see each other again the following summer, me holding some gilt-edged certificate with an amazing verse count recorded in purple ink, them waving good-bye and swearing they'd spread the word of what that towheaded boy in Cambridge had accomplished.

Of course, I never saw Bill and Jane again, and whether or not they were incarcerated somewhere down the line, or gave up traveling to form a permanent cult, or simply found some other, truly astounding idiot savant to tour with them is beside the point. For they had validated a suspicion that had begun to present itself to me, as it does to so many of us at about that age; and while I had the good sense never to actually utter the words out loud, I went away from that meeting with Bill, Jane, and my parents absolutely and unutterably convinced of, perhaps even mentally chanting, the bright adolescent's mantra: *"I am hot shit."* People who did not know me or my parents, who had no expectation of personal gain from participating in this pleasant fiction, had essentially said so, and, looking back I can say that Bill and Jane gave me the same kind of unadulterated, adolescent ego boost I experienced later on when unknown editors at far-flung and obscure journals began to accept, and say kind things of, pieces I had written.

Furthermore, the mindless endeavor that Bill and Jane had led me into eventually paid more substantive dividends. It had gotten out, what I'd managed to remember that summer, and for a long time after, I was to be used as a kind of human concordance by my Sunday School teachers and even by my family. It went beyond the level of curiosity. For my teachers, I became the kind of object lesson that Bill and Jane had envisioned; and for one of my uncles, who was fond of quoting scripture to justify his many opinions, I was a profound convenience at family gatherings: "Come 'ere and tell 'em what the Bible says about (insert any topic), Lessie."

All that went away when I stopped going to Sunday School and made sure to stay out of Uncle Beany's sight at the reunions, but the verses lingered on, whirling up into my consciousness at the oddest moments like cloud banks of mental weather scudding in from nowhere. The rhythms of speech, from the Psalms and elsewhere, might intrude as I performed some mindless task like sweeping the porch: "The Lord is my shepherd," *swish/ swish,* "I shall not want," *swish/swat.* Or I might find myself suddenly replaying one of the narratives as I sat in school, drifting off in the middle of the class recitation of the times tables to envision myself as right-minded Jacob upholding the principles of law and respect for family, scorning the churlish Esau who was so simple and shortsighted as to trade his birthright for a bowl of soup. I found endless pleasure in such revisitation of the stories I had stored away.

On a deeper level, I suppose I was unconsciously practicing what I would come to as a profession years later, much as you learn to play the piano by running the scales and playing the basic tunes. But at the time, I think I was also using the narratives to place myself in the world. And I did so in an uncritical and unhesitating application of the conventional, conservative readings that Bill and Jane and my well-meaning Sunday School teachers had supplied along with the text. That I superimposed my own visage on that of Esau as readily as I placed it on Jacob's during my daydreaming was something I was not really aware of until much later. At the time, I bought into the prevailing party line, that smooth was good and hairy was synonymous with dumb, and the lawyers would inherit the earth. After all, the way I read it, Esau disappeared into history, recipient of an afterthought of a blessing from Isaac, and doomed to live with some god-awful sounding group called the Edomites, while Jacob got to found the twelve tribes of Israel.

Such an interpretation makes sense to me, in retrospect. The way my mind worked in those days, abstractions, particularly the grand abstractions such as heritage, liberty, democracy, brotherhood, had much greater weight than particulars, and birthrights were clearly not things to be traded in casually for potted meat. It also seemed to me, then, that if Jacob could swing a birthright and his father's real blessing with some mild cunning, ending up as the keystone of the Israelite nation, also two wives, compliant maids, and a big ranch with plenty of stock, then God must in fact favor the businessman. That's how I figured the story, with Esau, careless as he was, lucky to get off as well as he did, comfortable place in the country and all.

How else could I have read it? My Sunday School teacher sold used cars for H. L. Cross Chevy-Olds, and was the nicest, most avuncular man I knew. All he did was relate the story, all he had to do.

When I think back, I can't hold it against the teacher, or even think less of him. We both grew out of that heritage, the meek inheriting and their lawyers skimming eighty percent. I finally shelved the story as simple-minded truth, letting it, and all that was really there, fade from that coulda-been-another-Elmer-Gantry memory bank. I moved in a self-centered way through high school and college piling up memory coupons of a different sort, stacking them until I had a wad that I could trade for a ticket to law school. Columbia, it was grandly called. And it sat in New York City, the glitteringest setting of them all, at least for a hairy boy from Ohio.

As it happened, law school did not work out (New York did not for Nick Carraway, either, of course). Following a towering argument with a Professor of Legal Method—"Young man, one of these days you will find out there's a great difference between justice and The Law"—it was agreed that the-President-to-be would be allowed to exit the halls of learning and spend the rest of the year off "finding" himself, readmission guaranteed.

Many years later, law school readmission long forgotten, aspiration to higher office as well, the process of "finding" myself continues. I've come to admit that it is likely to continue for a lifetime; and ironically enough, it is a process carried out primarily in terms of storytelling. Furthermore, I seem to have discovered that storytelling has as much to do with reexamination of the old stories—of the myths—as it has to do with inventing anything new.

And this may explain how I come to a reconsideration of Jacob and Esau while sitting on a bar stool in the midst of an author tour. Could it be possible that, as the old storytellers well understood, I find myself stumbling into a career, balancing the desire to write, to explore the self, against the ambition to succeed, i.e., promote the self? Nor is it a surprise to me to consider such parallels between a story and my "life," for as I say, stories, or myths, are life distilled. It's a process I follow every day of my writing life, following my fictional knight out into the fearsome wastelands (South Florida in my rendition) to see if what he's learned and gleaned will be of help when he goes up against the dragons (we have many of those in this part of paradise). The fact that it's a well-worn path doesn't make it any less interesting to me at all. I find something new around every familiar corner.

Let's go back to that story about the hairy man and his birthright. Hungry Esau, who has spent all day roaming the fields, searching out game, responds to cunning Jacob, who has spent all day over a hot stove in

Mama's tent: "My birthright? For a bowl of soup? Well, I don't know. But maybe if it's a big bowl . . ." So Esau eats, Jacob gets the birthright . . . and I find myself wondering these days who really got slickered after all? Granted, Esau is not a man to make minute distinctions. He works hard, comes home starving, his mind on food, not upon the finer points of the law . . . and what the hell is a birthright anyway, some abstraction that you can give away with a few words over the dinner table.

Having become a writer of stories myself, having taken great pains to construct narrative which embeds its meaning in its very shape, it occurs to me to assume the same intention on the part of the author of the story of Jacob and Esau. Instead of lifting out a portion of the narrative to regard as a parable with a convenient proscriptive meaning, why not read the entire piece, taking everything into consideration.

Looking at the story this way, I go on to consider the blessing that Isaac bestows on Jacob some years after the soup-for-birthright incident. Poor old blind man, about to die, Isaac asks his wife to send Esau out to bring down a deer for a final, favorite meal. Instead of sending Esau, however, Rebekah finds *her* favorite, Jacob, sends him into the pen to slaughter a couple of domestic goats, and dresses him up in sheepskin.

Though Isaac thinks it's Esau in the tent with him, it is of course Jacob —that wolf dressed in woolly sheepskin, whom his aged hands roam over —and the blessing is mistakenly bestowed. One more for the clever guy, I once thought. But wait. Consider that Isaac, twenty years or more after the birthright incident, is still calling on Esau as his favorite, Esau the dummy hunter. And swindling one's brother out of a birthright must not have led to much after all: here's Jacob, at forty, still taking orders from Mama, and still, apparently, needing to connive in order to secure his father's blessing.

Furthermore, even with the success of his kid meat and sheepskin masquerade, Jacob has not taken everything. Esau asks his father, once the ruse has been discovered, the all-important question: "Hast thou but one blessing, my father?" And blind Isaac responds, delivering with his second blessing evidence of an implicit justice in the human condition. It is impossible to read the story as an adult and not perceive that this is the essential motif of the Jacob-Esau relationship, and that this is surely the aim—or at the very least, the effect—of an artfully told story.

Following the story onward through Genesis only underscores the point. Though the chapters that follow say little of Esau (and little *was* said in my Sunday School class, to be sure), that's the importance of taking a second, more critical look at a subtly told tale. The verses trace Jacob's journey through the lands of his mother's people, where Jacob labors twenty years for Laban, his mother's brother, getting in return a herd of speckled cows and sheep and two wives, the best of whom he doesn't appreciate, the beauty a barren vessel. Reading this, smooth Jacob's bargains begin to look worse as time passes. When he finally leaves Panandaram for home, lovely wife Rachel steals her father's icons, hinting at the ultimate distance between her pagan heritage and that of her husband, and reminding us just how faulty Jacob's judgment is.

When Laban catches up with the fleeing Jacob, who has built his herds up at the expense of his uncle's stock, the two slicksters have their obligatory back and forth, very much, it now seems to me, like a pair of movie Mafia dons trying to make up without anyone losing face: finally they build a pillar as evidence of the peace agreement, just as Jacob earlier felt it necessary to erect a monument to mark the spot where he dreamed of his ladder and promised to tithe to God. In this universe, it appears, a man's word may be one thing, but a stone marker is forever.

Jacob is a cautious man, with an eye for the value of a contract, to be sure. Hardly has he got things straight with Uncle Laban than he must prepare to meet his long-lost brother. Understandably uncertain as to how he will be received, Jacob sends out an advance party with bounteous gifts —cows, sheep, goats, horses—hoping to mollify any stored-up urges for revenge on Esau's part. While he waits alone to see how his peace offering will be received, Jacob is visited by the angel of God. The two of them are wrestling, and once again, Jacob proves what a slippery fellow he is. He's got God in a headlock, and he isn't letting go until another blessing is bestowed.

God complies, and Jacob turns him loose, hoping that this bodes well for his encounter with his brother: the two men meeting again after twenty years, both of them in their sixties now, approaching each other under a hot sun on the dry side of a mountain pass, Jacob with his women and children arrayed behind him in a shameless bid for mercy, bowing and scraping his way toward Esau—if it were a movie, it occurs to me, like a dog coming to be whipped. He's absolutely blind to Esau's bewilderment at the evidence of wealth before him, for despite the material gains Jacob has amassed, he has gained no spiritual capital. "What will Esau say first," is the only thing on Jacob's mind. For all he knows, he is coming to meet his death.

Though I never got to this point when I was twelve, or somehow missed it if I did, this encounter constitutes the archetypal reckoning between the smooth and the hairy, or so it can seem: the slick one who has dealt all his life in appearances, making deals, exacting promises, taking advantage of his trust, building tangible monuments to his sincerity, and generally setting himself apart from the world around him . . . and the innocent man of short memory, apparently without guile, the eternal prey.

And yet it is Esau who has the power today, this is *his* turf. Jacob knows it, knows that power is all, regrets his life, nothing now without the power. . . . And what does Esau say to groveling Jacob but, "I have enough, my brother; keep that thou hast unto thyself." What this suggests to me is that while Esau may lack guile, he is no fool. Esau does not covet his brother's wealth. And while he may well remember all the past injustices done him, he is free of any impulse toward vengeance. In fact, Esau is willing to do something that seems outside his fearful brother's ken. In granting Jacob his forgiveness, Esau presents himself to me as that most blessed of creatures, a man at peace with himself.

Jacob, though relieved, worries that there must be a catch. Surely justice will be served here at this barren pass. Surely he will get what is coming to him, he who has admitted he is unworthy for even "the least of all the mercies".

Even after he has been spared, after Esau has gone, has left him with his blessing, Jacob still doesn't get it, never really internalizes those last key words of his brother. In his relief, it seems he's only caught the note that means he can walk away from this meeting unscathed and disregard the point on into Canaan, there to build another monument, this one a temple honoring his narrow escape and the magnanimity of Esau. He's missed it entirely, that final sentence of unassuming, guileless Esau, who stands before a fearful, twisted man and repeats the credo that has sustained a simple hunter's life, the maxim that transcends all the temples, and accoutrements of success, and protestations of faith: "What needeth it? Let me find grace in the sight of my lord."

Jacob, drawn back home by a spiritual call toward wholeness he does not fully understand, has missed his final opportunity in my way of reading it and cannot grasp the lessons he might have taken from his brother's example. Tragically, he has lost the last opportunity to change his ways, and so ends the story, with Esau finishing his days among the Edomites and Jacob playing administrator to the end, the fitting denouement. There is eternity and there is eternity, after all.

I don't really resent that the story as I "studied" it so many years ago came to me in a truncated form, nor that somehow certain essentials were glossed over. For reasons I have already explained, to remember that I once considered Jacob the "hero" of this story surprises me only a little. We dealt in essentials back then: the kid with the most verses wins, success equals the presidency, and who were the Edomites compared to the twelve holy tribes? Only now, aided by experience, by the attempts to tell the stories myself, do I begin to appreciate what has been there all along.

That I didn't understand Esau's strength and quiet dignity reminds me that there is the Jacob inside me too. That's the part of me that gets riled up when the turnout is especially low on the author tour, that idles away time at the computer keyboard urging a publisher or an agent to find the angle that's going to have us all rolling among handmaidens and speckled cattle. I suspect that somewhere in the psyche of the most guileless of storytellers there lurks the buried Jacob, that part of the self containing a certain ambition that it may take a lifetime to recognize. There is the comforting image of the battered knight who sallies forth to spread the word for the word's sake . . . and then there is that clever fellow who yearns to make a Veg-o-matic dance. The trick is to understand that he's there, that you have to keep an eye on him and what he's up to, do your best to keep him under control.

Perhaps most ironic, given what I've come to be doing with my life, is my present-day awareness of that ancient, original author—that person who, by design or by intuition, laid in long ago all that I have come to discover so late. I like to imagine him, or her, reaching out from the grave, yearning to slap this twelve-year-old towhead upside the head (they were stern in the Old Testament, weren't they), calling out in this ghostly voice, "Dammit, don't listen to them, read the whole thing for yourself. Pay close attention, get a better translation, if every word wasn't important I wouldn't have put them all in . . ." that sort of thing. The best response I have is: O.K., O.K., I'm older now. I'm trying. I'm beginning to get the idea.

Which seems to me the important thing about reexamining the stories, and the necessary thing. The best ones remind us that these human crises are familiar, that they've been occurring for a long, long time. That we encounter them today, just dressed in different clothes. That we can prevail at times, gain rewards we did not anticipate, even without the best attorneys on our team.

So finally, and even though I've yet to become President, I can still pay my check, give the bartender a smile, stroll out of the central Florida bar, and face whatever's coming next. There's no great mystery about how I've come to find myself among that eighteen percent, those of us with our simpleminded audacity to hope that tomorrow might be better. We look around. We pay attention. Again and again, we tell ourselves these old stories. We hope there's still time to get it right.

Psalms and Gospels

D A V I D   B R A D L E Y

It was Easter Sunday 1959 and I was losing Jesus.

This would have been a trying moment for any one raised in the Christian tradition. It was especially so for me. Christianity was the way in which I had been trained up to go, not only in life but in livelihood. To put it crassly, Christianity was supposed to be my business.

It has always been my family's business. My clan's primogenitor, my great-grandfather Peter, had become a preacher in the African Methodist Episcopal Zion Church while still a slave, and continued once he became a freeman, in 1836. One of his sons, Mark Anthony, became pastor of an A. M. E. Zion church in Hempstead, New York.[1] His other son, Daniel, my grandfather, eventually became what Methodists call a presiding elder, an overseer of a group of churches.

Before that he had been a pastor to several, including one called Mt. Pisgah, in a hamlet called Bedford, in rural Pennsylvania. That had been around 1915; forty years later his son, David, my father, also became Mt. Pisgah's pastor, but for him it was an unpaid avocation; his vocation was General Officer for the A. M. E. Zion denomination—he edited a church magazine, directed its historical research, and traveled the nation organizing Christian education seminars.

My father's career confirmed clan myth that ministry was destiny for at least one male in each generation. His ambition had been to be a history professor, and to that end he had earned a master's degree and taught in a small black college in the South. But eventually God had him swallowed up by cetaceous circumstances. Heeding his thus revealed call, he abandoned the Tarshish of Academia for the Nineveh of the Church, or so family lore had it. Where it had me was lent unto the Lord, whether I liked it or not. It was not only that I was the sole male child in my generation. I was also a son born to my father's second wife after much prayer and many years of barrenness.[2] My clan elders—grandmother, uncle, father—therefore expended much effort to ensure I found my identity in the Scriptures. One of my first memories is of my grandmother telling me my name was taken from the Bible (a fact of which I was obnoxiously proud, until I figured out almost everyone I knew also had a "Bible name") and that my namesake had been a direct ancestor of Jesus. I delighted in stories about how David, though only a poor, unarmed shepherd boy, knocked Goliath out cold with a sling, became the friend of the king's son, and married the king's daughter.

I was often put to bed with these and other Bible stories, sometimes told extemporaneously but frequently read to me from a big Bible storybook; my first lessons in literacy were based on Daniel in the lions' den and Samson and the Philistines and Moses in the ark of bulrushes—my interest in the last was not blunted by the fact that Moses had been dead a considerable time. My first school was Sunday School, my second a summer Bible School. Before I heard the Declaration of Independence or learned the Pledge of Allegiance I had by heart the Lord's Prayer, the Apostles' Creed, the Ten Commandments, the Beatitudes. And before I heard of Franklin or Jefferson or Lincoln I knew all about Jesus.

I didn't just know about Jesus in the Manger. I knew about Jesus in the Wilderness and Jesus on the Mount and Jesus on the Sea of Galilee. I knew about the Jesus in whose sight all the children of the world (red and yellow, black and white) were precious; who raised a girl from the dead,[3] who borrowed five loaves and two fishes from a boy to feed the five thousand,[4] who told his disciples to "suffer little children, and forbid them not, to come unto me: for of such is the kingdom of heaven."[5]

Heaven I thought of as being like the Big Rock Candy Mountain; Jesus I thought of as my friend. Not an imaginary playmate, for though of those I had many, I knew they were chimerical; Jesus was *real;* a warm, meek, silent (I was religious, not a schizophrenic) presence saving me from danger by day, and, at night, making sure the alligator stayed beneath my bed. He wanted me for a sunbeam, and loved me, for the Bible told me so.

Many children learn this, of course—or used to. But unlike most children, I attended not only Sunday School but church, from "The Lord is in His holy temple" to "The Lord bless thee and keep thee," and thus was exposed to not-so-childish things. Though I found the scripture lessons and responsive readings largely incomprehensible, I got a sense of dark and complex mysteries from hymns and spirituals. When Ezekiel saw the wheel a turnin', I imagined a truck tire and a car tire twirling, but understood that there was a relationship between human faith and the Grace of God— whatever grace was. When Moses told old Pharaoh to let God's people go, I understood, from the minor key, that the Exodus was no jaunt into the desert, but a desperate escape. Although I thought " 'Tis midnight and on Olive's brow" referred to the forehead of a man named Olive, I did grasp that my friend Jesus was suffering in the garden, and understood that despite the joy that Christmas brought to the world, the true focus of my clan's faith was not Advent, but Easter.

In 1959 I was still a child, only six months beyond my eighth birthday; obviously only something serious could have brought me to doubt. In fact, what was transpiring on that Easter Sunday morning was worse than a total loss of faith. I did not doubt that Jesus was the only Son of God, or that, though crucified, dead and buried, he had arisen and ascended. Nor did I doubt He would one day come again to judge the quick and the dead. Though I did not know who the quick were, I had full faith in the divinity of Jesus; it was humanity I was starting to doubt.

The prime mover of all of this was the African part of African Methodist Episcopal Zion—not that anybody in the church, certainly no member of Mt. Pisgah, called him- or herself an African. My family preferred the term "Negro," not because we were ashamed of the African past, but because we were more concerned with our American past and present. Most local blacks, who would not, then, have been comfortable with being called black, were, then, quite comfortable with being called colored.

That was the term most adult whites used publicly. Some, the more refined, used Negro, albeit awkwardly; they could never seem to understand that the initial vowel was a long e and not a short i—which suggests what they might have said in private. A few, the less refined, used that suggested term in public, but even of these few would have used it to a black person's face; in Bedford even the bigots tended to be polite. The children of bigots were another matter. I first heard the word nigger on the playground, on my first day of public school. I had no idea what it meant, which greatly frustrated the boy who used it; accordingly, he defined the term for me with a punch to my proboscis. Fortunately, battery did not prove common; verbal assaults, however, did; and threats were usually appended to the epithets. As most often no action ensued, I was able to adhere to the universal kid's code of silence.

Eventually the matter came to light when mother noticed deep bloody scratches on my legs, and I was forced to explain that just that day, one assault had become terrifying physical. A pair of beefy twins had bulldogged me, stripped my pants off, and whipped me with briers, while calling me a nigger. This revelation led to a general disclosure.

Oddly, the verbal abuse concerned my elders more than the physical. My mother did telephone the mother of my flagellators—who, apparently, did unto them what they had done unto me—but her plans to call other mothers ended when one of them called *her* a nigger. My grandmother called my mother's efforts foolishness; I would have to learn, she said, to ignore white trash, and she taught me how to hold my face impassive so as to deny said trash satisfaction. My father told me sticks and stones might break my bones, but names would never hurt me, and taught me how to walk away with dignity. My uncle Peter John, called John, the clan's eldest male, who lived afar, added his advice when next he visited: "Son," he said, "don't worry what they call you, so long as it ain't late to dinner."

What I did do was retaliate with nastier names. My grandmother had supplied one basic formulation; by listening to the less pious black folk in the town, I amassed a lexicon of racial insults—redneck, peckerwood, offay —and behavioral innuendo, few of which I understood, but all of which I learned to hurl as if they were David's five smooth stones. Though none of my foes fell unconscious, most backed off.

Verbal self-defenses proved effective during my first two school years, but by September of 1958, when I turned eight and started third grade, this effectiveness was decaying. Indeed, my invective now seemed to enrage my tormentors, possibly because they had learned, as I as yet had not, what that foul language meant. As some of the boys had grown in strength and aggressiveness, assault more often evolved into battery, mostly with fists, but sometimes with handy implements, like rocks and baseball bats. Christmas brought *de facto* truce; cold often kept us inside, and snow made the secluded, and therefore dangerous, areas of the playground inaccessible.

But as winter waned, life grew dangerous. By Ash Wednesday the playground had become a battleground.

As Lent progressed I tried to cope. First I tried verbal escalation; I decided it would be acceptable to preface my expletives with "God damn" because the commandment said not to take the name of God in vain and I wouldn't mind if God got involved, though I didn't expect it. But my tormentors were unintimidated by my maledictions; my only profit on it was I now knew how to curse. Then I attempted physical resistance. But though I too had grown, I lacked both moral conviction and combat experience, and so succeeded only in getting myself minorly lacerated, contused, and abraded—and majorly humiliated. Then I decided to try prayer. I knew what to pray for, too: to be delivered from mine enemies—that, I knew, had been the perennial plea of the Children of Israel. Though my mental image of that deliverance had Jehovah riding to the rescue in a truck like the milkman drove, I also knew David had cried out to be delivered, so I searched his psalms for model language. The language of Psalm 144 seemed so appropriate I wondered if there had been playgrounds in Bethlehem when David was growing up. But though I prayed with plagiarized perfection God failed to "Rid me, and deliver me from the hand of strange children;"[6] instead I was further lacerated, contused, abraded, humiliated —and, now, confused.

For I was, I thought, a good boy; I did no damage unto others, and couldn't see why God was allowing others to do damage unto me. I knew the Children of Israel did not always get delivered, but that was because they did things they weren't supposed to do, like . . . worshiping graven images. I wasn't sure what a graven image was, but I knew I hadn't worshiped any; surely I had no gods before God—although I *was* a little confused about the Trinity . . . And I was pretty clear on the rest of the commandments. I may have taken the name of the Lord in vain, but it wasn't *my* fault God hadn't actually damned anybody. I always kept the Sabbath—I had the gold stars to prove it. If ever I failed to honor my father and my mother they corrected me so promptly I doubted God even heard about it. I hadn't killed anybody. I didn't know what adultery was, but it sounded like something I *couldn't* do. I hadn't stolen anything, except freshly baked cookies. I hadn't borne witness—I had a mental image from "Perry Mason"—at all. I had coveted a red English racer bicycle, but I had repented immediately. Besides, the Children of Israel were always warned by a prophet before bad stuff happened; though many men in Bedford were old and hairy enough to pass for prophets, none had said so much as "Woe unto thee" to me.

After pondering all this in my heart it came to me: perhaps I wasn't being punished, but tested, or even refined for some great purpose. But then it occurred to me that I might be a member of that third or fourth generation upon whom the iniquity of the fathers was to be visited— though I couldn't imagine anybody in the patriarchal line hating God. Eventually, I gave up and laid the matter before my father.

I did this not because my father was my father, but because he was a spiritual leader. I had heard him preach hundreds of times, not only at Mt. Pisgah, but at churches in places like Pittsburgh and New York and Chicago. I saw him as a modern-day St. Paul, traveling as he did. However, he was also my father, and I had the same expectations of him most boys have of their fathers—that, among other things, they will know how to handle the rough-and-tumble of the world, in rough-and-tumble style. So when I spoke to him I not only phrased the business theologically, I also asked him would he please teach me to fight.

This was a request my father had long anticipated, and dreaded. Unfortunately he had also prepared for it, as he prepared what he called his Sunday "meditations"—he found the word sermon pretentious. But what he said seemed as pretentious as the worst of sermons. First he repeated that old saw about sticks and stones. Then he warned that if I got a reputation for fighting I would become *persona non grata*—which was Greek, not Latin, to me. Then he quoted Jesus, according to the

Gospel of Matthew: "all they that take up the sword shall perish with the sword."[7] Then he told me to read my Bible; specifically, that Gospel, Chapter 5.

Though it seemed my father missed my point—these little Philistines were using sticks and stones—I took his. For, though I had from a child known the Holy Scriptures,[8] and though I loved to read, I was not yet a reader of the Bible, and I had long known this was a flaw. Bible reading was a Christian duty, especially for a Methodist. Nor did my youth excuse me, for, if Jesus at twelve was amazing rabbis, at my age he must have been reading scrolls forward. Long before the crisis on the playground I had tried to rectify myself. I'd decided to celebrate my birthday in September by reading the life of David, which I knew was to be found in the Books of Samuel. But I foundered on the names—Ephraim; Elkahnah; Zuph. I barely got past Ramathaim-zophim and never reached Gilgal, much less Bethlehem. At Advent I'd resolved to read the Christmas story in all four Gospels; I thought the reading might be easier since I already knew the plot. What really made it easier was that two Gospels didn't mention the Birth of Jesus; I breezed through the four chapters of the two that did, and, thus encouraged, followed Mark's reference to Isaiah. But the Prophet's images —wounds, bruises, putrefying sores[9]—reminded me painfully of the playground, and I put the Bible down.

Contributing to this was the fact that my family did not favor vernacular translations; all the Bibles around the house and in the pew racks at Mt. Pisgah were dedicated to the Most High and Mighty Prince James, by the Grace of God King of Great Britain. Though I could read well for my age, I was only eight, though I preferred to say, almost-nine; even the adverb-laden language of Victor Appleton was more comprehensible than the King's English. But now I wondered if preferring Tom Swift to the Pentateuch might not be like having other gods before God. So I followed my father's guidance and took the Bible up again.

My father's guidance did help in tackling the text; focused reading revealed several relevant verses from Matthew, who quoted Jesus as saying:

> Ye have heard that it hath been said, An eye for an
> eye and a tooth for a tooth:
> But I say unto you, That ye resist not evil: but
> whosoever shall smite thee on the right cheek, turn
> to him the other also.[10]

and:

> Ye have heard that it hath been said, Thou shalt love
> thy neighbor and hate thine enemy.
> But I say unto you, Love your enemies, pray for
> them that curse you, do good unto them that hate
> you, and pray for them that despitefully use you,
> and persecute you . . . For if ye love them which
> love you, what reward have ye? do not even the
> publicans the same?[11]

Though I wasn't sure what a publican was, I didn't need Matthew to tell me of the rewards for not doing what they did: in general, blessedness; specifically, the meek would inherit the earth,[12] the peacemakers would be called the children of God,[13] and those who were persecuted would get the kingdom of heaven.[14] Nor did I need him to remind me:

> Blessed are ye, when *men* shall revile you, and
> persecute *you,* and say all manner of evil against you
> falsely, for my sake.

> Rejoice and be exceeding glad: for great is your
> reward in heaven; for so persecuted they the
> prophets which were before you.[15]

But I did need him to tell me how Jesus related Judaism to Christianity:

> And whosoever shall compel thee to go a mile, go
> with him twain.[16]

I did know what twain meant, and so I had it, good news and bad. My pain was no punishment called forth by a transgression of the Law of Moses, but part of a persecution that began before I was born. Nonetheless, I had transgressed, for if I wanted to be a Christian, I had to reach the higher standard set by Jesus. I had to abandon thoughts of fighting, and of counter-cursing, too; clearly such was the teaching of Jesus according to the Gospel of Matthew. What wasn't clear was what I was supposed to do to keep myself from getting beaten to a pulp.

About this time my uncle John made one of his frequent visits. He observed my confusion and wormed my quandary out of me. It seemed he had not realized the full extent of the problem when he previously gave advice. Now, he was appalled. And though he agreed that I should turn the other cheek, he pointed out that Jesus did not say what you should do should you be smitten there. Then he taught me a few punches; these he enjoined me to use only in the clearest case of self-defense.

The lessons gave me confidence, which I apparently projected at school, in a demeanor threatening enough to deter physical assaults. This gave me great heart; perhaps by looking sufficiently ferocious I could escape both the sin of fighting and the pain of persecution—if so, loving my enemies was something I could surely do. Accordingly, though I still prac-ticed jabs and hooks before a mirror, I also worked on glowers, grimaces, and steely-eyed scowls. Which worked—for a while. But came a day when facial ferocity proved impotent.

It happened during Holy Week, a time, ironically, when catholic events brought to Bedford a certain ecumenical—and incidentally interracial—harmony. The initial event was a Palm Sunday concert, featuring an appropriate oratorio sung by a community chorus. A Tuesday prayer luncheon, the last in a series of such held during Lent, saw the collection of Easter "gleaners"—slotted cards, distributed to parishioners on Ash Wednesday, now filled with dimes—as an Offering for the Poor. At midnight on Maundy Thursday the bells of all churches were rung to signal the end of the Last Supper and the beginning of the watch on the Mount of Olives. On Good Friday, during the traditional three hours of Crucifixion, an interdenominational service was held, at which the legendary Seven Last Words of Christ became the texts for prayers and sermons by different ministers. Though most Easter Sunday festivities were separate but equal, they began with a dramatic dawn service on the shores of a nearby lake.

These public rites were embellishments to what I truly loved about Eastertide: the rituals of Mt. Pisgah and my clan. These commenced with a Maundy Thursday communion service, incorporated attendance at the Good Friday service—Mt. Pisgah's members would not ordinarily have set foot in a white church. Saturday morning and afternoon were given to preparations for a clan feast—the baking of hams and roasting of ducklings, the stuffing of shad, the laborious preparations that produced fresh coconut cakes. Saturday saw the coloring of eggs. Easter Sunday started with the lakeside sunrise service, which seemed all the more mystical to me because I was usually half-asleep. Then came the Easter baskets, full of goodies that were only to be sampled, for the next event was Easter breakfast—steaming mounds of sausage and scrambled eggs and waffles dripping with butter and syrup, and icy, frothy milk, all of local origin, and so unimaginably fresh and pure. Then came Sunday School and Easter services at Mt. Pisgah, the usually small congregation aggrandized by seasonal attendees and emigrants returned. Then came the family feast, an orgy of food and not-often-seen relatives. Finally, there was Mt. Pisgah's evening Easter Program, at which I and my fellow Sunday-Schoolers recited doggerel and received the gruff praise and gentle criticism that told us both how much we were loved and how much was expected of us.

Even given habitual pageantry, Holy Week 1959 was special. My mother had sung a featured solo in the Palm Sunday oratorio. My father was to speak at the Sunrise Service. Though I was too devout to admit this made me proud, it did; though I was too young to see it as a symbolic breakthrough in local race relations, older black folk understood it was; their rising hope was infectious. My father apparently saw this as an opportunity for cultural outreach and augmented Mt. Pisgah's traditional Maundy Thursday grape juice and matza communion with a preservice Seder sampler—*karpas,* lamb, *maror*—and a meditation on the oft-overlooked obvious: that Jesus and his Disciples ate these foods not because they were having the Last Supper, but keeping Pesach; that they were in the Upper Room not because they were Christians but because they were Jews.

By Good Friday morning all this recent and anticipated celebration had me fairly fevered, a mood that was hardly cooled by the fact that school would let out well before noon. Other children were excited by this short day too, especially as most of the time would be taken up by a mid-morning recess and Easter pageant, complete with cross and Centurion—in those days no decree had gone out that the state should deny the church.

Perhaps it was that, distracted by all of this, I fell back into meek mien; certainly, on that Good Friday, I was in no mood to act tough. Or perhaps my family's current prominence made me a target. Or perhaps the lives of other children led them to see Easter not as a festival of light, but as an orgy of sadism and blood. In any case, a *minyan* sought me out at that mid-morning recess and stoned me with the foulest biological, genealogical, and racial epithets I had ever heard; clearly they'd been saving up.

Confounded by their number, disoriented by this sudden injection of ugliness into what I thought saw as the most glorious season of the year, and simply frightened beyond thought, I forgot fighting and fled. This satisfied the mob; they let me go. But one boy—a Goliath-like piece of piss-poor protoplasm, who had spent two years in each of first and second grades—pursued. He hounded me even unto the farthest reaches of the playground, where a copse and a culvert concealed us from the sight of anyone but God. There the fence forced me to turn to bay.

There I cowered while he reviled me and cursed me, said all manner of evil against me, and promised a dire physical fate. He did not vow to kill me, but I could not see how I could survive the promised atrocities. Desperately I prayed to my God; but God, it seemed, had quite forsaken me. Then I realized my tormentor was actually doing nothing, other than curse me and demand that I "put 'em up." Suddenly it came to me: Christ was at work here; this boy was unwilling to attack unless I agreed to violence. Salvation lay in not resisting evil, just as Jesus said.

I stopped cowering. I faced my enemy. I told him firmly I would not fight. He cursed me for a coward. I said "God bless you" as if he'd sneezed. He promised more direful damage. I said I would forgive him whatever he did. That rendered him speechless. Filled with a confidence that came, not from the Marquess of Queensberry, but from the Holy Spirit, I went that second mile: I told him I loved him.

Afterward, I could not remember if he actually smote me on my cheek, or if I turned unto him the other. If I did, he smote me there, for he smote me everywhere. I could not remember the individual blows—how my nose was bloodied or my teeth loosened, but I could remember being beaten, badly beaten, and thinking that I was going to die, like the prophets which were before me, like Jesus Himself. I could not remember going down, but I could remember lying on my back, not with my arms and legs outstretched like Jesus on the Cross, but drawn up and raised, like a submissive dog. I could remember crying out, not fine words of forgiveness, nor even a prayer, but a plea, not to God, to my attacker; try though I did, I could never forget I begged that brutal little bastard for mercy. Nor could I ever forget his response: he laughed, and kicked me in the side.

I could—and can—remember how the pain from insult and injury mangled my sensibilities: how I felt him stepping back, and tasted his satisfaction; how the dirt beneath me smelled soft; how my pain itself was a slow red roll—rhythmic, grotesquely comforting; how when he spoke I saw the words as if through a veil, written in air: STINKING CHICKEN-SHIT MONKEY-FACED NIGGER. That was when I went mad.

It was a truly biblical moment. Power invaded me; filled me with the strength of ten thousand. I did not get up, I *rose* up, as if with wings of eagles. My emotions simplified: I felt no doubt, no fear, no anger, but a pure, crystalline fury. My senses clarified: I felt the molars rolling in my mouth, tasted my blood, salty and metallic, saw his smirk fading as it dawned on him that the situation had changed. My pugilistic practice puri-fied into one inspired tactic: I went at him screaming, and before he could fight or flee, I was on him like black on night.

I remember how I sat astride him, my knees pinning his arms. I remember my fists punching, and my blood dripping down and mingling with his blood welling up from his nose and lips. I remember spitting blood and loose teeth into his face, and calling him every foul name I knew. At first he tried to free his arms, but gradually he gave up struggling for anything but air. But I remember his lips moving, and realizing that, though he didn't have breath to speak, he was still calling me nigger. And I remember how I then dispensed with punching and cursing, and grasping him by his ears, pounded his head against the ground, deliberately, method-ically.

I do not remember how long I continued pounding. At some point my fury drained away—probably then my pounding lost some force. But I kept on. I did not even think of stopping. When I did stop, it was for no kinder reason than that which would have made me stop playing tag or baseball:

the school bell rang. I rose from his body without ceremony and started up to the school, trotting, as if coming in from the outfield. I did not look back to see if he was coming, or conscious, or even still alive. All I knew was that *I* was still alive; indeed, despite the pain, I felt more alive than ever I could remember. I felt peaceful and sated, as if the last pang of hunger had been exactly satisfied by the last morsel of food. I felt the keenest, sweetest, profoundest ecstasy that I had ever known.

Fortunately, he was still alive, and came up after me. Fortunately, he kept the universal kid's code of silence, and told no man. Fortunately, my teacher asked no questions; I would have told the truth, exultantly. But her name was Grace and she had the wisdom of Solomon; she only told me to skip the Easter pageant and go get the bleeding stopped. That I did, before catching the school bus home. There I sneaked in and washed and changed for the Good Friday service, concealing my rent and bloody garments beyond all discovery. Of course my mother discovered them, before the day was out. Solomonic in her own right, she did not confront me herself. Nor did she bring my father—who spanked first and asked questions later —into it. She waited until the next day, when my uncle John arrived.

Saturday afternoon, while we cracked and drained the coconuts, my uncle and I reasoned together. By then there was no need to tell me my sins were as scarlet; as a result of the Good Friday service, exultation and ecstasy had been replaced by visions and guilt and shame. As one minister had described the Roman soldiers torturing Jesus in the Praetorium, I had seen myself spitting and cursing and smiting that boy's profane head. As another had spoken of Pontius Pilate washing his hands I had seen myself in the boys' room, cleansing myself of blood. When the final minister had intoned "It is finished" I had felt my soul rending as if it were the Temple's veil. Full of guilt at having eaten the bread of wickedness and drunk the wine of violence, I only toyed with supper. By Saturday I was hungry for absolution and I told my uncle . . . everything.

He let me talk without interruption. When I was finished he told me nothing, but rather questioned me[17] about what led to my anger and ecstasy. Answering lightened my heart a bit, for I had been so guilty about the denouement I had forgotten the prolegomena; now I recalled that I had been the victim. Still, I welcomed my uncle's chastisement, though in fact it puzzled me, for it seemed he was most concerned not that I had become violent, but that I had lost control. This seemed, I said, the least of my sins, and cited the Gospel of Matthew. My uncle shook his head slightly, and told me a few chapters in the Old Testament I should read.

That night, after the eggs were colored, I huddled under my blankets with a flashlight and a Bible and discovered the savage roots of Judeo-Christianity. I learned that Moses' first act of liberation was not to tell old Pharaoh anything, but to kill an Egyptian overseer.[18] I fought through the seventeenth-century language to see what happened when Samson "smote them hip and thigh with great slaughter"[19] because "As they did unto me, so have I done unto them."[20] I noted that Daniel did not object when his persecutors were tossed to the lions, along with their wives and children. And I read how David—who, I found, stole a sword when he had a chance, cut Goliath's head off, and went galumphing back—did not woo his bride with a harp, but bought her with the foreskins of two hundred Philistines.[21] Though I had only a vague idea of what a foreskin was, my guilt was relieved, for clearly David killed and mutilated those Philistines; what I had done was nothing to that. And what I had done had been achieved with the Power of God; what other source could there be? I fell asleep with my guilt abated. Men of God, it seemed, did not mind shedding blood from time to time; nor, indeed, did God Himself.

But Easter morning, as I waited on the lakeshore for the sunrise, I recalled the words of Matthew and realized that I had no reason for relief. For I was supposed to go the second mile, to forgive, not seven times, but seventy times seven.[22] If I wanted to be a Christian I could take no comfort from the behavior of Jews, or of any human. For Jesus said, "Be ye therefore perfect even as your Father which is in heaven is perfect."[23]

The sun rose. My guilt returned, and doubled. And redoubled, as the service began with the reading, from Luke's Gospel, of how two men in shining garments spoke the words that are the essence of Christian belief: "He is not here, but is risen."[24] Then my father began his meditation, which was based on the moment in the garden when Simon Peter[25] drew his sword and cut off the right ear of Malchus,[26] one who had come to take Jesus into custody. I knew what happened then according to Matthew: Jesus chastened Simon Peter, saying "all they that take up the sword shall perish with the sword,"[27] and for a horrible moment I thought my father knew what I had done. But the text was not Matthew, but Luke; there Jesus chastens not, but touches Malchus's ear, and heals him.[28] This was, my father said, the highest expression of Christianity. And I wanted to shout out, No!

Actually, of course, I shouted nothing, but I screamed rejection in my heart. For despite my training something atavistic in me told me this was *wrong*. Forgiving enemies was one thing, but *healing* them? No; that was not a second mile, that was too far by a mile. Love also was too far; it was enough simply not to hate those who'd hurt me. And so what if I did hate them? I only hated them because they clearly hated me. If they stopped, I would. Even forgiveness went too far, considering that those who'd harmed me had not repented. But all right; if they stopped I would forgive them for what they'd done. But I would never love them. I would not even try.

Such was my thinking on the lakeshore, in the damp and chilly dawn. But my bravery vanished with the dew. By the time I was seated in the family pew at Mt. Pisgah, I was appalled at my own apostasy, literally shivering with fear, expecting at any moment to be struck down. And I was horribly lonely, because it seemed that Jesus, not my God, but my Jesus, had forsaken me. For it was Jesus who enjoined me to forgive, to love, to be perfect, but Jesus just didn't *understand*. Maybe it wasn't His fault. Maybe they hadn't had playgrounds or bullies in Nazareth. Maybe no child ever made fun of His having been born in a cattle trough. Maybe the first time anybody mocked or beat Him was in the Praetorium.[29] Maybe when Jesus had talked of turning the other cheek, He didn't know they'd smite you on that one, too. Maybe when He cried out, "Father, forgive them; for they know not what they do,"[30] He didn't understand they knew exactly what they were doing. But when they finished doing it, Jesus was crucified, dead and buried; surely then He understood. Yet, when He appeared after the Crucifixion He'd told the Disciples not to take revenge on Judas . . .[31] Then understanding struck me: Jesus *could* not understand, for Jesus was divine.

Jesus was the Son of God—*and he knew it.* When Joseph rebuked him for staying behind in the Temple, He'd said, "wist ye not that I must be about my Father's business."[32] When He came out of the river after being baptized by John "there came a voice from heaven, saying, Thou art my beloved son, in whom I am well pleased."[33] And he knew that, despite the mocking, the scourging, the dying, he would rise from the dead.[34]

All *I* knew was, I was the only son of Harriette and David Senior; not begotten, but conceived in sin and born in iniquity—whatever that meant. I knew that if I meekly let myself get crucified, I wasn't going to be *around* to inherit the earth; I was going to be six feet under it. So now it seemed I had been tricked by my friend Jesus. Tricked into wanting to be like Him, when I was not and could not truly be. Tricked into trying to act like Jesus when that had gotten even Him killed. Tricked into feeling guilty about failing, when all I could do was fail, or die . . . or both. And, though now I might be undeceived, still I had to go on trying to be like Jesus. For He said: "no man cometh unto the Father, but by me."[35] Jesus had me, coming and going. Do it My way, kid, or go to hell.

This did not make me love my enemies; it made me resent Jesus. For it seemed to me He was taking and getting credit for what was for Him easy stuff. Easy to die when the tomb is temporary. Easy to say, "Take no thought for your life"[36] when you are immortal. Easy to say be perfect when you already are. Easy to ignore insults when you know *your* mother was a virgin. Easy to forgive when you can as easily damn. Easy to slum about as the Son of a man when you know you're the Son of God.

What might have proceeded from these thoughts is hard to imagine. Even at the moment they did not make me happy; before the day was out I would no doubt have been seriously depressed. Nor would I have been able to confide in anyone; I knew, without knowing the word, that this was heresy. Fortunately the meditation my father had prepared for the parishioners of Mt. Pisgah focused not on the garden, or Golgotha, but on the Temple, where Jesus passed much of the time between Palm Sunday and Maundy Thursday, pointing out the offenses of the Pharisees. The scripture lesson began with Luke, Chapter 19, verse 45: "And he went into the temple and began to cast out them that sold therein, and them that bought; Saying unto them, It is written, My house is a house of prayer: but ye have made it a den of thieves."[37] I had heard those verses before, of course, but this time, I saw the action implied by the words: when Jesus "cast out" these people, he *threw* them out. With force. Could, I wondered, this be true? Could Jesus have . . . kicked butt?

Recalling that the Gospels gave differing accounts of Christmas, I began to wonder if Luke, who omitted Advent altogether, might not be in error. So, during the lifting of the Offering for the Poor, I took out the pew Bible and looked at other Gospels. My wonder increased; this riot in the Temple was something on which all Gospels agreed. As Matthew had it, Jesus not only "cast out all them that sold and bought in the temple" but "overthrew the tables of the moneychangers, and the seats of them that sold doves"[38]—Jesus wrecked the place. According to Mark, His fury was premeditated; He went to the Temple and "looked round about upon all things,"[39] thought about them overnight, and then went in the next morning and cast out and overthrew.[40] According to John, He did more than think; He made "a scourge of small cords" with which He "drove them all out of the temple, and the sheep, and the oxen; and poured out the changers' money, and overthrew the tables; And said unto them that sold doves, Take these things hence."[41]

The offertory ended; the service went on. I made all the right responses—stood and sat and bowed my head at all the proper times—but I was oblivious to ritual. My mind was full of a vision I could barely believe: Jesus, in His flowing robe—I thought of a blue bathrobe—chasing the high priests with a *whip* in hand, driving men with the cattle, driving men as if they *were* cattle! Barely believe? I could *not* believe. Yet there it was, in Holy Writ, as surely as "forgive them; for they know not what they do."[42]

I did not know what to make of this Jesus. He seemed inconsistent; I had been taught to think of Jesus as constant, immutable, as a solid rock on which to stand, while all other ground was sinking sand. And yet it seemed that this inconsistent Jesus was something—no, *someone*—I could understand. It came to me then that I had been unfair to Jesus, thinking He had failed to understand me, when I had not even *tried* to understand Him.

So I did try. Ignoring my father's meditation, focusing instead on my own, I tried to think of Jesus as not God but man; tried to appreciate the pain He had endured, despite His divinity. Scourging surely had to smart. And never mind what my father said, being mocked was painful. Then I saw what must have truly hurt Jesus: knowing that Judas would betray Him and Peter would deny Him, and Thomas would doubt Him. And even though He did not have to fear death, He must have feared failure, especially as success depended on the likes of Peter and Thomas—of me. Then it hit me: perhaps what had happened, there in the Temple, was that Jesus *had* failed.

For there had been Jesus on the mountain, meek and mild, preaching forgiveness while the high priests schemed. There had been Jesus, coming down—leaving the idyllic mountaintop, leaving the calm sea and the pure wilderness—into the teeming city, riding through Jerusalem on a braying donkey, knowing how those shouts of hosanna would soon become demands for his head. There had been Jesus, in the Temple, forced, just when He knew His hour was at hand, to see the worst of those He was going to die to save. Maybe what happened was Jesus grew angry and afraid—as I had. Maybe, though, as I had, He tried to follow His own philosophy, He found it for a moment, at least, inappropriate. Maybe Jesus the man tried to be like Jesus the god—and found that He could not. Perhaps what had worried Him in the garden was that that big-voiced Father of His would not be so well pleased by His behavior in the Temple. Perhaps—and this thought struck me so forcefully it was like a pain—perhaps what Jesus had been praying for when He asked for the cup to pass from Him was not deliverance from death but escape from His destiny. Maybe Jesus just wanted to go back to Nazareth and live in peace; maybe He no longer wanted to be about His Father's business. I felt a strange warmth come over me, then—not some grand religious conversion, nor any breed of ecstasy. I just found myself feeling *sorry,* very sorry, for Jesus.

And suddenly I had Him back—though He was a different Jesus, to be sure. A Jesus who had a temper. A Jesus who was patient, but who could get fed up. A Jesus would surely understand, if not entirely approve, if I got fed up too. And when we stood at the end of the service to sing "He Lives!" I sang out lustily, for I believed, that I did indeed serve a risen savior, who was in the world that day.

Now, looking back, I marvel at the pure innocent strength of my belief, and wish I could have kept it. Such was not to be. This was not Jesus' fault; in His new guise He did not fail me or forsake me.[43] Convinced that Jesus would have understood, when I returned to school I systematically selected the weaker bigots and engaged them in combat. I had enough success that the stronger bigots decided beating on me was not worth the cost—especially since they saw what had happened to the boy who had really gotten me angry. I probably did become *persona non grata,* I also got out of elementary school alive.

But after I escaped from sixth grade I did lose Jesus. It didn't look as though I was doing that—it appeared I was becoming more, rather than less, involved with Christianity. In a sense I was. But my involvement was not with the Gospels but with the Epistles, not with Jesus but with the Church—and increasingly, with theological commentaries that said little of Jesus in the Temple, while concentrating on Jesus on the Mountain and Jesus on the Cross and promulgating what I have come to call the Doctrine of Jesus the Wimp.

As I was completing junior high school that doctrine gained odd credence in the secular world. It was used to give non-Christian notions, like Ghandi's *satyagraha* and Thoreau's civil disobedience, a Christlike authority, and to make ministers seem a legitimate source of political leadership. Though by then I was in many ways abandoning pious behavior I still believed in Jesus, and agreed with the ideals of Martin Luther King, even though my family found his advocacy of interracial *agape* radical—as my father put it, what could you expect from a Baptist, especially one who believed in full immersion? Yet I could not help but see that what I still thought of as Christian ideals were no protection against slavering dogs and high-pressure hoses; that the pure armor of righteousness was a poor breastplate when the bad guys had cattle prods; that to forgive unremorseful, unaltered, and unmitigated hatred was to devalue redemption; that to love an enemy who would bomb a church was to cheapen the idea of love. I understood such thoughts were quite unchristian, and worried that they were the reason Calling me did not seem to be high on God's To-Do list. I also gave thanks that this seemed so; I could not imagine how I could preach meekness when in my heart I understood violence so well.

Then came Eastertide 1968, three days before Palm Sunday,[44] when King—who surely did not take the sword, surely perished by it.[45] As I watched news footage of the riots that ensued, I recalled how my mind had left me during that long-ago playground battle, and though the violence seemed no fitting tribute to a man of peace, I wondered if the rioters did not understand what had happened on that balcony in Noph[46] better than those of us who mourned in more seemly style. And what, I wondered, made solemnity so seemly? Had not an earthquake followed the Crucifixion?

Before the year was out I found myself confronted by the teachings of a man who, though far more religious, and far more holy than I could now claim to be, had rejected not only nonviolence but Christianity itself. I read the *Autobiography of Malcolm X* and moved on to other of his writings, I realized Malcolm had found in Islam and Allah exactly what I had wanted when I was almost-nine; what I still wanted, in fact: a faith that seemed attuned to the reality of being a black American, a God who did not force His followers to deal with the world He had created with their hands tied behind their backs.

Though I had no interest in becoming a Muslim, I saw the sense of Malcolm's argument against nonviolence, against Christianity itself. For indeed it did seem strange that a society born in rebellion, that worshiped its history of resistance, that elected wartime generals to peacetime presidencies while worrying that a Catholic chief executive would be unduly influenced by his faith, would yet defer to a minister like Martin Luther King. Or it seemed strange until you noted that King was supposed to lead black people, that nonviolence was a tactic recommended for black people, and that, while salt-of-the-earth white men drove around with gun racks in their pickup trucks, black men were to eschew arms—until they were drafted. Then they were to take up the M-16—and probably perish by the AK-47.

I found I envied Malcolm his belief, albeit not his religion. I found I envied my younger self the belief I had once had. I went back to the Gospels, trying to find Jesus again. But the more I read the more it seemed that, speaking socially, Jesus did not take the narrowest way. Though He told parables about Samaritans He did not come as one, but as a member of the Chosen. Nor did He come as an ordinary Jew but as a member of the aristocracy, of the house and lineage of David. And in the end, He did not even bear his own burden; the Romans impressed a man named Simon, of Cyrene,[47,48,49] which is to say, of Africa, to tote Jesus' cross up Calvary.

This Simon was probably not a Negro—although he might have been —but it seemed he might have had a thing or two to say to Jesus. Like: Look, bro, if You gonna be forgivin' these Roman bastards You can carry Your own damned cross. Certainly I felt I had a thing or two to say. For it seemed to me that, while Jesus may have been God-Made-Man, He was not God-Made-Black-Man. Had He known even the little trouble I'd seen, though He might have said to forgive seventy-times-seven transgressions, He would have recommended war if the bastards did it again. Had He been privy to the tribulations of even so fortunate a family as mine, He would have found you could get up to transgression number four ninety-one in about a week. Had He an inkling of the pain and despair of my less fortunate brothers, He might have found a scourge of small cords too minor a weapon; certainly He would have said, Verily, verily, I say unto you, enough of this shit.

Such thoughts were not merely heretical and hubristic, they were so cynical they frightened me. They were also bitter and disappointed. For I still wanted my Jesus, as desperately as ever. Even now, though I no longer feel desperation, I still feel the desire.

And now, returning to the Scriptures after a time away, I find myself recovering some measure of faith. For, now conversant with the ironies of literature and the conundra of historiography, I see that some of my quandaries about Jesus sprang from errors often made. The fact is, despite the implication of the word ''gospel,'' nobody knows what Jesus actually said; only what others said He said. Only two of those sources are primary; Matthew and John, who were of the original Twelve Disciples, may have heard the words as He said them. Mark, if he ever saw Jesus, did so when he, Mark, was but a child; and though he probably got his information from Peter, he did the research thirty-some years after the Crucifixion;[50] the data was not fresh. Luke, who was neither one of the original Twelve, nor of the second wave of Seventy,[51] acknowledges that his Gospel is a compilation. Though he claims to quote those who "from the beginning were eyewitnesses, and ministers of the word,"[52] he gets no more specific, and, though he purports his Gospel to be a "declaration of those things which are most surely believed among us," he recounts details that go unconfirmed by Matthew, John, or even Mark. For example, all Gospels agree that somebody cut off somebody's ear in the garden (John supplies the identities of Simon Peter and Malchus[53]); Luke alone has Jesus healing the wound.[54] Luke, of course, was a physician; this bit of lore, then, may come from Hippocrates, who was a surgeon, rather than from God who only *thinks* He is a surgeon.

To point this out is hardly heresy. For even if one insists that the Scriptures in general and the Gospels in particular are divinely inspired, it is clear the inspiration was inconsistent. Luke, for example, omits the line about taking up the sword, altogether. Nor did inspiration extend to fully drawn context; when Jesus told Simon Peter that "they that take up the sword shall perish with the sword,"[55] He may have been expounding a general principle, but He might also have been pointing out that resistance was suicidal considering "a great multitude with swords and staves"[56] had the Disciples surrounded.

To make it all more complicated and confusing, both Mark[57] and Luke[58] were companions of the man we now call Paul, whose words, from various Epistles, are nowadays quoted by Christians as frequently as the words supposed to be of Jesus. This is sheer insanity. Though Paul claimed to be a servant of Christ and to have been called by Jesus Himself,[59] it was not Jesus in person, but Jesus in disembodied voice, which, as Paul admits, no one else present heard.[60] Worse, before his dramatic conversion, Paul was a creature of the most extreme Pharisees;[61] in defiance of the logic of his own teacher, Gamaliel,[62] Paul spent the first years after the Crucifixion "breathing out threatenings and slaughter against the disciples of the Lord."[63] He later admitted he "persecuted this way unto the death, binding and delivering into prisons both men and women,"[64] and that he was "consenting" in the stoning of Stephen—not that Paul stoned anybody; he just held the coats.[65,66] In fact, he may actually have been among those crying for Jesus' Crucifixion; it is ironic that in his First Epistle to the Thessalonians he condemns "The Jews who both killed the Lord Jesus and their own prophets."[67]

And as for all the meekness ascribed to Jesus, like so much else in the Gospels, it has roots in prior prophecies. Jesus, of course, quoted Scripture; the phrase about the Temple, "a house of prayer" becoming "a den of thieves"[68] is a revision of Jeremiah 7:11 ("This house, which is called by my name, become a den of robbers in your eyes,")[69] mingled with Isaiah 56:7 ("mine house shall be called a house of prayer").[70] Much of Christianity, like Jesus, is of the house and lineage of David. One of the more interesting details in John's account of the Crucifixion, that Jesus' legs were not broken, as was customary—"these things were done," John writes, "that the scripture should be fulfilled, A bone of him shall not be broken"[71] a reference to, among other texts, Psalm 34, which is commonly attributed to David. Although biblical attributions are a chancy thing, other passages in similarly attributed psalms provide what could be called a prophecy of the Crucifixion, or a blueprint for it, or, at least a crib sheet for Gospel writers. Psalm 69, for example, includes the detail "In my thirst they gave me vinegar to drink,"[72] while Psalm 22 includes "They have pierced my hands and my feet"[73] and "They part my garments among them, and cast lots upon my vesture,"[74] and one of the most despairing of the legendary Seven Last Words: "My God, my God, why has thou forsaken me?"[75] Although Psalm 22 also includes this language: "The meek shall eat and be satisfied,"[76] a clearer formulation is in Psalm 37: "But the meek shall inherit the earth; and shall delight themselves in the abundance of peace."[77] Who knows, then, if meekness was anything more than a family norm, handed down not from Jehovah but Jesse.

"What is truth," asks Pontius Pilate in John's Gospel albeit only in the Vulgate version.[78] If there is an answer I think perhaps it lies in that same place. For John, it has been argued, knew Jesus best,[79] and who, it should be noted, spoke, in his own voice, only of loving brothers, not enemies.[80] Wrote John: "Beloved, now are we the sons of God, and it doth not yet appear what we shall be: but we know that when he shall appear, we shall be like him; for we shall see him as he is."[81] This, then, is my new article of faith: that Jesus as He is would make perfect sense, to my world, my life, and me, if only I could see Him without a glass, and brightly. And when He comes to judge the quick and the dead He will do so with both the wisdom of Heaven and His knowledge of earth. He may well act as executor to the legacy of the meek. But He will also feed those who do hunger and thirst for righteousness.

NOTES

1. Rally Day Advertisement, c. February 1, 1918. Bradley Archives
2. cf. I Samuel 1:1–28
3. Mark 6
4. John 6:9
5. Matthew 19:14
6. Psalms 144:11
7. Matthew 26:52
8. cf. II Timothy 3:15
9. Isaiah 1:6
10. Matthew 5:38–39
11. Matthew 5:43–47
12. Matthew 5:5
13. Matthew 5:9
14. Matthew 5:10
15. Matthew 5:11–12
16. Matthew 5:41
17. cf. Mark 8:11

18. Exodus 2:12
19. Judges 15:8
20. Judges 15:11
21. I Samuel 18:27
22. Matthew 18:22
23. Matthew 5:48
24. Luke 24:6
25. John 18:10
26. John 18:10
27. Matthew 26:52
28. Luke 22:51
29. John 8:59 reads: "Then took they up stones to cast at him: but Jesus hid himself, and went out of the temple, going through the midst of them, and so passed by."
30. Luke 23:34
31. John 21:23
32. Luke 2:49
33. Mark 1:9–11
34. Matthew 16:21; Matthew 20:18–19: "Behold, we go up to Jerusalem; and the Son of man shall be betrayed into the chief priests and unto the scribes, and they shall condemn him to death, And shall deliver him to the Gentiles to mock, and to scourge, and to crucify *him,* and the third day he shall rise again."
35. John 14:6
36. Matthew 6:25
37. Luke 19:45–47
38. Matthew 21:12–14
39. Mark 11:11
40. Mark 11:16
41. John 2:15–16
42. Luke 23:34
43. cf. Joshua 1:5
44. King was killed on April 4, 1968. Easter was April 14 that year.
45. Matthew 26:52
46. King was killed in Memphis, Tennessee. Noph was the Hebrew name for Memphis in Egypt.
47. Matthew 27:32
48. Mark 15:21
49. Luke 23:26
50. *The New Analytical Bible* (Chicago: John A. Dickinson Company, 1950) p. 1129
51. *The New Analytical Bible* (Chicago: John A. Dickinson Company, 1950) p. 1157
52. Luke 1:2
53. John 18:10
54. Luke 22:51
55. Matthew 26:52
56. Matthew 26:47
57. *The New Analytical Bible* (Chicago: John A. Dickinson Company, 1950) p. 1129

58. *The New Analytical Bible* (Chicago: John A. Dickinson Company, 1950) p. 1157

59. Romans 1:1

60. Acts 22:7–10

61. *The New Analytical Bible* (Chicago: John A. Dickinson Company, 1950) p. 92

62. Acts 5:34–39

63. Acts 9:1

64. Acts 22:4

65. Acts 8:1

66. Acts 23:20

67. I Thessalonians 2:14–15

68. Luke 19:45–47

69. Jeremiah 7:11

70. Isaiah 56:7

71. John 19:36

72. Psalms 69:21

73. Psalms 22:16

74. Psalms 22:18

75. Psalms 22:1

76. Psalms 22:26

77. Psalms 37:11

78. *Oxford Dictionary of Quotations*, 2nd ed. rev. (London: Oxford University Press, 1966) p. 63

79. *The New Analytical Bible* (Chicago: John A. Dickinson Company, 1950) p. 1199

80. First Epistle of John 2:9–11; 3:15–18

81. First Epistle of John 3:2

Genesis (Eden) and John

J O Y C E   C A R O L   O A T E S

The first time I saw an adult man cry was in a country Methodist church in Pendleton, New York, in spring 1950. One moment our minister, Reverend B———, a man of probably no more than thirty-five, "old" to me, was preaching to the congregation in an impassioned, soaring voice, of sin and hell and Jesus Christ's suffering on our behalf; the next, he'd broken down, and was choking back sobs. His lean face was flushed and streaked with bright, terrible tears. His eyes seemed to have lost their focus, and gone inward. Many in the rows of hardwood seats, the women especially, began to weep with him out of reflexive sympathy and unease; others, like me, stared in embarrassed silence.

I was twelve years old. I was an emotional child, yet frequently detached, strangely analytical, judging. In my limited experience, *adult men did not cry*. Men closest to me, my father and my grandfa-

ther, and all the male relatives of my acquaintance, were the kind of men to scorn such behavior—such "weakness"—in other men. (In women, crying and "carrying on" might be tolerated, if barely.) My family, lapsed Catholics who would return to Catholicism after my grandfather's unexpected death, did not approve of my attending Methodist Sunday School and services in a country town two miles from our home, though apparently they did not forbid it. A girlfriend in my seventh-grade class who rode the school bus with me had one day invited me to come with her to her church, and I'd accepted the invitation, eager to be included, hopeful of an adventure. Over a period of months I'd not only become a regular churchgoer, I'd even been enlisted to play the organ, an ancient, wheezing, foot-pedal instrument, when the congregation sang hymns. In Sunday School, as in school generally, I'd been the brightest, most cooperative, and, how to say it?—most *hopeful* of young people, astonishing our teacher, Mrs. B————, with having memorized no less than one hundred Bible verses in a regional competition among Methodist churches, with the reward of a free week at Bible Camp near Olcott Beach that summer. (Selections from the Gospel of St. John: *In the beginning was the Word, and the Word was with God, and the Word was God . . .*) My religious yearnings, like the emotions of early adolescence generally, were powerful, disturbing, and inchoate; I did not know what I believed, or if I was capable of any sustained belief. Certainly I *wanted* to believe—something. I *wanted* to be what I perceived as normal, happy, adjusted, *chosen*. I was enchanted by the brisk, thumping hymns I played on the organ, like military marches—"A Mighty Fortress Is Our God," "Rock of Ages," "The Old Rugged Cross"—and by the language of the Bible, so new to me, mysterious and incantatory and vaguely terrifying, its cadences quite apart from its meaning. (Its meaning, I was told, was exactly what it was: just what the Bible *says*.)

I did not, of course, speak of such private things to anyone, not even my friend Jane. Certainly I did not speak of Reverend B————, my fascination with him, my doubts about him, this embarrassment for him, to my family.

To this Protestant man of God, whose faith seemed to exude from him like incandescent heat, Jesus Christ was not a distant historic or mythic figure but a living presence: Jesus was close beside us, Jesus was in the room with us, Jesus was watching us at all times. Jesus could be "hurt" by us, His heart broken, if and when we failed to live up to His ideals. God the Father, His Father, was a living presence, too, though invisible as the wind, and never illustrated in our Bible pictures; God was wrathful, unpredictable, less inclined to forgive than Jesus, perhaps because He knew us more thoroughly than Jesus did, and, never having been human, still less crucified, He had little patience with human weakness and hypocrisy. Indeed, as Reverend B——— was always warning, God was a jealous, judgmental God, forever observing mankind, apt to punish for the slightest infraction of His law. Jesus Christ was needed to intercede between God and man, bringing "salvation" to man after our first parents, Adam and Eve, committed sin, willfully disobeying God in the Garden of Eden. Of course, this wasn't enough—prayer, good works, a constant awareness of Jesus Christ in our hearts were necessary, though they might not be enough to make us "blessed." (Why did Reverend B——— break into tears that Sunday morning? Because despite his and his wife's tireless effort in the community, the Methodist congregation remained small; it may have been, that particular morning, that attendance was down. This was an unmistakable sign of God's displeasure with Reverend B———: he hadn't worked hard enough that week.)

How simple life was!—if you knew the code.

To Reverend B———, as to all deeply committed Methodists, the personae of the Bible—Adam and Eve, Moses, Jacob, Daniel, Samson, Solomon, the disciples of Jesus Christ, Mary, Martha, Paul, Peter, Pontius Pilate, above all Jesus Christ—were historic but "real" figures whom he seemed to know intimately. He and Mrs. B———, who taught Sunday School with the sunny earnestness of a kindergarten teacher, spoke of them with certainty. Of course, they spoke of all things pertaining to the Bible without ambiguity, and without irony; one quickly senses, in the company of such good people, how irony is not a tonal possibility for true believers of any faith. (No doubt, this is a large part of the appeal of "blind" faith.) Prayer for these Methodists was never formalized, but a personal, direct discourse; a one-sided communication perhaps, but unquestioningly heard, and responded to, by God/Jesus Christ. *How are our prayers answered? In ways we can't always know.* What was thrilling about the Methodist services with their boisterous hymns, emotional sermons, tearful witnesses for Christ, was that they were in no way ritualized, but had the air of the unpredictable, the spontaneous, even the dangerous, like a play in early rehearsals in which "authentic" elements intrude.

After the sudden death of my grandfather, my parents made a decision to return to Roman Catholicism, and I stopped attending Methodist services forever.[1] From my position as church organist, I was demoted to anonymity in a family pew; in the Latin mass, in the hypnotic/soporific recitation of rosary beads, my adolescent religious yearnings, if that was what they were, were lost. From the age of thirteen to approximately twenty I would attend hundreds of masses in numerous churches and would hear, or half-hear, as many sermons by Catholic priests, but few of these priests ever betrayed any emotion that seemed to me genuine. At communion, when, in theory, the "body and blood" of Jesus Christ are supposed to be *literally* (not merely symbolically!) present in the communion wafer, the priest's role is rarely other than coolly functional. The Catholic priest, as priest, is not an individual in the sense in which a Protestant minister is an individual, but rather a living symbol, exalted and impersonal. So too the Bible, traditionally, to most Catholics, is mediated by the Church, and its mysteries interpreted by authority. Of biblical mortals, only Mary, "Mother of God," is granted a significant presence, and an extraordinary status, having been "immaculately conceived"—that is, conceived in her mother's womb free of original sin. Biblical tales, especially the high drama of the Old Testament, have been generally ignored.

Rereading Genesis and the Gospel of St. John, so many years after my early experience, I am struck by several things. Primarily, could these works, now so hallowed, so universally known, have had single authors? Could these authors have known—if not known, sensed, hoped, fantasized —how their words would be preserved, cherished, fought over, imprinted in the memories of countless millions of people? Impossible! The wildest megalomaniacal vision could not have yielded such a possibility. Yet the biblical authors recount their tales, present their "histories" with such certitude, even the skeptic is inclined to believe—almost. *If this did not, could not, have happened in quite this way, surely it happened in some way, of which this version is the symbolic representation?*

All readers of the Bible are struck by its incantatory music. Cadences may vary from book to book, author to author, subject to subject, yet the music of authority underlies all. Human words are nets to contain the unnamable. *In the beginning God created the heaven and the earth. And the earth was without form, and void; and darkness was upon the face of the deep. And the Spirit of God moved upon the waters.* It is difficult to imagine more thrilling words. And a more assured narrative, at once quickening its pace as it moves through the days of creation, and God acquires a voice, in tenor how very like our own, though exalted: *And God said, Let the waters under the heaven be gathered together unto one place, and let the dry land appear: and it was so.* There are introduced into the narrative, as onto a stage, certain living creatures, among them mankind: *And God said, Let us make man in our image, after our likeness.* In the Book of St. John, of another biblical era entirely, language is rather more abstract; words echo words of earlier texts, including Genesis. The vision is more focused, the imagery more refined, concentrated. *In the beginning was the Word, and the Word was with God, and the Word was God*—the innermost secret of the writer's heart! To read this magisterial opening of the Gospel is, for me, to immediately hear an inner voice, my own voice of late childhood, for verses of St. John are deeply, irrevocably imprinted in my soul. *The same was in the beginning with God. All things were made by him; and without him was not any thing made that was made. In him was life; and the life was the light of man. And the light shineth in darkness; and the darkness comprehended it not.* Reading such words, led by them into tales of divine punishment, divine forgiveness, the redemption of our entire species, we are struck by the knowledge that religion belongs to the childhood of the race, when human wishes could be given a communal, codified objectivity; a self-declared authority it would be unthinkable to doubt. In even its abstract, philosophical propositions and promises, as in its more primitive tales of faith rewarded and "sin" punished, the unconscious urgencies of religion seem to us fantasy-driven. At its core is the simple wish that the perishable "I" endure, and by extension the family, the tribe, the blood-clan ("gene pool" is the scientist's less romantic term); about this yearning, an entire cosmos must be created through language. Heaven, not a concept very much developed in Judaic tradition, becomes the center of Christian thinking; the world is a "vale of tears" from which mankind must be delivered. This, the most transparent of all wishes, has as its polar opposite the phantasmagoria of hell, a region of unspeakable suffering. The good Christian is in terror of being damned, thus cast into hell with the wicked, and with "enemies" of the faith. (To be a fully reverent Christian, one must have an extraordinary capacity for cruelty—to postulate, even in fantasy, such sufferings of others!) The biblical figures of Adam and Eve are childlike and credulous, scarcely "like us," yet in the reading of these early chapters of Genesis, we identify readily with them, because in the mysterious infancy of the race, they are us.

Of course, all cultures are said to have their creation myths, and their tales of a lost paradise. Once, there was an Age of Gold, now, an Age of Lead, or worse. Once, there was a harmony of nature and man, now there is disharmony, even chaos. Paradise inevitably yields to the "fallen" world, the garden yields to the wasteland, for how else to account for our human lot of pain, confusion, tragic mutability? The quiet authority of Robert Frost's poem has its biblical echoes—

> Nature's first green is gold,
> Her hardest hue to hold.
> Her early leaf's a flower;
> But only so an hour.
> Then leaf subsides to leaf.
> So Eden sank to grief,
> So dawn goes down to day.
> Nothing gold can stay.

"NOTHING GOLD CAN STAY"

The God of Genesis seems to us the God of an ecologically harmonious world in which all units function with purpose. Like magic, with the pulse of poetry, "day" and "night" are made to appear; and a "firmament" in the midst of the waters; and Earth, and the seas; and creatures that have "life"; and man, in the mysterious "image" of God. (What, precisely, does this mean? If, as we must assume, the author of Genesis, Moses, is a mortal man, is he not staking his, and our, claim for a kind of godliness, at the very start of time? For man in the image of God is an elevated creature, blessed with dominion over all others.) Each stage of creation is marked with the incantatory refrain *And God saw that it was good;* there is an air of the improvised, the unpremeditated, about the discovery, as if, though God is omnipotent, He did not know beforehand how *good,* how *very good,* His creation was to be in His own eyes. Here is a design of sheer perfection, its interior order suggesting the psychic unity that presumably precedes consciousness. It is significant that the *naming* of creatures is Adam's responsibility, for man is the creature gifted with language, here a single, univocal tongue fitting for the Garden of Eden.

Of course, tales of paradise are inevitably tales of paradise lost. It is the creation of "man"—which is to say, self-consciousness, rationality— that introduces fatal disorder into God's world. As soon as we hear God's enigmatic instructions to Adam, *Of every tree of the garden thou mayest freely eat: but of the tree of the knowledge of good and evil, thou shalt not eat of it: for in the day that thou eatest thereof thou shalt surely die* (Genesis 2:16–17), we know that the command will be broken, just as a parent's sternest warnings to a child assure temptation. Out of what fissure in God's plan, what shadow-self, did the serpent arise?—this creature *more subtle than any beast of the field which the Lord God had made.* We wonder: is the serpent not one of these beasts created by God? Is he a prefiguring of the (yet-unnamed) Satan? Why does the serpent alone of beasts possess language? Is language somehow synonymous with disobedience, rebellion? And why is the serpent apparently more intelligent than Adam and Eve, those dull-normal humanoids, made in God's image?

God's terrible curses upon Adam and Eve strike us as but the enlightenment of adulthood; the expulsion from the garden is but the crossing-over into the world as mankind has always known it. Not a dream of infancy, but a stark, wakeful vision of what *is*. The author of Genesis brilliantly anticipates the world of the future, as in a *coup de théâtre* in which we have all been participants, unknowingly. Eve is told that God will *greatly multiply thy sorrow and thy conception: in sorrow thou shalt bring forth children: and thy desire shall be to thy husband, and he shall rule over thee.* Adam is told *cursed is the ground for thy sake; in sorrow shalt thou eat of it all the days of thy life: thorns also and thistles shall it bring forth to thee . . . ; in the sweat of thy face shalt thou eat bread, till thou return unto the ground; for out of it wast thou taken; for dust thou art, and unto dust shalt thou return.*

What powerful images—the agony of childbirth, the thorn- and thistle-ridden earth, man as dust, *mere* dust! However many times we may have read this passage, we are likely to experience a shudder of recognition. Clearly this God is not a God of love, nor even a God of justice, but a God of nature in its primary, Hobbesian sense, in which life is nasty, brutish, and short; and there is no transcendence—no promise of heaven, nor even of hell. For, out of *dust,* if that is all that man is, how can spirit arise? These paradoxes are never articulated, never resolved. ''Paradox'' is the province of philosophy and religion, not the province of literature; literature gives us narratives, or skillfully embodies narratives out of our communal imagination, but is under no obligation to answer our questions, only to stimulate them. So out of the early chapters of Genesis, as out of the proverbial ''Pandora's box'' of Greek antiquity, spring countless questions that cut to the heart of the human predicament. *What is the origin of suffering? what is the origin of evil? is simple disobedience tantamount to self-destruction? and if so, why?* Interesting to note, for the reader who is no theologian or biblical scholar, that the concept of ''sin'' has not yet been introduced in the Bible. The storytelling concerns of the author of Genesis are immediate and dramatic, not abstract.

Read by a nonreligious observer of religion, as I would characterize myself, the great story of the Garden of Eden is the most haunting of all such stories of paradise lost with which I am acquainted. Surely it parallels, in wildly inflated, nightmare terms, the loss of childhood's innocence and the inevitable (and desired) expulsion from the parental home. The young *must* be expelled from their parents' homes, that the next generation be conceived, free of incest, inbreeding; this is evolutionary wisdom, writ in the genes. Yet, still, expulsion is a fearful thing; growing up means losing one's child-self. That evolution's logic is rendered as a God's curse vividly dramatizes our problematic relationship with adult consciousness itself, for to *know,* to possess *knowledge,* as adults, is to surrender happiness, and court disaster; yet to remain blissfully united with nature, as in the womb or at the breast, is hardly possible. God's curse is both damning and enlightening: *Dust thou art, and unto dust shalt thou return.* Out of the riddle of human consciousness, the chronicler of Genesis created a drama of tragic resonance.

I find it interesting to note, too, that Adam and Eve, our "first parents" in the Judeo-Christian tradition, are so painfully vulnerable, finite, limited in intelligence; theirs was not a race of giants or nobility or demi-gods from whom lesser generations have descended. If the Garden of Eden is a "golden age" of a kind, as in classical antiquity, it can't be claimed that humanity itself has reached a peak of evolution. And this portrayal of early mankind as limited in reasoning ability is surely far more accurate, as a gauge of evolution itself, in which human intelligence grows, like the brain that generates it, with the slow, slow increment of time. In this cautionary tale, the act of disobedience, or sin, is introduced to the world, and death, to be underscored by the first murder, that of Abel by his brother Cain in the next generation. Out of nowhere, too, angels appear, instruments of God's wrath, in a cinematic flourish: *So he drove out the man; and he placed at the east of the garden of Eden Cherubims, and a flaming sword which turned every way, to keep the way of the tree of life.*

In the Methodist Sunday School, the story of the Garden of Eden was presented as literal, historical. It was not something that might have happened, as a way of explaining "original sin" and suffering; it happened as Moses said it did, in words given to us to be read (in what we children did not know was "translation"). The most popular Bible scenes lent themselves to illustrations on cards, in bright colors: Moses in the bulrushes, Moses and the burning bush, the parting of the Red Sea, David and Goliath, Daniel in the lions' den, Jonah in the whale; the birth of Jesus Christ, witnessed by the three wise men; the Sermon on the Mount, the miracles of Jesus, the betrayal and crucifixion of Jesus. These cards were given to those of us who did well on Bible drill and Bible memorization. We did not ask questions, nor were probing questions put to us. We were *told,* and perhaps we were grateful for the telling, which did not after all tax our minds. The story of the Garden of Eden was a simple one: Adam and Eve disobeyed God, and were suitably punished; the serpent was Satan, bent upon tempting *us,* too; if we succumbed, we would commit sin. However, unlike Adam and Eve we would not return to mere dust and nothingness, but would go to hell—unless of course we'd accepted Jesus Christ into our hearts, as our savior.

One of the less exciting Bible cards depicted Lazarus, a gray-haired man in grave clothes, being raised from the dead by Jesus Christ; it was less exciting, to a child's critical eye, than more active scenes involving younger people. Yet the miracle of *raising the dead* was a considerable one, apparently refuting the curse of Genesis, as Jesus Christ the Savior would seem to answer the quest of the Jews for their Messiah. (For some reason, Christ's raising of the dead daughter of Jarius, who was only twelve years old, and would have been of interest to young people, was not discussed; this miracle of Christ's is virtually unknown set beside that of the raising of Lazarus.) Miracles were naturally a favorite subject of the Bible cards, with their appeal to children. That Christ's most persuasive "power" is not spiritual so much as a public demonstration of a kind of magic suggests the primitive nature of such religious yearning, in which reality is suspended, or denied altogether; the lame and the halt, the leper, the plague-stricken and the blind, the very dead are made well. What hope, then, for the rest of us! The miracle of Lazarus, however, is singular, in being emotionally integrated, as in a skillfully organized story, with the narrative of Christ's personal life, for his role is two-fold: Christ is both a friend of Lazarus (who is Martha's brother) and the miracle-wielding and rather brashly exhibitionistic "son of God." Hearing of his friend Lazarus's illness, in John 11, Christ declares confidently: *This sickness is not unto death, but for the glory of God, that the Son of God might be glorified thereby.* When Christ arrives at the cave in which Lazarus has been entombed, allegedly dead for four days, He cries with a loud voice for the man to come forth: *And he that was dead came forth, bound hand and foot with graveclothes: and his face was bound about with a napkin. Jesus saith unto them, Loose him, and let him go. Then many of the Jews which came to Mary, and had seen the things which Jesus did, believed on him.*

Raising Lazarus from death anticipates, too, dramatically, the resurrection of Christ after His crucifixion. In John 11 and 12, Lazarus and Christ are pointedly linked, as the chief priests of the Pharisees conspire to kill both men. They reason: *What do we do? for this man [Jesus Christ] doeth many miracles. If we let him thus alone, all men will believe on him: and the Romans shall come and take away our place and nation.* Yet a prophecy is made that Christ should die not only for that nation but for all of mankind: *He should gather together in one the children of God that are scattered abroad.*

Following the miracle of Lazarus's rising from the dead, the crucifixion of Christ appears inevitable.

The teller of these tales, known to us as "St. John," is a deft, invisible narrator; his storytelling skills are so inspired, one is led to conclude that there is no story-"teller," no mere human agent at all. This is the highest employment of the art of literature—there seems to be no literature per se, only the most reliable reportage. And when one reads the story of Lazarus from a critical perspective, granting its (fantastic?) premises, one is impressed with its writerly qualities, its drive. Of course, we are trained to think symbolically in such instances: the story of Lazarus must *mean* something, and probably what it *means* has to do with the power of human faith to resuscitate the spiritually moribund; just as the more acclaimed resurrection of the crucified Jesus Christ might indicate the possibility of human rebirth, "resurrection" in spiritual and psychological terms. It is a measure of the richness of these Bible tales that they speak to us through the transparency of their creators' storytelling skills, through the centuries. The stories, after all, came first; "theology" and "Bible interpretation" much, much later.

Genesis (Eden) and John

God is indeed a jealous God—
He cannot bear to see
That we had rather not with Him
But with each other play.

EMILY DICKINSON

W. H. Auden wryly warns against those who "read the Bible for its prose." But most of us, after all, are of that category. It is the Bible's prose —at least, as translated—that compels us to read, and reread, through a lifetime.

The aged, water-stained Bible permanently on a bookshelf close by my desk at home is a *found object,* and therefore of special significance to me: where I found it, a long time ago, discarded in some public place, I don't exactly recall. The fairly small book itself was printed in London, no date given; I might in fact have found it in London, in 1971 or 1972 when we were living there. The edition is, of course, as the quotations I've used indicate, the magisterial King James version—one of the incontestably great literary works in our language. (Other, more recent and vernacular "translations" of the Bible, meant to make it accessible to the very young and the minimally educated, are painful to read: when *mystery* is exposed in monosyllabic elementary school English, it becomes something of an embarrassment.) And when I travel, as I do frequently, staying in hotels and motels, I often read in the Gideons Bible, which continues still to be supplied with such amazing generosity. What comfort, to open the drawer of a bedside table, and to see the Gideons Bible inside, whether one reads it that night or not! (A preliminary draft of this essay, for instance, was composed in a suite at the Sahara Hotel in Las Vegas, in May 1994, with the help of a pristine-looking gilt-stamped Gideons Bible: outside, glaring sunshine and a temperature approaching one hundred degrees Fahrenheit by mid-morning; inside, air-conditioned metallic-tasting coolness, an air of purposeful unreality in an immense "luxury"-appointed living room with its own "wet bar." What more appropriate place than Las Vegas, a mecca for those who yearn to believe in miracles, for the writing of an essay on the Bible?)[2]

Writing in the quick-waning years of our tragic twentieth century, what can one hope to say about the Hebrew Bible, and the New Testament, that has not been said countless times already? and by biblical scholars and commentators so much more qualified for making significant judgments than amateurs? (Though, in a sense, we should all be "amateurs" at religion; one dreads to imagine what a "professional" of religion might be.) Since my days as a preadolescent Methodist, a member of a church I could not have known might be categorized as "American fundamentalist Protestant," I have retained my original fascination with the Bible, but it has long become a purely poetic/metaphorical/psychological fascination. Apart from its prose, what *is* the Bible? Has any book, however "divinely inspired," any existence, any ontological weight, apart from the language that constitutes it? (My avid Methodism itself began to wane during the disappointing, stupefyingly dull week at Bible Camp I had anticipated with so much excitement. *I don't really like this,* I began to think almost immediately, *why am I here?* Most shocking to me, my fellow campers, girls and boys, were not especially nice: conspicuously Christian, perhaps, but not especially nice. My years as a nominal Roman Catholic were largely endured in the daughterly service of honoring my parents' wishes, or anxieties; as soon as I became independent of their household, like many young Catholics I abruptly stopped attending mass. It struck me as a wonderful irony when, a few years ago, I casually asked my parents about our old church, the Good Shepherd Church of Pendleton, New York, and they told me they'd stopped attending mass years ago, having simply ceased believing in Catholicism at about the time the "vernacular" mass replaced the Latin.)

Though I honor, and, in fact, am fascinated by, the religious convictions of others, it is not possible for me to believe that the Bible is holy writ; or, indeed, anything more than an astonishing compendium of mytho-poetic "history," written by countless men (and women?) over a consider-able period of time, these writers certainly inspired, but not divinely so. My Christian faith could not be sustained against a ceaselessly active curios-ity and skepticism that began in adolescence; I find it impossible to believe, and to wish to believe, in the proposition that there is a supernatural agent in the universe with which a tiny fraction of *Homo sapiens* has intimate contact, and a tiny fraction of that number actually represents. This "faith" or credulity is the basis for all organized religion, and it appears so egomaniacal, so improbable, as to be beyond respectful comment. Orga-nized religions and their pseudohistorical documents and traditions are secular phenomena, adhesive of a kind binding people together, designed, perhaps unconsciously, to provide consoling fantasies of immortality for those to whom reality is too painful, or insufficiently miraculous; more disturbingly, they are designed to closely monitor minds, women's bodies, and the young. At their most malevolent, these religions are power- and profit-motivated, hierarchical structures resembling businesses and profes-sions, in which careers, by tradition careers for men exclusively, are forged. Yet more dangerously, these religions can be virulently tribal, and intolerant of rational dissent; their "holy wars" are but priest-sanctioned terrorist rampages of slaughter of which our world, particularly the blood-soaked twentieth century, has had more than enough. A prayer for the next millennia might be: *Deliver us from all religions, and make us "merely" human!*

Yet I continue to read in the Bible. There is no anthology of voices so heterogeneous, so rich in stories, characters, wisdom. (Though, to a woman, biblical wisdom is not always so appealing as it may be to men.) In the Gospels, I am repeatedly struck by the brilliant aphorisms of that mysterious figure known to us as "Jesus Christ," which bear comparison with La Rochefoucauld, Montaigne, Nietzsche, and Oscar Wilde for their astute, uncommon good sense in succinct form ("Woe unto you, when all men speak well of you!") and aggressive idealism ("Judge not, and ye shall not be judged: condemn not, and ye shall not be condemned: forgive, and ye shall be forgiven.'')

Not miracles, but the humanly possible, and the inexhaustible riches of mythopoetic storytelling, are the Bible's enduring literary strengths.

Notes

1. My dreamlike, to me strange and "unprecedented," novel *Son of the Morning,* written in the mid-1970s and published in 1978, is evidently my valentine to that lost faith, those lost years. It was written during a period of obsessive immersion in the reading of the Bible as if I were not myself but the young male hero of the novel, a "bastard" begot upon a virgin, who becomes a celebrated evangelical minister.

2. Why was I in Las Vegas? What a good question! The annual conferences of the Horror Writers Association and the Antiquarian Booksellers were held there in 1994, and I was the recipient that year of the Bram Stoker Award for Lifetime Achievement in the field of horror writing, given by the Horror Writers Association. But that is another story.

PART
TWO

Ecclesiastes

R O B E R T   C O L E S

Most of the time my mom would choose not to bring her Bible to the dining room table at suppertime. She would call my dad, who was usually in his study reading the newspaper, and he would, in turn, summon my brother and me in a terse but friendly exhortation that I can still hear: "Bobby and Billy— dinner!" We'd come running, and often I remember quickly scanning the table—not for evidence of what we'd be eating, but for the presence or absence of Mother's Bible, one given to her when she was a child in Sioux City, Iowa, by her parents. About once a week it would be there (and not necessarily on a Sunday)—a rectangle of black that prompted curiosity, anticipation, concern, and not rarely, apprehension: what will happen as a consequence of that book being opened, its words recited, then discussed? Even now, as I write these words, I can see my brother and me eyeing each other as we both considered what had prompted our mom to take that ominous presence of sorts (that mere book, in fact—yet, its authority and power!) down from her study's bookshelf and carry it into the dining room, place it, invariably, at her left side, next to the knife. Even now, I can hear Dad saying "Oh!" as he, also, observed the Bible as our "guest" (he once wryly called it). Soon he'd be cutting the bread, always the first move made at the table— whereupon our mother (no longer our mom) would cut through any banter, or usually, a certain edgy, compelled silence, with the invariable rhetoric of request: "Would you three mind if I read from Scripture?"

As if we had any choice—and as if she expected us to reply! The word "Scripture" commanded utter acquiescence. We never so much as nodded —and anyway, we knew what to expect: a relatively brief spell of her voice, not raised, often lowered, actually—as if she was certainly respectful, maybe herself a bit fearful. Why not—hadn't she once told me that the Bible was God's "word"? In that regard, I would, a while later, tell my dad what I'd recently learned, whereupon he smiled, mused a moment, and asked this out loud: "I wonder whether God has ever spoken?" It would take me years, of course, to appreciate the mix of earthy common sense and philosophical savvy that informed that casual (only implicitly polemical) inquiry. When I told my mom of Dad's remark, she was neither surprised nor offended: "Your father is a scientist, and so he's learned to be a skeptic." She, too, wasn't thereby dismissive; she was trying to explain something to herself, never mind me—so I realized even as a boy of say, eight or nine, when I began to understand that my parents, quite happily married (they died in their middle eighties, within a month of one another, after a marriage of over sixty years), were by no means of the same religious background or belief or sensibility.

My mom had been brought up Episcopalian, and loved the old Book of Common Prayer. She liked, as well, the rituals and traditions of a particular church, though she often told us that the "best moment" in Christianity was "the first moment," meaning Jesus and His comrades and their families and the values, the intense and holy spirit to which they in their sum bore witness: a churchless cadre of vulnerable, brave, feisty souls, ardent in their espousal of "the beloved community"—a radical communitarianism that defied so many of this world's (actually, *all* of its) "principalities and powers." I recall, early in my life, hearing Mom say something else that, only later, had a more family-centered significance: "Jesus was one of the first of the Reform Jews"—to which Dad said nothing, but smiled. Later, I'd learn that his father was a Jew whose family belonged to the ancient Sephardic community of Ferdinand and Isabella's Spain; that his ancestors had left the Iberian Peninsula's persecution for Holland, then England, where Dad grew up (in Yorkshire—he came to the United States at eighteen to attend MIT, became a learned engineer, physicist). His mother was of French Catholic background, but had "lost interest" in the Church, even as his father had forsworn his Jewish faith, so our mom, somewhat sadly, had told us. Dad was quite reticent about his childhood, but he did press George Eliot's *Daniel Deronda* on my brother and me when we were older (along with other novels); he also talked about his early adolescent years in an English monastery—he'd caught tuberculosis, had been sent away for the only treatment then known: country air, country rest. "They were fine men"—his repeated word-for-word salute to the Benedictines: a secular accolade, I'd later understand. With great insistence he would seek out Benedictine monasteries on various continents, all the while refusing any motive other than the aesthetic: "such restful and lovely places."

Back to the table, though: once we were all seated, we'd be quiet—the Bible as the great silencer. Mom had various passages she'd favor, from Isaiah and Jeremiah, from Amos and Micah (she was utterly partial to prophetic rather than convenental Judaism), and she ranged freely over the four Gospels of the New Testament, as well as Paul's various letters—but there were certain messages she especially wanted all three of us (wanted herself, maybe, most of all) to hear and hear, to keep close in memory: the thrust, for instance, of "Ecclesiastes," from which she'd read portions of all twelve chapters, though concentrating on chapters one and three, the latter (I'd later learn) well known to many, but for my brother and me, then, something only taken to heart by our mother. Dad would often gaze out the window as she reminded us (out of the King James Bible) that "to every thing there is a season, and a time to every purpose under the heaven"—and, as the great lyrical preacher pressed home the details ("a time to get, and a time to lose," "a time to love and a time to hate") our father stared impassively, even as my brother and I oscillated back and forth, loyally keeping a timely watch, while deep down other impulses surged only so far: "a time to obey and a time to disobey" would race across my mind and disappear into the temporary oblivion of the uncon- scious, only to reappear the next time and the next time, a child's secret fun, an assertion of cleverness bound to earn a future entry to hell. Some- times, when Mother got to verse thirteen of that third chapter ("And also that every man should eat and drink, and enjoy the good of all his labor, it is the gift of God") Dad (unself-consciously? unwittingly? quite deliber- ately?—I'll never know) reached for his fork. Mother either ignored him or attended him with her voice: a faster clip—but she never stopped there, as his gesture surely suggested might be appropriate. She ended not with the particular chapter read in its entirety (the third chapter, or fourth or fifth), but with certain excerpts from the first, or the eleventh, which she'd tack on (the editor's privilege) even when they had been spoken earlier as part of the read verse—choruses we came to learn by heart: "vanity of vanities, saith the preacher, vanity of vanities; all is vanity," or "cast thy bread upon the waters, for thou shall find it after many days. . . . Truly the light is sweet, and a pleasant thing it is for the eyes to behold the sun. But if a man live many years and rejoice in them all, yet let him remember the days of darkness, for they shall be many. All that cometh is vanity."

Days might (mercifully? blissfully?) pass—with no Bible on that old pine table, covered with tablecloths our Midwestern grandmother had made and dispatched to us, with notes written in an intimidatingly neat and precise hand. Then, all of a sudden, the book of books—and this time chapter twenty of St. Matthew, a favorite, with the analogy of "the kingdom of heaven" as "like unto the man that is an householder." He hires laborers to work in his vineyard, promises them a penny a day, and as the laborers hired first keep toiling in the fields, he sees "others standing idle in the marketplace," and hires them—and keeps doing so during the hours of sunlight. When he pays up, as it were (starting with those hired last) he gives as he said he would give: all had been promised a penny, and all get one—but those hired first, who had worked longest, felt more deserving, wanted more. Jesus rebukes them—even insists in a memorable and pointed and ever so provocative comment: "So the last shall be first and the first last: for many be called, but few chosen."

That comment is also offered in Luke and Mark, as Mother often reminded us, a bit of exegesis that was meant to underline the import of the message. But she and Dad never went beyond that—never discussed the meaning of that comment of Jesus. The same with Paul's first letter to the Corinthians, another favorite—over and over, across the years, we heard Mother read the well-known thirteenth chapter, heard her pronounce at the end, "faith, hope, charity," heard her extol, through Paul, "the greatest of these," charity, but got no postlude, no footnotes, no follow-up discussion. Years later, when I came across the triad of "faith, hope, love" in the New English Bible, I was jolted—even as I'd *sort* of figured out, as a youngster, that the word "charity," as used by St. Paul, had to do with a rather substantial exercise of generosity and concern with respect to others. Still, we were children and we knew of the conventional "charities" which our parents discussed, and to which they gave their annual contributions— and somehow that climax of St. Paul's felt suspect, hollow to us, for the good reason that our parents, who knew better of it, never let the subject matter come to the resolution of an exchange of words.

Indeed, that is my major memory (and point, here): an agnostic scientist awaits his meal with mute patience; two small children know to sit still, keep their mouths shut, their ears open; a person known to be deeply religious goes for days with no apparent interest in the Bible or in church (and can skip Sunday attendance of the latter with no evident anxiety or qualms)—but suddenly, a hush over the table as the words of the Hebrew preacher, or of that itinerant rabbi (and His followers) who shook up history so unexpectedly a couple of thousand years ago, get spoken; and afterward, the steak or the lamb chops or the chicken and the vegetables and the desserts come our way, even as Dad makes remarks about Franklin D. Roosevelt or Harry S. Truman, both of whom he cordially disliked, and Mom (now quite voluble and explicitly passionate and more audible than was ever the case when the Bible was in her hand) rushes to a vigorous affirmation of "FDR," as she called him, whom she admired (to Dad he was Mr. Roosevelt, always), and "Eleanor," whom she also admired (*Mrs.* Roosevelt, Dad would counter), or Harry Truman, whom she also *very* much admired ("that fellow Truman," Dad said dismissingly), and "Bess Truman," whom Mother compared to *her* mother ("The President's wife," Dad said, not deigning to use her name or accord her the dignity she eminently deserved). As we grew up, that is, we heard politics discussed, savored, argued—but the Bible: it was handed down with considerable but controlled feeling, at random intervals, with no subsequent effort at moral or emotional integration, so to speak, no attempt to connect ancient assertions to a present-day family's life, its values, its ideals, its aspirations and worries.

Rather obviously, as I grew older, entered adolescence, I began to *think* about what I'd hear my mother read—and too, think about her, seemingly without rhyme or reason, choosing to make us listeners at the dinner table before her delicious cooking made its way to our hungry mouths. Gradually, I began to realize that what she occasionally said then, at six o'clock in the evening, had kept echoing through my mind at other times, often to my consternation and frustration. For example, I was her son, my dad's son: they had gone to college, and they wanted me to do likewise. Put differently, they wanted my brother and me to study hard, to perform well on tests, to be very good students, to achieve one or another kind of "success" in the conventional, secular sense of that word—and yet: the profound distrust of that very prospect directly, emphatically offered in both the Hebrew and Christian Bible. Ecclesiastes, or the preacher, is a fatalist; takes the largest view possible; casts grave doubt on the worth of so much that gets called a win, a victory, an accomplishment in today's world, in any world, maybe. Jesus, also, told His listeners that He wasn't going to hold to the usual categories of approval and disapproval, of inclusion and exclusion—rather, He was prepared to shake things up quite decisively, radically: in Nietzsche's memorable phrase, "a transvaluation of values," a topsy-turvy, even apocalyptic insistence that just about everything (and everyone) will be dislocated by this coming from on high. That is, finally, history revealed him to be Him—but what is a teenager or a young man in his twenties, living in the second half of the twentieth century, to do with all that, as it has been handed down countless times over the dinner table?

As I look back at my life, I realize how much of it has been spent trying to answer that question—trying to integrate the biblical lessons my mother posed to herself (hence her hesitant, soft-spoken, tentative, perhaps fearful and only occasional predinner readings), never mind us. I also realize that in his own way, and for his own reasons, my dad wanted, needed, to hear her challenge various "principalities and powers"—he whose wisdom was derived from a continual reading and rereading of George Eliot and Thomas Hardy and Charles Dickens, those three Victorian novelists who could move from irony to unashamed scorn as they looked at a (then) mighty nation's warts and worse. No wonder, then, it was hard for me to be quite as entranced with psychiatry and child psychiatry and psychoanalysis, my chosen profession, as were many of my fellow residents or our teachers; and yes, I fear I did have the proverbial "problem" (one with "authority") that was summoned in explanation of the foregoing by those teachers—an inclination toward misgivings and more misgivings that wouldn't quite go away, no matter the "training," the "control [psycho]analysis," the informal requirement, frankly, that one keep relatively quiet about one's reservations for the sake of graduating, being certified. I surely knew how, in that last respect, to shut up, but my mother's voice, my father's willingness to hear her out, even sometimes to nod knowingly, never really left my memory, my consciousness.

All the time, actually, I go back, by indirection, to those childhood days, to the Bible on the dining room table, and then in my mother's hands, to the chants of Ecclesiastes, to the drastic revolution in our assumptions, our thinking, that Jesus of Nazareth expressed in His brief teaching and healing life. A while back, I attended a psychoanalytic conference on narcissism—in recent years a lively subject of discussion, argument. As I listened to three psychoanalytically trained psychiatrists agree and disagree on this or that concept, on "narcissism in personality development," as one of them kept putting it, I heard Ecclesiastes in my head—heard my father taking my mother's biblical warnings and making of them the stuff of his bemused, if not sardonic worldview: there is the narcissism of theory, the narcissism of patients, and not least, the narcissism of the one who (narcissistically) propounds the significance of narcissism. Moreover, one kind of vanity not mentioned in Ecclesiastes is the vanity of the person who points out and by implication denounces vanity in his preaching, as in that book of the Bible! No sooner does such a line of thinking cross my mind, than I feel remorse—as if I'm incurably tied to a certain melancholy ruefulness, a crankiness, really, that compels distance from all wholehearted enthusiasms, social, political, cultural, professional, historical, even biblical—with no small number of hazards or dangers as a consequence: the vanity of one who spots all too keenly vanity everywhere, all the time; the smugness of one who remembers that according to the Lord's Son (so millions and millions have claimed to believe, do believe) many of those who seem to be doing right well will topple, and many of those who seem to be under this or that boot will rise to moral, spiritual triumph—though one can't help wondering when and where such will happen.

It is not hard for me (all grown up, if such is ever the case, and my children in their middle to late twenties, and so, also grown up), to turn away from the childhood moments I have been mentioning here—even as my parents lived a reasonable, American, bourgeois version of the proverbial long and happy life. Ecclesiastes didn't stop them from having a comfortable time of it, nor the warnings of Jesus. The clinician in me is all too tempted to say that my parents were, *on the whole* (that clever qualifier!), quite well "adjusted" (that dreary encomium of our time), even if they did, Mother especially, slip into temporary spells of moodiness, when the Bible's messages became for them a means of self-expression: this isn't such a good day for me—so, "all is vanity," and besides all will be turned upside down, and besides, it is "charity," or "love" that matters, not one or another thing pressed upon us by the assorted whims and fads of a given age. Maybe so, actually—the Bible as a vehicle for alienation and isolation and despair, not to mention their clinical analogues: anxiety, depression. But the doctor's diagnosis can be given its own tough scrutiny—the vanity of such a designated posture, and too, the moral vulnerability of those who are "first," who have and use the power to banish others into the realm of the sick, while ignoring their own blind spots, and worse—covering them up as "within the limits of normality." Indeed, when I think of the doctors who worked so willingly with Hitler, with Stalin (helped the latter's Gulag by shooting up suspected political dissidents with psychopharmacological drugs) I think I know a little of what my mother had in mind as she let the admonitions of a Jesus soon to die (to be killed) worry her from time to time: respectability and authority and power as potentially devilish accomplices to a particular life.

Yes, we need to walk carefully through any book, the Bible included —use a certain common sense and careful judgment as we consider with regard to our own lives various remarks made many centuries ago, under vastly different circumstances. Yes, we need to be immersed somewhat, at least, in life's daily flow, as workers and as parents, as friends and as neighbors, lest we take everything with a grain of salt, become all too self-consciously indifferent to the things of this world, not to mention the people. Still, and at the risk of that "sin of pride," that "vanity of vanities," which my mother, through her biblical forays, put before us as a constant threat, we also need to pull back on ourselves, even on others, even on others dear to us, from time to time—take note of the phoniness and pretense, the smugness and complacency that can inform our lives, and surely so among those at the top of the world as well as those living toward the bottom. Once, annoyed with my mom for giving me one of her reprimands (I'd forgotten to do some chores), I complained with no small outcry of self-pity: give me a break! To my great surprise, she had second thoughts—apologized with a considerable and obvious felt passion. She *had* been a bit hard on me, she let me know. Next came an observation (self-observation) I can still hear her making: "Pride is a constant shadow to all of us, I fear." By then I was twelve or so, well used to ("socialized," with respect to, as some would put it nowadays) such a manner of thinking and talking, both. By then, I could agree heartily with her—that she could be and was being all too sure of herself, all too ready for someone else to take the fall, while she pointed the accusing finger. Yet, she'd turned around, confessed—and even if *that* could be worked into the devilry of pride (the pride that goes with acknowledging pride!), a boy could feel relief and gratitude; and could remember the moment as a gift as well as a warning: "vanity of vanities," to be sure, as a necessary remonstrance that tells all of us about our rock-bottom inclination toward what George Eliot called "unreflective egoism"; but "vanity of vanities" now become an ironic instrument of saving humility, my mom's offered me in such a telling way that here I am remembering it.

Jeremiah and Revelation

KATHLEEN NORRIS

The Benedictine monks of St. John's Abbey in Collegeville, Minnesota, practice what is known as *lectio continua,* listening to entire books of the Bible at morning and evening prayer. They read through the entire New Testament in this way every year, and during the time I've spent with them—eighteen months over the last three years—we also listened to Genesis, Ruth, Tobit, Esther, Job, the Song of Songs, Hosea, Jonah, and large portions of the books of Exodus, Samuel, Kings, and Isaiah. Probably the most remarkable experience of all was plunging into the prophet Jeremiah at morning prayer in late September, and staying with him until the beginning of Advent, in early December. Reading for about ten minutes a day, we got through the first thirty chapters. It's one hell of a way to get your blood going in the morning; it puts caffeine to shame.

The monastic discipline of listening aims to still body and soul so that the words of a reading may sink in. Such silence tends to open a person, and opening oneself to a prophet as anguished as Jeremiah can be painful. On some mornings, I found it impossible. Like one of my monk friends, who had the duty of reading the prophet aloud through some particularly grim passages, I felt like shouting "Have a Nice Day!" to the assembly. Easier to mock a prophet than to listen to him.

On other days, I became angry, or was reduced to tears, perhaps a promising sign that something essential had gotten through. The command in Jeremiah Chapter 4:3, "Break up your fallow ground" stayed with me long enough to elicit a response in my journal. With the desert fathers and mothers in mind, I wrote, "and as I take my spade in hand, as far as I can see, great clods of earth are waiting, heavy and dark, a hopeless task. First weeds will come, then whatever it is I've planted. I feel the struggle in my knees and back."

One beneficial effect of *lectio continua* is that it enables a person to hear the human voices of the biblical authors. It becomes obvious, for instance, that Paul's letters were meant to be read aloud, and this allows one to take an unaccustomed pleasure in the complex play Paul makes of even his densest theology. To hear the joke working its way through 1 Corinthians 1:21 is to get the point. Hearing the passage read slowly one night at vespers, I laughed out loud: "For since in the wisdom of God the world did not come to know God through wisdom, it was the will of God through the foolishness of the proclamation to save those who have faith."

Listening to the Bible read aloud is not only an invaluable immersion in religion as an oral tradition, it allows even the scripture scholars of a monastic community to hear with fresh ears. A human voice is speaking, that of an apostle, or a prophet, and all the concerns critical to biblical interpretation—authorship of texts, interpolation of material, redaction of manuscript sources—recede into the background. One doesn't forget what one knows, and the process of listening may well inform one's scholarship. But in communal *lectio,* the fact that the book of Jeremiah has several authors matters far less than the sense that a human voice is speaking, and speaking to you. Even whether or not you believe that this voice speaks the word of God is less important than the sense of being sought out, personally engaged, making it possible, even necessary, to respond personally, to take the scriptures to heart.

Jeremiah 20, containing some of the most bitter language ever uttered by a prophet ("You seduced me, O Lord, and I was seduced") went straight to my heart: I staggered home after morning prayer and went back to bed. I'd been depressed anyway—a friend's brother had recently become homeless, others close to me were in a bad way, I was shaky myself —and the wild movement of that chapter simply wore me out. It begins with a dire prophecy of the Babylonian exile, and shifts abruptly, but appropriately, to Jeremiah's own vocational crisis, the folly of his urge to *not* prophesy ("I say to myself, I will not mention him / I will speak in his name no more. / But then it becomes like fire burning in my heart / imprisoned in my bones").

Jeremiah then assesses the public scorn that his prophetic role has earned him ("I hear the whisperings of many. . . . Denounce him") and makes a defiant prayer ("But the Lord is with me, like a mighty champion") that ends in a doxology that feels more ironic than not, followed as it is by: "Cursed be the day on which I was born . . ." The chapter ends, finally, on an anguished cry: "Why did I come forth from the womb, / to see sorrow and pain, / to end my days in shame?" Swallowed whole, the chapter is a vivid depiction of what it can mean to fall into the hands of a living God. It is not something one chooses.

I would not have chosen to listen to Jeremiah in the fall of 1993, but as it turned out, he was a good companion. It proved to be a difficult season, one in which I was made to suffer for who and what I was. Such times come to us all sooner or later, and most of us find ample means of escape. For a number of reasons, my means of escape were very few, and Jeremiah led me into the heart of my pain, forcing me to recognize that to answer a call as a prophet, or a poet for that matter, is to reject the authority of credentials, of human valuation of any kind, accepting only the authority of the call itself. It was as a writer that Jeremiah spoke to me, and it was as a writer I listened.

"When you look for light," he said, "he turns it into gloom, / and makes it deep darkness . . ." Those lines in Jeremiah 13 brought back to me a childhood image of God, which had led to nothing but trouble in my cheery, 1950s' Protestant Sunday school. We'd been asked to paint a picture of heaven and my effort, an image of God's throne surrounded by dark clouds, was a dismal failure. The cheap paper wrinkled under all the layers of paint I'd given it, before I finally realized I couldn't get the clouds dark enough. It wasn't until I stumbled across Gregory of Nyssa in my thirties that I discovered that my childhood image had a name, a place within the Christian tradition.

Many people experience such otherness in childhood, but I suspect that those who find this otherness integral to a calling—to religious life, to ministry, to the arts—have the hardest time of it. The journey to adulthood, toward realizing one's identity, can be difficult and dark. Jeremiah's darkness helped me define the odd and disagreeable situation in which I found myself that fall, in which I experienced, full blast, the scorn of academics for a poet in their midst. "The substance, the means of art is incarnation," Denise Levertov once wrote, "not reference but phenomena." To be a maker of phenomena, to speak as a poet, without reference to authority, but simply because the words are in you, like a fire, is not necessarily welcome in academia. I found myself misunderstood, spurned in public, and, as soon became obvious, ridiculed behind my back.

It was the prophet who helped me understand that there wasn't much I could do about all this, except wait it out. I watched ice form on the river outside my window and felt a loneliness more intense than any I could remember. And when it became too much to bear, words came to me. I wrote a poem entitled "The Silent Day" that ends with an image of a "necessary other, a reminder and reproach; the ground of winter, watchful and chill, no longer looking for what it is not there." I found the image curiously hopeful.

I realized that the Benedictines had led me to a new and strange place, in which I had come to depend on Jeremiah to help me understand my own life. I know better than to make facile comparisons between myself and a prophet. I relate the story only because I believe it illuminates the workings of *lectio*. Monastic life is an immersion in scripture, and over time the texts that invite you to commune with them can come to serve as a mirror. But the reflection is larger than you expect. As personal as my response to Jeremiah was, I was also forced to recognize, in the months that we took his body-blows at morning prayer, the public dimension of his prophecy and of our response. Jeremiah's lament over a land so ravaged that even the birds and animals have fled has a powerful resonance in an age in which species are rapidly disappearing, and the threat of nuclear warfare remains. His bleak image of death "cutting down the children in the street, young people in the squares, the corpses of the slain like dung on a field, like sheaves behind the harvester, with no one to harvest them" (9:20–21) could have come from a *Newsweek* story on Bosnia, or Rwanda, or inner-city Detroit.

The contemporaneity of Jeremiah made me reflect on our need for prophets; I'd sit in the monks' choir and think, *it really is this bad, and if people heard it they would want to change; they'd have to change,* and of course it was Jeremiah himself who'd bring me back to earth, to the bitterness of his call, when God tells him: "You shall speak to them and they will not listen; you shall call and they shall not answer." (7:27) Yet a prophet speaks out of hope and, like all the prophets, Jeremiah's ultimate hope is for justice, a people made holy by "doing what is right and just in the land." (33:15) As the carriers of hope through disastrous times, prophets are a necessary other. And we reject them because we don't like the way they make us look at the way things really are; they don't allow us to deny our pain.

Spending several months with the Book of Jeremiah reminded me that pain is something that we can't push aside, or go around, but must go through. It reinforced my admiration for the bravery of Benedictines, in late twentieth-century America, in a culture of denial, to try to listen to a prophet at all. The response of the monks was illuminating, and sometimes comical. "Know what you have done," Jeremiah shouted at us one morning (2:23), but before we could get over the ferocity of that command—it's so much easier to live *not* knowing what we've done—the prophet had gone on to a vivid depiction of Israel as a frenzied camel in heat, loudly sniffing the wind, making directionless tracks in the sand. This was imagery we could smell; the poetry of scripture at its earthy best.

"Stop wearing out your shoes" (2:25), Jeremiah said, and we sat up straight. Monks are not used to being compared to camels in heat, but they took it pretty well. I noticed eyebrows going up around the choir, and then a kind of quiet assent: *well, there are days. . . .* Monks know very well how easy it is to lose track of one's purpose in life, how hard to maintain the discipline that keeps (in St. Benedict's words) "our minds in harmony with our voices" in prayer, the ease with which aimless desire can disturb our hearts. Jeremiah's warnings were like something a crusty desert father might have said to a recalcitrant young monk who thought that some other monastery might suit him better, or whose restlessness was preventing prayer: get hold of yourself, settle down. *Stop wearing out your shoes.* Good advice for us in America, where seeking the holy has become an end in itself, not to mention big business.

One day, not long after we'd begun to read Jeremiah, and it was dawning on us that we had a long, rough road ahead, a monk said to me: "We haven't read a prophet for a while, and we need to hear it. It's good for us." Another said he was glad to be reading Jeremiah in the morning, and not at evening prayer, when there are more likely to be guests. "The monks can take it," he said, "but most people have no idea what's in the

Bible, and they come unglued.'' The ignorance of the Bible that is common even among seminarians and students of theology is, I suspect, a result not only of the secularism of our society but also of a deeply embedded cultural literalism.

This literalism is reflected in different ways by both fundamentalist and liberal voices within the American Christian church, which, like American culture, is marked by the denial of whatever is unpleasant or uncontrollable. As a writer, I know how unpleasant, even scary, metaphor can be. It doesn't surprise me that people try to control it in whatever way they can, the fundamentalists with literal interpretations of prophetic and apocalyptic texts that deny the import of its metaphorical language, the liberals by attempting to eliminate metaphoric images—Father, Lord and servant, the heavenly court, and even the cross, let alone camels in heat—that are deemed depressing, degrading, or politically incorrect.

Evidence of this curious symbiosis of fundamentalists and liberals may be found in the way that the liberal church tends to cede to fundamentalists the literature of apocalyptic vision. In some circles you can be labeled a fundamentalist just by admitting that you like the Book of Revelation. It was the Benedictines of St. John's who steered me around this dilemma. As we had read Jeremiah in the fall, we read straight through the Book of Revelation at morning prayer during Easter, and I was forced to listen.

The Apocalypse, or Revelation, of John begins sweetly, blessing both ''the one who reads aloud'' and ''those who listen to this prophetic message and heed what is written in it.'' (1:3) This presumes a communal context, in which a reader reads and others listen and respond, a context similar to the one in which I found myself in the monastery choir. Benedictines practice *lectio*—loosely and inadequately translated as meditative or prayerful reading—both privately and in common. Benedict considered private reading so important that he allowed several hours a day for it in a monastery's daily routine. As *lectio* is not a matter of literacy so much as a

287

disposition of the heart toward prayer, Benedict expected illiterate monks to participate by musing on the words of psalms and the Gospels that they had memorized.

In communal *lectio,* I found that it helped to listen to the Book of Revelation *as* an illiterate; to keep in mind that its primary impact is visual. The poet Diane Glancy once said to me, "As an Indian, I like Revelation because there's so much to look at, so much that resonates with Indian culture. The colors, the horses, the eagles. The four directions, the four winds." The Book of Revelation does not make for easy listening, but Diane's comments reminded me that I could simply shut my eyes and let the pictures unfold. To my surprise, I found it a relief to listen to John's baffling, wild, beautiful, and often frightening images without resisting, without always seeking to make sense of them. Slowly, I began to grasp the consoling and even healing power of apocalypse. Most importantly of all, I saw the need to reclaim it as poetic turf.

The word "apocalypse" comes from the Greek for "uncovering" or "revealing," which makes it a word about possibilities. And possibilities are poetic territory. Both poetry and apocalyptic literature explore the limits of speech, and must rely on intensely metaphoric language, as well as visual imagery. Revelation was Emily Dickinson's favorite book of the Bible for a good reason. "Uncovering" and "revealing" appeals to poets; it's the reason we write.

But metaphoric language, the language of revelation, is dangerous, especially when one attempts to force it back into the literal. Such interpretations of apocalyptic metaphors have often led Christians to construct a boogeyman God. Roberta Bondi, one of my favorite theologians, once described this God, the one she was raised with, as "the God who loves you so much He's gonna getcha if you if you don't watch out!" This God is an understandably human construction, one that allows us to assume the comfortable position of knowing exactly what God is up to, who's he's gonna get and who's gonna make it past those pearly gates. All too often, it has tempted Christians to pass judgment on other people. Hearing John's Apocalypse read aloud, I was astonished to find how little support there is for such a position. Judgment comes, and it's a terrifying spectacle. Judgment is up to God, and that's the good news. All evil is vanquished, and justice is done. The story reflects what we know from experience; that the point of our crises and calamities is not to frighten us or beat us into submission, but to encourage us to change, to allow us to heal and grow.

Emily Dickinson, who experienced the scriptures much as Benedictines do, reading them not only in private but hearing them read aloud daily at home (and in church until she was in her early thirties) came to be a shrewd, if severe, judge of preachers. She knew when a preacher was using apocalyptic literature to his own ends. Of one pastor who had preached a terrifying sermon on the Last Judgment she said, "The subject of perdition seemed to please him, somehow. It seems very solemn to me." The idea of judgment, being called to task for the way in which we have run our lives, and the world itself, *is* solemn, and terrifying, and apocalyptic language rises to the challenge. That's a cause for celebration, in my book.

Hearing Revelation read aloud, I felt challenged, as a writer, to reexamine the way I'd always stereotyped the book as "hellfire and damnation." I found that engaging the book as a listener made me think instead about metaphor, and how consistently it defeats our attempts to keep it under control. It revealed to me the extent to which, in our culture, we define metaphor as lying. We do not value it as truth, a unique truth approachable only through metaphorical means.

And that is precisely what John's Apocalypse seemed to be, as I heard its images unfold: uniquely true, true in its own terms, and indefinable—or just plain silly—outside them. Its images radically subvert our desire to literalize them, and also expose the flimsiness of our attempts to do so. Both liberal and fundamentalist Christians, it seems to me, try to control the images of apocalyptic literature, the former by denying them, the latter by interpreting them as prediction. But the Book of Revelation comes with a built-in irony. Whether one believes that John wrote the book, or regards God as the true author of all scripture, to interpret its images literally is to show a strange disregard for the method its author employed in order to get the message across.

And what in the world is the message of apocalyptic literature? We often use the word "apocalypse" to mean catastrophic destruction—and cosmic upheaval is evoked in Daniel, in the Book of Revelation, and several Gospel passages, in images of earthquake, fire, and plague, of the sun and moon darkening, the sea turning to blood, and stars falling from the sky. But destruction is not what the word "apocalypse" means, and it is certainly not the heart of its message, which is hope for persecuted or oppressed communities in crisis, hope for those on the losing end.

As I listened to the Book of Revelation over several weeks I was astonished to discover a healing vision, a journey through the heart of pain and despair, and into hope. And I was consistently reminded of how subtly this vision works on us. Apocalyptic literature asserts that the evils of this world are not incurable, that injustice does not have the last word. And that can be terrifying or consoling, depending on your point of view.

Like prophetic language, the images of the apocalypse are meant to make us uncomfortable. That is their value to us, especially in a society that has come to worship comfort. Using the lens of apocalyptic literature, one might say that the desolation of a slum reveals who we are as a nation, a people, far better than the gleaming stores of a shopping mall. The apocalypse forces us to look at what remains when pretense, including our pretense to affluence, is taken away. But apocalypse as a form of prophecy not only reveals the fault lines of the status quo, it takes our true measure with regard to it: the discomfort we feel when the boundaries shift is the measure of our allegiance to the way things are.

Apocalypse takes us far beyond the usual boundaries of language and custom. If you've ever experienced the strangeness of being a healthy person in an Intensive Care Unit, or a hospice or nursing home, then you have experienced apocalypse in this sense. The world turned inside out, revealed as radically different from what we thought we knew, all the things we value so highly—productivity, control of mind and body, the illusion of personal autonomy—suddenly swept away. And our response to this revelation—whether it depresses us and makes us want to run, or whether we can discern hope, and love, and grace in this strange, new place—is a measure of our true condition. It reveals us to ourselves.

And isn't this one of the goals of writing? Contemporary writers live at a far remove from John of Patmos, whose identity as a writer was inextricably bound to that of his community. Artists in the late twentieth century have come to lament the loss of a communal role. Yet it has not entirely eluded us; in times of crisis, apocalyptic times, people still look to artists for *something,* maybe even hope. There is the story about the Russian poet Anna Akhmatova standing in the long lines outside the prison in—I'll call it St. Petersburg—waiting to leave letters and packages for loved ones caught up in Stalin's purges, not even knowing whether they were dead or alive. Recognizing the poet, a woman approached her and asked, "Can you describe this?" Akhmatova replied, "I can," and notes that "something like a smile passed fleetingly over what once had been her face." Akhmatova at that moment fulfilled a prophetic role, as well as an apocalyptic one: *I can describe this.* Just the act of describing can be defiance, in the face of terror; it allows the powerless a glimpse into another reality, one in which words and images (not guns and prisons) have power.

Writers have no more power than their readers are willing to grant them. Akhmatova's story suggests that writing is an inescapably communal act, as it depends on both writer and reader (or listener). The writer must be willing to see, the reader to hear. Listening to John's Apocalypse day in, day out, I began to notice how much of it is concerned with the acts of seeing and writing. In the very first chapter a voice like a trumpet says to John: "Write on a scroll what you see." (1:11) When John turns to face the voice, he sees a figure that he describes, memorably, as holding seven stars, with a sword coming out of his mouth, and a face as bright as the sun. On touching John the figure says: "Do not be afraid. I am the first and the last, the one who lives. Once I was dead but now I am alive forever and ever. I hold the keys to death and the netherworld. Write down, therefore"—I love that "therefore"—"what you have seen, and what is happening, and what will happen afterwards."

Moving with the unfathomable logic of a dream, which requires only that you give yourself up to it, the book continues, giving us angels who direct John to write, to not write, and even to eat the words of a little scroll. The angel who offers John the scroll warns him that "It will turn your stomach sour, but in your mouth it will taste as sweet as honey." (10:9) This passage echoes both Isaiah and Ezekiel, and serves to remind the listener of John's prophetic call. The transition that follows, the word "then" sounding clear as a bell when one hears the passage read aloud, is a further reinforcement of John's authority as a prophet. He says: "I took the small scroll from the angel's hand and swallowed it. In my mouth it was like sweet honey, but when I had eaten it my stomach turned sour. Then someone said to me, 'You must prophesy again about many peoples, nations, tongues and kings.' " (10:10–11)

The Book of Revelation concludes as it began, with a blessing invoked on those who hear it. This time, a warning is also given, against anyone who would add or take away from the words of the prophecy. The passage concludes: "The Spirit and the bride say, 'Come.' Let the hearer say 'Come,' let the one who thirsts come forward, and the one who wants it receive the gift of life-giving water." (21:17)

It seems to me that the crux of this passage is the invitation given to the one who *hears* the book, which echoes an earlier invitation to John to come and witness the endless praise and worship that takes place in heaven, around God's throne. Now the listener is asked to become an active participant in the continuing process of revelation, to speak up, and invite others to receive the words of the book. As John was an evangelist, exiled to the island of Patmos, he tells us, for "giving testimony to Jesus," (1:9) this is not surprising. What might be surprising to people conditioned by cultural literalism is the way that the apocalypse of John functions as a radical act of biblical interpretation, or, as the *Oxford Companion to the Bible* puts it, "a rereading of biblical tradition in the light of the death of Jesus."

Visionaries like John are at the mercy of what they see, and their visions push them up against the boundaries of metaphor, of language itself. But John is also a writer working out of a tradition. He tells us that his book is a record of what he has seen and heard, but clearly it is also a fruit of his own *lectio,* his imbibing of the Hebrew scriptures, and probably the literature of the Gospel traditions as well. The *Oxford Companion* tells us that the Revelation may be seen as "a scriptural meditation, based perhaps on the Sabbath readings from the Law and the Prophets which has been cast in visionary form. Probably it is a mixture of genuine experience and literary elaboration. Biblical metaphors and images—dragon, lamb, harlot, bride— come to new life in his imagination."

Isn't "new life" the point of the religion? And don't we get there by a mixture of experience and metaphoric exploration? Not by "adding" or "taking away," but by continually reinterpreting what we've been given? And aren't metaphors part of that given? Jesus describes the kingdom of God in terms of mustard seed and yeast. The nineteenth-century mathematician Bernhard Riemann once said, "I did not invent those pairs of differential equations. I found them in the world, where God had hidden them." When I stumble across metaphors in the course of writing, it often feels as if I jump straight from stolid ignorance into blazing revelation, the words and images choosing me, not the other way around. While I manipulate them in the interest of hospitality, in order to make a comprehensible work of art, I have to give up any notion of control. The little scroll of the perfect poem that appears in a dream eludes me in the morning; the words that come so sweetly turn bitter once I've ingested them and sent them off to find their import in the world. Yet these are the words I am called to say, inviting others into communion with them.

For a long time I had no idea why I was so attracted to the Benedictines, why I've kept returning to their choirs over the past dozen years. Now I believe it's because of the hospitality I've encountered in their communal *lectio,* a hospitality so vast that it invites all present into communion with the text being read. I encounter there not a God who rejects me because I can't pass some dogmatic litmus test, but one who invites me to become part of a process, the continuing revelation of holy word. Heard aloud, the metaphors of scripture are roomy indeed; they allow me to relax, and listen, and roam. I take them in, to my "specific strength," as Emily Dickinson put it in her powerful poem "A Word Made Flesh Is Seldom." And I hope to give something back.

Toward the beginning of the Book of Revelation, John is called to say to the church at Ephesus that God "[has] this against you, that you have abandoned the love you had at first. Remember from what you have fallen . . ." (2:4–5) These are words of conversion; taking hold, they can change a life. When I first heard them in the monks' choir, tears welled up in me, unexpected and unwelcome. I remembered how completely I had loved God, and church, as a child, and how easily I had drifted away as a young adult.

I realized suddenly that I'd been most fortunate in being given another chance to encounter worship, in middle age, in a context that restored to me the true religion of my childhood, which was song. For me, participating in monastic *lectio* has meant rediscovering a religion that consists not so much of ideas or doctrines, but of song and breath. It's encountering the words of scripture in such a way that they become as alive as the people around me. As Emily Dickinson put it, words that "breathe."

And listening is the key. Isaiah 52, which echoes throughout Revelation 21, the "gemstone chapter" that is known to be Dickinson's favorite in the Bible, says simply, "listen, that you may live." Listening to the hard stuff, the words of Jeremiah and John of Patmos, I was able to return without fear to that other childhood god, the one my fundamentalist grandmother Norris had unwittingly imposed on me, and hear a different message in the metaphors of judgment and terror. "Who can stand?" (6:17) John asks, in a grim passage depicting the world's powerful scrambling into caves and behind rocks to hide from the wrath of God. *No one,* is the answer, and it's a comforting one—at the end of human power, of human control, we find a God of love, who desires to dwell with humanity, and "wipe every tear from [our] eyes." (21:4)

Somehow, the simple magic of having the Bible read aloud to me opened my eyes to recognize the extent to which I had, in the words of Teilhard de Chardin, allowed "the resistance of the world to good [to shake] my faith in the kingdom of God." A secular worldview, terribly sophisticated but of little use to me in the long run, had taken hold of me in my early twenties, and in Chardin's words, I had come "to regard the world as radically and incurably corrupt. Consequently [I had] allowed the fire to die down in [my] heart." Writing kept the fires of hope alive in me during the twenty years I never went near a church. In the Benedictine choir, as I allowed the words of John's revelation to wash over me—to be repulsed, offended, attracted, and moved to tears of grief and anger, joy and wonder—my full sense of the sacredness of the world revived. I had begun to learn to listen as a child again.

The radiant faith of childhood demonstrates that the opposite of faith is not doubt but fear. Children don't doubt; they fear. Throughout John's Apocalypse, as the frightening images unfold, all the angels and the figure of Christ himself continually tell John: "do not fear." I find the angels of Revelation refreshingly terrifying—calmly they stand at the four corners of the earth, holding the four winds; they plant one foot on land, one on the sea, and, roaring like lions, invoke seven thunders. No warm, fuzzy gift-shop angels, nothing for the New Age or "personal spirituality" market, nothing marketable at all. I love the story of the red dragon with seven heads and ten horns, and his defeat at the hands of the archangel Michael, and wonder if all this would interest children more than Barney the dinosaur. (In a childrens' sermon, in a mainstream Protestant church, I once heard Christianity described as a version of the Barney song: Where is John of Patmos when we need him?)

At the moment when the new heaven and earth are revealed to John, Christ speaks from a great white throne: " 'Behold, I make all things new.' Then he said, 'Write these words down.' " (21:5) Hearing this in the monk's choir, I gasped. No wonder this chapter is Dickinson's favorite. Christ's commission may well have helped her define her calling, her vocation as a poet (and I would claim, one of the great biblical interpreters of the nineteenth century). I gasped again, as a phrase entered my mind: "Ezra Pound thundered, 'make it new,' and Jesus said, 'I will.'"

I had just experienced a healing, a joining together of what had been pulled apart in me for many years, when I thought I had to choose *between* literature and religion. It was in encountering the Benedictines, after I had apprenticed as a writer for many years, that I learned otherwise. Much to my surprise, their daily liturgy and *lectio* profoundly intensified my sense of metaphor as essential to our capacity to hope, and to dream (not to mention to transcend the banalities of the Barney song). And it was free for the asking.

The poetry of apocalyptic literature takes us to the limits of metaphor, of human sense, the limits of imagining and understanding. It pushes us against the boundaries of language itself and suggests that the end of our control—our ideologies, our plans, our competence, our expertise, our professionalism, our power—is the beginning of God's reign. It asks us to believe that only the good remains, at the end, and directs us toward carefully tending it here and now. We will sing a new song. Singing and praise will be all that remains. That's okay by me. As a poet, I can relate to that.

WORKS CITED

The books of Jeremiah and Revelation, in both NAB and RSV translations. Also:

St. Benedict, *The Holy Rule*
Teilhard de Chardin, *The Divine Milieu*
Emily Dickinson, *The Complete Poems, The Complete Letters*
Richard Sewell, *The Life of Emily Dickinson*
The Oxford Companion to the Bible

Habakkuk and Romans

PETER SCHJELDAHL

As it is written, "the just shall live by faith."

ROMANS 1:17, CITING HABAKKUK 2:4

Is this not a joyous exchange—the rich, noble,
pious bridegroom Christ takes this poor, despised,
wicked little whore in marriage, redeems her of all
evil, and adorns her with all his goods?

MARTIN LUTHER

"Not my will but Thine be done."

JESUS PRAYING, LUKE 22:42

Martin Luther loomed in my small-town boyhood. He often wore monk's robes, which confused me. I realize only now that I had monks mixed up with convicts. But I believed what I was told, that Luther loved children in a special way. He was like a reliably benevolent, vaguely sinister uncle who breezes in the door with dazzling heartiness and a mysterious, cold smell about him. Luther vanished from my consciousness along with God when at the first high tide of puberty I became an atheist in nothing flat. Today, fifty-two years old, I am tired of atheism.

Anyway, Luther. Reentering my mind now, as for the first time I read his writings, he occupies a space that, I find, stayed vacant for the four decades of his absence, as if he held a lease on that matrix of neurons for my lifetime. He is unchanged, though embroidered with grown-up knowledge. He still loves the child in me, his hyperaware face beaming between robes and tonsure.

I have learned that Luther believed fervently in the devil, expected the Second Coming soon, became savagely anti-Semitic, cheered the suppression of peasants who took his message for a call to revolution, and was regularly a hothead who couldn't tell the difference between an honest disagreement and a showdown with the hounds of hell. But even as a kid I knew he was dark.

I did not know that Luther was so good a writer, though I would see his name above the great hymns ("Away in a Manger," we sang with quaking sweetness at Christmas, and "A Mighty Fortress Is Our God," thundering each Sunday). I could not imagine that hymns were "written" by anyone, much less the monk with strange eyes. Now I delight to discover Luther's clarity, audacity, and lyrical compassion, as in his characterization of the human soul: "this poor, despised, wicked little whore" whom suave Christ marries. Luther presents the soul's good luck with chuckling wonderment, as if each of us were Julia Roberts in *Pretty Woman*.

Besides his famous scatology, there is lots of sex in Luther. I remember fighting with Catholic kids who sneered their Church's old line that the Reformation was Luther's trick for keeping his priest job while getting laid—not that I knew what *that* meant. They had a point. It was his own point, in a real way. He deemed it preposterous that God, who made us as we are, wanted us to renounce our human nature in His service. If we are unworthy of God's love, Luther reasoned, God must love us precisely as unworthy beings—not because we're good, but because He is. Were it otherwise, the bloody sacrifice of His Son would not make sense.

He He He. God's super-masculine cast posed a problem for little me. I certainly was not aware of it as a problem, but now I see how it boosted my apostasy the moment a more convincing force declared itself in my groin. Simply, I never encountered a living man—not my father, not among my teachers and preachers—even remotely reminiscent of how God was supposed to be. Women seemed stronger. I got that I was bad in God's eyes, but I had no example from my life of a paternal wrath worth fearing, as a consequence, or a paternal mercy that could be counted on, in the event that I wanted to square myself.

Reading Luther now, I find a satisfying fatherly principle—demanding and loving in the right ratio—along with much else that got lost in transit from Saxony in the sixteenth century to Minnesota in the 1950s. But I also detect a prophetic weakening of patriarchal rigor that may have come with trashing the Pope.

Abandoning the Augustinian order, he took a strong-minded ex-nun, Catherine of Bora, to wife. They lived and made their six children in his former monastery. (When you think about it, this had to give a certain, well, savor to their bedtimes.) Luther seems to have had his own trouble with male prerogative even as he assumed it. There is murmur of guilt-ridden propitiation in his transvestite image of the soul, his own soul, as a pitiable trollop. His Christ is a principle of anxious concern—also passion, active love—for the female.

In one amazing passage, Luther ponders at length the hypothetical case of a woman with an impotent husband. While accepting the rule of husbands, he opens a Chinese-box series of loopholes for wives. The woman with an unperforming mate should seek a divorce. If denied, she should ask to sleep regularly with a relative or friend of her husband, any consequent children to be raised as the husband's. If the husband vetoes that, she should propose to "contract matrimony with someone else, and flee to some distant and unknown region." If turned down again—here a seedling of Ibsen's Nora springs from the Reformer's brow—she should go anyway. Just leave. Martin Luther says it's okay.

Then there is the erotica of a letter to a friend on the occasion of the friend's marriage. "On the evening of the day on which, according to my calculations, you receive this," Luther wrote, "I shall make love to my Catherine while you make love to yours, and thus we will be united in love." Isn't that wild?

What would knowing such things about Luther have done for me at a certain age? It might have scared me to death, I suppose. No one who has come of age since the fifties can imagine how opaque sex could be to an isolated kid back then. I came into sexuality with a sense that I was inventing it. It could have nothing, but nothing, to do with religion. Now I read Luther's words that denying sex is like "preventing nature from being nature, fire from burning, water from being wet." I had no idea.

It was the Renaissance out, a warm front bursting upon northern mists with thunder and lightning. Luther steps into history as a somewhat naive, scholarly polemicist against the Roman Church's sale of indulgences —weasel-worded salvation insurance peddled to yokels for the financing of such things as some ceiling decoration Michelangelo was busy with. If Italian clerics were not so addicted to paintings, I might have had another kind of childhood.

Like an addict, the Church came back at Luther with lazy defensive bullshit, marking time until they killed him—as they meant to and would have but for local political complications. He never got over the shock of encountering, in the Church he had revered, the leer of urbane and lethal Roman cynicism.

In 1517, thirty-three years old, Luther took one of the two actions that excited my imagination as a child. (The other—shying an inkwell at the devil—evidently never happened. Such close encounters with Satan as Luther had were apt to occur not in the hush of the study but amid the stinks of the toilet.) The deed was nailing his *Ninety-Five Theses,* proposing a debate on indulgences, to the door of the Castle Church in Wittenberg. I heard it mentioned often, and it worried me. I didn't know what theses were. The word did not sound interesting, though I liked the big number ninety-five: Luther must have had more theses than anyone! I could understand getting in trouble for pounding a nail in a church door. Such vandalism seemed steep even for a monk/convict.

As I understood it, higher-up monks tried to make Luther feel bad for what he had done. He said, "I cannot and will not recant. Here I stand. I cannot do otherwise. God help me. Amen." He would not say he was sorry about the nail. Things got blurry at that point. The result was that I was a Lutheran, the best thing to be. The Catholic church down the block was bigger, but Catholics worshiped idols, it was said. I couldn't imagine anyone doing that. I thought that if they tried to make me worship an idol, they would have to kill me first. I daydreamed about how gloriously I would die.

"No one is sure of the reality of his own contrition," begins the thirtieth of the *Theses.* When I read that recently, I drew a box around it and dog-eared the page, it revolted me so much. It reminded me that I have a long-standing beef with Lutheranism, for which I used to be sure I had Luther to blame. "Every man his own priest," he said elsewhere. He kept hitting that awful point of the soul's solitude before God: needing only grace, but with no one and nothing to aid or confirm the transaction.

As a kid and then an adolescent, I was lonesome enough already, thanks. It may have been refreshing for Luther, sprung from the monk barracks, to feel on his own, but I wanted tender loving reassurance. Church socials and groups—our teenage auxiliary the Luther League, hilariously militant name for the sorriest bunch of acne breeders imaginable —didn't avail.

I envied the Catholic kids. I admit it! They had an earthy glee and an unbuttoned sorrow for which I thought I felt distaste, but it was more than half longing. Later, Jews transfixed me. I learned from the radio and from our snowy television set that in New York people had invented an incredibly funny way of talking. I thought it was special broadcast talk, and when on my first day in New York, years later, I heard that sound on the street, I couldn't believe it.

Any sort of family where people yelled at each other and laughed together made me ache like a ragamuffin outside a bakery window. Blacks, Italians, Greeks, and Hispanics took turns sending waves of vicarious warmth across the clammy porcelain of what I took be my Lutheran soul. How much did I hate Lutheranism? How much can you hate anything?

I see now that the source of my malaise was an emotionally pinched second-generation immigrant style that didn't match up with anything vital in postwar America. Add the effects of a mean small town on a hypersensitive, grandiose misfit, and you have me. It wasn't Martin Luther. It was a frosty Norwegian mentality only partly thawed in the melting pot of mass culture.

In 1956, Elvis Presley came on the Ed Sullivan Show. My grandmother Lena said, "Disgusting!" When Elvis finished, I started walking to my friend Richie's house. Richie was walking toward my house, and we met halfway. I asked what he thought. He said he didn't know and asked what I thought. I said I didn't know. Together we confronted the new America, two stunned loiterers on Oak Street in Farmington, Minnesota.

In that moment, it became too late for me to be impressed by the knowledge, which I did not have, that Martin Luther loved singing, eating, drinking, cardplaying, and good times generally. Rebellion became my job in life. Every value I had received got turned upside-down, becoming a sign of the obsolete, common, and stupid. I still stumble on debris of that inversion. When my wife took up gardening a few years ago, I hated some of her choices—peonies, lilacs, lily of the valley—that turned out on reflection to be standard tastes of yard gardens in my childhood. Now I am relieved to acknowledge that something my parents liked can be, after all, perfectly lovely.

Anyway, Luther. I wish I could have gotten my Lutheranism straight from him. He really was terrific with kids, apparently. They were at the core of his ardor for Christmas. He more or less invented the modern Christmas, complete with the lighted tree. The moment of God becoming flesh was Christianity's central miracle for him. He seemed almost to prefer the humanity to the divinity of Jesus. The doubts of Jesus at Gethsemane moved him at least as much as the Resurrection, and the Baby Jesus in the stable—a site smelling of animal shit, hence in devil's face—moved him most of all. I would have liked having Luther talk to me about the Baby Jesus.

Luther's was a worldly religion, leaving the fearful Middle Ages for a life of enjoyment and service to others. He aimed to relieve the Christian's anxiety about salvation—funny how that got turned around, giving me the opposite impression—and thus to make goodness gratuitous, a gift freely received and given. He was doctrinaire, a theological policy wonk in his incessant fine tuning, but pointedly never moralistic. "Life is as evil among us as among the papists, thus we do not argue about life but about doctrine," he said to caution his followers against self-righteousness.

Luther declined huge opportunities of political power. German historians lament his lost chance to unify Germany into a modern state three centuries before Bismarck. But he was about bettering the world soul by soul, not changing it.

Luther was a friend of great artists, of Dürer and the Cranachs. In the

Frick Collection you can see Holbein's late portrait of him as a grumpy-looking bourgeois, his mood perhaps owing to the physical ills that plagued his last years.

As an intellectual debating with Erasmus, he was the archetype of a democratic plain speaker calling down an academic mandarin.

Modern thinkers have not known how to cope with him. Heinrich Heine tried to consign him to ancient history by means of praise: "It would be unseemly to complain of the limitations of his views. The dwarf who stands on the giant's shoulders can indeed see farther than the giant himself, especially if the dwarf puts on his spectacles. But notwithstanding our broader perspective, we miss that lofty intuition and giant's heart, which we cannot acquire."

In one respect, it is too bad that Luther would not stay in the past that the Jewish Heine so generously upholstered for him.

I refer to Luther's unforgivable anti-Semitism, no merely ambient prejudice of the time but a personally evolved conviction. It grew from his resentment of Jewish imperviousness to Christian conversion. Early on, he had seemed friendly to Jews, noting repeatedly that Jesus was Jewish and brushing off the medieval view of Jews as Christ-murderers. By the end of his life, he was urging civil authorities to burn synagogues. Four centuries later, his words appeared in Nazi propaganda.

Woefully, Luther's anti-Semitism had roots in the core of his theological revolution.

The key Bible verse for Luther is Romans 1.17: "For [in the Gospel] is the righteousness of God revealed, as it is written, 'The just shall live by faith.' " Not often quoted is the preceding verse, Romans 1.16: "For I am not ashamed of the Gospel: it is the power of God for salvation to every one who has faith, to the Jew first and also to the Greek." "To the Jew first" Luther did associate evangelism, and Jewish resistance enraged him, seeming to him proof of the devil's mobilization in the Last Days.

With the scalpel of justification by faith, honed on Paul's epistles,

Luther excised the spiritual primacy of the Catholic Church, relocating the whole mystery of this world and the next in the simple self-surrender of the individual. This Copernican shift spawned all manner of chaos, some of which horrified Luther and some of which, through hating parties who would not go along with it, he himself fomented. Luther generally accepted chaos as a prophesied, natural precondition of Christ's return.

Luther derived the ideology of faith from Paul, who reveals its Ur source in the Hebrew minor prophet Habakkuk. The verse cited in Romans 1.17 (and again in Galatians 3.11, ". . . we read, 'he shall gain life who is justified through faith' ") is Habakkuk 2.4: ". . . the righteous man shall live by his faithfulness." It comes in a context that feels very Lutheran.

Habakkuk reports an oracle in which he complained bitterly to God of the apparent triumphs of evil in the world. "Why dost thou let me see such misery, / why countenance wrongdoing?" In answer, God promises a reckoning, "a vision for the appointed time. / At the destined hour it will come in breathless haste, / it will not fail." The mark of that time will be the justification of the righteous by faith.

Confronting evil is what faith is for, the Book of Habakkuk suggests. Though indirectly, Luther makes more of this point—in a way, he makes everything of it—than Paul does. He binds Paul more closely to his Hebrew roots than Paul bound himself. From Habakkuk to Paul to Luther to us, the faith doctrine has to be the greatest three-cushion shot in theological history. It dazzles me. Moreover, I feel that it is true.

The good and bad of Luther come down to his identification, with Habakkuk, of faith as the power specific to fighting evil, which was absolutely embodied for Luther in the devil. We can't get around Luther's conviction on this point, so upsetting to modern sensibilities. Preenlightenment, with one foot in the medieval, Luther was on intimate terms with faith's tireless enemy.

Satan gave Luther an explanation of anguish and misfortune among the faithful, solving the problems of both Habakkuk and Job. It is only reasonable, he pointed out, for the devil to be most exercised where faith is strongest, not among the already fallen. To be closer to God is to be more a target of the Evil One. Luther recommended an attitude of familiar contempt, a sort of antiprayer, toward that hounding, implacable power. His more spirited sallies against Satan come down quite literally to this: ''Eat shit.''

Again, when growing up Lutheran, I had no idea. As I recall, the pastors of even our fairly conservative synod were evasive in references to the Prince of Darkness. I don't think the devil was ever real to me, even for a moment. I take this as a sign that Lutheranism was terminally denatured by the time it tried to take my young soul in hand.

It is a stretch to regret the modern ebbing of Satan to fundamentalist fringes of Christianity. As seen in Luther himself, devil-belief has a way of attaching sooner or later to people who annoy the believer. It can be homicidal. And yet, there is an ''and yet.''

Don't we suffer from a catastrophe of watery modern humanism that lacks a theory of evil? Between ''blaming the victim'' and indicting ''the system,'' we move evil around at abstract distances from ourselves, and evil thrives. Aren't we tired of dutiful, scrupulous, therapeutic conscience, trying to overcome in our heads a fundamental sense that something is wrong with us?

Reading Luther, I get hints of something salvageable from the wreck of Lutheranism for the cure of my own soul. It is Luther's sense of evil and redemption. He downplayed original sin and had no truck with predestination. With Paul, he deemed humans sinful by dint of the Law, the Old Testament standards, that are beyond any human's capacity to live by. So God, with one hand, all but ordains humans to sin. With the other hand he reaches down to the ''wicked little whore,'' to pluck up. Luther's point is that only by being lost do we come into God's saving hand at all.

I can't be a Lutheran. I can't even be a Christian, or anything else that starts with a capital letter. The Bible is fiction for me, though fiction with rays of light leaking through it. No religion is believable that does not explain actual life in the contemporary world. This leaves the field today to sects that posit hostility between believers and things as they are. Being inclined, with Luther's approval, to enjoy the world, I won't have that. My theory of evil must be personal.

Evil was always at work in me, from early childhood, because I am human. Being human, I am capable of faith and may by that means, and through no other merit, find grace.

I have a snapshot of myself aged twelve or so with backpack and cold-weather gear, about to head off to a Boy Scout camp. My frightened eyes in the picture seem to foresee that the camp will be a nightmare, but I am grinning gamely and snapping off the three-fingered Scout salute. That is some sad kid, whose gaze meets the gaze of a sadness unchanged in me. But what intrigues me is the kid's eagerness to be a bright and shining camper.

I recall a Luther League retreat, around the same time, where we each threw a twig into a fire to signify our self-abandonment to God. I threw my twig with fierce, rather hysterical devotion, hysterical probably because I already knew that it was no soap. I would choose myself, my sexual and willful being, over God, an inevitable choice under the circumstances, but accursed.

Luther persuades me that my very eagerness to measure up, my will to be good as well as somehow splendid, explains what is unhappy and destructive in my life. It has been my Law, which condemns me. All the while in my ear has come the whispering of the Deceiver, egocentrism, counseling anger and despair. There is a solution. It resides in the prayer of Jesus at Gethsemane after he has succumbed to fear, as a human being like us, and has begged to be released from His destiny. He says, ''Not my will but Thine be done.''

The prayer works whether I am sure of God's existence or not. Paul assumed belief but emphasized faith, which is different. You can have faith while waiting to believe. There is no time limit on the wait, not even death. Faith lives outside time, as nearby as my heartbeat.

SOURCES

My main sources are the biography *Luther: Man Between God and the Devil* by Heiko A. Oberman, 1982, trans. Eileen Walliser-Schwarzbart, New York: Image/Doubleday, 1992, and *Martin Luther: Selections from His Writings,* ed. John Dillenberger, New York: Anchor/Doubleday, 1952. I must also acknowledge William James's *The Varieties of Religious Experience,* which I read only recently and whose wisdom in general and quotations from Luther in particular had a very big effect on me. Thanks to David Rosenberg for illuminating Habakkuk. This essay is dedicated to J.G.

Gospels

E L I Z A B E T H   H A R D W I C K

We are asked, those of us collected here in *Communion,* to reflect upon some book or story or other commanding aspect of the Old or the New Testament, or both. I thought to challenge myself by directing my thoughts to the figure of Jesus, rather than to contemplate other biblical moments that have a narrative and psychological interest to me, such as the rape of Tamar or certain "amusing" details in the Widow Ruth's seduction, if that is an acceptable word, of the rich, old Boaz. With a sense of jumping into a pit of indiscretion deepened by ignorance, I have chosen the life of Jesus Christ, or perhaps we can speak of it as his career or calling, self-chosen or ordained by God—in any case a record notable for concentration of mind and talents put to use.

I hoped it might be of some instruction, at least to me, to think of this Divine, Son of God, Messiah: all that he is to the many

Christians throughout the world and all that he claims to be to non-Christians. Believers and nonbelievers are never to be rid of the daunting statistical success of the Other. Jews, Christians, and Moslems live eternally in a communion, in many respects a communion of dissent, with the Jews reigning under the law of primogeniture and, after Jesus, Mohammed the combative younger son.

It is one thing to read here and there in the Bible for whatever purpose is at hand, be it as a source of faith, consolation, inspiration, mystery, or to read the books as "living literature" divided into the rhetorical modes of composition. But it is quite another matter to make a composition of whatever thoughts occur to one. There lies folly, and most of all, banality: the twin born when one tramples on the ground where so many have labored to bring forth knowledge, fact, imagination, and much else. The long centuries of biblical study, the commentaries, the dating, if possible, the authorship, the anthropology, archaeology, the excruciating demands of Hebrew, Aramaic, and the curriculum listing known as New Testament Greek. Lack of mastery of these labors is not a deterrent to reading the Bible, but a deterrent to expressing what you find therein.

Preachers and pastors read out, without much show of anxiety, one or another of the opaque texts and expound for a few minutes before moving on to moral advice for those gathered in the pews, reflections on the current state of the secular landscape, anecdotes, real or imaginary, about "running into a fellow who told me . . ." So it goes or so it went in the various Protestant denominations I have had cause to drop in on. There are hymns drifting out into the Sunday morning air, and, of course, the offertory, the collection of quarters and dollars for the maintenance of the church and staff. Perhaps a new organ is needed or a new furnace, reminding us that the House of God is also a house. There are needs for foreign missions and nowadays the "global mission" of the evangelists for bringing them the heathen or the doctrinally misguided or fallen away, bringing them to Christ by the most expensive and extensive electronic possibilities. The hymns often make the most striking impression. For one brought up in the Christian faith, history seems to run from "Away in a Manger" to "The Old Rugged Cross."

In the Christian faith, the birth of Jesus is celebrated on Christmas Day and the year is given as A.D. 1, the beginning of the Christian Era. Scholars would set the date between 8 B.C. and 4 B.C., calculated by the time of Herod and other historical data. The designation of December 25 as the month and day was not set until centuries later. Whenever the birth may have been in historical time, the circumstances were exceptional and miraculous since Jesus was born to a virgin, his mother, named Mary. The child was conceived not by Mary's husband, Joseph, but by the Holy Ghost. And marvelous was the Coming far and wide. A star in the East led Herod's three wise men to "O Little Town of Bethlehem" and, instead of following Herod's commission, they fell down to worship the child and to deliver gifts of gold, frankincense, and myrhh. That is the story in the Gospel of Matthew. In Luke's Gospel, an angel of the Lord appears to the shepherds in the field, watching their flocks by night. The angel's message was: "For unto you is born this day in the city of David, a Savior, which is Christ, the Lord." This is the moment of "Hark, the Herald Angels Sing." The humble circumstances of birth by Immaculate Conception have a charming, sentimental endurance in the crèche, with its leaves and twigs, sometimes a lamb, the wise men and the shepherds. And, of course, the Babe in a cradle watched over by the Virgin Mary.

Jesus was circumcised in the Jewish tradition. And then there is a gap in which he seems to have little time for childhood with the family. We find him at the age of twelve running away on his own, as it were, troubling his parents until they meet up with him. He has, he tells them, "been about my Father's business," that is disputing with the scholars in the Temple, showing in his reasoning a special intellectual force, that of a prodigy with a challenging confidence.

He was baptized by the wandering prophet John the Baptist, who deferred to him, you might say, as a superior, the one who would be Our Savior, the Messiah. Then the progression of the life moved into tragedy with the Agony in the Garden and the gruesomeness of the Crucifixion—the nails, the thirst, the blood. He was crucified by the Roman governor, Pilate, and mocked as the King of the Jews. (The poet Robert Graves wrote a naughty novel called *King Jesus* in which he asserts that Jesus did in fact want worldly power and thus was both a religious and civil disturbance.)

Crucifixion was common in the ancient world and perhaps the populace could accept that the state, Roman, along with doubting Jews, would exact the ultimate punishment, the death sentence, not always alarming to Americans in our own day. In the New Testament, the horror of the Crucifixion is mitigated by Christ's escape from the tomb, a rising from the dead to appear to Mary Magdalene, his mother, Mary, and to the Disciples. After, in a pastel scene of blue skies and light he ascended into heaven to sit on the right hand of God the Father, from whence he would come to judge the living and the dead.

The martyrdom and Resurrection are the heart and soul of the Christianity that spread through Rome and beyond. The Resurrection of a particular prophet, Jesus, is the everlasting conflict between Jews and Christians. My telling of the story here is of obvious crudity, lack of precision and narrative detail, not to mention true knowledge of the Bible itself and the great store of critical examination and interpretation. The telling is not far from that given to me by innocent, only casually knowledgeable, ladies in the Bible Study classes of the Presbyterian church I attended.

As Jesus goes about his life among his brothers, and some think a sister, he does not appear to be interested in the singular fact of having been born of a virgin, if indeed he knew of the claim that would be made after his death in the picturesque accounts of the Nativity in Matthew and Luke. Still, a virgin birth, so violently contrary to the experience of the rural world of Jesus and, of course, before that and after, is the first of the inexplicable events in the New Testament chronicle of the life and deeds of the Messiah. However, the querulous and the questioning are nearly always at hand as the incredible is revealed to us in the Scriptures.

Mary herself, a modest Jewish woman, had much reason to wonder at the time of the Annunciation: in the Gospel of Luke, the angel Gabriel appears to her to announce: "Hail, thou art highly favored, the Lord is with thee; blessed art though among women." Mary was "troubled" by the greeting and "cast in her mind what manner of salutation this should be."

The angel proceeds with the spectacular nature of the child that is to be born to Mary. "He shall be great, and shall be called the Son of the Highest; and the Lord shall give unto him the throne of his father David. And he shall reign over the house of Jacob forever, and of His kingdom there is no end."

Mary asks: "How shall that be, seeing I know not a man?" The angel explains that the Holy Ghost shall overshadow her and that "the holy thing that shall be born of thee shall be called the Son of God." Without wishing to sound too contemporary a note, perhaps to be *overshadowed* by the Holy Ghost is as near as we can come to a somewhat realistic notion of man and woman in the act of conception.

The virgin birth had, like so much of the New Testament, its roots in the Hebrew Bible: Isaiah 7:14. "Behold, a virgin shall conceive, and bear a son, and shall call his name Immanuel." In addition, remember that Jehovah can confound common experience at the other end of the scale in the birth of Isaac to Abraham and Sarah when they were "old and stricken with age, and it had ceased to be with Sarah after the manner of women." In all parts of the Bible, the way of nature, here so nicely expressed in "it had ceased to be with Sarah after the manner of women," can be overwhelmed when the divine purpose is at stake.

Charismatic prophets, the founders of religions, and of contemporary cults of meager distinction, act and pronounce with outstanding presumption; this is their mission, their inclination, and sometimes their profession. Jesus was indeed the object of much astonishment in his claims to the grandest elevation in his personal being and in the supernatural powers by which he embodied the claims. The news of his precocity and of his miracles spread about and again we find him in a synagogue amid the village skeptics. The Gospel of Mark records the scene and the questions: "From whence hath this man these things? and what wisdom is this which is given unto him, that even such mighty works are wrought by his hands?"

The questioners knew Jesus as a neighbor, more or less, and thus they speculate: "Is not this the carpenter, the son of Mary, the brother of James, and Joses, and of Judah, and Simon? and are not his sisters here with us?" The answer given by Jesus is perhaps evasive, although it is delivered in words of wisdom: "A prophet is not without honour, but in his own country, and among his own kin, and in his own house."

On the matter of life after death, personal resurrection, the Sadducees confront Jesus with a conundrum of simple practicality. They tell of a man who dies leaving no children. According to custom, the brother is to take the wife, but he too dies, leaving no seed. At last all seven brothers have taken the wife and left no seed and she too dies. Should there be life after death, they want to know, whose wife she shall be of them, for the seven have had her to wife. Jesus rather wearily explains that in heaven there is no marriage, no giving in marriage.

With Jesus we are far away from the infinite "begats" of the Hebrew Bible. Jesus, as a prophet of luminous dominance, seeks followers who give up all to follow him. The rigid structure of families tilling the soil, the generations with their duties and privileges, the intensity of blood bonds and attachment to familiar places, all of this is hostile to the evangelistic spirit governing the primitive Christians. The converted are to be brothers and sisters in Christ.

Still, the vehemence of Christ's messages on the matter is quite striking in Matthew: "Think not that I am come to send peace on earth; I come not to send peace, but a sword. For I am come to set a man at variance with his father, and a daughter against her mother, and the daughter-in-law against her mother-in-law . . . He that loveth mother and father more than me is not worthy of me." The severance from the family is in great part a necessary severance from the Jewish faith. Later in the practice of the Roman Catholic Church perhaps we can say that the Adoration of the Virgin unites the sanctity of mother and child.

The Sadducees were troubled by the domestic arrangements to be adjudicated in the densely populated hereafter promised by Jesus. We note that the word "home" is in popular use for the Kingdom of Heaven, popular particularly among the fundamentalists. The preacher Oral Roberts, grieving about the insufficient financial support for his various colleges, schools, and churches, climbed up on the steeple of the church and threatened to stay there until "God calls me home." He at length, or in short, at last came back down to his usual home or homes.

There is the resurrection for the multitudes firm in faith and, in a different tone, the original Resurrection of Christ as the sign of possible redemption from sin for the righteous. We find a rather forlorn Paul in his journeys forced, like a teacher facing over and over an unlettered class, to insist on the absolute centrality of the doctrine of the Resurrection. "But if there is no resurrection of the dead, then Christ is not risen." And "if Christ is not risen, then is our preaching vain, and your faith also vain."

The end of the world is at hand. The brilliant, perfervid poetry of Revelation, the mysterious patterns of seven, the gorgeously fluent imagery of destruction for many and bliss ever after for the faithful and obedient: these foretellings can, we sometimes read in the press, still send folks out into the fields to await the Apocalypse determined by some obscure calculation to arrive on a night in perhaps July or September. They wait and then must gather their goods and return to face the disappointment that was the lot of the Disciples and many early Christians. Others will in time gather with a like expectation. Modern science can produce dire calculations about the uncertain future of our universe, the threats to our planet, but such theories or knowledge arise from an abandonment of Creationism, the story in Genesis in which God created heaven and earth. Mathematics, physics, and astronomy have a beauty of their own as an exercise of human intelligence; still it is easy to see why many cling to the beauty of: *let there be light and there was light.* "Literalists," as the fundamentalists, Pentecostals, and other denominations name themselves, take upon themselves a task to be master of allegory, symbol, the outrageousness of myth, the ambiguity of narrative which is the wonderful freedom of imagination in the Scriptures. For the rest of us, perhaps the Holy Books from Genesis to Revelation may be thought of as literally *wondrous.*

I have dealt here, sketchily indeed, with some of the "problems" occasioned by the happenings and assertions in Christ's mission. For contemporary Protestants of a liberal theological leaning one sees a movement away from the divinely mysterious in favor of an egalitarian Christ. Blessed are the poor, blessed are the meek, suffer the little children, drive the money-changers from the Temple. The miracles of rescue, the healing of the halt and the blind, the feeding of the hungry, the "embrace," if you will, of the sinner Mary Magdalene—all of this, along with the splendor of such parables as the Prodigal Son and the Good Samaritan are a balm for the sons and daughters of the Enlightenment. Also, the Hebrew Bible and the New

Testament are rich in ethical grandeur that can, if you wish, supersede the incomparably imaginative improbabilities. On another level there is the appeal of Renan's *Life of Jesus,* a sentimental, heartthrob account, described with some asperity by Albert Schweitzer as "gentle Jesus on his little donkey."

To account for the spread of Christianity, the historian Gibbon offers, among many other complex conditions, the reaction against the exclusiveness of the Jews by the poor, the ignorant, the criminal, the masses who were gathered in by the Christian message: the Jews "shunned, instead of courting the society of strangers. Christianity, on the other hand, offered itself to the world, armed with the strength of the Mosaic world, and delivered from the weight of its fetters."

Dan Jacobson in his book *The Story of the Story* speaks of the "remorseless retribution of Yahweh," although in the end he finds ways of coming to terms with the tradition. Religion-obsessed Simone Weil, born into a Jewish family, was offended by God's rejection of Saul when he did not exterminate the Amalekites down to the last man; also by the subjection of the people of Canaan. She was attracted to the Roman Catholic Church, but never baptized. Here, again, her contentious nature, or her scrupulosity, rejected the doctrine of "no salvation outside the church," and the fact that certain of the saints approved of the Crusades.

I had these readings in mind as I went through the New Testament, but there one could not overlook the sounding of "Woe unto you!" again and again, the revengeful accent of evangelism. The violence in the Hebrew Bible was not brought to an end by the triumph of Christianity. After the Reformation, the rupture between the Roman Catholic and the Protestant Church was one of the foundations of the bloody disputes in the Thirty Years War. On a lighter note, I read recently of the historian A. J. P.

Taylor's delight in an anecdote about the actress, Nell Gwynn, mistress of Charles II. When she was walking in the streets with some of her colleagues, the police were rounding up Catholics and Nell cried out: "Sirs, I am a Protestant whore."

For myself, I admire many of the English and American dissenters from the Anglican Church. The "inner light" and "covenant of grace" that banished Anne Hutchinson from Massachusetts; Dinah, the wandering preacher in *Adam Bede* who wants to bring "Christ's message to the poor." Then there is Edmund Gosse, an English man of letters, who tells about his father, a distinguished marine scientist of radiant, humble piety. The elder Gosse spent long years to write a long book trying to make fossils, the remains of prehistoric plants and animals, so important in the development of the theory of evolution, agree with the story of creation in Genesis. His notion was that God had created the fossils by design. The poor man's labors were greeted with a derision by his fellow scientists that broke his Christian heart.

In English fiction we have the scandal of the "livings" in the Anglican Church by which members of the landed gentry held the right to appoint curates, village pastors, who would thereby have a secure stipend and a house, the parsonage. Mr. Bennet in *Pride and Prejudice* has to face that his pastoral privileges, not opulent, would go by inheritance to the odious and obsequious Mr. Collins. The novels of Trollope also concern themselves with the "livings," which did not improve the character of the titled who could grant them nor that of the clerics who wished to receive them. The Anglican Church was at last cleansed by dissenters, the distinguished Clapham Group, largely from Cambridge University, and others.

I note in the evangelistic mode of today the stress in the phrase: Do you accept Christ as your *personal* savior? The stress on personal may be securely orthodox since Jesus himself did not preach to institution, clan, or tribe, but to the individual convert. On the other hand, the Jesus who said, *Noli me tangere,* to Mary Magdalene when he appeared outside the tomb is nowadays transmogrified into a tousled, stocking-footed house companion. The bearded ascetic is in the kitchen of a morning, in the afternoon showing preference in the Little League game, forever hearing briefs for parole from the consequences of ordinary mistakes in judgment. He is urged to further wishes for advantage in the mingiest uncertainties of a moment almost two thousand years beyond his own time. Thank you, Jesus! rings out as one of the television evangelists slaps someone on the head and in a hurried miracle pronounces his arthritis or cancer abated. Instead of making us more like Jesus, the evangelists want Jesus ever to be shaped in our own image: foolish, greedy, shallow, trapped in the mundane, there to be beseeched as a partisan in the most vagrant aims of citizen and nation. In God We Trust and even God Bless America are suitable locutions, but the austerity, the loneliness, the mystery of the biblical Jesus is curdled by many of the overheated practices of the contemporary Protestant.

Entering a Protestant Church is much like a visit to a high school auditorium, although some of the older New England churches are of pure, simple, and elegant proportions and design. There was an aesthetic and visual loss when the Reformation countermanded the Stations of the Cross, much of the elaborate ritual of the Eucharist, the great processions in the Roman Catholic Church that mark the liturgical year, Palm Sunday and Easter, especially, also the High Mass at midnight on Christmas Eve. Some of this remains in High Church Episcopalianism, but the Low Church and the dissenting denominations give us a rather utilitarian and sparsely evocative spiritual meeting place and service.

I have attended Easter services in Italy with the knocking on the door before the procession, the priests in their moth-eaten velvets and furs, the release of the dove, or pigeon, from the altar. I have also visited as a tourist some of the grandly eloquent mosques in the Middle East. And I have been in Jimmy Swaggart's compound, perhaps the word for his spread in Baton Rouge, Louisiana, on his first Sunday to appear after his unfortunate lapse into whoring. I can say that I like going to churches, which is not the same as Going to Church.

Amos and James

S C O T T   R U S S E L L   S A N D E R S

Long before I held my own copy of the good book, a gift from the queenly grandmother who wore feathered hats and drove a white Cadillac, the Bible entered me from the air of my childhood as words spoken or sung. Sitting on the bare wooden benches of Methodist churches, I heard ministers quote chapter and verse in country accents, heard choirs chant Psalms and congregations bellow hymns, heard men in starched shirts and women in cotton dresses read the Bible from pulpits as plain as milking stools. At the supper table, head bowed, I heard snatches of scripture offered in thanks for our fragrant food. Alone in bed, on the brink of the dismaying darkness, I murmured every scrap I could remember from God's word.

The word became not flesh but substance for me on my twelfth birthday, when my mother's stepmother, paying a rare visit from

Chicago to our Ohio farm, climbed out of that creamy Cadillac wearing a hat festooned with the downy feathers of quail, and presented me with my first Bible. Zippered shut, bound in fake black leather, no heavier than a meatloaf sandwich, it barely filled my outspread hand. Yet when I tugged at the brass cross that served as the zipper pull, and the book sprang open of its own accord like a set of jaws, I found inside a thousand whispery thin pages containing everything that God had seen fit to say, from the long-ago days when God still spoke in a clear voice.

Now, thirty-seven birthdays later, the onionskin paper baffles my fingers and the minuscule print baffles my eyes. But at age twelve I read the book from cover to cover, a few pages each night, not understanding half of what I read, yet pushing on, line by line, from "In the beginning" to the final "Amen." Although the title page informed me that I was reading the King James version, "translated out of the original tongues," I had no idea whose tongues those were, nor who King James was, unless perhaps a kinsman of Solomon or David. I had no notion that this eerie language, with its thee's and thou's, had come down from the time of Shakespeare. I thought I was eavesdropping on God.

Every now and again I would pause in my nightly reading to gaze at the blank ceiling or the black window, the better to see the ancient stories. I supplied my own geography, using Lake Erie for the Red Sea, the Mahoning River for the Jordan, a sand and gravel pit for the desert, our wooded hills for the mountains of Israel, our garden for Gethsemane. I attributed my fears, my hopes, my hungers to the biblical characters, and I gave them the faces of people I knew.

Amos, for example, that unwilling prophet, "an herdsman, and a gatherer of sycamore fruit," wore the gaunt face of an old farmer named John Sivy, a neighbor of ours, who spoke to me of dirt and crops and salvation while we forked silage into the troughs for his cows. When God uttered warnings through Amos, I heard Mr. Sivy's voice, earnest and gruff, sweetened by the lingering music of his native Swedish: "I will sift the house of Israel among all nations, like as *corn* is sifted in a sieve, yet shall not the least grain fall upon the earth." He was a thrifty man who built his own barns and kept the roofs tight and knew the difference between straight and crooked work, a man who could easily have said, "Behold, I will set a plumb line in the midst of my people Israel: I will not again pass by them anymore." I took the sycamores of Amos to be the same as those that grew along the river bottom on Mr. Sivy's land, their white limbs writhing up through the darker branches of maples and oaks. I could not imagine why anybody would want to gather their fruits, those spiky balls that pricked my bare feet when I walked under the trees. But there were many puzzles in the Bible that I had trouble solving.

To stick with Amos, who strode through my imagination wearing Mr. Sivy's neatly patched overalls, what did he mean by saying on the Lord's behalf that "a man and his father will go in unto the *same* maid, to profane my holy name"? The maid I understood to be one of those servants for rich folks, but I could not decipher the going in unto her. And what did Amos mean by saying, "The virgin of Israel is fallen; she shall no more rise: she is forsaken upon her land; *there is* none to raise her up"? The only virgin I knew about was Mary the mother of Jesus, and I thought the label was part of her name, Virgin Mary, like the Babe in front of Ruth. For that matter, I could not make heads or tails of all those italics, which were scattered over the pages like a trail of bread crumbs that led nowhere: "And ye shall go out at the breaches, every *cow at that which is* before her; and ye shall cast *them* into the palace, saith the Lord." All I really caught hold of in a verse like that was the cow, and the slanty letters made even the cow seem mysterious.

The one italicized word that rang through loud and clear from the pages of Amos was *punishment*. It matched the one emotion that rang out from the hubbub of strange names and the litany of sins: God was angry. God was fed up. God was fit to be tied. God was going to make Israel pay for its wickedness: "Therefore thus saith the Lord; Thy wife shall be an harlot in the city, and thy sons and thy daughters shall fall by the sword, and thy land shall be divided by line; and thou shalt die in a polluted land: and Israel shall surely go into captivity forth of his land.'' Although puzzled by the harlot, the captivity, and the dividing line, I could still hear the terrible fury in this curse. Reading Amos was like listening through the closed door of my bedroom to my parents quarreling. The words were muffled, but the fierce feelings came through.

Why my parents fought is another story, and a long one, featuring too much booze and too little money. For this story, I can only say that their shouts and weeping drove me to scour the Bible at age twelve in search of healing secrets. I was also compelled to read those whispery pages by the onset of a desire I could not name and by the dread of death. The desire gathered in me like a charge of electricity, gathered and gathered until it arced out in a blaze of feeling so bright that I feared others must surely see it, sizzling toward a bush heavy with purple lilacs, toward a hammer gleaming in my father's hand, toward a snorting palomino ridden by a neighbor girl whose blond hair matched the horse's mane, above all toward the girl herself.

What should I do with this intense yearning? ''Hate the evil, and love the good,'' Amos advised me. But how could I tell the one from the other? My body was an unreliable guide, with its craving eyes, itchy fingers, growling belly, and willful cock. In any case, my body was going to die. I learned that with piercing certainty a few months before my grandmother gave me the Bible. While undergoing surgery, I suffered an ether nightmare that would stay with me for over ten years, until I was married and sharing a bed with someone whom I could lay my hand on in the dark. Although the surgery was minor, I nearly died from loss of blood. From the moment I came to, encircled by anxious faces in gauzy masks, I realized that I was temporary, a loose knot that would come untied.

Where could I hide from death? ''Seek the Lord, and ye shall live,'' Amos told me, and Mr. Sivy told me as well. I sought the Lord passionately but also fearfully, because he was so often mad, waving his sword, calling down locusts and flood and fire. During my first journey through the Bible, the God of the Old Testament seemed to me like a peevish giant, hard to please and easily riled. If you were perfect, you might slide by unhurt. Otherwise, look out. This was the God who threw Adam and Eve out of the garden, sent Cain off into the wilderness, drowned almost everything that lived, kept Moses from setting foot in the Promised Land, turned Lot's wife to salt, sucked Jonah into the belly of a whale, buried Job under a blizzard of misery, slaughtered whole tribes, burned up cities, dried up crops, shook the foundations of the earth.

The Psalms were soothing, of course, and like anyone needing ointment for aches I returned to them over and over. But even the Psalms often sounded like cries from the bottom of a well, as though the singers were pleading, Haul me up out of this misery, Lord! At the very end of his prophecy, Amos tossed out a few scraps of comfort, foreseeing a day when the people of Israel would be restored to their land, and the cities would be rebuilt, and the gardens would bear fruit, and the mountains would drip with wine. Yet those five hopeful verses were preceded by one hundred and thirty-nine menacing ones, and that seemed to me about the right proportion for this cantankerous God, who offered an ounce of mercy for a pound of pain.

My church taught me that the history of the Hebrews was a long preparation for the good news of Christ; I know better now, but as a boy I could read their history in no other light. While I crept through the tangles and terrors of the Old Testament, I knew that Jesus was coming, like the promise of spring after a hard winter. But I would not allow myself to skip ahead, so I was well along toward my thirteenth birthday before I reached the New Testament.

From the opening chapter of Matthew, I could sense a change in the divine weather. Storms would break out again later on, especially in the letters of Paul and the Revelation of John, with judgments as dark as any known to Amos or Jeremiah. Before voicing a single threat, however, Matthew told us about the gift of a miraculous baby, who entered the world bearing a name that meant "he shall save his people from their sins."

Although I could not have drawn up a list of my sins, I had no doubt that I needed saving. I suspected there was a flaw in me that caused my father to drink, my mother to fret, my older sister to be lonely, my younger brother to cry. Why else had I almost died from a simple operation? What else but some flaw in me could explain why I was gripped in nightmare by the whirlpool of oblivion? Why else did I wake with fists clenched and cock stiff and tears on my cheeks? What was wrong with me? Jesus would know. Jesus would see through me with his X-ray vision, find the crack in my soul, and mend it with a touch. To read on through the onionskin pages was to be laid bare before the gaze of Jesus; yet only in such nakedness was there hope of healing.

What I drew from that first reading of the New Testament is easier to recall if I pass over the weighty gospels and Paul's bewildering sermons, and if I speak instead about the letter of James, a book so brief that I could hold it all in my head at once. I figured the author was the same person who showed up on the title page of my zippered Bible as King James, and therefore his words must be of uncommon importance. Whoever this James might have been, he knew what I was up against. He knew about death: "For what is your life? It is even a vapour, that appeareth for a little time, and then vanisheth away." He knew how it felt to be split down the middle by doubt: "A double minded man is unstable in all his ways." He knew that a flaw in the soul can lead to family strife: "From whence come wars and fightings among you? come they not hence, even of your lusts that war in your members?"

Lust was the name, I decided, for those desires that gathered in me like electricity, the wild longings that blazed out from me toward lilac or horse or girl. Surely everyone close to me could hear the whine of a turbine in my belly, could see the flicker of sparks beneath my skin, could smell the scorching flesh. Women especially, with their penetrating eyes and delicate noses, would be sure to find me out.

During the visit when she gave me the zippered Bible, my grandmother took us for a drive in her white Cadillac, to show us how, at the push of a button, she could make the car rise on its springs, the better to negotiate our rutted country roads. She wore the quail hat, and it was all I could do to keep from reaching out of the backseat, where I sat with my sister and brother, and stroking those iridescent feathers.

Riding up front, my mother at one point mused aloud, "What on earth can we do about Scott's feet? They've begun to smell dreadfully."

My brother giggled and my sister stared at her lap.

"He should wash between his toes," Grandmother declared, lifting her voice so that I would be certain to hear. "With soap, mind you. Then rinse thoroughly and dry with a clean towel."

"Do you hear that?" Mother asked me sharply, for she had been giving me the same advice for months.

All during those months, I had been scrubbing and rinsing and drying until the skin between my toes was raw. Yet still by the end of each day my feet stank, and so did my armpits and crotch. It was as though a rebellion had broken out in the provinces of my body. James knew about this rebellion of the members, knew about simmering desire: "But every man is tempted, when he is drawn away of his own lust, and enticed. Then when lust hath conceived, it bringeth forth sin; and sin, when it is finished, bringeth forth death." That seemed to be my fate, laid out with the economy of a fortune in a Chinese cookie: You will be overcome by lust, fall into sin, and die. Was there any escape?

Well, James suggested, I could comfort orphans and widows. That was hard advice, because the widows on our back road scared me with their bent loneliness, and the only orphan nearby had been adopted by a carpenter's family, had been smothered in gifts, and finally had run off to California with a banjo player. Well, then, I could love my neighbors as myself. The trouble there was, I had some ornery neighbors—folks who shot deer out of season from the windows of their trailers, wives who cheated on their husbands and husbands who beat their wives, kids who chewed tobacco and kicked their dogs—and besides, I could not very well love my neighbors as myself without first learning how to love myself.

Was there an easier way to save my soul? "If any man offend not in word," James assured me, "the same is a perfect man, and able also to bridle the whole body." I just might manage that. I could guard my tongue, never sass teachers or parents, never swear. When ugly words rose in me, I could seal my mouth and swallow them.

What else could I do? "If any of you lack wisdom," James wrote, "let him ask of God, that giveth to all men liberally, and upbraideth not; and it shall be given him." If there was one thing I lacked, it was wisdom, which I took to be the power to distinguish good from evil, and to choose the good. "Resist the devil," said James, "and he will flee from you. Draw nigh to God, and he will draw nigh to you. Cleanse your hands, ye sinners; and purify your hearts, ye double minded." I could more easily imagine drawing nigh to this God of the New Testament, who would not fly off the handle at the least little sin, than to the peevish giant of the Old Testament. I could risk praying to a God who was not armed to the teeth with floods and plagues and thunderbolts. Pray, then, said James, for "the prayer of faith shall save the sick, and the Lord shall raise him up; and if he have committed sins, they shall be forgiven him."

Here was the medicine for me. Here was the balm I drew from James, and more generally from the New Testament, the assurance that within me and beyond me, embracing my flawed, wavering, temporary self, there was an enduring and generous Power: "Every good gift and every perfect gift is from above, and cometh down from the Father of lights, with whom is no variableness, neither shadow of turning." Because my own life was shot through with darkness, I hungered for a God without shadow. Reading on beyond James, seeking a pound of mercy for my ounce of pain, I decided that Jesus had come to redeem not only us mortal sinners but also that old inscrutable tyrant.

Eight years passed before I read the Bible again from cover to cover, beginning on the first day of January 1966. By then I was twenty, a junior in college, a year away from having to choose either jail or exile or Vietnam. If my first reading had been provoked by family turmoil, dread of death, and fear of my own rebellious body, my second reading was provoked by history. The personal drama of sin and salvation still played inside me, but it had been shoved onto a back stage by the public drama of civil rights marches, antiwar rallies, the burning of draft cards and bras, sit-ins at nuclear weapons factories, environmental protests, bombings on campuses, riots in the cities, body counts on the nightly news. How should I live my precious life in the face of so much confusion and suffering and need? What should I study? What work should I do? How should I answer when Uncle Sam called me to go fight in that wretched war? And where did that *should* come from?

Those were the questions that weighed on me as I trekked once more, line by line, from "In the beginning" to the final "Amen." For that second reading I put away my grandmother's Bible, which now seemed childish in its zippered jaws of fake black leather, quaint in its Jacobean English. Instead, I bought *The Oxford Annotated Bible,* a hefty volume that offered the Revised Standard Version in a padding of headnotes, footnotes, indexes, historical surveys, and maps. The translation was more dependable, yet I could not help finding this modern English, stripped of *thee*'s and *thou*'s, to be rather bland by comparison with the version approved by King James. That the Bible was a translation, not a transcript of God's own speech, would have been news to me at age twelve. At twenty, I realized that the Bible was a ramshackle anthology, the work of many hands and centuries, bearing human stains on every page. By age twenty, I realized that God was not a bearded man in the sky, neither Lord nor Father, nothing that would fit inside the mind's frames, but instead the source and urge of everything.

During the eight years since my first reading, I had solved some biblical puzzles. I had learned, for example, that the Middle Eastern sycamore was in fact the humble fig, not the gigantic tree with white branches gleaming along riverbanks in Ohio; so now I could understand why Amos gathered sycamore fruit. Although I had still not slept with a woman, I knew what it meant for a man and his father to go in unto the same maid, and I knew the distinction between virgin and harlot. I had figured out that when Amos railed against cows, he meant selfish women "who oppress the poor, who crush the needy," and not the harmless Holsteins I used to milk in Mr. Sivy's barn.

This time when I read Amos, I did not think of Mr. Sivy. I thought of Martin Luther King, Jr., with his prophet's voice so much louder and richer than the old Swedish farmer's, his face and body so much more expressive of holy anger. "Take away from me the noise of your songs," I could imagine Dr. King saying,

> to the melody of your harps I will not listen.
> But let justice roll down like waters,
> and righteousness like an ever-flowing stream.

When the God of Amos denounced Israel

> because they sell the righteous for silver,
> and the needy for a pair of shoes—
> they that trample the head of the poor into the dust

of the earth,

and turn aside the way of the afflicted,

I heard the resonant, grieving voice of Dr. King rising from the steps of the Lincoln Memorial or a dusty road in Mississippi or a jailhouse in Alabama.

Although I could locate on the maps in my Oxford Bible all the nations condemned by Amos, I was not interested in their ancient quarrels; the only country I brooded on was my own. The indictment of Israel sounded in my ears like a judgment on my wicked tribe:

Behold, I am setting a plumb line

in the midst of my people America;

I will never again pass by them;

the high places of Washington shall be made

desolate,

and the sanctuaries of New York shall be laid waste,

and I will rise against the house of Johnson with the

sword.

My own people seemed to me guilty of every sin cataloged by Amos: wars against the weak, neglect of the poor, sexual dalliance, drunkenness, empty religious ceremony, ostentatious wealth, taking of bribes, cheating in business, idolatry, injustice, greed. If the God of the prophets was still keeping track, there would be hell to pay for so much wickedness. The editors of the Revised Standard Version had gotten rid of all those bewildering italics, yet even without extra emphasis the word *punishment* still rang out from the pages of Amos like a furious refrain.

At age twenty I had not lost my fear of the grumpy tyrant who vowed to slash, burn, enslave, and exile his unruly subjects. But I had come to recognize the tyrant as only one face of the Old Testament God, the image that a belligerent people would see when they looked in the mirror. Alongside the warrior chief, obsessed with rules and obedience, there was also the extravagant creator, raining equally on the just and the unjust, pouring forth the universe in grand indifference to our small doings. Amos knew this larger God, who

> forms the mountains, and creates the wind,
> and declares to man what is his thought;
> who makes the morning darkness,
> and treads on the heights of the earth.

In one magnificent passage, Amos caught both aspects of God, creator and destroyer:

> He who made the Pleiades and Orion,
> and turns deep darkness into the morning,
> and darkens the day into night,
> who calls for the waters of the sea,
> and pours them out upon the surface of the earth,
> the Lord is his name,
> who makes destruction flash forth against the strong,
> so that destruction comes upon the fortress.

So long as Amos was calling down destruction on neighboring countries, no one challenged him. But when he turned his sights onto Israel and its king, the high priest Amaziah rebuked him. "O seer," said Amaziah, "go, flee away to the land of Judah, and eat bread there, and prophesy there; but never again prophesy at Bethel, for it is the king's sanctuary." Amos fired right back: "I am no prophet, nor a prophet's son; but I am a herdsman, and a dresser of sycamore trees, and the Lord took me from following the flock, and the Lord said to me, 'Go, prophesy to my people Israel.' ''

When I read that exchange, I pictured Dr. King on the White House steps, preaching against the war in Vietnam, against the nuclear arms race, against racism and poverty and greed, against politicians and bosses who presided over so much cruelty and waste; then I pictured Dean Rusk or Robert McNamara or some other minion of President Johnson rushing outside to say, "Beat it, preacher, go deliver your message in some other country." Amos did not back down, and neither did Martin Luther King. A year after I graduated from college, Dr. King would be murdered in Memphis, the city of my birth. But in 1966 he still had a life to lose, and he kept risking that life by carrying the call for love into the precincts of hatred.

Would I have the courage to follow my own conscience when the summons arrived from my draft board? I knew that I could be trained to fight, and there were causes for which I would have fought; but I also knew that the killing of poor farmers in Vietnam was not such a cause. Behind the smoke and fog of politics, those farmers were defending their own land. Trying to imagine them, I recalled John Sivy pacing his fields. While I was away at college, those fields and the surrounding woods and much of my childhood ground had been flooded by a reservoir. Unlike the Vietnamese, I could not blame a foreign invader for uprooting me, yet I could feel some twinge of their anger and pain. To be torn away from one's land, as Amos prophesied that the Israelites would be, seemed to me a terrible punishment, worse even than prison. If I said no to the war, however, and if the draft board refused to consider me as a conscientious objector, I would have to choose between jail and exile.

The farther I read in the Bible that second time through, the more urgently I looked for passages to guide my choice. When I came to the Letter of James, for example, instead of worrying how to fool death or heal my family or save my soul, I focused on how he answered the question, "What causes wars, and what causes fightings among you?"

It was clear that James had in mind quarrels within the early church, doctrinal struggles that would lead to schism after schism during the next two thousand years. Yet his reckoning seemed to apply equally well to the mayhem in Vietnam, the nuclear arms race, and the pitched battles in our cities: "What causes wars, and what causes fightings among you? Is it not your passions that are at war in your members? You desire and do not have; so you kill. And you covet and cannot obtain; so you fight and wage war." Reading those lines at age twenty, I concluded that the root of violence was not the longing to touch, for which I had felt so guilty at age twelve, but the longing to possess. Possess what? Power and prestige, said James, but above all wealth.

Like his master Jesus, James was tough on the rich, because they took more than their share of the earth's bounty, because their luxury came out of the hides of the poor, and because they fancied their wealth would shield them against suffering and death. Think again, said James: "For the sun rises with its scorching heat and withers the grass; its flower falls, and its beauty perishes. So will the rich man fade away in the midst of his pursuits." When James called for us to "be doers of the word, and not hearers only," he took as his prime example service to the poor: "If a brother or sister is ill-clad and in lack of daily food, and one of you says to them, 'Go in peace, be warmed and filled,' without giving them the things needed for the body, what does it profit? So faith by itself, if it has no works, is dead."

To live our faith and not merely proclaim it, according to James, we should comfort the afflicted, befriend the lonely, house the homeless, speak the plain truth to all people, refrain from judging others, and never kow-tow to the rich: "Has not God chosen those who are poor in the world to be rich in faith and heirs of the kingdom which he has promised to those who love him? But you have dishonored the poor man. Is it not the rich who oppress you, is it not they who drag you into court?''

Not long after I finished that second reading of the Bible, my draft board threatened to drag me into court, unless I agreed to wear a uniform and carry a gun. I refused. I wrote a letter explaining my reasons, quoting Amos and Jesus and James, quoting George Fox and Thoreau, Gandhi and Martin Luther King. I told the draft board I would mop floors in a mental hospital, tutor children in a ghetto, ladle out meals in a soup kitchen, but I would not help kill peasants in Vietnam. You will report for duty on the date we specify, the draft board answered. My conscience would not let me do that, I told them. Well, then, they replied, your conscience had better get ready for a showdown with a judge.

I did get ready. I underlined with red pencil every passage in *The Oxford Annotated Bible* that supported my pacifism, while ignoring those passages that seemed to justify war. Thus I skipped over the dire warnings in Amos, which sounded so much like the evening news:

> For behold, the Lord commands,
> and the great house shall be smitten into fragments,
> and the little house into bits.

And I skipped over those notorious words attributed to Jesus by Matthew: ''Do not think that I have come to bring peace on earth; I have not come to bring peace, but a sword.'' Instead, I memorized the Sermon on the Mount. I rehearsed Paul's plea for a ''ministry of reconciliation.'' I took to heart the assurance in James that ''the wisdom from above is first pure, then peaceable, gentle, open to reason, full of mercy and good fruits, without uncertainty or insincerity.''

Was I so utterly sincere? the judge might ask. Could I really set my conscience against my country? Were my beliefs so firm? I would confess that I had my doubts. Whereupon the judge might quote James against me, observing that "he who doubts is like a wave of the sea that is driven and tossed by the wind." Yes, I had bobbed on the waves of uncertainty. But if there was any truth to the claims Jesus made about God, I would tell the judge, then we were called to lay aside our weapons and love our enemies, for "the harvest of righteousness," according to James, "is sown in peace by those who make peace."

In the end, I never got the chance to deliver my scripture-laden speeches in court, because the draft board, no doubt weary of my pacifist letters, decided to shut me up. Instead of saying yea or nay to my request for conscientious objector status, they classified me IV-F, the category for those who, by reason of mental or physical defects, must not be drafted under any circumstances. My body was fit for war; only my dissident, Bible-haunted mind was amiss.

My mind is still haunted by the Bible. How many times have I read it through since preparing for my showdown with the judge? Maybe three times, maybe five; I have lost track. Although the cover is scuffed and the paper is jaundiced, I have stuck with my copy of the Oxford edition, if only because so many passages are underlined, first in red pencil, then in green and blue. When I open the book today—as a man married more than a quarter of a century, with two children nearly grown—I still puzzle over death, over my father's drinking and my mother's grief, over sin and salvation; I still brood on war and cruelty and want.

But now in addition to those old concerns I also carry new ones. In James's tirades against the rich, I now hear an ecological indictment as well: "You have lived on the earth in luxury and in pleasure; you have fattened your hearts in a day of slaughter." In Amos's account of judgment day, I now see a foreshadowing of nuclear winter:

"And on that day," says the Lord God,
"I will make the sun go down at noon,
and darken the earth in broad daylight.
I will turn your feasts into mourning,
and all your songs into lamentation."

Here in the second half of life, I wonder less about my small self, more about my species, my planet, and the universe. How have we come to be these divided creatures, split between thinking and wanting? How should we live? On what can we ground our moral judgments? Are they only masks for desire? Are they merely stratagems for fostering our genes? Are they cultural conventions, as flimsy as fashions in clothes? Do we have any direct access to the source of things? Or must we rely on those clumsy guides—scriptures, history, popular opinion? What is the whole show about, if anything, and what is our role in it?

I no longer expect the Bible to yield definitive answers, to these or any other questions. Now I see this book as a record of one worthy tradition in the human search for knowledge, a search that seems to be our essential task. Now I think of God as the other side of the conversation that we have been carrying on with the universe since we learned to talk. Amos knew how we hunger for answers:

"Behold, the days are coming," says the Lord God,
"when I will send a famine on the land;
not a famine of bread, nor a thirst for water,
but of hearing the words of the Lord."

However scarce or abundant, the words of the Lord have never been clear. We have always had to contend with a power that speaks in whispers or thunder, in conundrums or codes. We raise our own voices to make up for the reticence of God. So Amos utters his prophesies; James composes his letter. Along with the many other witnesses in the Bible, they address an elusive One, who appears by turns as a tribal chief, an imperial judge, the Lord of all people, or the Creator of the cosmos.

I no longer have any use for the warrior or ruler or patriarch. I seek only the Creator, "who builds his upper chambers in the heavens," as Amos observed,

> and founds his vault upon the earth;
> who calls for the waters of the sea,
> and pours them out upon the surface of the earth.

From the surface of the earth we look outward and inward, seeking knowledge and more knowledge. "Of his own will he brought us forth by the word of truth," James insisted, "that we should be a kind of first fruits of his creatures." We are not first in time, of course, nor first in importance; but we seem to be first among the creatures in our potential for understanding. So far as we know, we are the only species capable of thinking about the universe as a whole. So far as we know, we alone are able to withdraw from the struggle for survival and the fever of reproduction long enough to gaze back at the source.

The quarrels that James lamented two thousand years ago are still splintering his church; tribal hatred and warfare still grip Amos's neighborhood; the rich still squeeze their wealth out of the hides of the poor; the downtrodden still cry for justice. If you take the brief perspective of recorded history, we seem to be set in our deadly ways. But if you take the long perspective of human evolution, stretching over a few million years, then we appear as a young and fast-learning species. Generation by generation, with many backtracks and wrong turns, we are making ourselves at home in the universe. As our senses of smell, hearing, and vision have evolved in response to the world's odors and sounds and sights; as our scientific models have come to agree more and more exactly with the behavior of nature; so might our moral vision be developing slowly, haltingly, toward congruence with an order that is really *there,* independent of us, in the grain of things.

If Creation began as the great, undivided "I AM," then poured outward into space and time and myriad detail, perhaps we are the frontier of consciousness, the expanding self-awareness of the cosmos. If this is so, then human utterance, in all its forms, would be Creation's way of articulating and celebrating itself. James knew the risk and responsibility that come with the power of speech. "And the tongue is a fire," he wrote. "With it we bless the Lord and Father, and with it we curse men, who are made in the likeness of God." Whether breathed into the air or inscribed on paper or broadcast into the depths of space, our words may curse or bless. The work of language deserves our greatest care, for the tongue's fire may devour the world, or may light the way.

Nehemiah and Matthew

M I C H A E L   D O R R I S

Ostensibly, the Palm Sunday gospel is
a blueprint for disillusion. Jesus and His apostles come to Jerusalem
and crowds celebrate by ecstatically waving fronds of a phony welcome that, within days, turns into an especially nasty execution. Jesus
knows this is going to happen, of course, lays out the highlights to his
apostles at the conclusion of the Last Supper, and then throughout the
text of Matthew's objective and unblinking narrative (Matthew 26:1–
75; 27:1–66), all inexorably comes to pass. As with virtually every
other preordained tragic fate in classical literature, prophecy affords
no protection against the inevitable.

At Louisville's Holy Spirit Roman Catholic Church in the late
1950s, I followed the words of the so-called Long Gospel via my
hand-tooled black calf leather *Saint Joseph Daily Missal*. A gift from my
grandmother on the occasion of my tenth birthday and the envy of my

parochial school classmates, it was a high-status item, the hottest and flashiest prayer book going, its end pages and my full name on the lower left hand corner of the cover embossed in ten-karat gold. According to the accompanying pamphlet,[1] the volume boasted a number of "distinctive features," including: "Latest indulgences—in accordance with the Latest Vatican Edition of the 'Enchiridion Indulgentiarum,' " and "over 40 black and white engravings plus 12 reproductions in *full color*." No major idea or scenario was left unexplicated.

Also included were a special powder blue three-ribboned (as in the Holy Trinity) bookmark "to eliminate the turning of pages when referring back to the Ordinary" and a set of complicated, small-print operating instructions, such as, "If there is a concurrence of Feasts, i.e., one in the Proper of the Season and one in the Proper of the Saints for the same date, consult a diocesan *Ordo*." Presumably, in those days, *Ordos* were always around when you needed them. With its 1,360 pages and weighing in at well over a pound, the *Saint Joseph* was a state-of-the-art how-to/what-to manual, a tome literally to conjure with, a definitive volume with enough far-sight to commence with a date-keyed Table of Movable Feasts (Septuagesima, Corpus Christi, Ascension, etc.) that stretched from 1955 optimistically through 1991.

Rules upon rules: I held in my hand the shorthand of two thousand years of accumulated codified law. But directions were not confined to the liturgy. There were unwritten protocols as well—customary laws or even functional superstitions governing the practice of faith—that somehow I had absorbed, not so cryptic cabala on the ways to *act* while praying in order to gain enhanced effects. And at Mass on Palm Sunday, the buzz went, a true believer could send the soul of one's choice from Purgatory to heaven by standing at full and immobile attention for the duration of the gospel reading.

What thoughts were supposed to pass through my brain, I wonder, when, head bowed over the words of Christ's passion and death, the rest of me sought to remain completely motionless? What were torture, humiliation, and isolation expected mean to a mid-twentieth-century boy in a newly air-conditioned church, a boy raised by three women—a grandmother, an aunt, and a mother—who practiced, by choice or default, the chaste lives of celibate, secular nuns? How did a placid lifestyle whose daily highlights were the "Mickey Mouse Club" and a peanut butter and jelly sandwich in the lunch bag reconcile itself with Middle Eastern scourgings, despair, and agony?

At that age, the sole personal tragedy with which I was even marginally acquainted—my father's Jeep-accident death at age twenty-seven in Europe shortly after the conclusion of World War II—was as pure an abstraction as Christ's torture. I never knew either man, yet the death of one had provided me my status—"the man of the house"—and the sacrifice of the other my putative philosophic stance: Judeo-Christian. The ironic parallels—a boy listening like a stone to the saga of the death of God's Son in order to claim an analogous eternal life for his own fantasy yet undeniably deceased father—were probably too sophisticated for me to appreciate. My quasi-religious, well-coached grief was sentimental, self-congratulatory, activated by the appropriate passages in my missal rather than by some genuine inner empathy or angst, some sense of actual horror drawn from empirical experience. I was an ingenue acting a bit part in a cosmic melodrama, bound by an orthodox script, to an audience that was both unseen and all-seeing. My performance was automatic, pure method, played to the locked Tabernacle. An outwardly passive listener, I was obsessed with my own narrow agenda, all but deaf to larger meaning.

A similar juxtaposition of content and context is recorded in the Old Testament Book of Nehemiah. The Jews, recently returned to their homeland after generations of Babylonian captivity, needed a refresher course on the codes of Moses, the moral laws inherent to leading a proper life.

Accordingly, the people are assembled, commanded to stand—thus, according to Jacob M. Myers's notes in *The Anchor Bible*,[2] inaugurating the practice of believers standing during the reading of Scripture (in my case, the gospel)—and listen "faces to the ground" while priests and Levites told aloud the words of the Law. Those listeners' ordeal—at least a full day's worth of nonstop Torah's greatest mythohistorical hits—makes the half-hour or so of my Palm Sunday gospel seem like a selected short subject, but then, all is relative.

The pedagogical idea, in both cases, is efficient mass aural indoctrination to a specific external order. A commonly held set of values is transmitted through a ritual whereby all members of society are simultaneously exposed to and presumably then internalize identical teachings. The significance of these texts is intensified in a number of ways: the public solemnity of the occasion, emphasized by collective cessation of all other activity; an insistence that the events recounted are not merely practical or logical guides to social intercourse but the exemplary words and deeds of God himself; and the promise of rewards, major and minor, for compliance in the ceremony. The confluence of message and medium constitutes an unusual type of societal opportunity, an extended intermission from mundane concerns with the added ambiance of a cram course. The intensity bars distraction and concentrates the focus of an otherwise disparate aggregate —old and young, men and women, rich and poor—on a record that's, frankly, foreign, bizarre, and scary. The Hebrews learned the consequences of not following the Law and I, the possible downsides of adhering to belief. On the other hand, the plot is so familiar that its deeper gravity is often buried by rote.

And attend we must, we are urged, for the survival of our very civilization is at stake. The alternative to enculturation—anarchy or, conversely, the specter of full assimilation into an alien worldview, i.e., the loss of our people's own hard-won identity—is devastating, unthinkable: either there *is* no ultimate controlling stability, or our ancestors' interpretation of cosmic management—which afforded them great advantage—has become irrelevant and we are no longer special. It's not surprising, therefore, that a congregation offered a straight shot of innately complimentary, though demanding, Truth is willing to be stationary for however long a period of time. The imprinted cultural glossary validates as well as explains, superimposing, the process, the everyday with the fabulous.

The parallels between Nehemiah and Matthew are striking. In both cases, suffering—with the eventual assurance of emancipation and homecoming —dominates much of the ethnohistorical accounts read by the priests. Human victories and triumphs are fleeting, the chroniclers inform us; don't trust them. We, the inheritors either of the early books of the Hebrew Bible or the latter of the New Testament, come from a legacy of captivity, humiliation, betrayal, and despondency. Only through utter confidence in the promise and protection of a divine scheme will we, in the manner of our far more miraculously endowed forebears, prevail. Like the decline of Job magnified to a grand scale, an entire population—or the Son of God himself—had to endure a test of faith by being deprived of all that was valuable and cherished in order to gain it back by stubbornly refusing to consent that apparent reality was in fact real.

This "news" of both Nehemiah and Matthew, moreover, was delivered not in the language or context of its origin but in temporal and linguistic translation, a reminder bulletin from the past aimed at shaping through metaphor and allegory behavior in the present. A formalized, condensed artifact of folklore, this bequest of carefully edited precedent was meant as a directory to conduct that extended far beyond its particularities. The Jews liberated from enslavement were no more likely to suddenly find themselves wandering in the Sinai than I was to have a crown of thorns shoved onto my crewcut head, but we were, all of us, to infer from an articulated antiquity renewed lessons governing our response to everything from predictable minor adversities to the giant, impossible, unavoidable conundrums of mortality and cosmology.

And, like the lollipop at the conclusion of a visit to the pediatrician, there was a prize for good demeanor if we persevered until the priest closed the book. Nehemiah bestows a sort of "Don't worry, be happy" message to his exhausted audience: "Go your way, eat the fat and drink sweet wine and send portions to him for whom nothing is prepared; for this day is holy to our Lord; and do not be grieved, for the joy of the Lord is in your strength." (Nehemiah 8:10) Jesus, also, avers an eventual recommencement of sustenance, albeit after a bleak intermediary period: "Now as they were eating, Jesus took bread, and blessed, and broke it, and gave it to the disciples and said, 'Take, eat; this is my body.' And he took a cup and when he had given thanks he gave it to them, saying, 'Drink of it, all of you; for this is my blood of the covenant, which is poured out for many for the forgiveness of sins. I tell you I shall not drink again of this fruit of the vine until that day when I drink it new with you in my Father's kingdom.' " (Matthew 26:26–30)

I can't say with any authority what Nehemiah's people took away from the preachings to which they were exposed or how they forged a bond between their fallible, average selves and the heroes and heroines of an epic legend. To paraphrase, they were told: You may not recognize this place you have arrived, but it's where you came from, where you should be. Pay close heed because this is how God wants you to act when you're not taking orders from someone else but are in charge of what you do. Don't expect to understand everything right away—file it for reference and adaptation when you need it. You have a fresh chance to be good. There will be no opportunity for questions, no deep analysis, just the facts as they have been revealed to and reported by your predecessors, who accumulated this data at great cost. Now stand still and listen up.

For me, the business of standing still most certainly interfered with my ability to actually hear Matthew. Perhaps that was not accidental. Without a psychological buffer, some mollifying obfuscation, the story is too shattering, too awful in every sense of the word to be comprehended by a child. Brought face to face with treachery, the vicious murder of God, the shaking of even Jesus' faith in redemption, how could I walk out the oaken double doors of Holy Spirit at the end of Mass and resume a normal routine? What did homework matter after the Crucifixion? What dent could I make in the injustice of the universe by brushing my teeth? In balance against the calumnies, insults, and assaults suffered by a gentle, helpless man, I could put on the scale . . . what? Being punctual?

Both those Jews of ancient times and I got a remarkably similar souvenir by which to tangibly recall the experience. "On the second day the heads of the fathers' houses of all the people, with the priest and the Levites, came together to Ezra the scribe in order to study the words of the law. And they found it written in the law that the Lord had commanded by Moses that the people of Israel should dwell in booths during the feast of the seventh month, and that they should publish and proclaim in all their towns and in Jerusalem: Go out to the hills and bring branches of olive, wild olive, myrtle, palm, and other leafy trees to make booths, as it is written." (8:13–15) This fresh exhortation to cleave to the old ways was a palpable link, a symbolic bridge that united past tradition and current custom in a way that sutured the space between and emphasized the "nothing truly changes" model essential to a seemingly irrational attestation to hypothetical continuity.

Catholics in Louisville, more than two millennia later, received a direct legacy from Nehemiah's mandate. Jesus had entered Jerusalem during a major festival, Passover, celebrated with full props, and though we had no obligation to reenact costumed tableaux from the days of Pontius

Pilate, we did come home with a similar kind of mnemonic relic. Palm Sunday was one of the few occasions that parishioners got a door prize: each communicant was presented at the altar rail with a dried, thickly braided palm wand, ideal for tucking behind a living room painting of the Sacred Heart—at our house it hung above the television set—where it remained until, twelve months later, it was replaced by a new one. Palms to us were exotic, tropical, emblems of another time and place far removed from the milieu of shopping centers and Little League baseball—just as the makings of primitive booths must have been to recent residents of metropolitan Babylon.

The meta-message of both events, and others like them, was self-evident. Not only could the future be ensured, but what had been lost could be reclaimed as well. Death was not necessary: neither the unremembered *was* nor the inconceivable *might yet be* need have a significant termination. Directed power was attainable to those ambitious and resolute enough to work for it. The obedient performance of burdensome tasks, tasks that ostensibly offered no immediate benefit, could, by their scrupulous repetition, become transcendent and potent. The Jews could reestablish the interrupted trajectory of their heritage; they could reinvigorate their tenet, in contravention of all available evidence, that they were the Chosen People and thus heir to all the proscriptions, prescriptions, and built-in benefits that implied.

And I? As a bona fide member of the new elect, I had at my disposal greater efficacy than, to look at me, anyone would guess. My attendance at Mass on the first Fridays of any nine consecutive months, for instance, guaranteed my "happy death," complete with a priest on hand ready to administer Extreme Unction. Once I paid off that peculiar installment plan, I was fully indemnified: I might be an apostate or a reprobate, I might marry a Methodist and neglect to extract her promise to raise our children within the teachings of the Church, I might eat meat every Friday for ten years, and yet, somehow, God contractually owed me a parting shot at paradise.

I could see it: I'm on my deathbed, my last gasp moments away, surrounded my grieving relatives. My unforgiven sins are legion and it's too late to get to Saturday afternoon Confession. What's that? A knock at the front door? "I'm sorry to bother you. I'm Father Kilkenny and I'm afraid I had a flat tire directly in front of your house. Funny, they were checked on Tuesday. Anyway, I wonder if I might use your phone? What? Oh, I'm so sorry to hear . . . why, yes, of course. I have my Last Sacraments kit in the trunk."

There were, of course, two sides to the coin. An unwillingness to submit to the Law of God rendered Nehemiah's Jews far worse off than any Egyptian or Mesopotamian gentile. The rejection of an opportunity to strictly obey God's wishes, once they were stated, was drastic. If God said, "Eat not of the Tree of Knowledge of Good and Evil," and the apple proved irresistible, good-bye Eden, hello sweat of the brow for you and all your descendants. If God warned, "Don't look back," and curiosity got the better of you . . . Pow! Pillar of salt.

The penalties for my own possible omissions and commissions were equally dire. Without so much as leaving my seat I was capable of condemning myself to Hades by mentally cursing God, whatever that meant. With a sentence or two of malevolent conversation I could give scandal, tell a lie, be disrespectful to my mother, or use the Lord's name in vain. By touching my body in the wrong spot or in the wrong way or at the wrong time I could make the Blessed Virgin cry. By looking at a condemned film, reading a book listed on The Index, listening to an agnostic speech, or drinking consecrated wine, I could buy a one-way everlasting ticket to The Bad Place.

I was a loaded bomb, dangerous, potentially nuclear, with a hair trigger, and most of the time I was scared to death of what I might inadvertently do. I walked a narrow corridor between unbending regulations, an amateur in a life or death game where every stop might turn up a Go Directly to Hell card and only lucky martyrs could legally cash in their chips when winnings were at their peak. In some traditional societies a menstruating woman is regarded as so possessed of untamed power that if she crosses a stream the fish will thereafter swim away in dread. During her periods she was well advised to remain indoors, thus keeping the world safe from her unintentional destructions. That's how I saw myself, too, except there was almost nowhere and no time I was sure I could be truly innocuous.

According to my grade school Ursulines' interpretations of the *New Baltimore Catechism,* the import of individual culpability was staggering. Jesus was crucified because of *my* Original Sin, to save *my* soul. Even my most throwaway naughtiness caused him pain, and since he never for an instant turned his gaze away from my activities, I was perforce a source of constant aggravation. Sooner or later I knew that I would mess up, ruin, disappoint—and then, woe betide me.

But I *could,* each year, stand still at the appointed half-hour, and that non-act, that *not* doing something, was all it took, according to Sister Stanislaus Kostka, my fourth-grade teacher, to accomplish the miracle that mattered most to me. If I didn't so much as shift my weight while that torrent of torment rained down from the pulpit, I could claim as *quid pro quo* for my sacrifice that a soul currently in Purgatory be immediately bumped up to glory. Passing stiffness seemed a small price for such a benefit, and though throughout each preceding Lent I gave careful and wide consideration as to whom among the many of the deserving I might spring, I—post-Hellenic, contra-Oedipal, secretly both bereft for the parent I had lost and guilty for the male primacy I had gained—inevitably returned at the start of that last week before Easter to my dad. I might not be able to restore him to flesh and blood, to be the father I had been denied, but I could make him happy and proud in absentia.

Nehemiah and Matthew

I remember the elation I felt the single time I made it unequivocally, all but blinklessly, through the Long Gospel. I had successfully borne the buzz of insects, resisted the call of a persistent itch, stifled the impulse to sneeze or yawn, ignored the flicker of intriguing tapping noise off to my right. I was positive that the rise and fall of oxygen in my lungs did not disqualify me, that the beat of my heart was sufficiently autonomic, that the course of blood through my veins was officially exempted since it was beyond my ability to dam. I had held myself bone-rigid, inflexible, unbending, flicking only a finger to turn the pages as the words ticked away. For encouragement, I cast my mind toward the one built-in reprieve, the one excuse for legitimate movement late in the reading, the one muscle-unclenching instruction in my *Saint Joseph,* the way a distance swimmer finishing a race anticipates the necessary last gasp of oxygen.

When Jesus is physically and mentally broken by all that has happened to him over the course of the preceding night and day, Matthew tells us, ". . . about the ninth hour Jesus cried out with a loud voice, saying, *'Eli, Eli, lama sabachthani,'* that is, 'My God, My God, why hast Thou forsaken Me?' And some of the bystanders on hearing this said, 'This man is calling Elias.' And immediately one of them ran and, taking a sponge, soaked it with common wine, put it on a reed and offered it to Him to drink. But the rest said, 'Wait, let us see whether Elias is coming to save Him.' But Jesus again cried out with a loud voice, and gave up His spirit." At this juncture there appeared in my text, parenthesized and italicized, *"(Here all kneel, and pause a little while.)"*

Today I might use that "little while" to ponder a parallel or two: as a writer, a person who attempts to describe, interpret, and get perspective on wider events, I am acutely in sympathy with the challenge that faced both Nehemiah and Matthew. What to include, what to emphasize, what to pass over in order to adequately convey to a nonpresent audience the impact and magnitude of cataclysmic events as they were observed in person?

Admiring of their craft, I might then contemplate without the blinders of enforced orthodoxy the two passages as pure story. Nehemiah paints a picture of a whole people striving toward homogeneity and consensus, an undoing of Babel, the reembracing of a collective consciousness. Matthew, in contrast, movingly portrays an individual who is increasingly isolated and alone, a man undone by his allegiance to an appealing set of radical precepts, a man who tolerated all but dishonesty, a man astoundingly young to have had such immediate and lasting import. Deprived of friends, stripped of all reenforcement save a determination for personal integrity, Jesus doesn't need to be God to be admirable. A martyr to belief, he defies death by remaining steadfast, stays forever vital in the present by refusing to snatch a future in which his ethical vision is compromised. Was Jesus *sure* he was going to resurrect in two days? There's nothing smug, nothing haughty about his demeanor to suggest such certitude. Instead, he's humble, resigned, brave, a man reduced to his own inner resources. How ironic, I would think at age fifty, how poignant, that so private an angst should be transmogrified into the root of such a quintessentially public spectacle.

But that's how I react now. Back then, thirty-three seemed immensely old to me and, anyway, equipped with absolute faith and historical retrospect, I knew Jesus' resolve had been amply justified: here we were, after all, as one sinking to the plush-padded planks that angled down from the pews. Relief simply to be in motion flooded my body, and probably some part of me thanked God for finally abandoning the struggle. During that "pause" of welcomed rest I remember taking pleasure in the realization that success was within my reach. Once we stood again, the three concluding paragraphs covering the quaking of the earth and the burial in the tomb were a piece of cake.

Yet, in the subjective convolution of history and memory, fact and fiction, literature and fable, wish and act, the core of the New Testament's hopeful message—the ringing echo of that of the Hebrew Bible—somehow did penetrate: life *could* be renewed, *could* prevail over death. Though most of the greater significances and meanings of Jesus' passion escaped me, I absolutely believed that the debt of my own birth was requited. Jesus expired so that my dad could rise from the dead, and, as the yoke between the two events, I had absolved myself of any lingering responsibility. I was born again, free. My father's gift to me of life had been returned with interest, for what he had bequeathed me was temporary, of this world, and now, thanks to Jesus and to will power, what I had granted him was eternal.

NOTES

1. Copyright © 1953, Catholic Book Pub. Co., New York, N.Y.
2. Jacob M. Myers, *Ezra and Nehemiah (The Anchor Bible,* vol. 14), New York. Doubleday, 1965, p. 151.

Book of Mormon and Isaiah

T E R R Y   T E M P E S T   W I L L I A M S

Turquoise has always been my color of communion. It is sky. It is water. It is a stone one picks up in the desert. It was also the color of my bandalo in Primary.

All Mormon children receive special guidance, teaching, and social experience through the Primary Association, one of the auxiliary organizations of the Church of Jesus Christ of Latter-Day Saints. Under the direction of women, our mothers and the mothers of our friends, we learned the principles of the gospel.

This is what I remember.

When I turned nine in the fourth grade, I graduated into a girl's only class known as "the gaynotes." Within the confines of our chapel, "the ward," I was presented with a turquoise bandalo made of felt. It hung like a chevron around my neck, its bottom resting slightly above my waist. In time, this would become my cultural necklace that would illustrate my advancement and proficiency in spiritual and domestic achievements.

At the bottom of the bandalo was a plastic insignia of a house representative of the power of the home. Above it diagonal lines of rhinestones were promised, each individual jewel tooled for a scripture learned "believing the Bible to be the word of God as far as it is translated correctly" and the *Book of Mormon* indeed the word of God. The *Doctrine and Covenants* along with the *Pearl of Great Price* are also sacred texts. A plastic circle about the size of a nickel holding the face of Christ or perhaps a long-haired girl reading scriptures would be awarded to us after a particular accomplishment, for example, memorizing *The Articles of Faith,* thirteen tenets of our religion beginning with *"We believe in God, the Eternal Father, and in his Son, Jesus Christ, and in the Holy Ghost"* and ending with *"We believe in being honest, true, chaste, benevolent, virtuous, and in doing good to all men; indeed, we may say that we follow the admonition of Paul—we believe all things, we hope all things, we have endured many things, and hope to be able to endure all things, if there is anything virtuous, lovely, or of good report or praiseworthy, we seek after these things."*

And so we, Mormon girls, advanced up our bandalos each year as a "gaynote," a "firelight," and a "merrihand," the corresponding plastic insignias glued securely on the turquoise felt. And with each year, more lines of rhinestones were earned and added. Our bandalos sparkled with the discipline of our people. We became spiritually literate.

We were also praised and decorated for homemaking skills.

In my gaynote year, I learned how to cross-stitch, creating a sampler that read, *"I will bring the light of the gospel into my home."* I chose silk threads of light blue and navy.

As a firelight, I learned to knit and did not fare so well. I managed to complete the backside of a sweater vest (in those days we called it a shell) and then gave up on the green yarn. I could never sit still long enough to master "knit one, pearl two . . ." I failed. My concentration was lacking in matters of the hearth.

And as a merrihand, my crochet techniques were worse. My teacher finally graciously passed me off on a simple red chain stitch belt while my classmates managed elaborate popcorn stitch circle rugs and comforters.

The boys our age had their own cultural incentives. They were moving toward eagle scouthood learning skills like building fires, building bodies, becoming acquainted with Indian lore, and gaining expertise in various entrepreneurial activities to raise money for camping trips. They had their merit badges. We had our rhinestones. Both sexes were being prepared for marriage within the Covenant. We were the templates of youth.

My grandmother wore a five-strand turquoise necklace that fell across her breasts like a waterfall. She had quietly purchased it through a layaway plan with Mr. Joe Fisher, who owned a rock shop and trading post in Mount Carmel, Utah. It took her two years to pay for it, after which he sent her the necklace through the mail with a note thanking her for never missing a payment. She wore her turquoise beads outside as well as in, a dramatic statement of her affection toward the Earth.

"I love the variation of color," she said as she ran her fingers through the strands. "No two beads are exactly the same."

"Who made it?" I asked.

"It was made by a Navajo named Jerald D. Yazzie," she replied. "Mr. Fisher sent me a photograph of him. His family lives in Aneth, Utah, near the Four Corners, not so far from here. Maybe one day we can go visit him."

This was my first introduction to the Navajo, the *Dine,* residents of the American Southwest.

My second introduction was through the *Book of Mormon,* a few months later. In Primary, I learned we called Indian people "Lamanites." We were taught that "because they rebelled against the truth, a twofold curse came upon them:

1. They were cut off from the presence of the Lord and thus died spiritually. Scales of darkness covered their eyes because they did not accept the saving principles of the gospel. They became apostates and the descendants of apostates. (1 Nephi 2:21–24; 2 Nephi 4:4–6; Alma 9:13–14)

2. "After they dwindled in unbelief," that is, after they had forsaken the Church and the gospel, "they became a dark, and loathsome, and a filthy people, full of idleness and all manner of abominations." (1 Nephi 12:23) So that they "might not be enticing unto the Nephites, the Lord God did cause a skin of blackness to come upon them." (2 Nephi 5:20–25; Alma 3:14–16) *Mormon Doctrine,* page 428, Bruce R. McConkie.

This was the "Lamanite Curse" and we were also taught the "Lamanite Promise." Again, from Bruce R. McConkie's *Mormon Doctrine,* ". . . the promise is that in due course they shall blossom like a rose . . . that is become again a white and delightsome people as were their ancestors a great many generations ago." (*D & C* 49:24)

Shortly after these teachings, I was staying overnight at my grandmother's house. I told her what I had learned about Indian people and the man who had made her necklace.

"Is it true?" I asked.

She looked at me. Her eyes narrowed. She got up out of her chair, walked down the hallway to her study, and pulled the black leather-bound book down from the shelf. She brought it back with her to the living room and sat down beside me. She quickly flipped through the delicate pages until she turned to *Doctrine and Covenants* Chapter 93 and read verses 36 through 37, "The Glory of God is intelligence . . ." She closed the scriptures and looked at me.

"I believe God has given each of us an independent mind, a mind that can think and act out of its own intelligence and conscience. You and only you can decide what is true or not. Intelligence lives in your heart. As for me, I do not believe God sees the color of a person's skin."

I felt confused. I was afraid of her turquoise necklace.

In May of 1973, I received a Second Place prize from the Linnie F. Robinson Poetry Contest sponsored by the Utah Poetry Society. I received a check for $25 and decided to do something special with the money. I went down to Sam Weller's Bookstore on Main Street and bought a brown leather "triple combination," the *Book of Mormon,* the *Doctrine and Covenants,* and the *Pearl of Great Price* and then had my name engraved on the leather in gold. I now had my own scriptures.

One month later, I graduated from Highland High School. With my diploma in hand, my grandmother gave me a graduation present. It was a turquoise bracelet with the initials "JDY" etched on the back of the sterling silver mount. I slipped it on my right wrist and marveled at the clarity and weight of the stone.

"It looks beautiful on you," she said.

There is a promise in the *Book of Mormon* given by the ancient prophet Moroni. It reads:

> When ye shall receive these things, I would exhort you that ye would ask God, the Eternal Father, in the name of Christ, if these things are not true; and if ye shall ask with a sincere heart, with real intent, having faith in Christ, he will manifest the truth of it unto you, by the power of the Holy Ghost.
>
> (*MORONI* 10:4)

I took my scriptures with me to Elk Creek Ranch in Island Park, Idaho, on the periphery of Yellowstone National Park. I went with a high school friend. We were hired as cabin maids. Before entering college that fall, I wanted to come to grips with what I believed and so each morning, I would rise early and read from the *Book of Mormon*. I would underline passages with my red pencil and ponder them.

> Yea and are ye willing to mourn with those that mourn;
>> yea and comfort those that stand in need of comfort, and
> to stand as witnesses of God at all times and in all things,
> and in all places that ye may be in, even until death, that
> ye may be redeemed of God. . . .
>
> *(MOSIAH 18:9)*

These were beautiful passages, passages that stirred my soul specific to my own culture, our own sacred texts, and then as the full, broad light of morning came forward, I would digress from the *Book of Mormon* and turn to the Psalms. I read these scriptures from the Old Testament not so much for theology but for the elegance of language. For me, it was the beginning of poetry. Hours would pass. I would put away my books, realizing the work I had not yet done, then dash into the cabins and change the beds.

During the afternoon, after my chores were complete, I would walk to the lake and fish. I would return to the ranch for dinner, cook the trout and eat the meat as sacrament. I was healthy and strong, tan, so tan, that when I bathed before going to bed and removed my turquoise bracelet, I wore another bracelet of white skin.

Toward the end of summer, I made the decision that I would take Moroni up on his promise. I took time off from work and went without food for two days. I walked to a favorite place of mine, studied and prayed, felt the sun on my face, listened to Clark's nutcrackers call to each other from the tops of lodgepole pines and watched an osprey fish, hovering high with a crook in each brown-and-white-checkered wing, eyes down, wings pulled back. She dropped like a bullet, feet first, splashed, rose with a trout in the grip of her talons, then sailed across the lake to her perch, a dead snag, rested, secured the fish, and flew to her nest. I read some more, returning to favorite passages.

> Let the mountains shout for joy, and all ye valleys cry aloud; and all ye seas and dry lands tell the wonders of your Eternal King! And ye rivers and brooks, and rills, flow down with gladness. Let the woods and all the trees of the field praise the Lord; and ye solid rocks weep for joy! And let the sun, moon, and the morning stars sing together, and let all the sons of God shout for joy! And let the eternal creations declare his name forever and ever! And again I say, how glorious is the voice we hear from heaven, proclaiming in our ears, glory, and salvation, and honor, and immortality, and eternal life; kingdoms, principalities, and powers!
>
> (D & C: 128:23).

I pressed petals of wildflowers between these pages, blue penstemon, scarlet gilia, and yarrow. The day was long and luxurious. I felt a humility rise out of my own hunger and that night in the solitude of a little cabin in Idaho, I prayed.

Terry Tempest Williams

I prayed I might find the truth of these things.

in horror of my darkness
in terror of inhuman space
exposed to a private death

totally vulnerable on the surface
of earth's
material matter . . .

then one of the seraphim
flew toward me
a live coal in his hand

a fire from the interior
of the earth
the core of my being

it was a burning stone
from the fire
on the altar

with the priest's tongs
he reached in the holy altar
and took it

and touched my lips
with it
and he was saying

you are seeing
the purifying fire of creation
burn up your past

ISAIAH 6

A POET'S BIBLE

DAVID ROSENBERG

The next morning, I telephoned my mother and grandmother to tell them I had had a vision. I told them a figure draped in a white robe had stood at the foot of my log bed. I was still shaking from the fear, the awe, the wonder of it all, the fire in me still burning. Neither one of them said much, but simply listened. I hung up the receiver and walked back to the ranch. By the time I had arrived in the kitchen to join the others for breakfast, my mother had already called and left a message. It read, "Kathryn and I are coming up to see you this afternoon. I love you, Mother."

This was no small gesture. It was a six-hour drive from Salt Lake City, Utah. At four o'clock, they arrived at Elk Creek Ranch. When I saw them I began to cry. They both held me and one of them said, "Let's go."

We drove to Mesa Falls, got out of the car, and walked to the edge of the cliff. The three of us sat down and watched the cascading water, the rainbow of light created by the sun.

I told them my story.

They listened.

And then as a young woman of seventeen years still unable to trust what I had just shared, I asked the women in my life who mattered most if they believed me, if they thought this apparition was about Mormonism or something else. The Church was true? Yes? Had I gone mad?

"Of course, you haven't gone mad," my grandmother said. "Whether the Church is true or not really doesn't matter. It's how you feel inside—"

My mother reminded me of the patriarchal blessing I had been given by one of the brethren shortly before I left. She had brought it with her. It read, *"Be not afraid to learn the truth of anything for no truth will be revealed to you as such that will be in conflict with God's kingdom. . . ."*

"It's all true," my grandmother said, looking out toward the landscape before us. "All of this—"

We sat on the edge of Mesa Falls together in silence, mesmerized, hypnotized, by the rushing water, the seemingly endless water, and I wondered about the source from which this water falls.

More than twenty years later, my mother is dead, my grandmother is dead, but my belief in a spiritual life remains alive.

My turquoise felt bandalo is tucked away in some box of memorabilia stored beneath our house. I do not cross-stitch, knit, or crochet. I do not believe Indian people are "Lamanites" and I deplore the idea that they are cursed, that one day through a "righteous path" they will become white. My grandmother through her own restraint taught me to recognize the insipid seeds of racism under the guise of Truth. Her turquoise necklace, my turquoise bracelet, have become talismans of integrity replacing rhinestones tooled in felt. But I must never forget, I must always remember, this is where my communion began—inside a ward house, learning the texts of my people, feeling the stability of soul within the safety of the shared ideals of a Mormon community.

This was the congregation of my youth.

The vision I had in Idaho after fasting and praying in the wilderness is the vision I had of the osprey—eyes down, wings folded in a free fall—the surface of the water breaks, holy food is within our grasp.

Job and Matthew

B I L L   M C K I B B E N

Through no precise fault of the pleasant suburban church where I was raised, I reached college in the year 1978 unaware that the Bible contained material that might shake me up. That is, I knew that the Gospels commanded compassion toward the poor, the hungry, the naked—but that was my politics anyway, for other reasons. (Good reasons, like the example of my parents, and mixed reasons, like a yearning for the sexy sixties.) I knew I was supposed to turn the other cheek, but so what—it would never have occurred to me to hit someone other than my brother anyhow. I was a good kid.

My leftism grew more righteous in college, but still there was something pro forma about it. Being white, male, straight, and of impeccably middle-class background, I could not realistically claim to be a victim of anything. (Not for lack of trying—in one short but loony phase I convinced myself that I was Irish-American and wore black armbands when Bobby Sands and his IRA companions starved themselves to death.) Mostly, I supported everyone else—marched in Take Back the Night marches, signed petitions for minority centers and Hispanic studies, conspicuously sat at dinner with gays and lesbians during gay and lesbian week. But I couldn't even claim the pleasure of enlightenment, as I was not a bigot or a chauvinist or a homophobe to begin with. I was, as I say, a good kid.

In those early years of the 1980s, with Reaganism ascendant and Lech Walesa busily proving to anyone who had not yet figured it out that communism was a stinking corpse, the only promising strain of ''leftism'' seemed to emanate from Latin America. And it was less the Sandinistas that fascinated me than the liberation theologians, who seemed to be issuing a coherent and genuinely popular response to the poverty and violence around them, a response perhaps not automatically fated to become a tyranny of its own. I can recall hearing for the first time about this ''new'' theology (in fact it was already a decade old but it had been slow, because it involved religion, to penetrate college reading lists). I haunted the library of the divinity school, where I'd never been before, trying to find the one title someone had written out for me: *Christology at the Crossroads,* by a Jesuit priest named Jon Sobrino. After several trips I finally found it on the shelf and grabbed it—only to find it dense going. I had no idea what Christology was, for example. (The liberation theologians piled the technical language of the left atop the technical language of the theologians, and most of it was translated from the Spanish to boot.) I kept reading, however, for I knew there was something vital beneath the jargon—it was during this period, after all, that Oscar Romero, archbishop of El Salvador, was assassinated for enunciating these complex ideas in the simplest terms. I can remember sitting in a leather chair in the library sounding out Gutierrez and Segundo, Boff and Cardenal, Miranda and Miguez-Bonino with a rising thrill, a feeling that this world of Christianity, to which I had at least a slight connection, was on a cutting edge sharper than any other around.

And yet it was still somehow removed from me. I believed that the Church should, in Gutierrez's key phrase, have "a preferential option for the poor." I believed that the poor should remake the Church and then the society to serve their needs. The poor, I read again and again, have to take charge of their own destiny. Praxis—that was one of the keys. I had no argument. But I was not poor. Not rich, certainly—by the standards of my college, halfway to shabby. But not poor, no more than I was gay or black. It seemed still as if a rooting interest was all I could muster. And part of me wished for something more.

The year I graduated school I left for Manhattan, where I found work writing magazine stories. At some point, for some reason, I decided I was actually going to read the Bible. (I am aware that this sounds absurd, that I should have read it long before I started digging into Latin American Christology. But I am well educated in a modern way, which is to say far more comfortable with commentary than text). To slow myself down so I'd actually *read* it, I decided to copy it out word for word in a notebook, beginning with the Gospels. And as I crawled along through Matthew, a chapter a day from my previously uncracked Comfirmation Bible, a blend of excitement and dread grew in me. This was addressed to me after all— amid the encouragement of the oppressed and scourging of the truly wicked, there was plenty aimed at the decent-but-complacent. That comes as revelation to no one else, of course, but it was the more powerful to me for coming late.

One story in particular startled me. It seemed to be my story, as if Jesus was one of those stage psychics who can pick people out of a crowd. First told in Matthew 19, it's not a parable, just an incident from Jesus' life.

A man approaches him while he is preaching in Judea and says, "Teacher, what good deed must I do to have eternal life?" And Jesus answers him—a little dismissively, or so it sounds—"Why do you ask me about what is good? One there is who is good. If you would enter life, keep the commandments." The man asks, "Which?" And Jesus—curtly still—says, "you shall not kill, you shall not commit adultery, you shall not steal, you shall not bear false witness, Honor your father and mother, and love your neighbor as yourself." Not that old list again—you can almost hear the young man's impatience. And mine too—clearly I was never going to murder anyone, and I didn't lie more than anyone else, and since no one I knew was married, adultery was not a great temptation. I was on good terms with my parents (which was enough of a rarity to make me feel virtuous). And I loved my neighbor, or at least said I did. I wanted off the sidelines. I wanted a real challenge.

So too with the man questioning Christ. "All these I have observed; what do I still lack?" Jesus—and you can feel the pause, feel the turn to look him straight in the eye—says this: "If you would be perfect, go, sell what you possess, and give to the poor, and you will have treasure in heaven; and come follow me." And, says Matthew, "when the young man heard this he went away sorrowful, for he had great possessions."

"If you would be perfect." Well, yes, that was one crux of it. I was yearning for some sort of moral heroism, and if I did not in fact have great possessions, I realized that my privileged life and connections and opportunities were a kind of capital, included in what Jesus was describing—I had been to Harvard, after all, and I was working at the *New Yorker*. It wasn't the "treasure in heaven" that interested me, since then and now I had only a mild interest in heaven. Instead, as usual, my attraction was for a mix of good reasons and bad. I am certain that the idea of renunciation appealed to my vanity. But perhaps I also glimpsed the possibility of a kind of *intensity* of life once one was free of the insulation from the world provided by money and belongings. That insulation had surrounded me always—an American suburb is a device for turning money into a kind of armor against experience: the experience of other kinds of people, of nature, of one's body. Maybe this was early-onset midlife crisis: the strong sense that there was something *more* and that the path to it lay through *less*. I had no idea quite how to go about it. Join a monastery? But I wasn't a Catholic, and anyway intense quiet did not yet appeal to me. Join the Peace Corps? But I couldn't actually *do* anything useful to anyone except write "Talk of the Town" stories. Still, I knew there were things I could have done.

But "went away sorrowful"—that was the other crux, the perfect description for my inability to take such a leap. Not "went away angry," or "went away scornful," but went away sorrowful, more than half-convinced the message was right, and yet unable to act on it. Exactly why I am not sure. It was early in the Reagan age, and Manhattan's streets were filling with homeless people—as a reporter I lived for a while as a homeless man, and then I helped start a small homeless shelter in the basement of my church, and frankly the fact of homelessness scared me. My profession seemed particularly economically insecure—my father, also a writer, had lost a magazine job when I was in high school, and I could still remember the fear when, for a while, he could find no other work. In retrospect my worries were exaggerated—but I was twenty-one, twenty-two, twenty-three at the time. What did I know?

The compromise that I reached, without thinking about it as such, was a strange one: I lived extremely frugally, and put the money I earned in the bank. In so doing I preserved both the option to do something heroic at a later date (only dimly sensing that the diving board would just get higher and higher with each extra dollar), and also the right to feel superior to my yuppie peers. When I say frugal, I mean frugal. One day, burglars broke into the sublet that I was sharing with a friend. They found him asleep, tied him up, and robbed thousands of dollars' worth of his belongings. From me they took two cardboard boxes. They dumped my small record collection out of one and used it to haul away David's computer. They dumped my dirty clothes from the other and carried out his VCR.

A few years later I quit my job and moved to the wild and distant Adirondack Mountains, and some of these concerns began to fade. Poverty is intense here, but it is not confrontational; no one begs, there are no spokesmen. And, too, I had met and married a wonderful woman; helping to care for a family on the precarious earnings of a freelance writer made me thankful for the money I'd saved in the city.

Most of all, though, I had finally found a cause in which to immerse myself. It did not take me long to fall in love with the natural world, a world more real and engaging than any I had known before. I bushwhacked up mountains, skiied lakes at midnight by the light of the moon, tracked coyote and deer across the ridges. And as quickly as my love for wild places grew, so too did my sense of their peril. My environmentalism began locally, fighting the constant threats to all the places where I hiked and canoed and lay out under the stars. It soon grew to encompass the globe, as I realized that the very climate of these remote Adirondacks was being changed by the habits of our species.

Such realization depressed me, of course: the title of my first book, *The End of Nature,* testifies to that despair. But this passion also allowed, finally, my full participation. Environmental change threatened me as much as any other human on the planet: white skin offered no special protection against the ultraviolet pouring in through the hole in the ozone layer. What's more, the greatest threat was not to humans at all, but to the rest of creation. And there seemed nothing paternalistic or patronizing about going to bat for bats, or wolves or hemlocks or salamanders.

I'd started going to the one local church almost as soon as I'd moved here, a tiny Methodist congregation with maybe twenty souls on a Sunday morning. The minister when I arrived was a recently released jailhouse convert, a Holy Roller who, as it turned out, soon returned to state custody after embezzling from one of his old lady parishioners. Though he was succeeded by a more congenial cleric, it was probably fortunate that I had begun to find my church in the woods and mountains, in a minor-key version of the religious ecstasy that marked, say, John Muir's first summer in the Sierras.

I might have turned into a full-fledged pagan had not my wife happened to give me a copy of Stephen Mitchell's translation of the book of Job from the Hebrew Bible. (The only way I've ever been able to understand the Holy Spirit is as that force which, out of all the books in the world, puts a particular volume in your hand at a particular time.) It shocked me at least as much as my first encounters with liberation theology: I sensed once more that the Bible had a great deal to say on subjects close to my heart, that it went beyond mere radicalism to roots.

The story of Job is, of course, familiar—a righteous man is felled by misfortune, reduced to living on a dungheap at the edge of town, his body a mass of oozing sores. In legend he is renowned for his patience, but in practice he is anything but. He rejects the counsel of his friends, who push the conventional wisdom that he must have sinned unwittingly and now is being punished. Instead he demands an interview with God, demands an explanation for his suffering. He gets the interview, but the explanation is not what he expects. Appearing in a whirlwind, God tells him zip about justice or righteousness or the meaning of suffering. Instead God taunts Job with his unimportance. ("Were you there when I planned the earth? . . . If you shout commands to the thunderclouds will they rush off to do your bidding? If you clap for the bolts of lightning will they come and say 'Here we are'? . . . Have you seen where the snow is stored?''). Job is being shown the limits of his human-centered logic; his affliction has nothing to do with his sins, because *man is not at the center of all things.*

Who cuts a path for the thunderstorm
  and carves a road for the rain—
to water the desolate wasteland,
    the land where no man lives;
to make the wilderness blossom
    and cover the desert with grass?

For me, living on the edge of the wilderness, this matched the newfound feelings flooding my senses: the glory of a true night sky, the loud piping of a life-filled marsh, the flight of a hawk. "Do you teach the vulture to soar and build his nest in the clouds," God asks Job. "He makes his home on the mountaintop, on the unapproachable crag. He sits and scans for prey; from far off his eyes can spot it; his little ones drink its blood. Where the unburied are, he is." I saw turkey vultures every day now, circling over carrion; this was the world I was coming to know, to relax into.

And the message of Job also meshed neatly with the ideas along the cutting edge of environmentalism: the "deep ecologists" and the "biocentrists" who were arguing convincingly that our entire ecological crisis stems from philosophical roots, from turning everything around us into "raw materials" and "resources" for us to use as we pleased. In a way, it was all a great relief: a worldview that went well beyond ethics and even morality. And this, of course, is one of the great cries against environmentalists; in my case, I deserved it.

For the only problem with God's message to Job was that it seemed to be less true with each passing year. The more I learned about the greenhouse effect, for instance, the more I realized that God's unanswerable taunts to Job were suddenly—in my lifetime—turning into the empty boasts of an old geezer. "Were you there . . . when I closed in [the sea] with barriers and set its boundaries, saying 'Here you may come but no farther; here shall your proud waves break.' " Job has to stand in humble silence, but not us. By pumping clouds of carbon dioxide into the atmosphere—clouds that rise from every car and furnace and factory—we are raising the temperature of the planet and hence its sea level. Collectively, the five and a half billion of us are large enough to take the measure of this bragging deity. Thunderstorms "R" Us too, and hurricanes; we are busy creating our own Leviathans and Behemoths with our genetic engineering, even as we wipe out the ones with which we shared the planet of our birth.

So I could read Job as a vision of what had been before history, and as a partial description of what remaining wilderness now resembled, and as a glorious picture of what the world might look like once again in the deep future. But this struggle requires more than vision; it demands, of course, that we acknowledge and deal with five and a half billion human beings. It demands that we deal with the wealth driving environmental destruction, and with the myth of the rich world that someday everyone else will be like us. There isn't atmosphere enough for them to be like us—so it demands, painfully, that we deal with ourselves.

Consider the following fact, tucked away in a recent paper by a Syracuse University research team led by Professor Charles Hall. "One way to view the relationship between economic activity and environmental impact is that each time a person spends a U.S. dollar approximately 3000–4000 kilocalories of energy (about 15 Joules, or the equivalent of one half liter of oil) is extracted from the earth and burned to produce the goods or services purchased by that dollar." Every time a liter of oil is burned, pounds of carbon dioxide waft into the atmosphere, increasing the amount of the sun's heat trapped near the earth.

In other words, our possessions are linked directly to the destruction of the planet: along with the size of human populations, and the efficiency of their consumption, the amount that they consume determines how much fuel is burned, how many forests chainsawed, how many marshes drained and hillsides mined. Spending twenty dollars on a book requires that ten liters of oil go up in smoke.

In other words, I'd come full circle, led myself back to the same place though from another direction. If we are to know the vision offered Job, the vision of an intact world where we are not at the center of things but instead a part of a functioning and glorious planet, then the advice of Jesus to the rich young man is a crucial prerequisite. We need to cease consuming at anything like our current rate, for our consumption drives the planet's deterioration. And, having ceased, we need to share with the rest of the world, now struggling to emulate our ways. For in a world where the average citizen of the First World has fifty-nine times the income of the average citizen of the Third World, it is no use denying our wealth, and no use denying its attraction.

The second time I crashed into this story, the collision shook me even harder. My mind had long since ceased dwelling on the advice to the rich young ruler; I thought I had escaped it. But now I was back to it, and from a very different angle. Christ's admonition echoed and anticipated, of course, the advice of a thousand other saints and cranks and gurus. Always for them the advice had been aesthetic, moral, personal, spiritual. And always, as in my case, it had gone too against the grain of the culture for more than a noble few to follow. Now it seemed to be converging with the very practical advice of scientists, of men clutching satellite data and computer printouts as they too made the case for simplicity and community and other religious joys.

This confluence makes it no easier to follow the injunction, and indeed I have taken but the first baby steps in that direction; I doubt my will to go very far down that road. But I do not doubt it is the right road, for reasons of nature and of social justice and of fulfillment. I reread the various Gospel accounts of the incident as I wrote this essay, and saw that although they are remarkably similar, Mark adds one clause. When the rich young man badgers him about what to do beyond keeping the commandments, Jesus softens; the man's zeal seems to touch him. "And Jesus looking upon him loved him," and said to him, change your life in the most fundamental ways. It is that tenderness that charges this story, that turns its seeming sternness upside down. It is that tenderness that makes it attractive, even seductive, not repellent. It is that tenderness that keeps it ever in my mind.

I read my words and think they must seem bizarrely literal—as if, having left the Bible mostly unread as a child, I now can read it only with a childish simplicity. I am not a fundamentalist, obviously. But the things that worry me—food and shelter for people who lack them, the gaseous composition of the atmosphere, a right life—seem to me fundamental. They seem literal. This story haunts me; may it always.

PART
THREE

Psalms and John

H E L E N   V E N D L E R

My days as a child invariably began with the morning Mass to which my mother took us. It was almost always a requiem Mass, sung in Latin, since deaths were commemorated a month afterward and a year afterward, and, in a sizable parish, such memorials crowded the calendar. My earliest memories are of the *Dies Irae* and, for some reason, of the long mournful strophes of the preface: *"Tuis enim fidelibus, Domine, vita mutatur, non tollitur; et dissoluta huius terrestris incolatus domo, aeterna in coelo habitatio comparatur,"* all sung to the plangent lifts and falls of Gregorian chant. At nine, teaching my seven-year-old brother the Latin responses to the Mass so that he could be an altar boy, I learned the Latin of the Mass more or less by heart, and this gave me the wish to learn Latin (I already knew Spanish, French, and Italian, which my father had taught us). It was in the text of the Mass that I first met the antiphonal rhythms of the Psalms: *"Introibo ad altare Dei, ad Deum qui laetificat juventutem meum."* At the same time, I was hearing the Psalms (the more amiable ones, naturally) read to us, in the King James Version, in my public school, one a day, before we pledged allegiance to the flag. Miss Fallon's low, harmonious voice is still in my ear, reading the obscurely satisfying cadences: "I will lift up mine eyes unto the hills, from whence cometh my help." But the Psalms were then no more than ravishing turns of phrase, whether in Latin or in English. I did not yet *need* the Psalms, or didn't know I needed them.

At ten, old enough for the streetcar, I was sent to the parochial school in the next parish (our parish had not yet acquired a school). Among many ungifted teachers, there was one uncannily inspired one, a young Lebanese nun who was (in spite of my having had two piano teachers) the first musical person I had encountered. She believed that a random group of mostly lower-class children could be taught to sing the Latin liturgy in Gregorian chant, and with her expressive eyes and her even more expressive conducting hand, she took us into the Psalms, notably during the long Holy Week service (now discontinued in the Roman Catholic Church) called *Tenebrae*. The nine Psalms of Matins and the four of Lauds for the appropriate day were sung: for Good Friday, for instance, this meant (in the Douay Bible numbering), Psalms 2, 21, 26, 37, 39, 53, 58, 87, 93, 50, 142, 84, and 147. I took to spending my spare time in the seventh and eighth grade learning Latin so I could follow the texts at least approximately; and since I was steeped in friendless adolescent misery at school, and the beginnings of appalled recognition of the life at home, the Psalms became my poems of reference.

I had had poetry read to me since birth by my melancholy mother (a primary-school teacher who, by marrying, had lost her fourteen-year career, since married women were not permitted to continue to work in the Boston school system); and I had read a fair amount of verse here and there on my own; but the Psalms were, I think, the first sublime poetry I consciously took on as my own. I didn't, even then, read them as the word of God. I don't believe I read them, or sang them, chiefly in an inner atmosphere of belief. I had already begun the rude questioning of the dogma and discipline of Roman Catholicism that led to my abandoning the Church forever as soon as I left my parents' house; and I was always of a skeptical temperament, impatient of all nonevidential talk of Virgin Birth and Resurrection (taught by the church as facts, not symbols).

When I try, now, to recapture my feelings at eleven and twelve, singing the verses of the Psalms, what I recall is the fierceness with which I appropriated the Psalmist's voice as mine. *I* cried out of the depths; *I* asked my soul, "Why art thou sad, O my soul? and why doest thou trouble me? Why go I mourning, whilst my enemy afflicteth me?" I was as likely to say it to myself in the language of the Mass—*"Quare tristis es, anima mea, et quare conturbas me?"*—as I was to read it in the Bible.

What did I gain, between ten and thirteen, from the Voice of the Psalmist? Equivalents for all my stifled and inarticulate feelings. I didn't often turn to those kinder psalms that had been read to me in public school. What I found were the wild psalms:

> I am poured out like water; and all my bones are
> scattered.
> My heart is become like wax melting in the midst
> of my bowels.
> My strength is dried up like a potsherd, and my
> tongue hath cleaved to my jaws: and thou has
> brought me down into the dust of death.

(2 1)

If anyone doubts that these are the emotions of adolescence, he has forgotten his youth. The insanity of stifled feeling, in my case, could only be stemmed by adequacy of expression, and since I had absolutely no adequate words myself for my own despair, I was abjectly grateful to the Psalmist.

The Psalms gave me, too, my first intuition of intertextuality. As I came on Psalm 21 for the first time, I remember being shocked, because I had had no idea, when I had heard the Passion read in church, that Jesus was *quoting* when he cried out, "My God, my God, why hast thou forsaken me"—the phrase that opens Psalm 21. If *he* could borrow the Psalmist's words and say them *in propria persona,* so could I. The psalm that best expressed my feeling of being sentenced to indefinite punishment merely by living as and where I did, in an atmosphere that permitted no personal freedom of thought or action, was 128:

> Often have they fought against me from my youth,
> let Israel now say.
> Often have they fought against me from my youth;
> but they could not prevail over me.
> The wicked have wrought upon my back: they have
> lengthened their iniquity . . .
> And they that passed by have not said: The blessing
> of the Lord be upon you: we have blessed you in
> the name of the Lord.

Lest it be thought that I exaggerate my feelings, let me add the fact that a poem I wrote at fifteen began, "Pitiless with repression, / They told me I must dwell / Within the narrow prison / They lived in." I was enraged, and helpless, and in prison; and I knew, in my twelfth year, no words but the Psalmist's to say my feelings for me. The Psalmist had satisfying curses,

a form not much encouraged in books for the young; the Psalms thus
became my first clandestine literature:

> May his children be fatherless, and his wife a
> widow.
> Let his children be carried about vagabonds, and
> beg; and let them be cast out of their
> dwellings . . .
> May the iniquity of his fathers be remembered in
> the sight of the Lord: and let not the sin of his
> mother be blotted out . . .
> And he put on cursing, like a garment: and it went
> in like water into his entrails, and like oil in his
> bones.

(108)

These words were for me like plasters applied to nameless wounds.
Almost everything I felt the Psalmist had words for. (The other feelings
found solace three years later, when I was fifteen, in Shakespeare's sonnets.) I don't know what I would have done with the grinding and self-
abasing and furious and lacerating feelings of my twelfth year without the
Psalms. They drew off the worst of the poison (by allowing me, among
other things, to put on cursing like a garment), and they filled my mouth
with language. A choking sensation in the heart, a smothering in the lungs,
a frenzy in the brain, an anger in the blood, tormented me every day, all
day, in those years. I had no one to confide in and no one to explain my
feelings to me. Only the Psalmist knew my soul, and I his.

Now, as I look back on that greedy ingestion of words by proxy, I see
that I was learning other things from the Psalms, two in particular: the

habit of intensive meditation proper to lyric poetry from the Psalter to Jorie Graham, and the basic intertextuality of all poetry. In the Psalter I found a repertory of most of the canonical lyric genres: the recapitulatory narrations by the Psalmist of Genesis (103) and Exodus (104) showed how to make lyric out of chronicle, and were models of the miniaturizing process necessary in short poems; the songs of praise, of triumph, of commination, of grief, of supplication, and of prophecy, taught me the thematic and tonal range possible to lyric. The Psalms are above all untimid; they are often sublime. They urge the lyric toward ardor and heroism and vision, avoiding the decorous, the small, the "merely" perfect. Because the speech of the Psalms is often choral, and because it was adapted to liturgical use, it never seemed to me language written with respect to gender. Rather, like most lyric speech, it was voiceable by anyone. I believe that poetry became for me the most natural of the genres because of the Psalms; and later, when I came to study poetry and write about it, I found that the web composed of biblical texts, the liturgy, and the hymnal extended its threads deep into the English lyric. Most readers are drawn to narrative, to the line that prolongs itself to an end; but I was drawn to meditation, to the ripples of intensification extending out from a center of thought. It is that concentric structure of the meditative lyric, from the Psalms to Wallace Stevens, that still seems to me the most compelling form of writing ever invented.

And the lyric reading provoked writing in me: first, a flurry of poems beginning in my fifteenth year and ending only eleven years later; and second, in my sixteenth year, my first extended critical writing, a long senior essay on Hopkins. Both sorts of writing made me happy, but my analytical bent, stronger than my imaginative side, made me finally a critic, not a poet. Though I loved, and love, the Psalms, I have not written about them; and that fact provokes me to ask why certain poems, certain authors and not others, bring forth critical writing from me. I think criticism is engendered in me principally by love of the mother tongue, as it strikes, with unnerving and uncanny power, some fault line in me which, surprised, cracks open in response. The liturgy and the Psalms, though not in English, laid down one such fault line of childhood imaginative experience, and left me—an atheist in adult life—vulnerable to religious language in lyric form, whether I encounter it in Herbert or Whitman, in Stevens or Glück. (Fairy tale laid down another such fault line, leading to my writing about Keats; and Shakespeare's plays laid down yet another, which led to my writing on his *Sonnets.*) As far as I know, my earliest drive to criticism came from the need to explain to my irreligious self, at sixteen, the power of religious lyric as I saw it in Hopkins (a poet whose work is permeated by the Psalms).

The Psalms were not the sort of reading given to young girls by schools and public libraries in my day—nor would they be recommended to twelve-year-old girls these days, either. Without disparaging the release of inchoate feeling offered adolescents by the Judy Blumes of the Young Adult shelves, I wish that our culture dealt out the wild verities of the Psalmist (and, to supplement him, the Shakespeare of the *Sonnets*) instead. Imagine a school system where every day a psalm and a Shakespeare sonnet were chorally recited by every class. When the end of the Psalter was reached, Psalm 1 would come round again; when the end of the *Sonnets* was reached, the cycle would rebegin. From, say, the third grade on, the whole Psalter, every year, and the 154 sonnets, every year: why, by Grade 12 the students would be literate. And, as a dividend, liberated in their hearts' passions.

The passage I choose from the New Testament is of another ilk. It is the story, in John 8, of the woman taken in adultery. This story was read aloud to me every year in church (it is the gospel for Saturday, the third week of

Lent). Since I didn't come to consciousness till eleven, and didn't begin my troubled questioning of my readings (and my life) till twelve, I assume I heard this story incuriously until I began to think about my own future. Though my future was wholly unknown to me in any positive way, I already knew what I didn't want: I didn't want restrictions on my freedom. Before me loomed the Roman Catholic Church's prohibitions of sex outside of marriage (I didn't know what sex consisted of, but I knew it was prohibited except to married persons); of "artificial" birth control; and of divorce. I was certain that I didn't want to spend all of my life on pregnancies and child care; and I wanted to be able to get out of a marriage that proved unhappy, and to be able to look toward a better one.

I began a series of angry and resentful and hectoring questions directed mostly at my mother, and received very unsatisfying answers in return; I began a series of readings in the Catholic authors (from Garrigou-Lagrange to Dorothy Day) that were to be found in the house, and found equally unsatisfactory answers. I could see absolutely no rational arguments against sexual freedom, birth control, or divorce. My anarchic temperament hated rules (and still does), especially rules invading one's private and domestic choices. When I became aware of the truly horrible possibilities before me as a Catholic virgin—early marriage, as many children "as God was pleased to send" me, and no divorce (not to speak of no sexual partners other than the first) I recoiled in full terror. That *could* not be my life; it would keep me from— From what? I had no idea, but the It that all the above would keep me from was, I knew, necessary to my very existence, whatever It was. (Nothing around me suggested what It was; the women I knew were either mothers or nuns.)

Therefore when I once again heard, with my newly awakened selfhood, the story of the woman taken in adultery, it produced in me mixed feelings. Jesus seemed not to side with the law punishing adultery by stoning. So far so good. On the other hand, he seemed to think adultery *was* a sin, since he said to the woman, "Go, and now sin no more." Jesus' remark assumed that the woman and he were in agreement that there was such a thing as a legally and religiously defined "sin," and that she had committed it. Yet the story also suggested that nobody at all was without sin, and that sin was part of the universal human condition—since the angry crowd of stoners had melted away (beginning, significantly, with the eldest ones) once Jesus had invoked the criterion, "He that is without sin among you, let him first cast a stone." On the whole, as an adolescent, I admired Jesus' acts and words, even though I did not like the Church and its prohibitions. But here was Jesus endorsing the public commandment against adultery, and endorsing the general concept of "sin." I wasn't sure I agreed with him. His position was better than that of the stoners, of course; but how much better?

The story presented one of the conundrums of behavior—especially female behavior—that, with pitifully little mental equipment, I was struggling with. I had no idea what made people commit adultery, how you did it, or how I would feel about it myself in the long run. I couldn't even imagine being married, let alone being adulterous. But since what I then wanted most in the world was freedom to live and behave according to my nature, I didn't want to preclude any potential exercise of that freedom. Maybe, in the future, it would include wanting or needing to "commit adultery" (that mysterious act) as the woman in the story had. Was I willing to let Jesus call it a sin and leave it as that in my mental economy—as a prohibited act? No: I wouldn't take anything on anyone's say-so.

These were the incompetent and feeble moral thoughts of a twelve-year-old girl. But insofar as this gospel story (and many others) were grids on which to hang my first intellectual struggles, they were incomparably useful. Now, of course, I see the story as one example of Jesus' avoidance of head-on confrontation with Mosaic law, even as he criticized the scribes and the Pharisees. But as a child, I was thinking only of the plight of the beset woman.

A few years ago, I was reading the title essay in Seamus Heaney's *The Government of the Tongue,* and lo and behold, there it was again, the story of the woman taken in adultery. But Heaney was using the story in a wholly new way. Beset, himself, by partisans on both the left and the right, in both Northern Ireland and the Republic, who wanted poets to take decisive political stands in their poems, Heaney saw the gospel story in a new light, as he focused on the two moments in the story where Jesus stoops down and, with his finger, writes on the earth characters neither described nor interpreted by the evangelist. Heaney comments:

> The drawing of those characters is like poetry, a break with the usual life but not an absconding from it. Poetry, like the writing, is arbitrary and marks time in every possible sense of that phrase. It does not say to the accusing crowd or to the helpless accused, "Now a solution will take place," it does not propose to be instrumental or effective. Instead, in the rift between what is going to happen and whatever we would wish to happen, poetry holds attention for a space, functions not as distraction but as pure concentration, a focus where our power to concentrate is concentrated back on ourselves.
>
> This is what gives poetry its governing power.[1]

It is not the plight of the woman that Heaney addresses, but the plight, one might say, of Jesus. Everyone is clamoring for action on Jesus' part—that he should ratify the Mosaic law or, falling into the trap that the scribes and Pharisees have set, repudiate it. Instead, Jesus writes. He writes twice, and in between the two moments of writing he invites anyone sinless to cast stones. He could have issued that invitation without the mysterious writing fore and aft. I, to my shame, had never even noticed or thought about the writing. But Heaney the writer had; and he had found in it a powerful metaphor for the worth of meditative writing in the midst of heated editorializing and violent acts.

It is the richness of implication in this story that has made it a favorite of writers and painters. It has the simplicity of parable, the suspense of drama, the ingenuity of riddle, and the unintelligibility (in Jesus' writing) of mystery. Remote though it was in time and space, it could catch up a child's heart and mind then, and a poet's attention now.

Among communities of believers, the Judeo-Christian inheritance can mean these days—as it did in my case—not only the discovery of memorable texts but also an encounter with superstition, sectarianism, censorship, repression, oppression, fear, and a disingenuous hermeneutic practice. Imposed as academic study in a course in the history of religion, it can be simply another set of obscure canonical texts to be mastered for an examination. It is no longer a heritage with a large living textual base in ardent practice (only fundamentalists, both Jewish and Christian, still seem to know the Bible intimately). The Hebrew Bible and the New Testament were once not only read but heard and studied and recited. That is why they became part of a living heritage. Now, even among the nominally religious in America, biblical texts are a dead heritage.

Can the biblical texts be resuscitated as an active part of American culture? I hardly think so. Our twelve-year-olds are not encouraged toward secret investigations of the Psalms or the moral conundrums of Bible stories. But, I tell myself, reading is often fortuitous: the literary young may be finding the Psalms through the poetry of Yehuda Amichai, or the story of the woman taken in adultery through the essays of Heaney. What is certain is that the hunger of the young to learn the truth about their own passions is as avid now as ever; and since any given piece of literature is always knitted, by a dozen strands, to others, the clue always leads into the same labyrinth, where the literary child will, sooner or later, discover the room containing the Bible.

NOTES

1. New York: Farrar Straus Giroux, 1988, p. 108.

Deuteronomy and John

A L F R E D   C O R N

In south Georgia in the mid-fifties, nearly everybody was fundamentalist even though no one used that term. Believing that the Bible was dictated directly by the Almighty was just practicing your religion. You didn't contradict your elders and didn't question the Word of God: some things went without saying, or, for that matter, thinking. Not too long after I ordered my Oxford University Press King James Authorized Version of the Bible, bound in pebbled black calfskin with my name stamped in gold in the lower right-hand corner, I became aware that a new translation called the Revised Standard Version was being hailed as the one for contemporary readers. Too late: I had my Bible—and besides was this new translation the real thing, the *Word of God?* The RSV couldn't help introducing a doubt, a challenge—which was dismissed by one old-timer this way: "I'm not going to read that thing. If the words of the

King James were good enough for Jesus they're good enough for me." I could see his mistake, and I could also see the Bible had stopped being an absolute for me. It was a work in another language, where the meaning of words and whole passages might vary according to who translated them.

I read my Authorized Version all the way through, now and then stopping to check with the RSV for clarification when I came to a verbal thicket. I preferred the sound of King James's English because that's what I'd grown up hearing; but I had become aware that his Bible contained errors. And if the AV did, wasn't it possible that the RSV had a few as well? In fact, could we ever be certain that any translation was error-free? Did no one have a chance of understanding the Word who couldn't read Hebrew, Aramaic, and Greek? Vexing questions for a youngster in an environment where it wasn't the custom to go too deeply into religious issues: obviously I was a melancholic bookworm in the making, creating problems for myself.

Just possibly the propensity to be troubled explains why I was especially struck, as I read my way through the opening books, by that scene at the conclusion of Deuteronomy, where Moses is refused entrance into the Promised Land and must instead die. It seemed so unfair. After giving up his comfortable life at the court of Pharaoh, after forty years in the desert, after shepherding the children of Israel through so many crises, after delivering the Ten Commandments and the Law to them, after so many rebukes delivered to backsliders, he was denied the triumph of a happy ending for his story. The honor of leading the Israelites home went to Joshua. Why? The explanation sounded capricious. While the Israelites were still wandering in the desert they came to a place called Meribah-Kadesh and suddenly found themselves without water. God told Moses that if he touched a rock there with his staff, water would flow. Angered by the complaints of his charges, Moses *struck* the rock with his staff. He opened a life-giving spring in the rock—but, alas, displeased Yahweh, who had ordained a scene of sanctification, not Moses' volunteer show of temper. And so Moses would not be allowed into the land accorded to the patriarch Abraham so long ago. Well, God's ways are not our ways.

Lit with less tragic grandeur, but also disturbing was the story (when I got to the New Testament two years later) of John the Baptist. Jesus' cousin, unmistakably a holy man, living like a hermit in the desert in his animal-skin clothes and diet of locusts and wild honey, John was held worthy to baptize penitents and cleanse them from sin. Nevertheless, he knew he belonged to the second rank. In the first chapter of John the Evangelist's Gospel, the elders come out to the Baptizer and ask him who he is. He answers, ''I am not the Christ,'' meaning he is not Messiah. Well, who then? ''I am the voice of one crying in the wilderness, Make straight the way of the Lord.'' The quotation refers his hearers to a short passage in the fortieth chapter of Isaiah, foretelling the advent of a certain wilderness prophet, a passage understood by John as foreshadowing this baptismal ministry several centuries later. (Understood by which John? The Evangelist or the Baptizer? First by the Baptist and then echoed by the Evangelist? But that's just it, we can't be certain.) John reports John as saying that though he comes first, the One who is to come *after* him will be preferred, the latchet of Whose sandals he is not worthy to unloose. If John baptizes with water, God's Son will baptize with the Holy Ghost. Eventually the forerunner performs his special rite on Jesus Himself, and proclaims Him the Lamb of God. In the third chapter of the Gospel, John says, ''He must increase, but I must decrease.'' Disparity between the two roles is accepted by the Baptizer with perfect equanimity, a single, faint demurral coming only after his imprisonment by Herod, when he sends word to ask whether Jesus intends to bring the Kingdom in soon and release him. But freedom never arrives; instead, he falls victim to Herod, who has him beheaded according to Salome's request. Once again faithful service, according to divine will, gets swallowed up in another person's more glorious triumph. Moreover, in this story, it is rewarded with capital punishment. God's ways are not our ways.

I still own my calfskin Oxford Press edition, which I actually do consult for the text of the AV; but reading it now is quite a different experience from those early encounters. I know that there are many, many translations of the work, beginning with the Targums, Aramaic versions of Hebrew scriptures made after the language was no longer spoken in the Near East; then the Septuagint, the Greek version that Alexandrian Jews provided three centuries before the Christian era; the Latin Vulgate of the Old and New Testaments done in whole or part by St. Jerome; Luther's German translation; then several English versions predating King James; and so on, up to the present. At the philosophical level, I know that texts are inert on the page; they become meaningful only in the minds of *readers,* each with a different *con*text, according to experience and learning. My own context includes not only churchgoing and a keen interest in Judaism, but also advanced degrees in literature, as well as an experience with editing a collection of essays on the New Testament *(Incarnation: Contemporary Writers on the New Testament)* similar to David Rosenberg's work on this volume and his earlier *Congregation.* A certain amount of unprofessional Bible scholarship is something I'm involved in on my own account because of its intrinsic fascination. Nowhere close to being a Gershom Scholem or a Norman Gottwald, I am nevertheless someone for whom the Bible is a thoroughly engaging object of scholarly study and criticism. The gathering of interior contexts that compose my identity includes a religious and a literary-scholarly one, both perpetually reading each other—which may explain why neither is especially conventional.

I have written a poem about Moses titled "The Author of Torah," even though I know that Moses is not the author of the first five books of the Bible and that Torah (or the Pentateuch, to use the Greek name) is the product of multiple authorship. As for the New Testament, I know that few scholars believe that John the Beloved Disciple is the author of the Gospel of John—for how could a Galilean peasant learn Greek well enough to write this book, which contains some of the most complex theological thinking and writing in the New Testament? Just possibly the actual author knew John and took down his account of things, but otherwise the connection to Jesus' disciple is moot.

To carry this notion of the internal context a step farther, it's probably necessary to note once again that Hebrew scripture is not for Jewish readers "the Old Testament." Quite apart from the differences in arrangement and detail between the Hebrew text and the one established in the Vulgate, specific passages in Tanach (the Jewish term for the sacred book) are not read the same way—because the interior contexts meeting them are not the same. The Christian reading occurs within the perspective of a later scripture, the "New Testament," which was composed in the spirit of retrospective interpretation. The original salvation narrative was understood as a predictive work, foretelling the appearance and ministry of Jesus Christ, various details concerning his life, and actions accounted for by the phrase, "so that the prophecy might be fulfilled." Some of those carefully signaled fulfillments arose from Jesus' consciously symbolic actions (for example, his recitation of Psalm 22 during the crucifixion); but others are the evangelists' discovery or invention. Sometimes these are highly ingenious, as with Luke's story about the imperial census, which took the Nazarene Joseph and his betrothed to Bethlehem, where Messiah has to be born if he is to qualify for the Davidic mantle.

Through scholarly study, I think I have nearly acquired the ability to lay aside the lenses of Christianity and read Tanach as Jews read it—as complete in itself and only occasionally concerned with predictions. Being able to do this, however, doesn't nullify an admiration and even a veneration for Christianity's transformation of its Hebrew forerunner text. On the contrary, Christianity's revision strikes me not only as the sole version of Judaic religion that would have had any chance of success among the

Hellenized peoples of the first century Roman Empire, but also as an extraordinarily brilliant instance of a process we see at work in nonreligious tradition as well. I mean by that the process whereby new writers reimagine the texts of earlier authors and transform these into something the later writers can claim as their own. A plotting of symbolic details in sequential order exists, I believe, in Tanach, but it was carried out much more resolutely by the New Testament writers faced with the task of making Jesus' advent and Messiahship seem to arise inevitably out of sacred history. "Typology" is the term used for this Christian exegetical approach. When speaking of resonant symbolic sequences in Tanach, perhaps we could call them "leitmotifs" rather than "types," to make the distinction. Of course Judaic tradition includes highly conscious instances of symbol-reading in the form of midrash, interpretation of scriptural passages made in full awareness that they go beyond the original author's intention (insofar as those intentions can be defined). It's possible to regard the New Testament and Christian theology as a large-scale midrash on the Hebrew scriptures as a whole, so long as we keep in mind that in Judaic tradition midrashim are always lesser in status than the texts they are based on, while the New Testament has full canonic status for the Christian faith.

I'm not certain how to define the following reflections on the two texts chosen for discussion. With no credentials as a biblical scholar, I can't propose any authoritative value for this essay—though it would be a lift to think that some scholars might find stimulating points of departure in it for more rigorous studies of their own. On the other hand, I have enough experience as a literary critic to produce an essay using traditional critical methods to arrive at a helpful synthesis based on what can be textually supported, irrespective of the authors' conscious intentions; and it seems important to me not to lose sight of the literary character of biblical texts. I suppose literary criticism has been in my case the natural outgrowth of my own work as a poet; a possible result is that purely professional critics would find an unprofessional intensity in literary essays of mine, in particular, that critical bugaboo, "overinterpretation." (And yet: who decides, according to what objective, eternal yardstick, what constitutes "overinterpretation"? And must the proof of professional adequacy be that interpretations are reassuringly obvious enough to be dull?) The normal human wish not to be regarded as a fantasist has to coexist in my mind with an acknowledgment that many issues raised in this essay have figured in poems of mine written over the past six or seven years. All right, but, for some poets, poetry is not entirely remote from cognition and reason; can be valued as much for its communicative as for its solipsistic aspect; and appeals to us because the experience embodied in it is recognizably like, even though quite different from, our own.

Readers will no doubt quickly perceive that my engagement with biblical texts is religious as well as literary, and it's fair to say so at the outset. In that framework, I can regard the following reflections as a form of midrash, with, needless to say, no status as scripture, but with, even so, some interest or instructional value to believers—at least, those believers with a literary bent. The gist of this essay would have to be put in simple, unscholarly form in order to become available to readers not practiced in textual analysis. Actually, I believe it already *is* available to them, in the form of uninterpreted symbols acting directly on the unconscious mind. For some of us, however, the process of making symbolic language *conscious* is meat and drink, with no presumption that religious potency or cultic aura is lost in the process. All things considered, this third description of what I'm doing—as religious and midrashic—is no doubt the one safest to adopt, since the verifiability requirements of midrash are the mildest. But I expect to go beyond the usual limits of midrash and bring in historical, linguistic, or literary categories whenever they seem pertinent to the discussion. Long before I was a poet or literary critic or unprofessional biblical scholar, I was a reader of the Bible concerned with exegesis, a reading process in which every word is weighed, paired with all its appearances elsewhere in the Book, and linked to an overarching pattern governing the whole. Biblical exegesis determined the kind of critic I became, but also the kind of poet, no doubt. (Leave aside the question whether it was a smart idea to compose poems all of whose meanings would emerge only after reading of a carefulness not common outside the practice of biblical studies, and *that* in an era when we lack time to read even the classics with much exactitude or attentiveness.) Like everyone else I plead the great tautology: I am the poet, literary critic, and biblical scholar that I am, with no sharp boundary between the territories. That proviso stated, I can now move to the subject of this essay.

Moses' story actually begins in Exodus, where we have the miraculous incident of his being spared from the death Pharaoh decreed for all male Hebrew children—a mass murder that foreshadows the last plague visited on the Egyptians just before the Israelites departed. An eye for an eye: when all the Egyptian firstborn suffered death Pharaoh was at last persuaded to end the Hebrews' long era of servitude. In Christian typology, the murdered Hebrew children are seen as prefiguring the Slaughter of the Holy Innocents more than twelve hundred years later, commanded by Herod when he heard that the Christ had recently been born in Judea. Typology also sees the Flight into Egypt (and the eventual return), when Joseph took Mary and the Child out of Judea to escape Herod's death sentence, as prefigured by the first Joseph's descent into Egypt and Moses' Exodus. These details and others tend to associate Moses with Jesus, just as Jesus is typologically associated with other heroic and prophetic figures like Joshua, Elijah, and David (his ancestor, according to the genealogies in Matthew and Luke). Another typological detail is the name of Moses' sister Miriam: ''Mary'' is an Anglicization (via Latin) of the Greek form of that name. A less superficial symbolic connection to Moses is found in Jesus' decision at the beginning of his ministry to spend forty days of prayer and fasting in the wilderness (or desert), which recalls the forty years of Moses' and the tribes' sojourn in the desert, as well as the forty days spent on Sinai, when the covenant was being delivered.

Moses' forty days and forty years also recall, within Torah itself, the leitmotif of the forty days and nights of rain that produced the Flood. (In the J account of Noah, the full period of the Flood is given as forty days, though not in the others.) Another leitmotif in Exodus 2 connecting Noah to Moses is the word designating the little wicker basket that his mother put him in before she floated it down the Nile for Pharaoh's daughter to discover. This word used is *tebah* (or, alternatively, *tebhah,* or *tevah),* which is the same word used for Noah's vessel. Just as his ark saved him and his family from the Flood, so the little basket saved Moses. Talmudic commentary attributes consciousness of the term's symbolic dimension to Moses' mother: she put him in an ''ark'' because she wanted to save him from destruction; she used wicker for the basket rather than Noah's ''gopherwood'' (or ''pitchwood'') because wood is too heavy and might break if the ark ran aground. In any case, the term *tebah* and the little Nile voyage to safety inscribe her act in a symbolic series beginning with Noah and continuing with the later passage through the Reed Sea.

Actually, the theme appears in many other contexts as well. Exodus 2 tells us that Moses was given his name by Pharaoh's daughter because it means ''drawn out'' (from the water, that is). Throughout the opening books of Torah, we discover a series of leitmotifs beginning with the Creation narrative, where dry land is separated from water, or a character passes through water to dry land as from death to life or from sin into righteousness. (The word for dry land in Genesis is *eretz,* which simply means ''earth'' or ''land''; and it is the term for the Promised Land also.) Besides the story of Noah, there is Jacob crossing the ford of Jabbok for his encounter with the divine being who gives him the name ''Israel,'' and Jonah's doomed sea voyage from which he is safely returned to land by a giant fish. The most important, the *defining* instance, is the Exodus from Egypt, the Egypt of fleshpots and an annually flooding Nile. Moses' escape was effected through the Reed Sea, which, Exodus tells us, opened for the Israelites but engulfed Pharaoh's pursuing armies. This epic event is the origin of Judaism's most joyful feast, the Passover, which is celebrated every spring the world over. Jews have been willing to make a sea voyage to settle in other countries, but they were not a seagoing people in ancient times, nothing like the Phoenicians or Greeks. Possibly the reason for that resides in a deeply internalized aversion for large bodies of water, as inculcated by the sacred book.

Moses' basket is not made of wood as Noah's ark was, rather, it is made of reeds or bulrushes—what we now call papyrus. (Exodus 2 is careful to note that Moses' mother coats the basket with pitch to make it waterproof—the same substance used by Noah on the first ark.) The Sea of Reeds through which Moses and his people pass is a wetland where reeds or bulrushes or papyri grow. The papyrus is better known as a plant used in paper-making than for basket-weaving. Moses, according to tradition, is the author of Torah, so his recording of his nation's foundational narratives and the code that gave it an identity and unity would be set down on papyrus (the one exception being the Decalogue or "Ten Words," which were inscribed on stone). Writing, too, is a means of survival, outliving any given author; and there is a sense in which any sacred book is an "ark," a vessel carrying the substance of salvation across the seas of circumstance to a safe destination. A fascinating instance of retrospective midrash is one offered in Talmud by Rashi of Genesis 6:14, which, in the AV translation, says, "Make thee an ark of gopherwood; rooms shalt thou make in the ark, and shalt pitch it within and without with pitch." "Rooms" translates Hebrew *kinim,* but Rashi says *kinim* are strips of papyrus used to fill in the chinks between the boards of the ark. And if Torah is an ark, what a brilliant metaphor for Talmud, the layered or compartmentalized series of midrashim (written on papyrus) that attempt to explain inconsistencies or ambiguities in the original text—in effect, to fill in gaps and make it seaworthy.

Eventually in the Deuteronomic narrative we are told that the scroll of laws recorded by Moses is placed next to the Ark of the Covenant in the holy tabernacle that accompanied the Israelites in their desert exile. It is a medium-size wooden chest, with angelic witnesses or guarantors present in the form of a pair of carved wood cherubim facing each other over the Ark's lid. Inside the Ark Moses placed twin stone tablets engraved with the Ten Words. The other laws, because not written on stone and not housed inside the Ark, were clearly regarded as less sacred—and yet only comparatively less. They were meant to be preserved in perpetuity also. The term "Ark of the Covenant" fits beautifully into the resonant series of leitmotifs outlined earlier: Noah's and Moses' survival (and by extension the survival of God's covenant with the people) culminates in this sacred object in which the holiest writings were contained. A very neat match—but it is a "midrash," an example of what might be called the "midrash of translation." For the Hebrew word in this context is not *tebah,* but *aron,* which means "box" or "chest." The mistranslation begins with the Septuagint, the first Greek-language version of Tanach, which was done in the third century B.C.E. by Diaspora Jews living in Alexandria, for a community that no longer understood Hebrew. Noah's *tebah* is translated with the Greek word *kibotos,* which means "box" or "chest." The same word is used for the *aron* of the Covenant. Meanwhile, Moses' *tebah* is translated as *thibis,* which simply means "wicker basket." Noah and the Chest of the Covenant are brought together, but Moses is dropped from the series. The Septuagint is now regarded as a rather haphazard effort, and so I may be mistaken to see any special intention or midrash here. And yet it is also difficult to imagine that scholars who knew Hebrew well enough to translate Tanach were unaware of commentary on the text's key words. If the Septuagint's translators had a midrashic intention, what was it?

To begin with, the wish to have a Greek-language Tanach for a Greek-speaking community already implies a perspective in which dwelling in the Land is not essential. Jewish history includes long periods of residence outside the Land, whether in Egypt, Babylon, or the Hellenic Diaspora. Meanwhile, the traditional significance of Moses' life is twofold: to lead the Israelites back to the Land and to convey the Law to them. But the Jews of the Diaspora did not accept residence in the Land as mandatory; they were not waiting impatiently to return. A sufficiently righteous life came from following the Law, which had been stored in and next to the *aron*. So the Septuagint translates Noah's ark and *aron* as the same word. The Covenant will carry its followers to safety.

The term *aron* is found in one other passage in Torah. Genesis 50:26, the last verse of the book, says (in the AV), "So Joseph died, being an hundred and ten years old: and they embalmed him, and he was put in a coffin in Egypt." *Aron* is the word translated as "coffin," but this tends to give a negative cast to a word also used for the container of the cult's most sacred writings. Perhaps the redactors of the original liked the suggestion established: what had been a coffin in Egypt became a powerful, life-giving ritual object in the Land. That is only a step from implying that the Law, if practiced outside the Land, would be a moribund affair, that it could only be abundantly life-giving in the Land. Jews living in Egypt, though, wouldn't be willing to accept the inference, and the Septuagint translates *aron* here with the Greek word *soros,* which means "funerary urn" or "coffin," dissociating it from the Ark of the Covenant.

Jerome's Latin Vulgate follows the Septuagint, so that Noah's *tebah* is Latin *arca* (etymologically, the source of the English word "ark"), as is the *aron* of the Covenant. But Moses' crib is only a *fiscella scirpea,* "a wicker basket." Wyclif, the first translator of the Bible (1380s) into English, follows the Vulgate, reserving "ark" for Noah and the Covenant, and calling Moses' vessel "a ionket of resshen," that is, "a basket of rushes." With Tyndale (1525) we have "basket of bulrushes," but Coverdale's translation (1535) reverts to "an Arke of reeds." In the King James AV (1611), this becomes "ark of bulrushes," so the full sequence of leitmotifs is maintained: Noah's boat, Moses' basket, and the container of the Covenant are all the same vessel. In a seagoing, colonial era, perhaps it was important to reinforce every association between religion and ships—after all, the conversion of New World peoples could only be carried out if the sacred Book was carried to them overseas. In this framework, Columbus's ships, and those of all the explorers and colonizers, were arks as well as all those that later traveled between the Old and the New World. Specific aims can always be debated, but at least it should be clear that translation is not neutral: it is always to whatever degree intentional—in effect, a midrash.

There is a problem, minor or not, depending on perspective, with the other half of the phrase "Ark of the Covenant." This translates the Hebrew *aron ha-berit,* which appears throughout Torah, sometimes in the variation *aron berit-YHWH,* "the Ark of the Covenant of Yahweh," as, for example, in Numbers 10:33. The word *berit* is used for the several covenants Torah records with the Lord, including Noah's, Abram's, Jacob's, and Moses'. But the Ark is also sometimes called the "Ark of the Testimony," which translates the Hebrew *aron ha-edut*—as, for example, in Exodus 25:22, where the command to build this "chest" first appears. The term means "testimony," or "pact," or "witness-pact," in any case, something less powerful than "covenant." At least one of the D sources is constantly concerned with YHWH's covenant *(berit)* and the container for it; but P, the Priestly redactor, prefers to call the box *aron ha-edut.* Why the difference? Or more specifically, why does P wish to decrease the suggestive power, the aura of the *aron?*

This question reminds us that, when trying to understand biblical writings, we have to consider not only the source but the intended audience. In what direction did the author/redactor want to take presumed readers of his writings? The latest scholarly thinking asserts that there were two major redactions of Deuteronomy, one before the Babylonian Exile and one after. If true, this explains why Deuteronomy seems to pull in opposing directions, on one hand asserting the importance of reaching the Land, and on the other moving toward an abstract, universal faith that can be practiced anywhere, far from the Land, far from the Temple—and far from the *aron*, which is only a ritual prop, certainly not the dwelling place of Yahweh nor even the repository of the *berit*. Moses' twofold role, as the leader of the Exodus into the Land and as mediator of the Covenantal Law, reflects this division. The Lawgiver's greatness does not depend on his going into the Land; and the sacred chest that does go in is, for P, the Chest of the Testimony, not the Covenant.

For at some point the *aron* disappeared, possibly when Jehoash, ruler of the northern kingdom of Israel, defeated Judah and plundered the Temple, but more likely during the Babylonian Exile. When the Second Temple was built after the return from that tragic and instructive expatriation, no one attempted to construct a new Ark. The cult could survive without it. In Solomon's Temple, the innermost sanctum or Holy of Holies had held the Ark, but in the Second Temple, that sacred space (in Hebrew, *debir)* was entirely empty except for a low stone platform. In 70 C.E., during the sacking of the Second Temple, Roman soldiers who hoped to find some fabulous golden trove inside it were apparently greatly disappointed. It was not a treasury; it was sacred space. The empty *debir* is one of a series of steps in the process of abstracting and universalizing the cult. The Babylonian Exile proved you needn't live in the Land in order to be faithful; furthermore, upon returning, one could manage without a sacred repository of the Covenant and the tablets inscribed by the Lord Himself; and, finally, it was even possible to do without a Temple (which also means forgoing animal sacrifice). Such was the conclusion of the rabbinic council that gathered in the town of Yavneh in 70 C.E. after the destruction of the Second Temple. (As an interesting sidelight, we might review the story of Rabbi Johanan ben Zakkai, the main architect of post-Temple rabbinic Judaism. He was, according to tradition, smuggled out of the burning city in a coffin—which recalls Joseph's Egyptian coffin and the *aron* of the Covenant.) In rabbinic Judaism, the shamanistic intensity of the Temple cult was much diminished, but there was a gain in the direction of universalizing intellect, as well as a final dispensation accorded to the people: they could live where they would, without fear of inadequate ritual performance.

Increased religious abstraction finds even so a countercurrent in a growing reverence for the sacred book (which has many copies), along with a reciprocal recognition that the faithful person is, in essence, an embodied text. The Jews did not begin as the People of the Book, but they did become that people. By the time of the first version of Torah around 400 B.C.E., members of the priestly class were able to find in it a powerful legitimation of their role. Jewish Diaspora in the Hellenized Mediterranean was a fact, a dispersal kept stable by the Book, which steadily increased in importance as residence in the Land diminished. The eventual centrality of Holy Writ is first hinted at in 621 B.C.E., when, during Josiah's reign, a sacred book of law was discovered in the Temple and went on to become the occasion of cultic and civic reform. (The story is recounted in 2 Kings 22–23.) Scholars hypothesize that an earlier version of Deuteronomy was the book in question. Whichever it was, the effect on Josiah was powerful and can only have led to increased respect for sacred writings, a respect that deepened throughout the period when Talmud was composed and the final canon of Tanach defined. In the aftermath of the Temple's disappearance, when the synagogue became a sanctuary for ritual enactments, the sacred book became the focus of devotion. The cabinet where the scrolls of Torah were kept, today known as the *aron ha-kodesh,* is understood as a replica of the original chest that was lost; in the Talmudic period, this cabinet was called the *tevah,* or Ark.

It's reasonable to think that the P writer's term *edut* ("testimony") really intended not the Covenant but the written *story* of the Covenant, which is not the same thing. P's view seems, in any case, to have been understood that way by Jerome, who translates the word *edut* sometimes as *testimonium* and sometimes (Exodus 30:26) as *testamentum*—which is the same term he gives to the Book as a whole, the first part of it *Vetus* ("old"), the second part *Novum* ("new"). The Ark of the Covenant appears twice in the New Testament, in Hebrews 9:4 and Revelation 11:19, and in both cases the Vulgate has *arca testamenti*. Wyclif and Tyndale each translate it as "arke of the testament," but the AV goes back to "Arke of the Covenant," losing in the process Jerome's symbolic connection of the Book to the old sacred container. In classical Latin, *testamentum* meant simply a testamentary will, so Jerome's decision to use it for *edut* and for the two books of scripture has midrashic force. And yet, like most midrashim, Jerome's gets at a truth. For isn't Torah presented as Moses' great legacy, his last will and testament?

The concluding chapter of Deuteronomy is a memorably staged presentation of Moses' death, taking him up to the top of a mountain (Pisgah for the D writer, Nebo for J), where he surveys the different parts of the Land he has been laboring so long to reach, knowing that entry will be denied to him. It is a magisterial scene, and several poets have used it as a subject for poems—Vigny in French, George Eliot and Robert Browning in English. In David Rosenberg's translation of J, YHWH's final words to Moses are: " 'This is the land I vowed to Abram, Isaac, and Jacob,' Yahweh said to him. 'To your seed I will give it,' were my words. It is revealed to your eyes, though your body cannot follow." Readers exiled from the Land could also "see" it, in this description of the scene; but their bodies could not go there. For them a text would have to do as an acceptable substitute for the Land; and if Moses could bear being denied entry then so could they.

God's command had been stated a bit earlier (in Deuteronomy 32:50) in the words of the D source: "And die in the mount whither thou goest up, and be gathered unto thy people; as Aaron thy brother died in mount Hor, and was gathered unto his people." It's the phrase "gathered unto his people" (Authorized Version) that solicits reflection, for, though the context shows that it means simply "to die," a milder expression for death is used, one that tends to undermine death. The Hebrew here is *v'hai 'ahsaif el amchah,* with *amchah* a word that originally meant "tribe," but brings in the idea of clan or close relatives as well, in short, "your forebears." Yet I think D intended an extra dimension of meaning here. For the Children of Israel are poised at the Jordan, ready to cross into the Land and inherit the Promise. Moses is also being taken to those tribes since they would not have arrived if he hadn't (within the perspective of the narrative) forged the opportunity for them. So "gathered to your people" has the flavor of futurity as well. Those who come later will inherit Moses' legacy, his testament.

Verse 6 of Chapter 34 also records God's burial of Moses: "And he buried him in a valley in the land of Moab, over against Beth-peor: but no man knoweth of his sepulchre unto this day." It might seem sad, at first glance, that Moses' tomb is lost. Talmud says that the absence of a tomb prevented idolatrous worshiping at it (or of it). Another inference is that tombs emphasize death, while the whole drift of the preceding passages had been to adumbrate a credible continuance for Moses' life. Instead of merely dying, he is "gathered to his people." For the generations coming after the one that knew him, the vehicle of that transfer is his book, his *edut,* his testament. And the D source must have wanted his own writerly destiny to be fused with Moses' here: his text will be taken to his future audiences in perpetuity, including all the later poets who build on his foundation. Just possibly D wishes to be regarded as the person foreseen in Deuteronomy 19:15, when Moses says, "The Lord thy God will raise up unto thee a Prophet from the midst of thee, of thy brethren, like unto me; unto him ye shall hearken." Within the "ark" of Moses' prophetic testament, the Deuteronomist will also be carried safely into perpetuity.

I said earlier that veneration for Torah steadily increased as rabbinic Judaism became the norm, and that the faithful more and more saw themselves as an *embodiment* of the Book. If so, they were only following the prophecy of Jeremiah, who in Chapter 31: 31–33 speaks of a new covenant that will unite the divided kingdoms of Israel and Judah. An obvious precondition is a cessation of dispute about the central location of the cult, whether in Shechem or Jerusalem: best not to have a single sacred precinct where the Law is enshrined if the separate tribes are to be unified. Jeremiah reports God as saying, "I will put my law in their inward parts, and write it in their hearts; and will be their God, and they shall be my people." This is as much as to say that the people becomes a book, and the same book everywhere. In reciprocal fashion, Torah becomes a person. For, in several religious ceremonies, Torah is taken out of the *aron ha-kodesh* and carried among the congregation as though it were a person walking the path ritually prescribed for it. Moreover, what is the process of responding to scripture in the form of Talmudic commentary or midrash than a conferral of the commentators' own lives and "inward parts" to the Book? An exchange is set up in which readers become textual and a text breathes with their life. I've often wondered if the Hasidic practice of growing long, cylindrical curls on either side of the face, apart from symbolizing uncompromised masculine *virtú*, isn't also meant to remind at least some viewers of the twin scrolls of Torah, which individuals have, by long study and practice, incorporated?

The French Jewish scholar Olivier Revault-d'Allonnes, in his midrashic book of reflections titled *Musical Variations on Jewish Thought,* has pointed out that the word *kerev,* the term for the space inside the Ark of the Covenant, is the same word for the space inside the human thoracic cavity. His midrash (following Jeremiah) transforms the human heart into Torah and the body into the Ark (or chest) containing it. It's clear that Paul, in 2 Corinthians 3:3, was using a similar metaphor when he said, "Forasmuch as ye are manifestly declared to be the epistle of Christ ministered by us, written not with ink, but with the Spirit of the living God; not in tables of stone, but in fleshy tables of the heart." "Torah" is usually translated as "Law," but the word actually means "the telling," or "instruction." Insofar as we become ourselves "a telling," a source of true instruction, an epistle to others, we become an embodiment of Torah.

Earlier I pointed out a few of the connections that Christian typology established between Moses and Jesus, details found in the Gospels or singled out for comment in the Epistles. Returning to the passage in the first chapter of John, we can also note typological similarities between Moses and John the Baptist. John begins his ministry in the desert, preaching repentance just as the Deuteronomic Moses does. The rite he initiated, immersion in the Jordan River, was not part of Israelite tradition—except in the sense that it was a symbolic reenactment of the water leitmotifs of Flood, Nile River, the Reed Sea crossing, and the crossing of the Jordan into the Land, which only the righteous deserve to inherit. As such, John-the-type-of-Moses represents the parent religion—a forerunner, but, for the Evangelist, not a sufficient salvation. That will come only with the Christ. His name, Jesus, is the Anglicization of the Greek form of "Yeshua," which in the Pentateuch is transliterated as "Joshua." Joshua-Jesus, the one appointed to carry into the Land the mission begun by Moses-John, is, surprisingly enough, willing to be baptized by his forerunner. Immediately afterward he is visited by the dove of the Holy Spirit whereupon the voice of God proclaims Him as His Son. Christ's dual nature is being signaled here: incarnate of a woman (Miriam-Mary) and subject to death, for which baptism is the sacramental symbol; but He is also Spirit, emerging intact from water, and as such continuous with the immortal and eternal God.

This is the same Spirit that came to Mary and engendered her son at the Annunciation, an event medieval typology saw as prefigured in the story of Noah and the Ark. Noah, aground on Ararat, sent out the dove a second time and saw it return with an olive branch, a sign that meant safe dry land awaited him outside. When the Dove of the Spirit came to Mary, she knew that she carried within her the Word of God, who is God's Son. Church architecture reflects this typology, the cathedral understood both as Mary's body and as a ship: "nave" is from French *nef*, "a ship." At the conclusion of the eucharistic liturgy, communicants are freed like the ark's passengers or "born" like children as they pass by the baptismal font of waters out the west door into the world, while the rose window above them remains intact, penetrable by rays of light but nothing else.

I don't know whether typology ever connected the Bethlehem manger, where Jesus was lain in swaddling clothes, with Miriam's little wicker basket, but the connection is there to be made. Neither Matthew nor Luke (the sources of the Nativity narrative) mentions any stable, but Luke's manger summons it into consciousness, and Christian tradition quickly made the stable, with its sheep, oxen, and asses, a standard feature of the story. Typology might have associated Noah's animal-crowded Ark as well with the stable, but I haven't so far found any instance where the symbol is developed.

It would have been more convenient for typology if John's name had been Moses, but the actual name allows for another typological resonance. John (in Aramaic, Yochanan) derives from Jonathan, Saul's son and presumed heir, who nevertheless was replaced by David, the shepherd from Bethlehem who became king and prototype of Messiah. Another typological resonance is discoverable, too, in the special affectional bond between Jesus and the later John, the Evangelist, known as the Beloved Disciple. As David loved Jonathan so Jesus loves the Evangelist—who, I think, was aware of the overlap of his name with Jonathan's and with John the Baptist's as a coincidence with symbolic potential for his Gospel. John's first chapter opens with one of the supreme passages in New Testament theology, a description of the Eternal Logos (or Word), which is to be understood as the Christ. Immediately after this abstract, purely spiritual flight, we are thrust into the concrete details of The Baptist's prophetic ministry. He is depicted as preaching but never *writing*, which is the reason that his story had to be told by someone other than himself. John the Evangelist (equated by tradition, though not by scholarship, with John the Divine, author of Revelation) has a kind of immortality not available to the Baptist, whose death is recounted in the Gospels, as the Evangelist's never is. John's Gospel narrates at much greater length the story of Jesus, the Christ, the Logos, and shows how baptism not by water but the Spirit allows the faithful person to partake of the Logos's divine nature and to become a "telling" oneself, (in John's case, the author of a Gospel). Catholic liturgy prescribes special reverential gestures such as bows and incense for the Gospel text, a reverence appropriate, in fact, to the divine Person. Doing so suggests that, as with Torah, the book has taken on divine life that can in turn be embodied again in hearers and readers.

During the period of the final redaction of John's Gospel, differences between the orthodox congregation and the Jesus sect, deemed negligible at first, had devolved into open hostility. The Birkat ha-Minim or Twelfth Benediction, a prayer against heretics once aimed at Sadducees, was, during the ascendancy of Raban Gamaliel II, redirected against Jesus' followers. Those attending services were required to say the prayer as a way of assuring that all present were of the same doctrinal disposition—a measure fiercely resented by congregants who venerated Jesus without wishing to give up traditional religious practice. By the beginning of the second century there were more Gentile members of the sect than Jewish, and John's Gospel is therefore an outright repudiation of the parent religion—which is saddening to contemplate, apart from the disastrous consequences of that repudiation for Jews in European history since the beginning of the Christian era. Where earlier Gospels had "the chief priests" or the "people" speak out against Jesus, John specifically names "the Judeans" (or "Jews") as his opponents, which cannot be accidental.

Actually, John's symbolic undermining of the older tradition begins much earlier—as early as the first chapter of his Gospel. Moses' twofold function in Deuteronomy is divided in the Evangelist's typology between

John the Baptist and Jesus (eventually, John the Evangelist as well). Insofar as Moses' mission is summed up in the trek to Canaan, he is the forerunner of John the Baptist. Insofar as he is mediator of the Covenant and "gathered to his people," he is a type of Jesus. For the Evangelist, Jesus is the new Moses, with a new covenant not attached to the Land, but instead available everywhere, to all people. If the doctrine were promulgated in purely abstract terms, it would have impressed few people, yet, during the Last Supper, Jesus was able to revise the Passover Seder into something new, with as much shamanistic intensity as Temple sacrifice. Designating bread and wine his body and blood and giving it as food to his disciples brought (and brings) with it the shiver of broken taboos. It also symbolically enacts the distribution of Spirit (or Logos) to the people, into whose bodies it is taken. The rite can be performed anywhere, but it is always concrete and physical, otherwise it would not be sacramental. Communicants are referred to as "the Body of Christ," and if the Resurrection occurred in no other way, then at least it occurs this way, one substance with living, breathing bodies. And the Communion must be an *exchange* between at least two people since the priest is not allowed to celebrate the eucharist alone —just as no one writes a text that is not meant to be later read, at least by the author and usually by others as well.

If we return to Revault-d'Allonnes's concept of the body as an ark of the covenant, the eucharist becomes a transfer of the substance of the covenant from its original maker to several subsequent "arks," who then contain it as a source of sanctity. Jesus' association with the Ark is found not only in the brief voyages he makes in fishing boats on the Sea of Galilee (sometimes preaching from the deck of the ship), but also in his most satirized miracle, when he walks on water, as recounted in the sixth chapter of John. In Matthew 14, Peter attempts to imitate him and manages fairly well until he begins to be afraid and starts to sink. Jesus holds out an arm and helps him back up, restoring to Peter the arklike ability to float above water, an ability dependent on faith. Many attempts have been made to account for this miracle rationally, either by translation (John's Gospel allows for the meaning "walked beside the sea") or by natural details, such as the notion that the Sea of Galilee has rocks just under its surface, on which Jesus could stand and seem to be floating. But if the incident is seen as one in a series of leitmotifs involving safe passage through water to salvation, the evangelists' decision to include a story so incredible as this will seem natural enough.

The account of the empty tomb is even more incredible, yet it, too, has a typological resonance, at least in the third and fourth Gospels. The single "man" remaining at the tomb on Sunday morning in Matthew and Mark becomes two angels in Luke and John. In each case, the message of Jesus' Resurrection is conveyed to the angels' astonished listeners. John portrays the angels as seated where Jesus' head and feet had been, with his discarded linen shroud between them. (One medieval term for "book," *incunabula,* means, literally, "swaddling clothes," which Jesus' discarded linens recall.) In John's described arrangement, the angels resemble the two cherubim that faced each other over the Ark of the Covenant, as detailed in Exodus. But Jesus' "ark" is now empty, as empty as the *debir* or Holy of Holies, just at the moment when the Covenant is gathered to all faithful people who remain on earth. This is the risen Body of Christ—each member thereof eventually leaving behind its own ark when the received content is turned over to others still present in the flesh, flesh "inscribed" with the Word. The Hebrew name for Deuteronomy, taken from the book's first sentence, is *Devarim,* which simply means "Words."

Song of Solomon

J   O   Y   H   A   R   J   O

I.

The first Bible I remember was the huge book, the only book, in my mother's parents' one-room house in northwestern Arkansas. My grandparents were sharecroppers, and owned very little. They had both come to that land via migrations. My grandmother's mother was Cherokee and had been forced to the area by the United States Government from the East in what is now North Carolina. She married an Irishman from Ireland who came to this country for land. My grandmother was born and raised in Oklahoma, on Cherokee assigned lands. My grandfather's people were immigrants from France and Germany. The Bible carried family records and was all they had because everything had burned in a house fire. I never witnessed anyone reading the Bible, but I did see my grandmother open it to verify the date of a death. It was a book of records. I'm not even certain how much either of my grandparents could read for I never saw either of them read, not even a newspaper. My mother's education ceased at eighth grade. Higher education was not perceived as an option. The opportunity belonged to another class of people. Hard work was seen as the only way to survive.

There was an aura of sacredness around the Bible. It was viewed as God's book, though when I imagine the sacred in that humble house I think of my grandfather opening a can of peaches. Peaches were bought with money from backbreaking work. He opened a can for me every time I came to visit and I understood it as an offering of the best he had.

I also experienced the mystery of the sacred there in the form of ghosts who wandered the land. One was a relative of my grandmother's who had murdered his whole family with a pair of scissors. Another was Pretty Boy Floyd, who my grandmother had given a drink of water from the well when she was a young girl as he fled from justice. The stories told by my grandparents pondered the questions of life and death. That ghosts survived meant something sacred and profound was going on.

A large popular print in a pine frame of two beautiful children walking over a bridge at night was the only artwork on the walls of their humble house. Before the children was a hole in the bridge they were sure to fall through in the dark, but an angel they couldn't see appeared to guide them safely over the danger.

I spent hours inside the mystery revealed in the scene of the children and the angel, and knew that it related to the mystery in the pages of my grandparents' Bible. I considered the appearance of angels and knew they were possible for I had seen them appear as lights in times of terror and uncertainty. Yet, the angels I saw did not have the human countenance or the immensity of wings as the angel in the print. I also wondered why those particular children warranted protection, when others didn't. Many of the most disturbing stories that were passed around in the family had to do with deaths of children. Perhaps the Bible mapped the puzzle of mystery, or gave counsel to navigate the paradox.

2.

My father's mother's father was a Creek Baptist minister. The Bible was brought to the Creeks by the many European nations claiming Muscogee lands as theirs, by right of the God in the Bible. (These nations included Spain, France, England, Scotland.) I imagine the Bible being carried as a sword through the various nations and tribes from the Middle East to Europe then across the Atlantic. It was a tool of righteousness weighted with the blood of many nations who fell to those who brandished it.

The Creeks (or Muscogees) already had a spiritual path laid down in the very beginning, given by the same Creator who inspired the Bible. We have our stories, our songs, rituals, and ceremonies that celebrate and praise God as well as instill within us an awe of the mystery of life. We know that the stars, land, animals, plants—all living things are a part of this larger beingness, this body and soul of God. We exist together. The presence of God the creator is embedded in each cell—the sound and meaning connecting us. Song and stories that make up ceremonies are our Bible, as is the meaning inherent in the process of a corn plant or the movements of deer. These events also document our history, from the creation story to our presence now in a land far from that place. This knowledge and recounting are inherent in every ceremonial aspect of living as a member of the tribe. Planting is or can be considered a ceremonial process—we take part in the birthing of the process of the corn, beans, or squash growing. The corn songs sung to ensure healthy corn are encoded with memory—of our relationship with the corn, and the garnered knowledge of what is needed to grow.

The Bible too is a rendition of sacred stories and songs that convey what is sacred as well as the how-ness of the sacred specifically to the peoples it was given to, to a particular shape and spirit of land and language. These transcriptions were given to sustain the spiritual health and direction of a people. I imagine these stories told, these songs sung in the context of particular place and history, a context that makes perfect meaning for the relatives and descendants of the singers. I think of the caution given at tribal ceremonies, by mother to child, uncle to nephew, grandparents to grandchildren (perhaps given by the ancestors of the Bible to their children): ''These rituals of songs and stories are powerful, they belong in this place, have power in this place. To use them otherwise is to abuse their power.''

The Bible carries within it great power, as do many of the song and story rituals of my nation. When this power is misused, it backfires, destroys rather than creates community. I am still confounded by the origin and great need of the destructive force that razed the tribal cultures of Europe and any country in the world where the Bible has been used as a tool of colonization. This process is ongoing. The Bible translators and missionaries go in just ahead of the multinational corporations, collaborate in the theft. Force does not unite people in faith, rather separates by distrust and suspicion.

I imagine my grandfather Henry Marsey Harjo as a young orphan as he attended and grew up at the Eurfaula Boarding School. Many children were orphaned after the forced migration from what is now Alabama, and were raised in the new Creek Nation. Christianity strictly supplied the tenents of education. I see Henry Marsey as a young boy, his fierce intelligence crackling around his head, but he is perhaps viewed as a soul with few resources, someone to be saved from his Indianness, a strain of Africanness. His intelligence and spirit are funneled through a version of Christianity that will shame him, turn him from his tribal beliefs; his soul will observe him from a bit of a distance. Marsey will later become a minister and he and my grandmother, Katie Monahwee, will travel many winters to Florida as missionaries to the Seminoles.

I have a photograph of my grandparents dressed stylishly in modern apparel, standing next to newly converted Seminoles in Florida who still wear the traditional turbans and coats. My grandparents embodied the hope of the industrialized world that everyone could become converted to a more "civilized" way of life or disappear. But as with anything that happens in this world, a people either adapts in some manner or is destroyed.

Katie was also orphaned and raised by Christians. I imagine a whole generation of Creeks disrupted after the displacement from our homelands. How do you rebuild in a place far from home, when your records are etched in the land and skies of another land?

For some, Christianity became a refuge, another way to understand the sacred that perhaps masked the loss. They found ways to incorporate Christianity, for ultimately, without the fundamentalism and agenda of the colonizers, the Bible allowed another way to speak of the sacred, especially when it was read without the judgment of fundamentalist sects. Other tribal members retreated into the hills to carry on the meaning of the sacred fire of the tribe, accounted directly for the losses, and began anew. A line would be drawn between these groups by the Bible teachers.

The Creeks developed their own form and style of Baptist worship. In the church of my great-grandparents the men and women were segregated. The hymns and preaching were in the Muscogee language, as was the Bible. Other stylized elements characterized the services, which always ended with a community dinner that included sofkee, a staple of the tribe made of corn, a dish rich with spiritual implications. This is true today; these churches are still active and are central to Creek communities.

I imagine Marsey Harjo in the office of his twenty-one-room house, a house bought with oil money discovered under his allotted land, reading the Bible as I read it as a young girl, with a hunger for the music and stories of peoples who were similar in many ways to his own people. They were a tribal people who suffered. The Creeks too suffered great tests. We were forced away from our home to a new land to deal with an imposed government and system. Perhaps he found comfort in relating to these struggles. Yet, there is always the paradox of the text, of its origins and how it was used to belittle his own language, his own memory.

The oral tradition informs the stories and songs found in the Bible and as a Muscogee person he was still close to those traditions, for even in the boarding schools the children found a way to subvert Christianity, to maintain their Muscogeeness, for the beingness of a people is maintained through centuries, since creation, and is not easily diverted.

I wonder what were his favorite passages, what stories moved him beyond the ordinary? I wonder what happened to his papers, what he had to say, and about the sound of his voice relating these stories to his congregations as well as his own children: my grandmother, aunts, and uncle?

I can imagine him reading the Song of Solomon in the context of the importance of corn for the Muscogees, as this morning I read Song of Solomon 4:11 (King James Version): "Thy lips, O my spouse, drop as the honeycomb: honey and milk are under thy tongue; and the smell of thy garments is like the smell of Lebanon. A garden inclosed is my sister, my spouse; a spring shut up, a fountain sealed . . ." This could be a love song to the corn, a song of praise so the corn will feel compelled to grow straight and thick, feel welcomed. In my tribe the corn originates from the body of a woman.

I hear Henry Marsey Harjo sometimes in my own voice, and have seen him standing nearby as I study, write, and ponder the mystery of the world. Perhaps all literature has a sacred source. Perhaps we are tools of the literature, being created by it. I believe it works both ways.

3.

I was lured to my own relationship with Christianity and the Bible as a kindergartener. Members of the Tulsa Bible Church congregation waited for us after school, on the sidewalk surrounding the public school just before summer vacation. They passed out announcements of Vacation Bible School, each flyer laced with a sucker. I loved anything sweet and figured there was more where that came from, and there was: Kool-Aid and cookies always followed the Bible lessons. And thus began my relationship with the church.

I became an orphan figure in that church. I came every Sunday for the morning Sunday school and church, then for Sunday night services, as well as for the Wednesday night services. I attended on my own, without my parents. My mother was exhausted with working two and three jobs as a waitress and/or cook. My father and then stepfather did not go to church. When my sister grew older I brought her with me, and my brothers attended more sporadically, but we essentially came without parents. The stories and songs became a refuge. They provided a structure of meaning in a household that had gotten caught in the whirlpool between colonization and tribal awareness. Many families got stuck and could not move either way. Colonization meant jobs working for others. Your work did not nurture the tribe, rather made money and power for an outside source. In strange times such as these the attention to the songs and stories can fall away from exhaustion.

As soon as I learned to read I read voraciously. I immediately read all of the books in the first-grade classroom, then went to the second-grade classroom. I loved the Bible and began reading the King James Version of the Bible when I was seven years old and read it through twice by the time I was fourteen. I loved the language in the Bible, for it was a language of song. The stories too embodied rich human drama. I loved the story of Ruth and Naomi and often referred to a painting in our living room, of Ruth and Naomi, a painting by my grandmother Naomi Harjo, Katie and Marsey's daughter. She had painted it in the early part of the century. I disappeared in that painting and walked the sandy hills of the landscape, pulled by the fierce story binding these women together. Ruth's entreaty: "for whither thou goest, I will go . . . thy people shall be my people"

(Ruth 1:16) always made me tearful as I imagined her refusing to leave Naomi and the family of her in-laws. I could imagine many leavings: the forced move to Oklahoma, my father from our family, my mother from us.

I soon began to realize the Bible was divided into the spoken and the unspoken: there were stories and songs that were used and reused in the church, and there were the stories and songs that were never spoken, because there was no place for them within the context of colonization in Oklahoma in the 1950s and later 1960s. Even the Bible had forbidden parts, including stories of the sins of figures who had been presented to us as saints, and other paradoxes of meaning. I had a gift for finding them and perhaps that's what spurred me on in my reading, as well as the sensual musicality of the reading, the smell of the ink on the pages.

I was shocked to come upon the story in Genesis 19 of Lot's daughters getting their father drunk and sleeping with him to make descendants. I read it to my mother one evening while she was bathing. We often had our deep conversations then. "This is what's in the Bible!" I told her. She didn't believe it at first, for her experience of the Bible had been through sermons in the Methodist church when she was young, stories of the Christ Child, the usual stories children are told. She did not know how to explain the story of Lot and his daughters. This was not the sacred book in her parents' house. We were both disturbed over this story of the taboo of incest. Later I understood there were undercurrents neither of us could yet touch.

The appearance of this story confirmed for me that the church had purposefully discarded what it couldn't explain in human behavior. Yet this story opened up all kinds of questions that discussed could deepen human knowledge. The world is rife with paradox, yet paradox was not allowed in the church, or rather specifically allowed when it came to concepts such as the Trinity. As a child of two cultures (or more precisely three and more), my belief system had to embody paradox or it would not be useful for navigating through this life. I didn't recognize any of this for some time and immersed myself in the system of the church to save myself. Yet, in the place of all-knowing we carry within us, I knew that though I appeared to be within the system I would always be outside it. I stood out because of my aloneness and differentness. I was one of the few Indians; worse, my mother appeared light and had married an Indian. (This had more serious implications than if she had appeared to be Indian. This was Ku Klux Klan territory as well as "the Bible Belt." The connection of terms makes sense now.) I was also from a family of divorced parents.

Yet, I became the hope in that church, the one who would become a missionary, much as Marsey and Katie became missionaries. I memorized Bible verses to win prizes, such as a Jesus on a cross that lit up in the dark, as well as my week at church camp. I became part of the choir and believed fiercely in this power called God who could save me from the disappointment in life I saw all around me. I craved mystery; I believed in the mystery of this power. It unfolded before me in symbols of light in the middle of the night around my bed, wove through my dreams. I knew things I had no way of knowing in the system in place in public school, in the community in which I lived. There was no context for that kind of knowing except in the stories that came to me from my parents (particularly my mother), and in the passages of the Bible that told also of visions and dreams. I remember in particular Jacob's dream of wrestling with an angel. I dreamed too and had experiences similar to Jacob's. The dream world was often more real in scope and truthfulness than this one I had found myself in. Sometimes I believed my life as a child in Tulsa, Oklahoma, to be a dream. Though we were told the story of Jacob's ladder in church, the church openly disparaged visions and dreams. They were not allowed, condemned as heathenism and fortune-telling, and were thought to be of the devil.

4.

"Behold, thou art fair, my love; behold, thou art fair; thou hast doves' eyes within thy locks: thy hair is as a flock of goats, that appear from mount Gilead . . . Thy lips are like a thread of scarlet, and thy speech is comely; thy temples are like a piece of pomegranate within thy locks . . ." (Song of Solomon 4:1, 3)

When I was nearing adolescence
I found the Song of Solomon.
It was a secret of beauty
in the wilderness of sin
though according to the keepers
of the book in recent history
sensuality was a sin.
To be born with a body
blessed with the gifts
of sensual pleasure
was to be born of sin.
Then why did God create us
to enjoy ourselves and each other
as representatives of God's
body, for aren't we the sons
and daughters of God?
I saw the spring grass enjoy
the little winds sliding through it.
Birds leaned into the flirting winds
and snuggled in

the haven of the nest
with mates.
Humans were born with fingers,
eyes, ears, a tongue and mouth
each to communicate
humanness.
We crave the comfort
of the song we make
with each other.
These songs were the secret of my secret longing
for the beloved. This urge
is born within each
human at the transformation of becoming
woman from girl
or man from boy.
For the transformation makes a song
that stirs us, similar to the corn
learning to sing as it grows
to the sky.
It is with this song we create our
own songs, poetry.
With this song language I could sing
of this thing
that was turning me inside out.
Within this song was the power of the corn growing
the deer dancing, the fire changing us
from stone, to animal to human animal
to spirit.
The holy ghost danced through these songs.
I knew it was not shameful

to be a human with a body,
how could I if I heeded
the lessons
of the wisest teachers?

5.

The summer of my fourteenth year I visited my mother's brother and his family in Joplin for two weeks. I didn't know much about them though I had met them at family gatherings and especially liked my cousin Mary, who was my age. She and her sister had to wear dark dresses that covered nearly every inch of skin. They went to church every night of the week. I showed up with my suitcase of shorts, jeans, and tee shirts and began a bit of a revolution in that household. Perhaps to make me feel more comfortable, the girls were allowed to shorten their dresses a few inches to more closely accommodate current styles. And we went to church every night during my stay.

My uncle Clark and his family belonged to "the holiness church," which was the cultural center of their lives. Every night my uncle carried in his guitar and amplifier and set up next to the piano.

The first night I didn't know what to expect. I knew from my cousin Mary that dancing was prohibited (as it was in my church) as was rock music or anything else associated with the pleasure of the senses. (She told me this as we tried to smoke cigarettes and listened to the rock station from Tulsa at night in her parents' car.) From my readings of the Bible I knew that music was central, for there was certainly music at the root of the songs of Solomon, and I knew David danced before the altar, but no one in my church would ever engage me on that question.

The service proceeded as any other Protestant service among sober people who have kept praise of life in check. Everyone's story was a version of my uncle Clark's—a life of poverty from a sharecropping family. For most it was a hard life with very little to celebrate. The preacher said a few words. An unraveling basket was passed around that collected the spare change of the congregation, who all seemed on the edge of exhaustion. It had been only twenty minutes and I was already yawning and twisting in my chair, and began to open my Bible to read Song of Solomon as I often did in those times.

And then the music started.

The church music wasn't particularly compelling at first. Neither the singers nor the piano were in tune, nor was there anything acoustically alert in that pine building. But something rose up in that little church, like a wave in an ocean headed to shore. From afar off it didn't look like much, but as it came into sight you either joined it, or it took you with it.

The transformation of the congregation had begun. This is what they had come for, what they had waited for as they had worked long hours in factories, or had done the family wash on wringer washers, or had watched television.

The piano player followed the voice of the preacher who answered to the moan of the piano.

"We are a sorrowful people, we have sinned," intoned the preacher as he held his Bible aloft. The people rose up out of their seats in response to the music.

"We need salvation," the preacher begged.

The pain of loss and sorrow from these people who were the descendants of the poorest of the immigrants, of the Indians who'd been caught in the destruction of industry, melted away as they embraced hope together in this spirit of community. Hope became the name of the piano player who pounded out redemption on the dancing keys. The formerly taciturn preacher became illuminated with hope as the promise of salvation washed over him. My uncle's worn-out body filled with music and the people began to shudder and shake as this collective celebration of salvation took them over one by one.

The whole congregation rose with this spirit and began dancing around the church in a conga line, singing and praising God. My cousin Mary whispered to me that they were being filled with the Holy Ghost, who sang and talked through them.

We watched as the most inspired fell to the floor, writhing and dancing with the power of this spirit, speaking in languages that were said to come from a paradise, a place in which God's believers would one day join Him.

I was amazed at this transformation and I couldn't stop thinking about the Holy Ghost, this strange invisible spirit of the trinity my pastor urged us to accept without question because no human could understand it.

I figured the Holy Ghost must be a woman. Why else would she be invisible in a church that told wives to be obedient and obey their husbands, as if they didn't have souls? I wanted to see this Holy Ghost.

The next few nights I brought my clarinet and set up next to my uncle and played with him to call forth this spirit who moved these people to dance in celebration and in sorrow in a church that outlawed dance or any other display of sensuality.

The fourth night I finally saw the Holy Ghost. By then I'd almost given up. I'd been looking for a shimmering spirit, like the ones who used to visit when I was a child, or for an angel-like presence to come floating out of the sky while the preacher was talk-singing. Instead, she appeared to me in the most unlikely place, in the face of a timid young woman who wasn't more than twenty but looked twice her age. She wasn't the face of the beloved I had imagined.

Her four children circled her as she shook in communal passion on the linoleum floor of the church. The Holy Ghost gave this woman her tongue, turned her into an orator who sang beautiful words in a mysterious and compelling language. We all paused to stare, to take part in her magnetic performance.

In her I saw the power of the fields, what made the corn grow. I saw the loved and the beloved. It was a power similar to that I have seen since, in the ceremonies of my Muscogee people as we prayed and danced together.

6.

I left my church that next fall, when the pastor told some children of Mexican immigrants, who'd been invited by members of the congregation, to leave because they were talking in church, something that the white children did regularly as they sat between their parents. I am ashamed I did not have the bravery to walk out with them. But my spirit left with them that day. I quit going shortly thereafter and left the Bible with the memories of that church.

7.

I did not open the Bible or consider the power and effect until several years later as I listened to Li Young Lee, who was conducting a workshop for my creative writing students at the University of Arizona. He is a fine poet, the son of a Chinese missionary father who was also displaced from his native lands and carried the Bible from one land to another. Li Young Lee talked about the influence of biblical language on his poetry and how history must inform poetry or poetry can become a shell of emptiness, as so much workshop poetry is in this age.

As I listened to him I watched the faces of the students gathered around him, as well as his countenance as he spoke his version of the journey to the end of the world, this time as a poet. I saw his father in him, propounding on elements of the word, how they related historically, spiritually to the well-being of the community. I saw Marsey Harjo, who was often mistaken for Chinese or Jewish when he was outside his community, as he spoke to his congregation. The words and actions of our ancestors continue in us; we are all traveling together.

I walked out into the balmy desert night thinking of the Bible and the words of the Bible that informed my language, of the history of how I came to be, very physically present, moving beneath the palm trees, listening to the gas lamps illuminating the dark with their hiss, tasting a distant rain, so far away from Oklahoma, the homelands of the southeast, even France or other lands I had never seen.

How did we begin? And how did we come to this place—that I could feel the delight of spirit moving in bones, walking through the dark rich with history, and at being able to use words to praise and understand this place, as if the words were taproots reaching out for rain, for sustenance? I considered the concantenation of voices, songs, words forming my bones as I walked.

I had never forgotten the verse at the beginning of the book of John: "In the beginning was the Word and the Word was with God, and the Word was God." (John 1:1) Years ago as the pastor pounded out a sermon based on this verse I saw a God who looked much like him, an angry man who was infused with a sense of self-rightenousness. I imagined the Word as the tablets in Moses' hands as he came down from the mountain. Yet in this place many years later, after many tests, I felt the Word as the spirit galloping in my heart, the particles of rain approaching the mountains.

In the years and in the stories and songs since that separation at fourteen from the Bible, I realized I could not separate the history of the Bible from the Bible, just as I could not separate my own painful and disturbing history from this exact moment in the desert. I had to make peace with the paradox.

I recognized the rhythms of speaking and singing from the Bible informing my history, my poetry, just as I could hear the current of the powwow drum, and turtle shells shaking beneath the current of the poetry, of this life. There would be ongoing paradox—and paradox can never be solved, only pondered, like the simple action of my grandfather opening a can of peaches when there was no money for peaches, or the appearance of songs when there are no words.

Isaiah, John, and Luke

T   O   M   C   L   A   R   K

MEDIATED

Not that I gave it much thought at the time, but my early experience of the Bible was largely secondhand. The message of scripture came in highly mediated form, processed through those baffling layers of good intention and institutional game plan, the doctrines and ceremonies of the Catholic Church. The evangelists' accounts of the life of Jesus, a great floating bank of stories and sayings, so drenched the catechism, classroom instruction, and liturgy as to accumulate, by the time one got through the early grades of parochial school, into an undifferentiable agglomerate of myth and legend one had little choice but to accept more or less uncritically as gospel truth. And this is not to speak of the variously eccentric, sometimes vividly mystical spin-doctoring which individual teaching clergy often applied to biblical text in the course of hands-on instruction. At this point there emerges out of deep waters of Lethe, like a horrifying nightmare permutation of the hand of the Lady of the Lake brandishing Excalibur, the withered arthritic fist of my religion teacher, Mother Marie, clutched tightly around the wooden ruler with which was meted out the punitive chastisements that managed to exact from even the most recalcitrant fourth-grade spitball-throwers, in their little Buster Brown shirts and ties, something close to undivided attention.

As testimony to the industrious and efficacious transmission of this composite message, one was inculcated at a relatively tender age, when perhaps most inclined to appreciate and least able to resist it, with a powerful sense of the mystery of things. Just as the daily life of the parochial school was visibly saturated with the imprint of divine meaning (one had only to contemplate the classroom decor), the universe as a whole was permeated with it. There existed an otherness, perceptible in secret ways if one knew the secrets, yet never entirely palpable as empirical fact—except of course in the not entirely uncommon case of miracles, which, far from restricted to the long-ago lives of Jesus and the saints, were still going on all the time. One was informed of this on the authority of those who'd allegedly witnessed all sorts of strange things: visions of the Virgin Mary were widespread, cancers were known to have been cured by pilgrimages to Lourdes, and so on. (By the age of eleven or twelve I must have been forced to sit through a half dozen parish-school auditorium showings of *The Song of Bernadette* in all its excruciating 150 minutes of persecuted-mystical glory, with Jennifer Jones paying the same hard price for having the Virgin strike up a miraculous spring by melting out of a rock in front of her every time.) The idea that not only in and beneath but outside and beyond the mechanical order of things (the rational order, that is, of the atheists, whom one heard about but seldom ran into, though privately one suspected certain soi-disant Protestant acquaintances might in fact be cunning atheists in disguise), there lay another order which was paramount: every school kid who could understand the difference between eternal hellfire and fluffy lambswool clouds irradiated with gold and pink light had no choice but to take that for granted.

The Bible had shown, one was told, that the world had a spiritual history which underlay as well as dwarfed in importance its physical history —a sort of (as it were) unhistorical history of which the language of scripture filtered through doctrine and ceremony was the memorial storehouse. In the strict and proper ritual sense, as well as in the practical sense, as it happened, that language was the Latin of the Vulgate, preserved in bits and pieces in the choral responses of the Mass, which as an altar boy I naturally got down by rote.

While in truth all I recall now of that lost language is a few fragments of ancient lingo-babble distorted by the line-noise of a lifetime of forgetting, underneath, like some ineradicable strain, the primitive bedrock imprinting of early memorization still creates odd echoes. I haven't been inside a church in more years than I can remember, yet *Kyrie Eleison, Gloria in Excelsis, Sanctus, Agnus Dei,* choral pieces from the ordinary of the Mass that incorporate fragments of the Vulgate, are tunes that still occasionally waft through my bedimmed middle-aged mind, triggering a kind of over-conditioned response, out of which comes a flood of strangely confused images and feelings bearing very little reference to the actual meanings of the Latin words. It never really occurred to me as a child that the gospels, which contained the story of Jesus' life, might be considered as literature. They were stories of a special kind, eternity directives with a stable signification, arrows that pointed into one's heart. It wasn't one's job to interpret them. That was the concern of others.

But now I'm on my own, just another strange and lonesome reader. Are hidden messages from ancestors entombed in these lost scrolls? Puzzling over a past I'd thought as remote as another planet, I'm overcome by curious sensations of familiarity perhaps similar to those impressions of having been through another life, somewhere up the line, which presumably persuade people of the reality of reincarnation. But so far I haven't died, only changed: or have I? How deep does the plummet of ''early conditioning'' go? Coming back to the gospels now, I feel the rough brush of a chilly wing as I turn the pages, a cat's-fur feeling like a static charge.

The traveling French-Canadian retreat priest, in his fanatical war of attrition against the dark angels of self-abuse, with his little theatrical sideshow of hokum wonders and gimcrack miracles, sliding wooden panels, invisible photoelectric fields, a lit-up, bleeding Jesus jumping out at you from a black screen: turning the pages of Luke's account of the Agony in the Garden, I recall that priest's baleful imperative glare, and a vague connection way back in the graveyards of memory between Jesus' sufferings and their ostensible cause, the jacking-off of all those billions of adolescent boys down through all that history which hadn't happened yet. Why had God made nature so sinfully irrepressible? Reserved for that offensive nature was the unspeakable hell of tortures which Mark (9:43) called ''the fire that never shall be quenched.'' Luke, who seems to have seen money as the root of all evils, saved the unquenchable flames for the rich man, but our retreat priest, on his mission to the boys of the eighth grade, insisted that the actual entryway to hell lay in the depths of the pockets of our grubby corduroys.

Leafing through the Book again, I experience the old cold shudder of mortal fear; make out a light somewhere, bright and warm, but notice behind the chiaroscuro glow a deeper darkness in which that light drowns. I hear semiaudible sounds, the echo of nuns' voices in the black whispered sibilance of the litany. I feel the hardness of the kneeling pads in the wooden pews, sense the light falling diffusely through colored glass, smell the cloistered air mixed with a whiff of incense and traces of body odor, see the candlelight reflecting in the sightless eyes of the plaster image of Virgin and Child, am swallowed up by the shadows of the confessional, taste the papery dryness of the Host on my tongue, stare without blinking at the nails in the statue's wounds, can't help wondering if the spear in the side of the dying god is mine, and witness once more the guilty spectacle of Thomas the Apostle, my namesake, forever shamefully doubting.

Quite honestly the Book remains as much as ever less text than trigger and test, though now in ways that are quite different from the arcane, ecstatic, terrified ways of childhood. Sorting through all this fragmentary floating detritus of a canceled faith is an oddly unsettling project.

Here and Now

One was taught the Bible as a kind of ultimate guidebook on how to get out of all this alive—and not get scorched too badly later. Though life on earth was not portrayed in the available parochial school interpretation of the scripture as particularly pleasant, the carrot dangled from the stick of institutional promulgation (intermittently used to beat on you) turned out to be quite a package: eternal life. "I go to prepare a place for you," Jesus had promised the faithful in John 14:2. That other, better place up above, expansively extrapolated from the sacred page in picturesque colorations of endlessly reiterated ritual and liturgy, hymn and story, was almost as prominent in the teachings as that still other, much worse place down below, declension to and habitation of which were succinctly conjured, for example, by Luke's hellbound rich man, who cried out to Father Abraham, "Send Lazarus, that he may dip the tip of his finger in water, and cool my tongue; for I am tormented in this flame." (16:24) In this program terrestrial existence was quite obviously reduced to the status of mere prelude.

Coming back to the Book belatedly, it's interesting to note how little play that other-life / other-world theme gets in the Hebrew scriptures of the Old Testament. Did it take Greek philosophy to make Elsewhere-thinking into the meal ticket that would purchase centuries of pleasure-postponing flesh-haters the kingdom of heaven? Traditional Christian teaching about salvation, evoking images of heaven and the hereafter, and of redemption and justification in various forms, finally rings false for everybody but subscribing true believers (which isn't true of the simple evocative pictorial beauty of many gospel stories and scenes—for example, Luke's account of the Nativity—or for that matter of the serene, compassionate, poised handling of dramatic events in Jesus' life throughout a good part of Luke's gospel).

The historical people on whom the gospel tales are based, one would gamble, couldn't have helped being above all interested in the here and now, if only because that's been the first attention of most people who've ever lived. Otherworldliness has always been an attitude cultivated by those who've given up on this one, or on whom this one appears to have given up. The phenomenon was common, particularly among women, in the Catholic parish ambience of my childhood; but then the history of human credulity is of course as old as the world. Suffering is commonly the cause, but then again, who needs immediate local consolation quite as much as one who's currently and presently suffering? As the seventeenth-century Cambridge Platonist Benjamin Whichcote, testing faith by reasonable good sense, put it, ''Give me religion that doth attain real effects.'' If the righteous were to become partakers of divine nature, Whichcote reasonably argued, it had to be in *this* life. The horizons of moral and spiritual vision are foreshortened, in such a view, from the hereafter and the out-there (potential realms of unlimited perfection) to a more immediate form of purification that's at once approximate at best, local if anywhere, and in the present tense if ever.

Ironically, in many respects this Platonist position actually harkens back to the older Jewish view. The imagery of the Fall and the Atonement, so prominent in the gospels and so fundamental to the traditional Christian idea of salvation and eternal life—and of course largely absent from the Old Testament, despite later claims of parabolically inclined Christian proselytizers like the evangelist Matthew—can't help making slightly uneasy any reader who believes that with death one's world simply and literally comes to an end. "And he that was dead came forth," saith John 11:44. But as it happens common sense tells us quite unequivocally that death is an event in life, not the threshold to some other place. The only locus into which one may ever come forth, realistically speaking, is the "eternal" here and now.

"If we take eternity to mean not infinite temporal duration but timelessness, then eternal life belongs to those who live in the present," as Wittgenstein proposed in his *Tractatus Logico-Philosophicus,* a work that in its profundity, brilliant compression, and cryptic serial form perhaps bears sufficient resemblance to some of the wisdom books of the Bible to be thought of as scripture for our time. "Our life has no end in just the way in which our visual field has no limits . . . Not only is there no guarantee of the temporal immortality of the human soul, that is to say of its eternal survival after death; but, in any case, this assumption fails to accomplish the purpose for which it has always been intended. Or is some riddle solved by my surviving forever? Is not this eternal life itself as much of a riddle as our present life? The solution of the riddle of life in space and time lies *outside* space and time."

"I go to prepare a place for you," John has his Christ intoning to the disciples. It would be cynical to suggest the Son of Man was selling them or anybody a bill of goods. But where words can't go, isn't it perhaps arrogant to suppose we will somehow, some way be able to follow?

A Prodigal Son

Luke's serene, poised compassion—the marvelous stylistic "personality" of the author, whoever he was—is the first thing that comes across in reading him now. Was he a devout Greek writing in "literary" Greek for Gentiles? I don't recall that historical surmise coming up in school, any more than the equally strong sense I get now that Matthew, with his lawyerish dueling citations from Hebrew scripture, was a man of the old law, intending his gospel for Jewish Christians. In school the only intent that mattered, and it was far less outright yet probably no less strong than Luke's or Matthew's, was the institutional spin put on their words by the stamp of ecclesiastical authority. If that spin, and the sparks that flew from my confrontation with it, led me and the spin doctors permanently to part ways, still there's no arguing the fact that, historically, it worked. That particular old-time religion is one of the great corporate success stories, as even a prodigal son has to have the grace to acknowledge. Of the perennial fifteen percent of the "fallen away," there are probably few who can ever finally say they are confident some stealthy soul-hunter is not still out there tracking them; because as Jesus said, the most precious soul is that of the one that got away. And besides it was always nice to feel wanted.

Nativity and Mariolatry

"And it came to pass in those days, that there went out a decree from Caesar Augustus, that all the world should be taxed." (Luke 2:1)

Luke's lovely tale of the Nativity: who could say no to it? Even if Luke invented the problematic taxation decree that gets his hero *in utero* from the plains of Galilee, where he would later take up his teaching career, to Bethlehem, for the sake of the Messianic prophecy, it is so splendid a piece of dramatic writing there seems no alternative reality one could prefer to

Luke's interesting fiction. With the addition of Matthew's Babylonian star in the east to illuminate the misaddressed European solstitial snowfall, no more was needed to set up one of sacred literature's most picturesque tales.

As cultural anthropology, certainly, Luke's story, with its emphasis on the internal life of Mary—was she really his source, as some claim?—is the indical text for the Catholic household. Was Luke's Mariolatry aimed at his Gentile audience? Luke, who may have been a doctor, is considerably more interested in women and their points of view than the other evangelists. Unlike Matthew's, his account of the so-called ''virgin birth'' permits one to take him as suggesting the conception might possibly have been natural after all, though of course such a suspicion could not have entered the mind of the youthful taker-on-faith of every word the nuns and priests said.

There the plaster figures lay, anyway, in the manger, amid the snow and animals, because there was no room at the inn. Certain poor shepherds (the populist Luke's contribution) and wisdom doctors (wandered out of Matthew) hung around the edges of the scene, just props, really, like Joseph himself, who might as well have been sent down to the corner to get doughnuts, for all the use he was. The fathers-are-stooges message came through loud and clear. Mary, on the other hand, had this independent power, a kind of special channel through to the top. It was well known she could whisk you in the back door of heaven, that's how heavy she was.

END TIME

If the Old Testament is a monument of historical consciousness, the New Testament ushers mankind out of history toward a Now in which increasingly time stands still. In this respect the Jewish apocalyptic tradition, flourishing in the final centuries before Christ and reaching a literary pinnacle in the Book of Daniel, is obviously transitional. The historicism of the Old Testament is dramatically depleted in the gospels. Of the four evangelists only Luke actually seemed to have had what we would now think of as a historical mind, and perhaps not coincidentally, he appears most wary of stopping time. Perhaps he was embarrassed by popular expectations of an imminent Parousia event—that tantalizing outbreak of End Time just around the corner, the promise of which had been keeping several generations of prophets in business—and wrote his gospel at least in part to apologize for the delay. Certainly the repeated unfulfilled predictions of their bolder forerunners had to be on the minds of those still speaking of End Time at a point when it must have seemed to have receded into the indefinite future. Luke is careful to have his Jesus holding off at arm's length the whole idea of the Second Coming. The end of time, he has his messianic candidate warn, "is not by and by" (21:9)—i.e., shortly, or any time soon. Luke's relatively tentative eschatology suggests a landscape from which the once-imminent Parousia event has faded somewhat as a realistic prospect.

But the idea of a sudden suspension and abridgement of history has an enduring appeal, tested against the variable credulity of people, and enhanced by their present sufferings and fears. During my early Cold War childhood, End Time was once again seemingly at hand. At school we dutifully crawled beneath our desks during the bomb drills. At home we were instructed to tack blankets over the windows to cut down the flying glass and the blinding effects of the nuclear flash. One's relative security was computed by one's distance from the prospective site of Ground Zero, in my own case about far enough to have a pretty good chance to avoid being instantly vaporized, but much too near to miss the even less enviable outcomes of frying like an egg or withering away hideously from radiation sickness.

According to the interpretation of Revelation proposed by one local

Irish Catholic businessman—a very successful bottled water mogul, who had spent his own money to publish a book about the coming Apocalypse—all the signs predicted by John the Divine were at hand: strange manifestations of the Northern Lights, spy planes, shakings of the fallen angels' robes in the Aurora Borealis, enemy bombers over the Aleutians, Stalin as the Antichrist, the rider on the red horse, armies from the East, lakes of fire and of blood.

Each successive potential confrontation between the naturally opposing superpowers—international communism as the Beast 666 staring democracy and the Pope hard in the eye—provided a new feast of symbolism for this macabre eschatology. Death on a pale horse rode through my dreams from the Korean conflict to the Formosa crisis. One night's television news produced a map of the Chinese coastline, with an arrow pointing to two tiny dots: Quemoy and Ma-tsu. Pretzels and milk were dispensed, then upstairs in my friend's room, under the steeply pitched attic ceiling, he told me how the devil had appeared at the foot of his bed and shaken it.

I had another friend who carried the Bible to school with him, and held it up like a holy shield as he berated other boys for taking God's name in vain. A powerful, intense, furious boy, and the first true intellectual I had ever met, he spent much of our playground time chasing foulmouthed classmates around the concrete yard. His father was a symphony cellist. I remember the day Stalin went into a fatal coma. The nuns openly celebrated the news in class. *De facto* belligerent playground camps were wearing Union and Confederate army caps at recess around this time, not because there were any actual Yankees and Rebels present, but to clarify targets for impromptu scrapping. Hostilities were suspended when my friend held up his Bible and announced the death of Stalin was a sign of the End, backing up his claim with a citation from Revelation. He later was inveigled by the class tough into a brief life of crime. They were caught breaking into a furrier's warehouse. The symphony cellist had a heart attack. Next I recall, my friend played jazz trumpet and subscribed to *Downbeat*.

DOWSING

How does one talk about one's experience of a language that is at least purported to be a pipeline to the Unsayable? That is nowhere a writer ought to want to go. Though as Wittgenstein suggested, it may be there comes a point in scaling the heights of philosophy when one throws away the ladder, abandoning the way back down (''what we cannot speak about we must pass over in silence''), literature is something else again (at least in theory). If there's no ladder, how does the reader get a handhold? Then again is the Bible really literature at all? Or is it rather a kind of inspired spiritual given—a donnée of spirit, key to divine meaning, record of otherness at work in the universe, storehouse of numinous values, testament of the world-historical incarnation of timeless truth-content—not merely reputed to be, but in fact sacred? What is the question to which these eloquent, inevitable-sounding, and inconceivably mysterious words are the answer? And how does one go about reading them?

Fortunately, the divining rod of scripture fits everybody's hand. In this sense it may well be true that that ravening magpie, the writer's appropriative instinct, entering the Bible as a raptor of its wonders, impatient with study, greedy for results, is actually proceeding very much like unnumbered generations of common readers over the millennia. Without a lot of time to spare, obscurely, irrationally ascribing the text a private dimension of meaning entirely divorced from public history, one hunts the sudden, illuminating answer to the impossibly fluid, endlessly inchoate question of *this* moment. Could it be that the quality we call ''sacred'' in a text has to do less with *it* than with *us*—the intensity of need we bring to it, determining all the unusual relations that ensue?

Opening the book, it's not long before one is visited by that cat's-fur feeling of brushed nerve-endings. A hushed expectancy arises in the half-dark study, and word associations waft up out of deep memory, each triggering its own little slow shudder of recognition. Skimming without plan, within minutes I find I have stumbled as if fated into the ruined country of the oracles of the foreign nations in Isaiah.

It is a remarkable spectacle. The full sweep of time is felt, and of a divine hand whose workings are manifest in history. From Nineveh to Tyre, Egypt to Asia Minor, Damascus to the Blue Sahara, one by one, the cities, homelands, and gods of Israel's enemies fall in their unfortunate turn before the profoundly wish-fulfilling, calmly vengeful reaper's stroke of an unforgiving LORD GOD of hosts.

Isaiah's several voices of threat and promise—the tonal disjunctions are only what would be expected in texts addressing widely different historical situations, and evidently composed over a span of several centuries (circa eighth century to sixth century B.C.), in effect in the tradition of, rather than actually from the hand of, the original prophet—are resonant with understanding of how apparent vicissitudes of events which effect human destiny always have a deeper meaning when looked at with the longer view of faith.

Isaiah brings vision to bear upon history, and requires time to answer unto spirit. Sieges, conspiracies, invasions, occupations, and the ultimate misfortune of exile—the sufferings befalling Israel—unroll before us, terrible scenes from the visionary scroll. In Isaiah's magisterial view of the great balancing rhythm of history, justice exacts pain and rewards faith according to laws one has no recourse but to trust, for they are the most ancient of laws. In this landscape of urgency and foreboding, alien powers who have for centuries rumbled practically at will across the territory of Judah, geographical token of God's covenant with his people, come to their own baleful reckoning. Here divination is the mouthpiece of righteousness at work in the blood-darkened fields of history.

The prophetic watchman of Israel's fate dolefully tolls the names of the threatened cities and nations in a mantic voice that moves from dread, fear, and dismay to ironic parry to quiet righteous judgment, building and subsiding as the pain of the exilic removals accumulates and is relieved by hope. The watchman's sense of portent weighs down the prophet's vision of retribution with a particular historical gravity, the weight of fatality that is the grand undertow of Isaiah.

In Chapters 13 and 14 the burden of the hegemonic imperial kingdom of Babylon, conqueror of the Fertile Crescent under Nebuchadnezzar, is foreshadowed along with the inexorable advance of the Lord's weapons of indignation toward it, "from a far country, from the end of heaven . . . to destroy the whole land." (13:5) Behind these words one summons the image of the coming down out of the north, like heat lightning on the horizon of a haunted summer night, of the armies of the Persian monarch Cyrus, first hint of the "anointed" descent of the redeeming sentinel who will later occupy Isaiah extensively. Here the shining glory of the proud Babylonian king now becomes the subject of ironic taunt: "How art thou fallen from heaven, O Lucifer, son of the morning." (14:12)

Late in Chapter 14, Isaiah (as constructed by his editor or editors) harks back two centuries to consider the long-prior Assyrian aggressor, raging through the nation of Israel in those evil days when the original prophet came back from his naked calling in the wilderness; the horrified eyes that saw Sargon roaring down the coast, Sennacherib laying waste to the nation, here look with satisfaction upon the Assyrians' ultimate shattering and fall. Chapters 15 and 16 pronounce the burden of Moab, its silencing and desolation, the overthrow of its heathen gods and faith. Chapter 17 declares the burden of Damascus, "taken away from being a city, and it shall be a ruinous heap." (17:1) The next several chapters promise woe and shame for Egypt, and for "the land shadowing with wings, which is beyond the rivers of Ethiopia." (18:1) Chapter 21, the curiously reverberating Desert of the Sea pronouncement, anticipates the fall of Babylon before Median and Elamite besiegers; the poet-prophet envisions the avenging force in history as a dust storm in the gales that rush through the Negeb Desert: "The burden of the desert of the sea. As whirlwinds in the south pass through; so it comes from the desert, from a terrible land." (21:1) There follow pronouncements against Dumah and Arabia, Tyre and its trading partners ("Howl, ye ships of Tarshish" [23:1]). And then come the verses into which I first fell in beginning this study, the striking portrait of the watchman in his tower (21:5–12):

> Prepare the table, watch in the watchtower, eat drink: arise, ye princes, and anoint the shield.
>
> For thus hath the Lord said unto me, Go, set a watchman, let him declare what he seeth.
>
> And he saw a chariot with a couple of horsemen, a chariot of asses, and a chariot of camels; and he hearkened diligently with much heed:
>
> And he cried, A lion: My lord, I stand continually upon the watchtower in the daytime, and I am set in my ward whole nights:
>
> And, behold, here cometh a chariot of men, with a couple of horsemen. And he answered and said, Babylon is fallen, is fallen; and all the graven images of her gods he hath broken unto the ground.
>
> O my threshing, and the corn of my floor: that which I have heard of the LORD of hosts, the God of Israel, have I declared unto you.
>
> The burden of Dumah. He calleth to me out of Seir, Watchman, what of the night? Watchman, what of the night?
>
> The watchman said, The morning cometh, and also the night: if ye will enquire, enquire ye: return, come.

Did I land on this passage because it was "meant"? What if the accident of meaning is the meaning of accident in reading—the unintentional discovery emerging from the purposeless search, the apparent accident in fact expressing certain mysterious unconscious contents, bringing out a motive whose true nature hasn't yet really been grasped, but of whose actual urgency there can be no doubt, because one feels it?

Only afterward did research fill in the background to Isaiah's oracles for me. My first attraction, as the pole attracts the compass, was to the engagement of the poet in history, in his lonely calling, in his solitary watchtower, with that uncannily resonant voice which has been sounding in the back of my head throughout the months of this study.

Genesis (Eden)

A N N   L A U T E R B A C H

I begin this essay in Denver, Colorado, sitting in a strange room in a beautiful Victorian house, facing West, where I can see a scrap of the Rockies rising beyond the rooftops. It is early January. I have come here for a ten-week stint of teaching, but really to try to recover a rhythm of concentration and work which had evaded me in New York. I have made several such visits to unknown American cities (Madison, Minneapolis, Iowa City), always with deep ambivalence, as I pack up my belongings and estrange myself from the familiar. And yet I should be used to this, since New York is nothing if not a continuous shifting from estrangement to intimacy, from anonymity to identity; where what is expected and what actually happens are always, in Emerson's phrase, in a "stupendous antagonism."

I.

Whoso would be a (wo)man, must be a noncon-
formist. (S)He who would gather immortal palms
must not be hindered by the name of goodness, but
must explore if it be goodness. Nothing is at last sacred but the integrity of your own mind. Absolve you
to yourself, and you shall have the suffrage of the
world.

EMERSON, "SELF-RELIANCE"

As the stories we tell about ourselves stiffen and condense, contracting
away from nuance of detail and from the often incommensurate gap between intention and action, we treat them more like familiar texts to which
we return. This return is not in order to recover something lost so much as
to reinvent what is found, to move the *already* into a place of continuance,
to extend our present boundaries. In a sense, we live in order to accommodate and interpret the choices we have made, and what we recall of those
choices narrates how we might proceed.

Eve made a choice to eat the forbidden fruit. The serpent, she said,
"beguiled" her. A poem I wrote when I was in graduate school ended with
this stanza:

> Call me indolent, self-indulgent. Ah yes, I crave
> an apple, peach and pear. I'll have them all
> and with each a slice of rare and aged
> cheese. That's the curse upon my sex, as
> someone said, we take an apple to our bed.

Genesis (Eden)

I'll not deny the truth:
I'm one with Cleopatra, Eve, and Ruth.

Strong appetite was not something readily condoned in women then (it was 1966) and I'm not sure this isn't still the case. Women feel wicked for their avidity, for their cravings, sensual as well as intellectual. We might need to say "he made me do it"; "I was seduced." We do not want to appear greedy; our curiosity is meant to stay within certain bounds. (Think of Hillary Clinton, as opposed to, say, Jacqueline Kennedy: the one seen as overstepping her place, the other an icon of feminine discretion.) Eve was the embodiment of female desire, the original transgressive sibling. At Columbia, entering students in the MA Program in English were told not to try to do anything "creative"; we were told to do a bibliography, perhaps, for our thesis. Women in particular were treated with consummate patriarchal condescension. Wanting to be a Namer of Things, I was told, in effect, that all things had already been named and I should just put them in order. I felt at sea, at a loss: overwhelmed and undersupported. Wanting to be nurtured by the Great Institution, I was told by the famous Miltonist that I was "afraid to succeed." I was ignorant, scared, eager. I didn't know where to begin, and so I ended, abruptly, after the first disastrous year.

The following September, I left New York for a three-week trip (Dublin, London, Paris), beguiled by the map of Dublin that my professor, a Joycean, drew on the blackboard. My imagination was rooted more in American transcendentalism and pragmatism than in Joyce's exalted, indifferent artist—God, paring his fingernails, but still, something must have spun in me, reading:

> 26 April: Mother is putting my new secondhand
> clothes in order. She prays now, she says, that I may
> learn in my own life and away from home and friends

what the heart is and what it feels. So be it. Welcome,
O life! I go to encounter for the millionth time the
reality of experience and to forge in the smithy of my
soul the uncreated conscience of my race.

A PORTRAIT OF THE ARTIST AS A YOUNG MAN

I was beguiled, also, by the elegant sorrowful cadences of Yeats. It was one
thing to read Yeats, another to want to write poems in a landscape which
seemed to give itself up to multiple meanings, temporal braidings, where
the mythic realm of the Fall—as in the poem ''Adam's Curse''—could
abide with a contemporary love story, Byzantium with old men.

I had been stunned by Beckett's stripped landscape, where hope and doom,
comedy and tragedy, seemed to dissolve into a single vision as iconoclastic
as it was universal. That in the suspended animation of *waiting,* of *delay,* a
whole linguistic world could unfurl. Vladimir and Estragon, Lucky and
Pozzi, marooned in Nowhere or Everywhere, in a dark Apocalyptic Eden
with a single tree, and no Eve.

I stayed away for seven years, forging a self with which to return.

2.

I cannot think of any poetry which adequately expresses this yearning for the wild. The *wilde.*

HENRY DAVID THOREAU, JOURNAL, *1851*

In the first story of Genesis, God creates each thing day by day, ''after its
kind.'' He invents categories as he goes. These acts of creation give him
pleasure, he observes their goodness. The days are counted; there is an

orderly progression. Repetition brings solace: "And the evening and the morning were the first day." "And the evening and the morning were the second day." "And the evening and the morning were the third day."

Growing up in New York, I experienced home as a wilderness. That is, the main figure at home, my mother, was herself a wilderness, if by wilderness is meant the opposite of order. The days did not unfold with expectancy, but with a constant heightened attention to the possible ruptures between what should be and what was, what could be and what wasn't, to protracted attention to certain cues or clues that would tell how far the day would drift away from clarity. The nights brought forth episodes of mystery which threatened to, and sometimes did, erupt into violence. At night, I imagined continually the sites of potential danger; I read each sign for discrepancy, for the rip or tear in the frail fabric of our domain. Sorrow and joy seemed to be woven together until they were indecipherable in their quixotic patternings. There was music, there were tears, there was smoke, footsteps, doors. There was the *stench* of chaos, sensuous and primordial. Outside, the city contributed its harmonic: sirens, the Third Avenue El rasping along black tracks, cats, a lugubrious foghorn, bells dividing the hours into part-song. The boundaries between *inside* and *outside* were porous, a mere skin. I lay awake and imagined another set of reals, in which everything had a place, including myself. I imagined a stasis, instead of constant mobility and discontinuity, as if the whole world were nothing but a threshold. I was vigilant, a deciphering angel of fatal anticipations.

When a child's home is already a wilderness, the problem of obedience, of limit, is not an easy one to solve. What is to be obeyed? Whose rules are to be followed? One is trying to find ways to impose order on chaos, but that imposition goes against the prevailing real. I was helpful. I dreamed up a second domestic frame with my dolls. I went for strolls down the long corridors, inventing trees as I went, holding imaginary conversations with passing strangers. I tried to be such a good child that my mother would want to enter my world, that my father might return to it. I painted pictures and played a violin, wanting to distract into focus, into attention. Secretly, I imagined escapes: sky dragons, adoptions, love, whatever. Secretly, I was the model of disobedience. Secretly, my psyche was a veritable dominion of punishments and rewards. When my father, who had been away most of my early childhood in what was called then the Far East, died of polio when I was eight, I knew the possibilities had dwindled precipitously and forever. Given some brightly colored *cray-pas,* I drew two multicolored winged figures: gorgeous visions of transformation and transportation. Part creature, part bird, part phantom, they seemed the very agents of escape. They seemed to embody a form of knowledge that somehow preceded and anticipated my own. Mute and unnamed, these figures nevertheless were emblems of my will to be Elsewhere.

Or so I now think. 10 January 1995, Denver. The evening of the sixth day. One must be careful of the inertia of stories. Floods in California. Begin to read Waiting for Godot *again and find it wildly funny. The mountains amaze, holding back the weather, or gathering it, as if winter could be kept in a huge rocky attic. How did it feel, to come across the country and see them for the first time, rising from the flat land, like great beasts lounging on the horizon?*

The common etymological root shared by exile and ecstasy is in the obvious prefix *ex-,* meaning "out of." Exile comes from the Latin *exilium,* banishment. Ecstasy combines "ex" with the Greek word for "to place." Both words imply a crossing of boundaries—geographical in the first place, psychological or spiritual in the second. In poetry, this idea is called metaphor, where "a name or descriptive term is transferred to some object to which it is not properly applicable."

In the second account of Creation, the one that we in the West have adopted as part of our inner iconography, there is a garden. "And the Lord God planted a garden eastward in Eden; and there he put the man whom he had formed." Most considerate Lord, to plant a garden prior to putting his man there! This garden had "every tree that is pleasant to the sight, and good for food; the tree of life also in the midst of the garden, and the tree of the knowledge of good and evil."

The night before I left on my journey, my friend Susan and I played a record of Paul Robeson singing the great "Jerusalem" hymn, in which Blake's soaring lyrics portray England as the prophetic "green and pleasant land." I was sure I was going to die, Icarus-like, in a flaming crash, before I ever reached the other side of the ocean. The *fact* of this other shore seemed to me hypothetical, irreal, a fiction.

3.

When I was growing up, there was an impediment to the forms of things. One was told not to do something, but the person who said "thou shalt not" was herself the very embodiment of disobedience, of transgression. *Forgive us our trespasses as we forgive those who trespass against us.* When I was growing up my father, a journalist, was off in the world *naming* it.

> 19 And out of the ground the Lord God formed every
> beast of the field, and every fowl of the air; and
> brought them unto Adam to see what he would call

them: and whatsoever Adam called every living creature, that was the name thereof.

The considerate Lord, having given Adam the garden to tend, realizes that
he will need "a help meet for him." Wonderfully, he then forms beasts
and fowl, and brings them to Adam "to see what he would call them: and
whatsoever Adam called every living creature, that was the name thereof."
This first linguistic event, the alignment of Thing to Word, this permission
to know the world through one's names for it, to be the *original* namer, is
an act of huge consequence, putting, as it does, the history of masculine
possession of the map of our readings into play, into place.

> 20 And Adam gave names to all cattle, and to the fowl
> of the air, and to every beast of the field; but for
> Adam there was not found a help meet for him.

And so the Lord put Adam to sleep, took one of his ribs, and "made him a
woman."

> 23 And Adam said, This is now bone of my bones,
> and flesh of my flesh: she shall be called Woman,
> because she was taken out of Man.

Adam gives birth to a woman. Is this the *first* immaculate conception?

Genesis (Eden)

4.

'Tis the best use of Fate to teach a fatal courage.

EMERSON, "FATE"

When I arrived in Dublin in September 1967 I was ecstatic. I felt exalted, as if I had been transported out of the literal into the imagined. As if the texts I loved had devolved from language to landscape. The scale shifted; time slowed; the light was sheer, instead of the tarnished gold of the light I knew; it was white light, radiant and sudden. I seemed to have escaped the present altogether and fallen backward into the future. I was Alice in Wonderland, Dorothy in Oz. Everything beguiled me. Women carried baskets to do their shopping along crooked narrow streets; in St. Stephen's Green the green was luminous with a wet lush sheen; everyone talked and talked and talked, giddy with speech, as if, indeed, speech itself were action. Ah, I thought, I will be a poet in Dublin, not a career girl in New York! I had the sense that now I held my own destiny because I would now be, or so I thought, in control of the story; my life was only what I might make of it, what I might tell of it. I was enthralled with a sense of powerful incipiency; I barely noticed how isolated and lonely and obscure I felt. The fall, when it came, was drear. I wrote my first "real poem" in a little room on Lower Hatch Street in complete desolation. By New Year's Eve, I left, destitute and afraid, and moved to London.

> *This is one way of telling this story. There are many others.*
> *This version omits almost everything.*
>
> Now the serpent was more subtile than any beast
> of the field which the Lord God had made. And he

said unto the woman, Yea, hath God said, Ye shall not eat of every tree of the garden?

2 And the woman said unto the serpent, We may eat of the fruit of the trees of the garden:

3 But of the fruit of the tree which is in the midst of the garden, God hath said, Ye shall not eat of it, neither shall you touch it, lest ye die.

4 And the serpent said unto the woman, Ye shall not surely die:

5 For God doth know that in the day ye eat thereof, then your eyes shall be opened, and ye shall be as gods, knowing good and evil.

6 And when the woman saw that the tree *was* good for food, and that it was pleasant to the eyes, and a tree to be desired to make *one* wise, she took of the fruit thereof, and did eat, and gave also unto her husband with her; and he did eat.

7 And the eyes of them both were opened, and they knew that they *were* naked; and they sewed fig leaves together, and made themselves aprons.

Sometime during my sojourn in London, I again became interested in Genesis, in the story of Eden, in the figure of Eve. I cannot now remember why; I do recall that I wrote a poem on the subject, about which I was particularly prideful and which I have, happily, lost. Perhaps I was thinking more about exile, about being an ex-patriot in bad times; I felt shame at forsaking the political extremity foregrounded by Vietnam. In London, the counter-culture was all show: Carnaby Street and the Beatles, sex drugs and rock 'n' roll.

I was aware increasingly of distinctions; one of the things the British are good at is making distinctions, especially between themselves and everyone else. I was interested in the function of "manners" as a way of keeping boundaries between persons, a way to ensure a slow unfurling of friendship, of keeping distance, in contrast to the American tendency to assume intimacy on the least provocation; I was becoming aware of how class structure limits mobility within a society; I was realizing that an individual could climb just so far up the social ladder, but not far enough to become the Queen, for example.

In any case, what I had not remembered, or perhaps I had never known, was that the two trees were the Tree of Life and the Tree of the Knowledge of *Good and Evil*. The forbidden Tree was, I thought, simply the Tree of Knowledge. Reading Genesis, I was astonished. It's a fable of adolescence, I thought; it is about the discovery of sexuality, of gender difference! The Tree of Life is the Tree of Unity, of Oneness, Wholeness, Sameness. If there is only the Tree of Life, there is no Death, no opposite, no Other, no Male and Female, distinct from each other. If there is only the Tree of Life, nothing is strange, and so, there is nothing to fear. What about this snake, this serpent, this subtle creature? It is itself a marker, a boundary, stretched out on the land, drawing a line. It is like a tongue, wagging, circumscribing, delineating. The snake is the symbol of speech itself, wherein the moral universe is born.

Where desire is, limit is sure to follow.

This is the morning of the seventh day in Denver. I am up early, before eight, having been dreaming of multiple leavings; a dream where I am split between leaving and staying. I cancel planes, I seek advice; I am a veritable whirligig of indecision and despair. This dream imitates life. Before I go somewhere (before I came here, for example), I am often in a state of frenzy that verges on paralysis; I feel I am being made to leave, rather than that I want to leave. I feel I am being abandoned, and my whole psyche resists. I want someone to implore me to stay. At these moments of departure, I think I am split between my mother and father: the one who leaves is my father, the one who remains at home is my mother, and both inhabit me: my mother's reckless, slow dereliction and decay, my father's flamboyant apotheosis and demise. Writing is a way of controlling beginnings and endings. In later years, I came to think that my mother inhabited my work as the idea of Wilderness, as my father inhabited it as Limit or Form.

> *3.4 And the serpent said unto the woman, Ye shall not surely die. 5 For God doth know that in the day ye eat thereof, then your eyes shall be opened, and ye shall be as gods, knowing good and evil. 6 And when the woman saw that the tree was good for food, and that it was pleasant to the eyes, and a tree to be desired to make one wise, she took of the fruit thereof, and did eat, and gave also unto her husband with her; and he did eat.*

Repetition brings solace; we return to the text, read it again. Writing, we travel outward, cross boundaries and thresholds, stitch the known to the unknown.

In the first place, the serpent does not tempt Eve, it simply reassures her by contradicting what God has said, or rather, explaining to her that the reason God has forbidden them to eat of the Tree of the Knowledge of Good and Evil is that they will become "as gods." Eve makes her decision based on her own observations, her own curiosity, her own "fatal courage." She decides she is willing to risk everything, life itself, for the rewards of finding out about pleasure, goodness, and wisdom. It is one thing to name things, objects, creatures, as Adam had, it is quite another to have names for the relations between them, to know an action by its consequence. No sooner have Adam and Eve eaten the apple, than they are made to suffer the consequences: they will cease to be mere creatures of God's delight in his own creative mastery and will become *human,* entering the chronic, the temporal, finding themselves in complex relations to each other and to the world: they will know labor, and sorrow, and enmity; they will struggle with obedience and fidelity; they will notice that they are different from each other. This strangeness will unfold its great history of desire and fear. Existence, henceforth, will be marked by the contingent. The serpent, of course, was wrong. Adam and Eve will, indeed, "surely die"; they will know the difference between Life and Death; they will be responsible for the form of their life; they will be moral agents.

Leaving, we begin again. This ruse, this idea of extension, of volume, of stepping across. To fall away, or into, renovating the spoiled encumbrances of the circumscribed. The anchor is hauled up over the bow. The engine is started; choice once again elicits our daring.

The precariousness of the unknown and distant was, in my case, preferable to both the initial disarray and disjunctiveness of my childhood and the ominous strategies of attainment and/or containment which seemed to configure the future. What held me was only an inchoate desire to write myself into a life, to be the maker of my own map. I was trapped in a punishing enclosure of self-absorption which I could not transcend by imagining any conventional route or role; only the vague fantasy of becoming a poet resonated, as if language itself could rescue me from a morbid vanity. I did not feel intact enough as a subject to join any group, any movement, any plan or purpose. Apparently Adam's last act as Resident Nominalist was to have named Eve *Eve*. This he does after God's severe abjuration.

> 3/20 And Adam called his wife's name Eve; because
> she was the mother of all living.

The causal relation between the name "Eve" and the fact of her being "the mother of all living" is not obvious without historical and/or etymological exegesis unless, of course, it is simply that the "eve" of a given day is anticipatory, prior, as in Christmas Eve. Eve thus, being Mother, is the one who anticipates; she is, in fact, the one who literally embodies the notion of narrativity (which carries its own nativity). Eve is the Mother of all Living because she is the Author of Discourse; the fall from Eden is the call into Language. It is in the initial separation between Self and (M)other, subject and object, that language forms, stretching the place between initiation and completion, coming and going, *(fort da fort da)* into our capacity to tell stories, to re-present ourselves to ourselves.

In a sense, when I left home I was pregnant with myself, wanting to find a way to turn my subjectivity into objectivity, to be outside myself. By making the world strange, my own boundaries became more pronounced, more noticeable—how I looked, moved, spoke—I was exotic, a young American woman untethered from her origins. In a little room in Lower Hatch Street, Dublin, I found in my extreme isolation a way to speak of myself as Other, and in so doing, I also found the astonishing properties of language to form and formulate the essential relation between Self and World. It was an almost visceral experience, in which words seemed to find their way toward the poem; I had the sense that the poem itself could make demands on language, could call upon it, and that I was merely the agent of this calling. I thought that if what you had to say was strong enough it would find the objects, the particulars, in the world to make it legible, readable; language was a kind of map of the mind, a way of finding your way.

> 3/23 Therefore the Lord God sent him forth from the garden of Eden, to till the ground from whence he was taken. 24 So he drove out the man: and he placed at the east of the garden Cherubims, and a flaming sword which turned every way, to keep the way of the tree of life.

The pen is mightier than the sword, or so it is to be devoutly hoped.

Jeremiah and Corinthians

L   A   W   R   E   N   C   E   J   O   S   E   P   H

I.

Now it was May. The Jesuit high school in Detroit. We were studying the Gospel According to John.

"Love. God. Is. God is love. Do you understand?" Father Born asked. "Do you? Each word means the same thing. That's what God is. Love."

"Tha-a-a-t's what love is m-a-a-a-a-de of," Czechlewski whispered across the aisle, imitating Smokey Robinson.

"In the beginning is the word. The word is with God. The word is God. And God is love. That"—Born took a deep breath—"is what this Gospel is about. There's a prophet. John the Baptist is a prophet. A voice crying in the wilderness. A witness. *Ut testimonium perhiberet de lumine.* One who provides testimony. As to what? To what is seen.

And what is seen? The light. And what is the light? The word. And what is the word? Made flesh. *Verbum caro factum est.* The word is made flesh, alive, among us. *Habitavit in nobis.* Part of us, part of our lives. The incarnation of the word of God. This and the redemption of every human being by the sacrifice of Christ on the cross—these are the central mysteries of our faith. Both have to do with love. Then, and now. Right now. The word, God, love, among us, alive, right now. Right, Czechlewski?''

Czechlewski was singing Marvin Gaye's ''Can I Get a Witness,'' pounding the song's beat out on his desk with flattened palms, loud enough for the whole room to hear.

''Right, Czechlewski?'' Born said again. ''Even you can see what I mean, can't you? Basic logic. God is love. God is the word made flesh. Therefore . . .''

''God is love—in the flesh,'' Czechlewski answered. Everyone laughed.

''No, really,'' Czechlewski said. ''Seriously. Back to what you were saying. All this about God and love and the word. Sort of abstract, isn't it? But what does it *mean?*''

Born was surprised by the question. He paused an instant, then smiled. ''Well, that is *the* question, Czechlewski. Good. We'll leave it at that. Enough for the day. This word business—well, it's serious stuff.''

''It *is* serious,'' Czechlewski said after class. ''I mean, what if Born is right. I mean, what if it *is* all words. That words are what we are. That what we do is what we say. ''Do-be-do-be''—he started to laugh—''now what I sa-a-y. No''—he paused—''seriously. What if what we say, how we say it, why we say it, when we say it—what if what we say *is* what *is*. What love''—he moaned the word the way Smokey would—''i-i-i-s. Think about that''—his voice was mimicking Lyndon Johnson's—''my fellow Americans. Think about it,'' he said, his voice almost fervent. ''God is, love is—words, our words. Right here, right now, in De-troit city, this year of Our Lord nineteen hundred and sixty-six . . . Damn!'' He stopped, shaking his head several times. "Have mercy! Getting a bit carried away now! I must admit, though," he said, suddenly smiling again, "the whole thing does, sort of, boggle the human mind."

2.

But that city, at that time, was, after all, a very serious place. Millions came there early in the century to work, many whose forefathers and mothers were slaves. A large working class. An industrialist class among the wealthiest in the world. Whole parts of the city sectioned into factory complexes. An inner city where the poor lived. A city of churches. A city of bars. Wide avenues named Grand River and Jefferson, Ford and Chrysler expressways, streets lined with oaks, elms, catalpas, silver and red maples. A river, actually a strait, between two Great Lakes (in winter often dark green with ice floes), bordered on one side by Canada. In the strait, a municipal park, Belle Isle, where there were deer. From there you could see ore boats, freighters, one after the other, pass by.

It was a violent place, too. The country was at war. My generation was being conscripted into the army, mostly from the lower middle class or the poor, a disproportionate number black. The streets were changing fast. Guns could be bought for almost nothing, and they were used, often by those who returned home knowing how to kill if they had to, many of them addicted to heroin, unemployed, while the economy boomed, inflated by war. When I was nineteen—1967—the city was set on fire, an insurrection whose magnitude no one could have imagined. I saw it: my father's and uncle's small grocery and liquor store looted and burned. Divisions of the armed forces, recently returned from Indochina, dispatched by the President. I had just completed my first year of college. That summer I worked night shift in a factory dry-sanding bodies of Chevrolet trucks as they came out of a primer oven. For me violence was unavoidable. I felt it. It was not all that I felt, and certainly not what I wished to feel, but there it was, in the foreground, manifestly part of things, something to be taken in, and understood—a matter of survival.

That was also when I began to feel that language was an integral part of the world I lived in. Where this sense came from I don't know, but I felt it physically—I was impelled by it. Every type of language I knew—including those languages of the Old and New Testaments I'd known since childhood—folded into issues of meaning. My faith by that time concentrated on the incarnation. The word of God alive in history. From the beginning of Genesis, the repetition of the words ''and God said let there be''—the word of God as part of creation. God's words appearing, on fire, before the prophet Moses. The word of God among those prophets—Isaiah and Jeremiah, Ezekiel, Daniel, Micah, and Amos—eight, seven, centuries before Christ; those books witnessing our deepest human troubles through heightened, hyperconscious, spoken language.

It was in 1969, I remember, around Christmas, when I found these opening verses from the Book of Jeremiah:

> Now the word of the God came to me saying,
> ''Before I formed you in the womb, I knew you;
> before you were born I consecrated you; I appointed
> you as a prophet to the nations . . .''

(the word of God directly spoken as part of the self—in the beginning—even before the self is formed);

> I said, ''Ah, LORD GOD! I do not know how to
> speak: I am only a child.''
> But God replied, ''Do not say, 'I am only a child.' Go
> now to those whom I send you and say whatever I
> command you . . .''
> Then God put his hand out and touched my mouth

and said to me: "There! I have put my words in your
mouth . . ."

(one who cannot or wishes not to speak stunned into conversation with
God, impelled to do what he will do);

"See, I have, today, set you over nations and over
kingdoms, to root out, and to pull down, to destroy
and to throw down, to build, and to plant . . ."

That following February (shortly after my father was shot during a robbery
in his store—"he was so hopped up on heroin," he said later of the man
who shot him, "he didn't even know the gun went off") I wrote:

I was appointed the poet of heaven.

It was my duty to describe
Theresa's small roses
as they bent in the wind.

I tired of this
and asked you to let me
write about something else.
You ordered, "Sit
in the trees where the angels sleep
and copy their breaths
in verse."

So I did,
and soon I had a public following:

Saint Agnes with red cheeks,
Saint Dorothy with a moon between her fingers
and the Hosts of Heaven.

You said, "You've failed me."
I told you, "I'll write lovelier poems,"
but, you answered,
"You've already had your chance:

you will be pulled from a womb
into a city."

3.

" 'Theology after breakfast sticks to the eye,' " a friend said, quoting Wallace Stevens, laughing after I told him that I'd been thinking a lot lately about the theology of the word. "The theology of the word? Take a look at Paul's epistles to the Corinthians."

I'd never read either of them all the way through. An epistle, a classical form; speaking in writing to another, or others, who are absent, somewhere else, about common issues: that's the form. Paragraphs of verse after verse written against the "wicked" in the city of Corinth are interspersed throughout both epistles: "Whatever you eat, whatever you drink, whatever you do at all, do it for the glory of God." But the prescriptive side of this language isn't what holds your attention. What you first of all feel is the illumination of good and evil by an openly changing intensity of expression—the writer's voice. Suddenly, for example, in the second epistle—shortly after Paul says that his epistle isn't intended "to condemn," that the Corinthians are "in our hearts"—he gives the following "suggestion":

. . . A man is acceptable for whatever he has, not for
what he does not have.
This does not mean that to give relief to others you
ought to make things difficult for yourselves:
it is a question of balancing what happens to be your
abundance now against what they need now; one day
they may have something to spare that you may need.
As it is written, "He who gathered much had none
too much, he who gathered little was not lacking."

A few pages later, after the writer boasts about his authority, we hear,
almost apologetically, "I am speaking as a fool . . . I am talking like a
madman." Then, near the end of the epistle, the tone switches again: "I
warned those who sinned before and all the others, and I warn them now
while absent . . . that if I come again I will not spare them . . ."

There is also talk about the meaning of talk itself. The distinction is
made between speaking in tongues and prophecy. "He who speaks in an
unknown tongue edifies himself . . . But he who prophesies speaks to
others, to edification, and exhortation, and comfort." The holiest language
takes account of others. It has to do with the world.

And for that Syrian rabbi versed in the prophets, blinded and rendered
speechless "when a light from heaven flashed around him" (God's voice
speaking to him outside his will, telling him he would be told what to do,
so transformed by the experience that his very name was changed)—it has
to do with love. Toward the end of the first epistle to the Corinthians his
testimony is this:

If I speak in the tongues of men and of angels, but
speak without love, I am simply a noisy gong or a
clashing cymbal.
And if I have the powers of prophecy, and understand

all the mysteries there are, and know everything, and even have the faith to move mountains, without love I am nothing.

If I give away all that I have . . . but am without love, I am no good whatsoever.

Love never ends. The powers of prophecy will pass away; the gift of tongues will cease to be; and knowl-edge—it, too, one day will pass away.

For our knowledge is imperfect and our prophecy is imperfect, but once perfection comes all imperfect things will disappear . . .

For now we see through a glass darkly, but then we will see face to face. Now I know in part; then I will know as fully as I am known . . .

So there are three things that last: faith, hope and love; but the greatest of these is love.

These lines I recognized right away. I'd heard them before. The first time, no doubt, as a child, during that part of the Ordinary of the Mass when the priest reads a passage from the Old or New Testament (not including the Gospels), a common prayer called the "Epistle."

4.

So on this past Feast of the Incarnation I reflected on the word made flesh.

A chilly wind slid through the green and blue morning air. I walked down to Battery Park. The harbor blazed with light. A woman and a man on the promenade were talking animatedly to one another, the words between them dissolving in the watery light. A man wrapped in blankets was talking to himself.

Not far from Coentes Slip and Water Street, a few blocks from Wall Street, there is a war memorial. Words of soldiers etched into a green glass wall:

20 Apr 70

Dear Gail,

You don't know how close I have been to getting killed or maimed. Too many times I have seen guys near me get hit and go home in a plastic bag . . . It is time to forget. But it's hard to forget these things. I close my eyes and try to sleep but all I can see is Jenkins laying there with his brains hanging out or Lefty with his eyes shot out . . . Then you stop to think, it could be me. Hell, I don't know why I'm writing all this. But it feels better getting it out of my mind. I love you, Pete

SP/4 Peter H. Roepke
A 3/506 Inf.
101st Airborne Div.
Thua Thieu

On a pier on the East River I look at a small book, these words of a poet: "Sometimes the 'you' is me, talking with myself. Other times 'you' is someone else I'm talking to, even the 'you' who created me. Other times it could be 'you' talking with 'you.' The 'I' also changes. It could be me, it could be someone else. And, when I say 'he,' sometimes I mean me."

Later that day I looked again at the Book of Jeremiah. "For this word is like fire, like a hammer that breaks the rocks into pieces," the prophet says. Yet the word is a joy to him—he eats it ("I found your words, and I ate them; and your word was the joy and rejoicing of my heart"); he is starved without it. Sustained by it. Physically dependent on it. Through words he is taken into God's indignation, love, sorrow. Nothing to do with a sense of doom—it has to do with a sense of judgment. The prophet doubts (as God, too, really doubts) what to do, how to do it. Detached not only from his own likes or dislikes, but from God too, with whom he quarrels, he speaks for those who have to live in, not make, history; his emotions are collective, sublimated, ironic—revealing those truths that struggle for expression in our hearts, sometimes in a code of which we take in only as much as we can.

"The language of the prophets? It's not that complicated," one of the people in this world I'm closest to said when I told her what I'd been thinking. "If you have to rethink the whole situation—which some of us seem chronically compelled to do—you need to invent a language to do it, don't you? That's what those books are about. Have you ever read Isaiah chapter by chapter? It's a book of poems. Light, and more light—and the sharper the light is, the more glaring the distortions the writer sees around him. The sense of the body charged with words—God-words, human words. The feeling of language making something new, or, at least, words made as intense as existence. Language sparked, transposed, transformed—creating. In that sense divine.

"Think of it," she went on, "think what 'In the beginning was the word' really means. Among the Jews were these bizarre moralists who knew, through this ongoing conversation in writing with one another, that the universe is revealed through words. The whole thing. Everything. Think of it. Biologically we are pure emotion. But, alone among the animals, we are given words. The result? The politician. The writer. And those Jewish prophets—and, if I remember right, in Catholic theology, Christ is the last among them—understood what this meant. The pressures of the word are overwhelming. To use words you don't hear much anymore —awe-inspiring. Like the feeling of life itself.''

I go back to the Gospel of John. I'd forgotten how it ended. *"And there are also many other things which Jesus did, the which, if they should be written every one, I suppose, that even the world itself could not contain the books that should be written."* The final verse of the final Gospel. A book beginning 'In the beginning was the word' ending in words that say no words can express the life of one person. A repeated sending-forth of words—Christ made alive by the transmission of his life into words—making its way into history, never-ending.

"Listen," you insisted, "just listen!"

I said I would listen.

"It was the last time I saw her. She was propped up in her bed in this —God, I can't even say the word. Home. We call them homes! A dwelling! Her hair white and wild, her body unable to move of its own accord. Then, suddenly, she began to . . . you couldn't really call it talk. I wiped her lips, they were parched from the medication. She began to . . . what's the word? What she was doing was making sounds. But she was looking right at me. She was *conversing. Communicating.* Suddenly, she began to sing, a kind of guttural chant, a song, I think, from her childhood. She was able to form only a few words I understood. 'You.' 'I.' 'Remember.' But it was mostly those sounds, intonations you might call them, from deep inside her —God, this woman who spoke so beautifully, who taught me my words. There she was, as alive as I'd ever known her, trying to say what she was feeling. There we were. And do you know what I think? There is no such thing as no language. Because that's what it was—language. What we say, what we don't say, what can be expressed, what can't be . . .''

"What happened?" I asked.

"She went on like that for about an hour. A woman, much older— she was crippled, I think—in the bed next to her, kept saying, 'She's talking! She's talking! It's a miracle! She's talking!' The more she got into those sounds, her eyes widened until they were almost transparent—they had color again, they'd changed from dark brown, almost black, to gray and green . . .''

"Her eyes changed color?"

"Yes. Her eyes had actually changed color! There she was—God, what a beautiful woman!—raising her voice, lowering it, trying to move her body, singing again, her face softening, her head slightly nodding up and down, tilting sideways.

"Then, suddenly, she closed her eyes, and never spoke to me again.''

Genesis (Abraham) and Gospels

D E N I S E L E V E R T O V

 hen I tried to decide what portion or portions of the Bible to write about for this collection, I found that many of the stories in the Hebrew and New Testaments which came to mind concerned or included an initial nonrecognition and subsequent revelation of an encounter with the angelic or the divine. Had these, I began to wonder, imprinted themselves in my sensibility early in life? An attraction to such dramatic moments is obviously not rare, and narrative literature, not to speak of the theater, is full of them— I'm not claiming it as a peculiarity of personal taste; but the fact that, as I've come to realize, my own work, even in the years when I would have identified myself as agnostic, is full of insouciantly made biblical allusions, allusions which were simply part of my natural vocabulary, makes me wonder if early exposure to the Bible didn't play a larger part in forming the character of my poetic development than I had realized.

Although I was a clergyman's daughter, I received far less of a religious education than might be imagined. My father did not have a regular parish and I did not attend any school or Sunday school. At home, there were periods when we had family prayers each morning, but then, for reasons unknown, the practice would be discontinued. I did, of course, attend weekly services throughout my childhood, but in my early teens I had developed some doubts and was generally disaffected and embarrassed by adult religious concerns. (These feelings fluctuated and there were times of religious emotion, I can remember, but they were sporadic and largely private.) More conventional parents would no doubt not have let me so absent myself, but mine, despite their own profound belief and commitment, were remarkably liberal (even, one might say, laissez-faire to the point of neglect in some respects, for they allowed my formal education, which was not very formal anyway, to peter out when I started to attend two ballet classes a day at the other side of London—a neglect for which on the whole I am eternally grateful). But though I had no oppressive insistences to cause me to rebel, I was inattentive to Bible readings even as a much younger child, and much preferred fairy tales.

Nevertheless, I heard a good deal of the Bible and heard it early; and what one hears, even without *listening,* no doubt enters one by a sort of osmosis. Thus, when long years afterward I at last began to read the Bible for my own interest and pleasure, and eventually as part of my regular practice as a believing Christian, I sometimes felt a dreamlike familiarity with episodes I was unconscious of knowing; and in others which I *knew* I knew, found a poignance that owed something to the resonance of earlier encounters.

No doubt, too, another factor in my relationship to the Bible has been the experience of biblically inspired music and art. When I was ten I went with my grown-up sister and some young German refugees to hear the St.

Matthew Passion at Southwark Cathedral, a major event in the growth of my sensibility. All my life I've spent a lot of time in art museums, where I have gazed at thousands of medieval and Renaissance depictions of Old and New Testament scenes. But these important experiences don't have particular relevance to the theme of "entertaining angels unawares," which I'd like now to look at more closely.

The obvious example in the O.T.—though not accepted in the Hebrew canon and thus possibly unfamiliar to some readers except as a subject in Renaissance visual art—is the delightful Book of Tobit. My mother must certainly have read or told me the romance of Tobias and his companion—not to mention Tobias's dog—and their adventurous journey, and how they bring back both the magical fish which will cure his father's blindness and —for the young Tobias—a lovely bride. The reader is told, from his first appearance, that the helpful traveling companion, Azarias, is in reality the Archangel Raphael. But the protagonists of the tale, though thoroughly grateful to God, have no suspicion of the angelic intervention, and in this instance not a sudden heightened perceptiveness but the deliberate confession of Raphael himself presents them with the joyful revelation.

The Infant Samuel hears the voice of God but naturally assumes that his human master is calling him. I was intrigued by this story as a young child, simply because it was about another child, and because of the detail concerning his mother bringing him a little coat each year when she visited —though I didn't like the idea of his being given away like that, to live with the old prophet. And at a slightly later stage I was irritated by Samuel's emphasized obedience, dismissing him as a goody-goody. But as an adult I became fond of the story, recognizing it as a parable of the call of vocation. I had taken my own poetic vocation as a given long before I had a word for it, but in later life I have often met gifted people who were timid or disbelieved in their own potential, and seemed to need, like Samuel, a mediator to assure them of their call. The recognition scene, in this story, differs from the others in this way: not little Samuel, who *hears* the voice, realizes its source, but Eli, who does not. Who can fail to see parallels in the many teachers—often obscure high school teachers, or merely competent musicians eking out a living instructing children reluctant to learn—who recognize talent or even genius in one lone pupil to whom it has not even occurred, yet, that such a gift might be his or hers.

Genesis 18, in which three strangers come to the tent of Abraham by the oak of Mamre, seems to me ambiguous in regard to when recognition occurs. Abraham has already had direct speech with God, yet when he addresses the obvious leader of the three as "my Lord," it is not clear to me that he's aware to whom he's speaking or, deferring to his evident status, and no doubt being in the habit anyway of offering hospitality at his oasis, is simply being courteous. The Jerusalem Bible points out that "in the most ancient texts 'the angel of God' is not a created being, but is God himself in a form visible to men." Does Abraham at first think he is entertaining a man, or a "regular" angel or an "angel of God"? By the time he pleads with his guest not to destroy whatever just men there may be in Sodom along with the evildoers, he seems fully aware (and grandly bold—providing a wonderful example of that tradition of arguing with God which is such a unique and moving element in Judaism). And Sarah—when she laughs at God's promise that, old though she is, she will bear another child, in whose presence does she, at that moment, think she is? She's embarrassed and denies her own laughter when challenged; but was she, too, daring to challenge Yahweh, or does she take the stranger for a mortal man? By the time she names her son, the following year, there is no doubt, and I like the amusement with which she says, "God has given me cause to laugh; all those who hear of it will laugh with me. Who would have told Abraham that Sarah would still nurse a child!" She sees the whole event as not only joyful but comical.

This story (the earlier part of which always reminds me of the story of Hermes and Zeus, disguised as poor and weary travelers, visiting Philemon and Baucis) does not quite fit with the episodes of belated recognitions, yet I count it among them, for if its ambiguity implies a *gradual* revelation, that too has parallels in my, and others', experience of wonder. Can one not live in the presence of something a long time before one begins to perceive its value? The ultimate admission may be dramatic but the change from taking-for-granted to astonishment and gratitude isn't always sudden. And this particular story has for me an indissoluble association with the D. H. Lawrence poem which says,

> . . . it is the 3 strange angels.
> Admit them, admit them.

—a call to open the door to inner change. One can indeed be taken by surprise again and again; discoveries and recognitions aren't once and for all, but recur in stages. One may regress to a previous state of ignorance, and need to be reawakened. It is sometimes nonplusing to a writer, who leaves more of a trail evidencing this than others do, to find much the same thing said in an old as in a new poem—unless the repetitions in a life are seen as akin to those in a musical fugue, in which each time a sequence of notes recurs the accretion of intervening passages results in some fresh nuance of form and effect.

Two more Hebrew Bible stories involve this matter of initial nonrecognition. One is the meeting of Joshua at the walls of Jericho with an unknown warrior with naked sword, of whom he demands, Are you with us or with our enemies?—only to find that it is "the captain of the armies of Yahweh"—an "angel of the Lord," that visible emanation of God himself. Then there's the endearing story about Balaam's ass—the humble donkey, so disrespected by humans, who surely represents not only animals in general and their different wisdom, but also the instinctive and intuitive in humans. This donkey can see perfectly well that angel, barring the way, whom Balaam is blind to. But for once the creature's mouth is opened to retort in human speech (and Balaam hears and replies as if too astonished to *be* astonished).

Finally—the Hebrew Bible story that I respond to more than any other—the great poetic event of Jacob's night-long struggle. The moment of recognition for Jacob is (again) unclear. Who does he at first think he is wrestling with? By daybreak, lamed but undefeated, who is it from whom he demands a blessing? Clearly he knows this is no mere man, but when he begs to know his name he is still uncertain. Only after he receives the blessing can he utter those words of awe and triumph, ''. . . I have seen God face to face and I have survived.''

I see a parallel in the New Testament (Acts 9) when Saul is on the road to Tarsus and, struck down as if by lightning, hears that voice speaking to him. He implores, from the dust where he lies, ''Who are you, Lord?'' —and I take it that by that address he expresses humility before a great power of some kind, but not yet an assumption that this is the Lord of All. Or does he indeed, remembering the direct encounters with Yahweh experienced by the leaders and prophets of old, at once know that God is the speaker? At all events, what he least expected must have been the reply, ''I am Jesus, and you are persecuting me.'' The zeal and passion of his previous antagonism don't obstruct, but rather seem to enable him to respond at the same level of intensity to the drastic intervention. (Could it have happened to a lukewarm person?) Saul becomes Paul; he discovers the Messiah precisely among those he had targeted for persecution.

In Acts 12 we do see an angelic intervention, not a theophany. When the angel delivers Peter from his chains and leads him out of the prison, Peter thinks he's dreaming: the recognition of physical reality comes to him only when the angel leaves him and he finds himself out in the street all alone, free. One significance this has for me is as a reminder that miracles have aftermaths: Peter now has to get on with whatever comes next on his life's agenda. Fancy presents miracles as culminating solutions, happy end-ings—whereas real miracles are beginnings, or gateways to continuance.

Wonderful stories; but the heart of the matter, in the New Testament, is of course in the Gospels. Reading the Old Testament, I find a great compendium comprising epic history, poems, legends, philosophy, proph-ecy; metaphor and parable are common to all its categories, and much of it goes back to times twice as remote from us as the first century A.D. Reading the New Testament, I find the biography (as told by several writers) of one person, plus a group of documents which expound the transformative meaning of that life, and recount the adventures and travels of the followers of Jesus to spread the news of his significance.

Because I am committed to the Christian faith, the New Testament necessarily has for me a different impact than the rest of the Bible; it's somewhat comparable to experiencing the beginning of a new movement in a musical work, a movement in which key and rhythm and even instrumen-tation change in a marked degree, although it forms part of a whole and takes up, in its new key, motifs already sounded in the preceding move-ment. And—as a believer—I respond more intimately, more intensely by far, indeed in quite a different way to this new music. The Gospel narra-tives, culminating in the Passion and Resurrection, together with the post-Resurrection appearances and the account of Pentecost in Acts 2, *combine* the historical and the numinous, and with unique force for those who believe them.

Among the New Testament episodes germane to my theme I don't count the Annunciation because there's no indication that Mary mistook for a single moment the angelic nature of her visitant. But at Jacob's Well (John 4:5—29) an unnamed woman simply sees a stranger sitting there, evidently a traveler, tired and road-dusty; and is surprised that a Jewish man deigns to speak to her, female and a Samaritan. Their exchange is a Shakespearian moment of comedy: Jesus astonishes her further by a quite theatrical, calculated display of omniscience. Though it leads to the lyrical image of "living water" I see a playfulness in the manner with which he leads up to the revelation of his own identity; and I value the significance of his choosing a woman—a woman from a despised group, an unlearned village woman, a woman who lives a turbulent life and has broken the code of virtuous behavior, to be the first to acknowledge him as Messiah. He knows not only all her mistakes but also her capacity for response. In its vivid evocation of the interplay between them the episode is more like a modern short story than any other Bible story I can think of.

It is after the Crucifixion that the most intense recognitions occur. Mary Magdalen weeps outside the inexplicably empty tomb, bereft of even a body on which to lavish her mourning, only that terrible emptiness; she rushes away from it to get Peter and John, they come running, look, and confirm that the body of Jesus is gone. She stoops to look again where Peter and John have already looked and have seen only the linen cloths discarded, and nothingness. She, though, finds angels there, one where the head and one where the feet of Jesus had lain, who ask her why she is weeping. She tells them, but is too dazed with grief to register them as signs of a hope she can't grasp. Reading this passage just now for the umpteenth time I suddenly get a faint stir of very early memories—the words read to me, " 'They have taken away my Lord and I know not where they have laid him' "—and my mother surrounding the story with her own words, paraphrasing, describing, depicting. I have been using the Jerusalem Bible translation while writing this essay, but for this the beautiful rhythms of the RSV translation demand my return:

> . . . I know not where they have laid him. And when
> she had thus said, she turned herself back, and saw
> Jesus standing, and knew not that it was Jesus. Jesus
> saith to her, Woman, why weepest thou? Whom
> seekest thou? She, supposing him to be the gardener,

saith unto him, Sir, if thou hast borne him hence, tell
me where thou hast laid him, and I will take him
away. Jesus saith unto her, Mary.

It is so quiet, tender, of deeper dramatic force than a thousand trumpets.

She turned herself and saith unto him, Rabboni, which
is to say, Master.

(JOHN 20:1—16)

Hearing the passage about the road to Emmaus must have made an
early impression on me, because I was always ready to suppose a person of
significance might be encountered unbeknownst. On the all-day excursions
into the Essex countryside my sister and I used to take, by bus and on foot
and by "getting lifts" (as a bit of hitchhiking, then so safe, was called in
1930s' England), we would sometimes see a certain tramp—a wayfaring
man—whom I decided was St. Ignatius going about doing good deeds.
(This was when I was between eight and ten years old.) I knew nothing of
St. Ignatius but his name; it was the tramp's appearance that the name
Ignatius seemed to suit: he had curly black hair, with a thick beard, bright
blue eyes and, though he never spoke to us, would flash us an engaging grin
of recognition. Years later, when I was a grown woman with a ten-year-old
son, I fancied that the broom-seller who appeared unexpectedly to sell us a
new broom just when we needed one (for practical but also for symbolic
reasons) was one of the Lamedvovniks, the thirty-six unknown just men
who at all times uphold the world in Jewish mystical belief. These are petty
and childish anecdotes to place near to a Gospel passage of serious significance; yet they belong here as examples of the way childhood impressions
reverberate throughout a life: in this case as a disposition, an openness to
acknowledge that there may be more than meets the eye in seemingly
commonplace occurrences.

Something else attaches, for me, to the Emmaus account (Luke 24). Often, when he was working at the Soncino Press's English edition of the *Zohar* (he is credited with the translation of one of the several volumes, but in fact contributed to others also), my father, descending from his study to partake of the midday meal, would be full of the passages he'd been translating during the morning, and would tell them as we ate. The subjects of debate, as Rabbi Hisdah and Rabbi Eleazar, Rabbi this and Rabbi that, walked and talked were far above my head, but I was left with a strong impression of the peripatetic nature of so many of these discussions, and a vivid mental picture of dusty country roads shimmering in the heat and two long-robed, bearded figures wending their way along them, deeply absorbed in conversation, gesticulating as they walked. At what stage of my life I perceived the similarity of this image to that of the two disciples on the road to Emmaus I don't know, but the one picture illustrates both for me—and when an unrecognized third joins the disciples it is simply an expansion and evolution of that picture. (Of course, the moment of recognition occurs indoors after they have arrived at Emmaus—but the outdoor scene flows as if with a panning cinematic shot into that interior.)[1]

Last of the passages I will cite, there's the appearance of the risen Christ on the beach (John 21). I have no early recollection of this, but when I read it quite late in life, after my turn from agnosticism to faith, I found it one of the most intimately moving. (I don't count the appearance among the disciples in the locked room—John 20:19, Luke 24:36—among the incidents of unknown identity, since although they at first think his condition is that of a ghost, not a living man, there is no question for them of *who* he is.) I think what I specially like about the meeting on the beach is the practicality with which a man on the shore, a shadowy figure in dawn twilight, or perhaps backlit by the rising sun, calls out to the disciples, who've been out fishing in the night and caught nothing, pointing out to them a spot to starboard where if they cast their net one more time they'll fill it. It seems in the half-light that he's just a man, a stranger. But the young John, loved by Jesus for his unusual sensitivity, suddenly knows: "It is the Lord!" he exclaims. And at that, impulsive Peter, who never stops to think but simply acts, gathers his cloak about him and jumps overboard. Most people would cast a cloak *off*, not put it *on* to do so! But to cover his nakedness before the Lord is a traditional gesture of respect, and paradoxically blends itself here with Peter's nonrational impetuosity. He doesn't wait to help tow the boat one hundred yards to the beach—I see him go splashing shoreward in his haste to get close to his Master. When they reach the shore the disciples find Jesus has brought some bread and has got a fire going, on which a fish is already cooking. "Come and have breakfast"— and he suggests they contribute some of the big catch they've just made. Peter climbs back in the boat and drags the big net onto the beach. It is all so factual, so full of concrete detail.

Disguises and revelations, maskings and unmaskings, are a familiar motif in myth and fairy tale; and my early reading experiences—listening experiences, rather—were far more densely packed with fairy tales than with the Bible, which was a background presence to me, constant but largely subliminal. The Andrew Lang compilations of fairy tales were much more prominent in my consciousness, as was Kingsley's *The Water Babies,* in which the barefoot young Irishwoman Tom meets on the road, close to the beginning of the story, turns out by the end to have been both the stern Mrs. Bedonebyasyoudid and her sister the gentle Mrs. Doasyouwouldbe-doneby—and something else besides, whose name she won't reveal, and which Tom and Ellie can't yet guess, but whom an adult can recognize as Lady Wisdom. Did the theme preoccupy me, wherever I found it? I think not; but the sense that things or persons may be more than what they seem did root in me early.

And was there no qualitative difference between biblical and nonbiblical stories, for me? How (or whether) I considered that as a child I cannot truly say. But as an adult I register a different intensity of affect in my response to the Old and the New Testament instances I have cited. Those from the former do have the ring of *fictive truth* whether or not they are historically true; some instances, e.g., Jacob's wrestling with the angel, I take literally as well as metaphorically: i.e., I think the force with which he struggled was embodied—why not? We may have lost certain faculties, such as the perception of such embodiments, through overconcentration on developing others. However, those from the New Testament have a more emotive and differently experienced power for me. The balance between what documents events the writers believe to have occurred, and what those events *signify,* is a different one. Because I believe the Resurrection was an event of historical reality, its mythic significance penetrates into my receptive imagination further than the myths of rebirth to be found in all cultures, and this gives a different weight to pre- as well as post-Resurrection anecdotes.

Whether the aggregate of these accounts, fictive and documentary, biblical and nonbiblical, of delayed recognition decisively influenced me early in life or whether I had an innate predisposition which made them particularly attractive to me, I can't say. It has become clear to me, however, that the possibility of "entertaining angels unawares" is integral to how I perceive. I seem to have had some conscious awareness of this for a long time. By 1946 I had written,

> I love to see, in golden matchlight
> Intimate contours of a face
> Like discovered innocence
> In dusty annals of disgrace

and in a 1960 book, a poem called "Pleasures" begins,

> I like to find
> what's not found
> at once, but lies

within something of another nature,

in repose, distinct.

That poem goes on to speak of certain natural objects—squid bones, the seed of a tropical fruit, and so on—but in fact the experience is of wider application. Over a lifetime it has to do with finding the more in the (seeming) less, with being found rather than arriving where one thought one was going. Less a theme than a quality, what much of the poetry I'm drawn to as a reader has in common, diverse though it is, is the revelation of the wonderful in the apparently ordinary. And the instants of heightened perception which often are what start me on writing my own poems are not simply responses to what is clearly beautiful, such as the almost reflex appreciation of a rose or a sunset, but have an element of surprise, of a curtain being drawn back, an opaque disguise becoming suddenly transparent.

NOTES

1. In a painting by Velázquez, now in the National Gallery of Ireland, a young servant-girl can be seen to recognize the identity of Christ a moment before the two men do so.

Matthew

R O B E R T P O L I T O

This was the summer after Sputnik, the summer of 1958, and the family was driving back from two weeks of swimming, fishing, and the nightly barbecue in a scruffy rented cottage—one of a colony of identical A-frames—near Buzzards Bay, Cape Cod. As he glided the car along the Southeast Expressway past Braintree and Quincy toward Dorchester, my father, who reinforced his aspirations of my growing up a scientist with astronomy charts, a plastic microscope, and a vast chemistry set beyond my seven and a half years, shifted the conversation to the Soviet launch of the previous November, space travel, and the possibility of life on other planets.

I joined his familiar car talk avidly—UFOs were our shared infatuation that year. But soon I found myself assaulting him with a confusion that had never occurred to me before. "If they find life on other planets, won't that mean the Bible is wrong?"

Both my parents seemed flummoxed by this abrupt question, my mother fidgety in the front seat, even angry. Turning his head back from the wheel of the two-tone, secondhand Oldsmobile we had scrubbed and waxed together early that morning, my father interrupted the silence. "I guess you're right . . ."

A few nights later, he revisited the drive home as he was tucking me into bed. My mother, he reported, wanted him to speak with me. She had telephoned the Monsignor, and what I said in the car didn't disprove the Bible. "God wrote the Bible about Earth," he said. "Those beings on other planets could have their own Bibles."

But he only sounded half-convinced.

The minor mystery here was not so much any precocious iconoclasm—my favorite aunt, already dead from cancer at thirty-nine, had served as a nun in the order of the Sisters of St. Joseph, and I still hoped to carry on her vocation as a Catholic priest—as it was how I managed to hear anything at all about Genesis. The Boston Catholics I grew up with during the 1950s and 1960s, the predominantly *Irish*-Catholics who inhabited St. Mark's parish, were not people of the Word or the Book.

Our house, the first-floor flat of a classic three-decker, contained a Bible, but it was not clear where it had come from, nor was it proudly displayed. Stiff, greasy from kitchen fumes, and so thick as to be unreadable except at a lectern, our Bible sat on the bottom shelf of a rear hallway under some cookbooks and the old electrical engineering and psychology texts my father studied in night school on the GI Bill after World War II, before he took a job with the Post Office.

One of the focal curiosities of my childhood involved an emphasis on education that flourished amid a blank renunciation of art and culture. From the start I was made to appreciate that I would attend the parochial grammar school at St. Mark's, where the Sisters of St. Joseph maintained academic discipline, rather than a lax local public institution; after that, if I worked hard, my parents vowed they would scrape and save to send me to a good Catholic high school, and on to college. Yet nowhere in our house could be discovered any of the obvious vehicles and gratifications of education. There were no novels or poetry books, few new books of whatever kind beyond my father's random popular science paperbacks, no musical recordings; we never went to the movies, and I don't think we even owned a TV. (My earliest home experience of television, as far as I can recall, was watching the inauguration of the first Irish-Catholic president, when I was nearly ten.)

Still, every afternoon after school my mother would sit down beside me with my homework, for upward of three or four hours as my friends played stickball in the parking lot behind the grocery store at the corner of our street. Her connections inside the Sisters of St. Joseph allowed her access to the answer keys the nuns relied on to grade our quizzes and tests, and her lessons often ran entire months ahead of my class—I became so bored and restless at St. Mark's that eventually the sisters sent me home with the diagnosis that I must have worms.

Beyond the conspicuous illustration of my parents' worldly ambitions for me, our daily rituals of learning also carried a quiet religious burden. Her relentless overpreparation reflected my mother's mournful sense of inhabiting a fallen world. Everything about her tone during these anxious sessions at the kitchen table over my schoolbooks seemed to say, "That world out there, it's hard, and you're going to need all the help you can get." And if her little scholar's attention wandered through the window and down the street, she yanked it back with a coat hanger she held poised in her right hand.

Dominated by my mother, and her mother—my Nana—the eyes our family set before that outside world radiated distrust. Their morning Masses, the visiting florid priests and pale sisters, their milky tea and soda bread, the St. Patrick's Day parades and memories of Eire, directed a social order as compact and impervious as any on Easter Island. Ethnic identities sustained an almost occult solidity. A typical conversation satisfied a scrutinizing, "What's he like?" with totemic classifications, "Oh, he's a Swede," or "He's German." My mother remembered that before she met my father, she "used to go with an English fella." The only "coloreds" I knew about were some letter carriers at my father's post office whose distinguishing virtue appeared to be that they "weren't like other coloreds." Some of their wariness extended to my Italian-American father. Nana could toll a domestic argument to a halt with the reminder that he was living in a house that her Irish husband had paid for.

The Bible receded on this mixed current of suspicion and self-contentedness to its remote storage beyond the kitchen. Invoked periodically as a sort of triumphant last word, usually against sin (an act or opinion was "against the Bible"), the book itself also came to be linked with a race of sinners called "Protestants," who, my mother and grandmother said, revolted against the Church and were condemned by God to hell. The Bible figured obscurely in that doom, but since we didn't know any Protestants, it hardly mattered.

Prior to the Second Vatican Council (1962–65) the Mass was spoken in Latin, and many of my early impressions of the New Testament arrived secondhand. One of our first English readers at St. Mark's summarized heroic episodes from the life of Christ, but my most consistent encounters with his story passed through the rhetorical filter of the Baltimore Catechism—named after the Third Plenary Council of Baltimore (1885)—that aligned the foundation of our religious study.

The introduction to the *Baltimore Catechism* vaunted its easy entry to the Bible:

> The teacher aims at presenting to the children the words of Christ and even more the Person of Christ, Who is *the* Word in which is contained all truth . . . The object is to introduce the child at an early age to the Bible itself where we have the Person and message of Our Lord Jesus Christ presented by the Holy Spirit Himself . . . If they learn to love the Bible, they will fall in love with Christ.

Each lesson accordingly opened with a brief illustrative quotation from the New Testament, in youthful paraphrase. But the lessons themselves seemed designed to transport the reader as far as possible from the verbal texture of the Bible. Emblematic of the catechism's indifference to the words of Christ as recorded in the Gospels was a declaration from the first lesson that the fundamental tenets of the Catholic Church subsisted in the Apostles' Creed—a mnemonic formula established at the Council of Trent in 1563, which derived more from Augustine than from the Bible:

> I believe in God, the Father Almighty, Creator of heaven and earth; and in Jesus Christ, His Only Son, Our Lord; Who was conceived by the Holy Spirit, born of the Virgin Mary, suffered under Pontius Pilot, was crucified, died, and was buried. He descended into hell; the third day He arose again from the dead; He ascended into heaven, sitteth at the right hand of God, the Father Almighty; from thence He shall come to judge the living and the dead. I believe in the Holy

Spirit, the Holy Catholic Church, the communion of
Saints, the forgiveness of sins, the resurrection of the
body, and life everlasting. Amen.

The language of the New Testament, or of Christ, proved incidental
to the catechism, as it marshaled its dislocated and disembodied content.
Unlike some Protestant or Jewish friends who would retain the inflections
of the King James or the Hebrew Bible as a kind of common interior
melody, the enduring tune from my religion classes pitched insistent questions against pat answers:

1. Who made us?
   God made us.
2. Who is God?
   God is the Supreme Being who made all things.
3. Why did God make us?
   God made us to show forth His Goodness and to
   share with us His everlasting happiness in heaven.
4. What must we do to gain the happiness of
   heaven?
   To gain the happiness of heaven we must know,
   love, and serve God in this world.
5. From whom do we learn to know, love, and
   serve God?
   We learn to know, love, and serve God from
   Jesus Christ, the Son of God, who teaches us
   through the Catholic Church.

The drawings and sketches scattered through the catechism—most
famously the full and empty milk bottles tracking the debasement from a

pure to a sinful soul—furthered this domestication of the Bible. A distinctly European Christ preached and performed his miracles surrounded by his European disciples and, often, a small troupe of American school children, our time-transported stand-ins who, for instance, mingled among the mourners at his crucifixion. Or Christ held the hands of a little boy and girl, each dressed in sporty 1950s summer clothing, as they walked a country road; the caption noted, "Jesus guides us on the way to heaven." Literalizations abounded—if Christ was our "Good Shepherd," his followers were envisioned as actual sheep on a real farm.

The catechism urged us to identify with the apostles and saints, and each of us tested our faith against Peter's denial at Gethsemane. For the young male reader, anyway, the catechism also encouraged a subtle identification with Christ, portrayed in both text and illustration as another white prince from our story books. It was not hard, neither blasphemy nor simple vanity, to make an imaginative connection to this boy who, with his ambiguous relation to his earthly parents, challenged his mother in a Jerusalem temple, as each night after supper I retreated from the grind of homework to the tiny lair down in the cellar where I kept my own books, toys, and an ancient radio, and hid out until it was time for bed.

When the moment of my First Holy Communion neared, my mother presented me with a small package wrapped in tissue paper and sealed with a purple bow that my aunt, Sister Mary Dionetta, put aside during her final illness. Opened, this contained everything one would need to celebrate First Communion, including a Latin missal inside a leather slipcase and a dazzling Rosary styled from heavy onyx beads and a wooden cross. My classmates, I noticed with insider's snobbery, would have to make do with the standard plastic facsimiles.

My aunt's touching, from-beyond-the-grave surprise shortly exploded in public humiliation and trauma. A few days before the much-anticipated May Saturday morning, the nuns called a formal dress rehearsal in St. Mark's Church, where the Sister Superior would inspect our First Communion clothes and kits. After leading us through the ceremony, which she coordinated with a Morse Code of clicks from the wooden clapper she carried inside her rustling habit, the Sister Superior asked to see each of our missals. When I explained about Sister Dionetta, she smiled— they had entered the order together, she said, and I must be proud of her now in heaven. But on a closer look at my missal, she began to frown, and snatched the book away. My missal was "heresy," she announced to the entire assembly of communicants. She would have to send it into the archdiocese, where it would be destroyed. I fled home in tears.

The crux, I learned after my mother phoned the school, was this. The imprimatur who signed off on my missal was Father Leonard Feeney, a recently excommunicated Jesuit priest my aunt had known years before when they both were associated with St. Paul's Church in Cambridge. Father Feeney, as I much later discovered, presided over the St. Benedict Center, which had evolved from the Harvard Catholic Club during the 1940s. Alarmed by a Harvard curriculum he saw as corrupted by Hegel, Freud, and Marx, Feeney directed an assault on contemporary liberalism that eventually advanced beyond Harvard to indict the modern Catholic Church. Evelyn Waugh explored the St. Benedict Center on the counsel of Clare Boothe Luce:

> [Father Feeney] fell into a rambling denunciation
> of all secular learning which became more and more
> violent. He shouted that Newman had done
> irreparable damage to the Church then started on
> Ronnie Knox's *Mass in Slow Motion* saying "To think
> any innocent girl of 12 could have this blasphemous

and obscene book put in her hands'' as though it was
Lady Chatterly's Lover. I asked if he had read it. "I don't
have to eat a rotten egg to know it stinks.'' Then I got
rather angry and rebuked him in strong words.

Father Feeney insisted that there was no salvation outside of the
Church, and eventually declaimed anti-Semitic speeches on Boston
Common.

Expounding the intricacies of Church heresy to a child probably was a
lost cause, and all that I could glean from my parents' halting clarification I
already understood too well: my aunt's prized bequest was destined for
archdiocesan fires. "Just politics," my father concluded, with the air of
someone piercing the veil of that day's headlines; but we must obey the
Church, my mother added. Neither my parents nor I possessed the wit or
courage to argue what was obviously spotty theology. If retrospect could
void Father Feeney's *imprimatur,* were all the marriages he performed while
a priest now invalid? All the dying souls he intoned the Last Rites over also
condemned to burn?

A more current missal was hastily purchased, and my First
Communion overcame the initial mortification. Cardinal Cushing officiated
at the Mass, at once magisterial and elfin in gold vestments, crosier, and red
suede boots. The high drama of the Latin Mass cannot be exaggerated. I
still recall a Good Friday Passion at the downtown cathedral where the
intense spectacle—choirs, incense, cloth-draped statues, an agonized
Stations of the Cross, and the cardinal, this time arrayed head to feet in
purple—would only be matched thirty years later by a performance of *Aida*
inside the Roman arena at Verona. The emotional pulse of Catholic
Dorchester, perhaps, shuttled between these twin poles: arrested instants
when private tragedies—my lost missal, my aunt's death—weighed less
than rain; and elevated occasions when any personal hurt or grief was
subsumed in the universal downpour.

The gravity of First Communion persisted into a fitful secret rite. The catechism account of the Eucharist mingled cooked semiotics ("The Eucharist is a sign") with raw hocus-pocus ("It is a sign which looks like bread and tastes like bread, but is really the Flesh and Blood of Christ as the food and drink of our soul."). Provoctions of magic connected the Eucharist to my favorite passages in our English reader on the life of Christ —the miracles: the wedding feast at Cana, the curing of the blind and paralytic, Lazarus raised from the dead.

A few months after First Communion, instead of swallowing the host at Sunday Mass I would surreptitiously pass it from my mouth to a handkerchief for preservation at home in a pickle jar I kept hidden among the liquids and powders of my chemistry set. My notion was that reserves of such potent magic could only prove useful someday—for or against what I can't say, as I don't think I ever moved beyond hoarding them. I must have ended up with about an inch of curled, crusty Eucharists before a neighbor, sitting in the pew behind us, informed my embarrassed mother and the jar was confiscated.

Through a misunderstanding of a phrase in the catechism, "the communion of saints," I transferred some of this magic to the pair of relics my grandmother displayed on her bedroom dresser. Chips of bone encased in glass and bronze, Nana's miniature reliquaries housed the partial remains of Pope Pius X and another saint whose long name started with the letters D-I-O-N before fading into illegibility. For a number of years, I believed the smear of bone and glue *was* Sister Dionetta, my aunt.

Still, bits of that magic stuck. Whenever I thought and think about an afterlife—a parallel life to the one we live every day—it is as a "communion of the dead," a conversation among and with dead friends

and family, my "saints." James Merrill's convocation of his dead friends
and literary ancestors over a Ouija board for *The Changing Light at Sandover*
probably reexposed this nerve when I first read "The Book of Ephraim" in
Divine Comedies, and eventually I wrote a book about it. As Merrill recorded
late in *Sandover:*

> Night. Two phantoms out of Maeterlinck
> Stand on the terrace watching the full moon sink.
> DJ: It's almost as if *we* were dead
> And signalling to dear ones in the world . . .

Louise Gluck in her acute essay "The Education of a Poet" describes
writing poetry as "attempting dialogue with the great dead."

Everyone's idea of a Catholic childhood—sex, sin, and guilt—infiltrated
through the unlikely cover of the weekly Catholic newspaper, the *Boston
Pilot.* There were other double agents, no less slanting or improbable, and
Mary Magdalene particularly incited flustered conjecture when she turned
up in our English reader. The nuns glossed her mysterious trespass as
adultery, a sin against the sixth commandment. The catechism predictably
shunned details. "By the sixth commandment we are commanded to be
pure and modest in our behavior. God the Holy Ghost lives in us. If we
bear this in mind, we shall always want to keep a pure and clean dwelling
for Him." (As late as freshman year in high school, purple metaphors
would still dominate our sexual indoctrination. A Dr. Lynch, imported by
the Jesuits from a Boston hospital, launched his narrative of our conception,
"Your father took a seed and placed it under your mother's heart. . . .")

Every Saturday the *Pilot* printed the Legion of Decency List, a classifi-
cation of current movies according to their "moral estimate." The infa-

mous Class C—Condemned—probably was our earliest introduction to adult sex, certainly to verbal sex. Along with many classics (from *Baby Doll* and *Never on Sunday* to *Jules and Jim*), the Condemned List chronicled the sort of stag film that played Boston's Combat Zone, no doubt salvaging many pulp-erotic titles from prompt oblivion—*Port of Desire, Mating Urge, Question of Adultery, Love Game, The Molesters, Sins of Mona, Love Is My Profession,* or *Liane Jungle Goddess*.

The critical annotations that sometimes accompanied the Condemned List flaunted a fierce probity: *"Five Day Lover* (French)—Objection: This film, immoral in theme because of its mockery of marriage and traditional morality, is further highlighted by salacious and indecent morality." But often the objection seemed less licentiousness than a refusal to be conned or ridiculed by the too-clever filmmaker: ". . . this film makes a false pretense to be moral in theme by the introduction of a patently contrived crime-does-not-pay ending." And the Legion of Decency similarly denounced "films which, while not morally objectionable in themselves, require some analysis and explanation as a protection to the uninformed against wrong interpretation and false conclusions." Many of the Condemned List movies, fascinatingly for us at St. Mark's, treated what looked like religious subjects—*Private Lives of Adam and Eve, Garden of Eden, Wages of Sin, And God Created Woman,* and *Magdalene*.

Around the fifth grade, one of my friends somehow chanced upon a stash of rain-soaked pornographic magazines during his walk home, and raced them back to the St. Mark's playground. Fear spurred our excitement, and scads of confused jokes. But as we were divvying up the photographs, however, for private study later, some older boys bullied the pages away from us. They left only a neat pile of tiny breasts and vaginas, each organ carefully ripped from its original body, with the taunting explanation that we could hide these more easily from our parents. (This was my initiation into the priority of context.)

Such episodes, and the "dirty thoughts" they inspired, demanded Contrition, Confession, and Penance. We were trained to prepare for the weekly recital of our sins to the priest with a strict examination of our conscience, a systematic review of our life since our last Confession. Penance was coded according to the frequency or magnitude of sin—three Our Fathers, seven Hail Marys, an Apostles' Creed.

Catholics grow up accustomed to looking at ourselves from the outside—no deed, after all, can escape an all-seeing God, our paradigm for the examination of conscience requisite to "a good Confession." Ingrained habits of self-analysis do not necessarily make Catholics moral or responsible, savvier at translating insight into action or kinder at forgiving ourselves; perhaps only more self-conscious.

By the time I reached the seventh and eighth grades, Nana was dead, and my family trailed "white flight" from Dorchester to the suburban South Shore. After the Second Vatican Council, Mass was in English, with freshly translated Epistles and Gospels—and a folk Mass for the young people every other Sunday morning. But we were listening to the Kinks, the Rolling Stones, the Beatles, and trying to look tough in sharkskin jackets that didn't quite tally with our red and gold school ties. The nuns at St. Ann's in Wollaston, here the Sisters of Charity of Nazareth, struggled to contain the historical wave. Instead of stories about Christ, the books at the back of our classroom carried titles like *Brass Knuckles,* and featured juvenile delinquents who renounced their gangs for the priesthood.

The Monsignor at St. Ann's, the Reverend Walter J. Leach, arranged a parish scholarship for me after I was accepted at Boston College High, a Jesuit commuter prep school. Because of complications with the funding, he told my parents, they should return to him $250 cash for each $500 check he wrote us. The scandal broke in the Boston papers some years after

I graduated. There were many parish scholars, it transpired; our kickbacks, among other church funds, found their way to a bank in Sweden. The money was for the Swedish Missions, Monsignor Leach maintained, before fleeing to Stockholm.

Even at B.C. High, the Bible preserved the equivocal status of a simultaneously privileged and off-limits text. With both Jesuit and lay instructors we kept circling Holy Writ in our classes—Ancient History, Church History, Theology, the Reformation, and Guidance. Although the comparative religion sequence of my senior Asian Studies course introduced us to the *Bhagavadgītā,* the *Mahābhārata,* the *Upanishads,* the *I Ching,* the *Tao Te Ching,* and the *Analects,* through four years of high school the Bible, except for a single vivid occasion, stayed a closed book.

But a Catholic high school in the late 1960s wasn't the tonic my parents envisioned. An ambitious young English teacher, fresh from graduate school, seduced us into serious reading for the first time with his resourceful assignment of Ian Fleming's *From Russia with Love,* and soon we were happily writing short papers for him about *The Waste Land,* Auden, Chinese poetry, or John Barth. Following his example, we started buying classical records, and covered the walls of our rooms with poster-reproductions of paintings. Some of us even furtively took to smoking pipes. Meanwhile, with each subway ride after school to Harvard Square for the secondhand bookstores, or on Sunday afternoons for the rock concerts at the Cambridge Common, the sway of Church and home receded a bit further, or, perhaps more accurately, moved underground.

I grew inventive at not attending Mass, except on unavoidable holidays like Christmas or Easter, and family supper-table discussions of religion shifted now to a symbolic turf—the Vietnam War, long hair, Malcolm X, the Velvet Underground. In Harvard Square I purchased a worn copy of Bertrand Russell's *Sceptical Essays,* and quietly debated whether to call myself an atheist or an agnostic. My mother would be appalled when she noticed I no longer went to church, my father more troubled that I also lost my interest in science.

The erosion of Catholicism was not without its chills or fevers. After more than one French class spent translating Camus and Sartre, I stood trembling at my locker, feeling that I was living on hydrogen. The *Baltimore Catechism* may have been silly, but everything in that world held its place. Irony, mainly glib yet sometimes surprisingly sour, composed our dominant religious stance. Over the obligatory applause and shouts that greeted the Jesuit hierarchy at B.C. High assemblies, my friends chanted, ''Give us Barabbas!'' as the priests and proctors scurried to descry the source. Our sneaky, feeble rebellion was itself, I suppose, inverted homage to the New Testament we scarcely knew.

That one irruption of the Bible at B.C. High could not have seemed more casual. We had just finished translating Book VI of the *Aeneid,* the descent of Aeneas into the underworld. Our Latin teacher decided to reward us by taking some time off, he announced, to remember other notable poems about hell. He read aloud a canto from Dante's *Inferno,* selections from Milton's *Paradise Lost,* and the entire Old English ''The Harrowing of Hell.'' You know Christ also descended into hell in the Bible, he added. We didn't. He then took up the last book from his pile, astonishingly—for us —the King James version, and read Matthew 12:38–45.

Matthew 12 opens with the hungry apostles foraging for food in a cornfield. When the Pharisees complain that ''thy disciples do that which is not lawful to do on the sabbath day,'' Christ stirs to their defense:

> 3 But he said unto them, Have ye not read what David
> did, when he was an hungred, and they that were with
> him;

4 How he entered into the house of God, and did eat the shewbread, which was not lawful for him to eat, neither for them which were with him, but only for the priests?

5 Or have ye not read in the law, how that on the sabbath days the priests in the temple profane the sabbath, and are blameless?

6 But I say unto you, That in this place is *one* greater than the temple.

7 But if ye had known what *this* meaneth, I will have mercy, and not sacrifice, ye would not have condemned the guiltless.

8 For the Son of man is Lord even of the sabbath day.

The edgy, doubled questions ("Have ye not read . . . Or have ye not read"), the crisp, almost taunting subjunctive clause ("But if ye had known . . . ye would not have condemned"), and the blunt, crowning declaration ("For the Son of man is Lord . . .") quickly establish *this* Christ as another order of being from the genial Good Shepherd of our catechism.

Bold enough to arraign the priests' sanctimony against his disciples' hunger, and to summon King David as the forerunner of his own kingdom, Christ proceeds directly into the Pharisees' synagogue. There, amid further clamors that he is violating the sabbath, Christ heals a man with a withered hand and "one possessed with a devil, blind and dumb." After the Pharisees accuse him of confederating with Beelzebub, he hones his rebuke:

25 And Jesus knew their thoughts, and said unto them, Every kingdom divided against itself is brought

to desolation; and every city or house divided against itself shall not stand:

26 And if Satan cast out Satan, he is divided against himself; how shall then his kingdom stand?

27 And if I by Beelzebub cast out devils, by whom do your children cast *them* out? therefore they shall be your judges.

28 But if I cast out devils by the spirit of God, then the kingdom of God is come unto you.

29 Or else how can one enter into a strong man's house, and spoil his goods, except he first bind the strong man? and then he will spoil his house.

30 He that is not with me is against me; and he that gathereth not with me scattereth abroad.

Christ casts the riddle of his identity as an ascending ladder of logical drills: "If Satan . . . how shall then . . ."; "If I by Beelzebub . . . therefore . . ."; "But if I . . . by the spirit of God . . . then . . ." But his examples intimate a condemnation—the Pharisees, too, dwell in a "house divided against itself"—that stretches to a dire judgment, nearly a threat or curse, "He that is not with me is against me." Informing the Pharisees that "by thy words thou shalt be justified, and by thy words thou shalt be condemned," Christ tags them "a generation of vipers."

Beaten down, the Pharisees can think of nothing else but to request "a sign." Christ retorts with a gust of prophecy, his own harrowing of hell:

39 But he answered and said unto them, An evil and adulterous generation seeketh after a sign; and there

shall no sign be given to it, but the sign of the prophet Jonas:

40 For as Jonas was three days and three nights in the whale's belly; so shall the Son of man be three days and three nights in the heart of the earth.

41 The men of Nineveh shall rise in judgment with this generation, and shall condemn it: because they repented at the preaching of Jonas; and behold, a greater than Jonas *is* here.

42 The queen of the south shall rise up in the judgment with this generation, and shall condemn it: for she came from the uttermost parts of the earth to hear the wisdom of Solomon; and, behold, a greater than Solomon *is* here.

43 When the unclean spirit is gone out of a man, he walketh through dry places, seeking rest, and findeth none.

44 Then he saith, I will return into my house from whence I came out; and when he is come, he findeth *it* empty, swept, and garnished.

45 Then goeth he, and taketh with himself seven other spirits more wicked than himself, and they enter in and dwell there: and the last *state* of that man is worse than the first. Even so shall it be also unto this wicked generation.

As Jonas fades to Christ, and the Old Testament jostles against, then blends into the New, horror drifts among the spare details—the enigmatic "queen of the south," that awful "last *state*"—much as the pathetic "unclean spirit" . . . "through dry places."

These were the lines our Latin teacher put next to the *Aeneid*. His performance had the effect of transforming the Bible into literature—not ''literature'' like at home, extrinsic and negligible, or purified and safe like the catechism, but Virgil, Dante, Milton—strange, wondrous, necessary, terrifying.

Perhaps sensing our shock, our excitement, he wound down with some passages from Revelation, including—if I'm remembering right—Revelation 1:18:

> I *am* he that liveth, and was dead; and, behold, I am
> alive for evermore, Amen; and have the keys of hell
> and of death.

By then the class hour was over. His reading would not be repeated.

Genesis, Psalms, and Gospels

L O R E N Z O   T H O M A S

This dream, O King, though seen under two forms,
signifies one and the same event.*

JOSEPH TO PHARAOH, AS RECORDED BY JOSEPHUS,
ANCIENT HISTORY OF THE JEWS II, 5

I.

In Jean Toomer's *Cane* (1923) there is a
weird old man who sits all but interred in a basement predicting
doom upon America in retribution for "th sin th white folks 'mitted

---

* Quoted in Sigmund Freud, *The Interpretation of Dreams*. Trans. by James Strachey (New
York: Avon, 1965), p. 369.

when they made th Bible lie.'' That character, driven to madness by his knowing, is not representative of all the generations of black Americans who managed to find their own truth in the Bible.

There are, for me, at least three biblical texts that resonate with a sort of hieroglyphic potency. Each has, of course, a specific interpretation and a personal significance; and each also seems to be laminated and illuminated in a palimpsest of deeper meanings connected to my own evolving sense of who and where I am. Part of being black in America, however, is the realization—not always bitter—that being so is not simply a public fact but an unavoidable dimension of what is called ''personal.'' This is true even in the usual confusion of adolescent alienation. Often subjected to academic scrutiny, this is not necessarily a type of schizophrenia (cultural or clinical) but rather a sort of enhanced self-awareness. What is important, crucial, is that the black person in America is not easily extricated from the history of black people in America.

And thus, some public history must come first. The public, or ''official'' history that follows is also my personal story, as I've come to know it.

Although it can hardly be said that slave-owners encouraged Bible reading, enslaved Africans surely identified with the situation described in Psalm 137:

> By the rivers of Babylon, there we sat down, yea,
> we wept, when we remembered Zion.
> We hanged our harps upon the willows in the midst
> thereof.
> For there they that carried us away captive
> required of us a song; and they that wasted us
> required of us mirth, saying, Sing us one of the
> songs of Zion.

How shall we sing the Lord's song in a strange
land?

(*PSALM* 137:1–4)

Though they could not sing its concluding verses of retribution for the
wicked, because of what DuBois called "the limitations of allowable
thought," the slaves nevertheless used their rudimentary English to create
an astonishing parallel to Psalm 137 in the movingly beautiful spiritual
"Sometimes I Feel Like a Motherless Child."

The descendants of these slaves, the children of the 1870s Reconstruction Era, saw the figure of John the Baptist as emblematic of the entire
African diaspora. They saw themselves as specially chosen. Just as John was
"sent from God . . . for a witness, to bear witness of the Light" (John
1:1–2), so were they destined to be leaders in the redemption of their
motherland Africa—in both the world's esteem and in material reality.
This reading of the figure of John the Baptist was essentially secular and a
proudly optimistic response to European imperialism and white supremacy
doctrines in the United States. In his *Philosophy and Opinions* (1923), black
nationalist leader Marcus Garvey succinctly stated the widespread attitude
of the period. "We the Negroes of this Western Hemisphere," Garvey
wrote, "are descendants of those Africans who were enslaved and transported to these shores, where they suffered, bled and died to make us what
we are today—Civilized, Christian free men." Africans in the West, so the
idea went, because of their opportunities for advanced education (including
the spiritual and moral advantages of being Christians) would be the ones to
lead their brothers on the "dark continent" into the modern, increasingly
industrialized age.

But the abolition of slavery was not an unmixed blessing and the
freedmen's hopefulness was not without challenge. "With the beginning of

the work of reconstruction,'' wrote historian William Wells Brown—
himself a former fugitive slave—in his 1874 book *The Rising Son,* ''the right
of the negro to the ballot came legitimately before the country, and
brought with it all the virus of negro hate that could be thought of.'' And
by the turn of the century W. E. B. DuBois registered some apprehension
about the popular John the Baptist metaphor in his story ''Of the Coming
of John'' included in *The Souls of Black Folk* (1903).

In DuBois's story John Jones, a young black man who has been away
to college, returns south to open a village school. His long-anticipated
arrival is a day of jubilee in the black community.

> And as the people were in expectation, and all men
> mused in their hearts of John, whether he were the
> Christ, or not;
> John answered, saying unto them all, I indeed baptize
> you with water; but one mightier than I cometh, the
> latchets of whose shoes I am not worthy to un-
> loose . . .
>
> *(LUKE 3:15—16)*

''It was several days later,'' writes DuBois

> that John walked up to the Judge's house to ask for the
> privilege of teaching the Negro school. The Judge
> himself met him at the front door, stared a little hard
> at him, and said brusquely, ''Go 'round to the kitchen
> door, John, and wait.''

When the Judge is ready to speak to John his words could have been
predicted by most readers:

"Now, John, the question is, are you, with your education and Northern notions, going to accept the situation and teach the darkies to be faithful servants and
laborers as your fathers were,—I knew your father,
John, he belonged to my brother, and he was a good
Nigger. Well—well, are you going to be like him, or
are you going to try to put fool ideas of rising and
equality into these folks' heads, and make them dis-
contented and unhappy?"

DuBois did not, of course, mean to discourage his readers. Early in the
story we see that John strengthens himself for the struggle by repeating
Queen Esther's words, "I will go in to the King, which is not according to
the Law; and if I perish, I perish." (Esther 4:16) And, though in fact the
fictional John Jones does perish, the importance of the metaphor in the
African-American community did not diminish for the next half century.

Because I had been taught to find the Bible relevant I heard the
signature of the black struggle in Psalm 137—as many thousands had before
me. Its repetition through the ages offered solace and instilled determination. It was a splendid gleaming thread that helped to fashion African-
American oratory and literature from Frederick Douglass through the Harlem Renaissance of Langston Hughes and Countee Cullen to the eloquent
James Baldwin. Psalm 137 was the grounding text of the Civil Rights
anthem "We Shall Not Be Moved" and the electrifying speeches of Reverend Martin Luther King, Jr.

In the galleries of Munich's Alte Pinakothek one can see that the early
masters of the Dutch school found John the Baptist a favorite subject in the
late 1400s. While Memling's prophet glows like an icon, Dieric Bouts
(1410–75) depicts a John much more familiar to my imaginings—a gaunt

man in a shabby cloak with matted locks and a facial expression hinting that his concentration is intent but elsewhere. This is, indeed, the pictoral counterpart of the Gospel Keynotes' John: "Just a voice (high high falsetto harmony) crying . . . in the wilderness."

In the depictions of the European masters, John the Baptist is an obvious outsider with matted hair and tattered loincloth. The look on his face is often more distracted than beatific, disturbingly similar to the alarming gaze of some homeless people along Main Street whose thoughts and communications apparently occur in a weird dimension unknown to ordinary passersby who are distracted, to a much lesser degree, merely by business and personal problems.

In the endless disputes that are the life of a city we may see the simple conflict of desires. This conflict need not be terminally destructive. We always have the choice between greed and the shrewd generosity of a man who learned how to be human and was honored for it.

In his suave dignity and handsomeness, King resembles the figure depicted in Jan Swart van Groningen's *John the Baptist Preaching* (ca. 1530) where the Bible tableau is presented with the preacher and the multitude in fine Dutch middle-class costume. Similarly, though he spoke of the upheaval of an unjust world, the 250,000 or more people Dr. King addressed on that day in Washington, D.C., were no enraged rabble but American people come to their nation's capital, on their best behavior, clad in their Sunday go-to-meeting clothes, citizens.

Keith D. Miller in *Voice of Deliverance: The Language of Martin Luther King, Jr. and Its Sources* (1992) identifies King's effective use of biblical allusion as "voice merging" and his discussion brings to mind similar techniques of quotation of musical motifs in African-American performance styles such as jazz; which, in turn, also suggests the spiritual "possession" of both the traditional black church in the South and earlier African religious ritual.

In King's most famous speech at the March on Washington in 1963 he alludes to Luke's gospel. "I have a dream," King intoned as he quoted Luke's citation of the prophet Isaiah. Added to this is King's own sly and dignified adaptation of the African-American rhetorical insult called "signifyin.'' In his ringing geographical litany even Georgia and Tennessee have mighty mountains from which King dreams freedom will ring, but bad old intransigent Mississippi is adorned with mere "hills and molehills."

As Miller points out, King's "expert application of biblical prophecy through folk preachers' techniques signified that God spoke through him.'' As millions of Americans—black and white—understood, rhetorical technique or not, King spoke the truth.

The Gospel According to John moves at the pace of a music video. The writer sums up the Creation in a few verses and fast-forwards to the announcement of Christ's coming in contrapuntal repetition and astonishingly mysterious imagery. Similarly, the changes in American society that seemed to swirl into the very air from King's oratory appeared dizzyingly rapid to many—but only because the brilliance of the figures often made listeners forget how long a time it had been coming.

In moments of frustration we would complain—as if every white man were his own George Washington or Edison or Charlton Heston—"the problem is black folks are always waiting for a leader.'' That's what we said when Martin was murdered; those were the words that pushed the tears away. Grief caused many to misread the age-old symbolic meaning of "the coming of John.'' We were forgetting in our stress, of course, what Frederick Douglass knew; that our mythology insisted that we were—collectively —the existential vanguard, fruit of the fruitful bough, the syncretized miscegenated Ephraims and Manassehs of the African peoples.

2.

Because my uncle Lloyd had his barbershop on New York Boulevard, the compass of my childhood world was enriched by our family's personal association with the local businessmen. At the northern edge, across the street from the barbershop, was Mr. Alves's office where he sold insurance and real estate and was a notary public. Then there was the candy store owned by Mr. Mendes and, southward, along the route we walked to school was the real estate office of Mrs. Welcome. She was a large and cheerful old woman who seemed to spend her business day watering the plants in her window and chatting at length with an endless parade of friendly nonclients.

I learned later that Mrs. Welcome and her husband, back in the 1920s, had been the first realtors to open the borough of Queens to African-American renters and home buyers and that they had used some of their profits and social prominence to support the politically aware, black nationalist magazine *The Colored Challenge.*

On the corner was Mr. Tolliver's unmentionable Crystal Casino tavern, which I thought quite fascinating simply because its very existence caused the grown-ups in my house to scowl and kiss their teeth.

For the first years of my life, I suppose I was a Catholic. My mother took us to St. Benedict the Moor's because, she said, in Panama she had herself grown up in the Catholic Church. But when Calvary Baptist Church completed its new edifice a block away from where we lived, that's where we went. My mother said she really was a Baptist, as her mother had been. My father, staunchly Episcopalian, attended neither of these churches (except occasionally for the whole family to be together doing the same thing today sort of thing) and took the subway all the way into Manhattan to St. Cyrian's early on Sunday mornings.

It was at Calvary, of course, that I was eventually baptized—somewhat embarrassed to be almost nude beneath the white baptismal gown, fearful that Reverend Pinn might lose his grip and I could drown. I attended Sunday School and church primarily because I was supposed to. In my early teens, like other boys my age, I learned to dawdle on my way upstairs so that I frequently was seated in the very last row of the balcony—as far away from the pulpit as possible. On summer Sundays I could lean toward the stained-glass casement window cranked open for air and distract myself from the sermon with the distant jubilation of the song rising from the Pentecostal church across the street where the congregation praised God with melodiously raucous voices, cymbals, and sometimes—amazingly—a trombone.

Reverend Walter S. Pinn was capable of preaching powerfully but he did not engage in extravagance; nor would his sedate, striving middle-class congregation have appreciated such a display. Our pastor was, appropriately, given to logical argument and sensible demonstrations of the relevance of the Bible to our lives. Sometimes a guest preacher from down South would bring an authentic ancient fire to the pulpit. I would, however, be more amused than awestruck by the notion of damned "sinners huh huh WAILING huh huh for Mercy! throughout ETERNITY! in their jail cells down in Hell!" The idea that earning the wrong afterlife was not much more terrible than a statistically possible fate in this life only inspired impish speculation: perhaps down there in hell's cellblock, Satan would only give harmonicas to the sinners who couldn't play.

In fact, the concept of eternal damnation didn't chill my soul until one afternoon, studying at the Schomburg Library in Harlem, I read the ancient Egyptian formulas of the Osirian judgment. In ancient Africa, it seems, those who had lived unworthy lives were weighed against the feather of righteousness and doomed to have the crocodiles digest their bones. In a cold sweat, I handed the book back to the librarian and headed home.

My father's pals were very busy men. Some of them had an extra part-time job or, like my dad, took night courses at Brooklyn College. Over glasses of scotch or rum on an occasional Saturday afternoon they would discuss old times in Panama or the latest events. Usually there was a lengthy and vigorous analysis of what the *New York Times* had seen fit to print—and why.

These men were not full-time intellectuals but their opinions always seemed to include a book or an article as reference point. And always, too, a personal anecdote about actual events that, to their appreciative and fascinated eavesdropper, apparently occurred in their own young lives in what seemed a distant century.

The Saturday afternoon Sanhedrin was never frequent but it was never less than charged with astonishing energy, laughter, and good-natured teasing, and dramatic moments when a single voice became urgent and oracular.

"What you do to-day that is worthwhile," wrote Garvey, "inspires others to act at some future time. Chance has never yet satisfied the hope of a suffering people. Action, self-reliance, the vision of self and the future have been the only means by which the oppressed have seen and realized the light of their own freedom." My father and his friends had read these words when they were first published, when they had been not much older than I was as I listened to them talk. I realized that every recollection had a reason, that every anecdote and joke was somehow an improvisation on that theme. Like a bebop quintet—five men who can actually hear a thousand melodies disguised within the silliness of "Sweet Georgia Brown" and actually play a dozen of them in three minutes—these men constructed worlds with words. Their talk, though only passing time, was full of dreams and possible realities somehow much more serious than the amusing and purposefully nonsensical debates that one could hear in Uncle Lloyd's barbershop.

There was, in other words, no way to grow up in my house without ambition.

We were not W. E. B. DuBois's "Talented Tenth," we were just ordinary people; but it was axiomatic among African-Americans in the 1950s that everyone's best efforts were required for the advancement of the race. That belief was such an intense and pervasive thing there was no need, really, to talk about it; which means, of course, that it was something we never stopped talking about.

I spent my introspective time before the mirror, massaging Murray's Day-Glo into my hair until the front rose above my forehead like one half of the Red Sea, with a flood of stiff curls gleaming behind it. Eager and egotistic, I saw myself in the mirror exactly as I was: too short, too smart, too boringly normal.

An extraordinary lady, Sylvia Friedlander, led me through Honors English and a thesis that required reading all of John Dos Passos. At the same time, I was being coaxed into acting as a speaker at youth meetings sponsored by the National Conference of Christians and Jews. The ladies on our street also seemed to find opportunities for me to come to their churches and recite something or other. I loved to read anyway and, thanks to Reverend Pinn and my Sunday School teachers, the language of King James and the somewhat less poetic Revised Standard Version was no puzzle to me. I approached the Bible as a great work of literature and even the scurrilous advertisements of the atheist proselytizer Joseph B———, who sold pamphlets that identified the "dirty parts," only quickened my appetite for reading the Good Book.

An ambitious kid, I spent much too much time, however, wondering what would become of my dreams.

3.

An echo of the wonderful psalm of the exile never fails to sadden my heart, when it is answered by the voice of one crying in the wilderness—Joseph's saga, for me, bridged the gap between public and personal exile.

In this *bildungsroman* we meet our hero first at seventeen when, due to his father Jacob's favoritism, symbolized by a special coat of many colors, he has earned the jealousy of his brothers. Eventually jealousy overrules sense and the brothers plot to kill Joseph and then settle for selling him into slavery, reporting to Jacob that the favorite son has been devoured by a wild beast. Transported to Egypt as a slave, Joseph eventually wins the favor of Pharaoh and rises to the office of a cabinet minister. When famine strikes the land it is to this Egyptian bureaucrat that Jacob's sons must appeal for aid. Joseph ennobles himself by not exacting revenge.

As with many folktales, the provenance of Joseph is complex and obscure. It pleased me to think of it as an African tale as much derived from Hebrew legend as from the ancient Egyptian "Tale of Two Brothers." It appealed to me also in its avoidance of the supernatural. I have never, in fact, heard or read a more powerful adventure story, nor one that was more tantalizingly resistant to a simplistic reading. To love the figure of Joseph as I do is, first of all, to admit to arrogance. To say that we are dealing with a modest arrogance that knows its limits still may not ameliorate the sin.

Reverend Samuel Sewall, a Puritan judge in *The Selling of Joseph* (1700), concerned himself with the legal illogic of slavery. For him, all men were sons of Adam regardless of race or nation and, as a practical man of morals, a shrewd New Englander with a conscience, Sewall warned the buyer of slaves to beware of trading in stolen goods:

> If Arabian Gold be imported in any quantities, most
> are afraid to meddle with it, though they might have it
> at easy rates; lest if it should have been wrongfully
> taken from the Owners, it should kindle a fire to the
> Consumption of their whole estate.

Reverend Sewall wondered why no such scruples attended the buying and selling of human beings.

" 'Tis pity," wrote Reverend Sewall, "there should be more Caution used in buying a Horse, or a little lifeless dust; than there is in purchasing Men and Women: Whereas they are the Offspring of God . . ."

It would not have surprised him that, in 1864, the African-American poet and preacher James Madison Bell saw the result of 240 years of bad karma in the Civil War:

> America! America!
> Thine own undoing thou hast wrought
> For all thy wrongs to Africa
> This cup has fallen to thy lot
> Whose dregs of bitterness shall last
> Till thou acknowledge God in man;
> Till thou undo thine iron grasp,
> And free thy brother and his clan.

To dwell upon Joseph and his secular success, to choose this Bible text above the many others that speak so beautifully of those who suffered because they loved the Lord, may be also to admit being unprepared to deal with that which is of ultimate importance. And it may be that evasion is the true theme of this story that so carefully, so relentlessly, explores the meaning of loyalty and duty.

The story of Joseph is emblematic neither of alienation nor assimilation but suggests that it is possible to avoid the snares set out by both. A grand drama of exile and ambition, Joseph was the story of one man and also the story of many people.

Today there are black urban neighborhoods that have been trapped in a cycle of famine upon famine for twice the seven years of Pharaoh's dream. The poetic voice arising from those places has forged its own mythology of ego, jealousy, and hatred that has in turn been alchemized by record companies into fortunes for their executives, flashy sports cars and empty mansions for the "stars."

Yet, as I grew up watching my parents, relatives, and their friends prosper in America, I knew that these men and women did not delude themselves that racial discrimination had not always decreed a limit to their achievements. Trying to understand Joseph, I began to understand them; and to unravel my own skein of resentments before it bound me. Everything is accomplished at some risk. Joseph is not Moses but a man who is faithful to his own conscience and responsible in the offices he accepts. I suspect that exacting a petty vengeance never really even crossed Joseph's mind.

If Joseph's story has not been as warmly embraced in the African-American consciousness as that of Moses or the psalmist's plaint by the rivers of Babylon, it is not difficult to understand why. The psalm of alienation is still relevant for too many of us while Joseph's successful progress in the world is something only the most recent African-American generation might actually achieve.

For that reason, if for no other, I would offer this great narrative to young men and women. I would rather even that they misread it and dream material dreams than that they go through life believing that the only song they have is one of sorrow.

Genesis and Revelation

H U G H K E N N E R

It's about sixty years since I read the first three chapters of Genesis on a January 1, to persist thereafter day by day clear to the end of the Bible, and arrive at the last three chapters of Revelation near the very end of December. A scheduler's rule of thumb is three chapters each weekday, five each Sunday; in a year that regimen would take you through 1,199 chapters, while by fortunate coincidence the 1611 King James Bible—Old and New Testaments, but minus the so-called Apocrypha—contains just under that number: 1,189. The fit is so neat a fundamentalist might be set to wondering if exactly ten chapters have maybe been mislaid.

One harvest of what I undertook (as an eager reader, moreover raised in a Bible-fearing family) has been a vivid sense of the Bible's encyclopedic variousness. Now and then a whole page is given over to the recital of some opaque list—

21 And the uttermost cities of the tribe of the children of Judah toward the coast of Edom southward were Kabzeel, and Eder, and Jagur,

22 And Kinah, and Dimonah, and Adadah,

23 And Kadesh, and Hazor, and Ithnan,

24 Ziph, and Telem, and Bealoth . . .

(JOSHUA 15)

Yet just a few pages later we're confronted by stark and vivid narrative—

19 And he said unto her, Give me, I pray thee, a little water to drink; for I am thirsty. And she opened a bottle of milk, and give him drink, and covered him.

20 And again he said unto her, Stand in the door of the tent, and it shall be, when any man doth come and inquire of thee, and say Is there any man here? thou shalt say, No.

21 Then Jael Heber's wife took a nail of the tent, and took a hammer in her hand, and went softly unto him, and smote the nail into his temples, and fastened it into the ground: for he was fast asleep and weary. So he died.

22 And behold, as Barak pursued Sisera, Jael came out to meet him, and said unto him, Come, and I will shew thee the man whom thou seekest. And when he came into her tent, behold, Sisera lay dead, and the nail was in his temples.

(JUDGES 4)

That sleek fellow, passing on his casual requests—"Thou shalt say, No"—
to the woman who in fifteen minutes will be driving a nail through his
skull!

One of my occupations in the ensuing six decades has been exploring the
categories: History of the world, history of the Jewish people, much cautionary rhetoric and much hopeful; numerous exemplary lives, much concern with inventory (ancestors, land allotments). The Bible is even, as I've
written elsewhere,[1] the *fons et origo* of the vast tradition of how-to, from
the Lord's specifications for the Ark (gopher wood, three interior stories,
one window, one door, dimensions 300 cubits by 50 by 30) all the way to
His layout of a post-Apocalypse City (12 gates, 12,000 furlongs square—
that's 144,000,000 square furlongs—a 144-cubit wall; what a mania for
dozens).

In its long domination of the mind of Europe, the Bible has been put
to use in every conceivable way. An odd instance is the big book John
Wilkins, D.D., F.R.S., published back in 1668. It is called *Essay Towards a
Real Character and a Philosophical Language,* such a language being a huge
taxonomic system, the kind Adam had registered when his prelapsarian
insight accorded the animals such (surely!) ordered names as the Babel-
babblers would replace by the jumble we've inherited. (Cat, tiger, lynx:
those words encode no trace of any family relationship. Adam surely did
better, and so must we.) Wilkins needed to be sure he knew how many
species of animals there were, lest his system get wrecked by a novelty
some explorer might fetch back from Africa. But God, who'd created the
animals, had also dictated the layout of the Ark, which would hold them by
pairs for the postdiluvian replenishment. So Wilkins had only to show, as
he did with a pull-out diagram based on a frenzy of calculations, how
twenty species of carnivores (and the 1,825 sheep that will feed them for a

year), plus twenty-six kinds of herbivores and their year's hay, plus the Noah family and the birds and the pots and pans, will all fit exactly into a three-storied Ark of the specified dimensions.[2] Thus a taxonomy can be guaranteed thanks to one of the few things humans know for sure, that, God being incapable of self-contradiction, the Word of God is internally consistent.

God's amanuenses too were clearly aware that the Book of the Word on which they were engaged would but mirror the coherences of the Book of the World. A familiar instance is Matthew's attention to such symmetries as the three sets of fourteen generations (Abraham to David, David to the Babylonian captivity, the captivity to Jesus), or to such correspondences as that between the return of the Holy Family from Egypt and an otherwise mysterious saying Hosea ascribes to Jehovah: "Out of Egypt have I called my son." What Hosea said has now been fulfilled. Fully sixteen times Matthew has recourse to that word "fulfilled"; as, for example,

> 22 Now all this was done that it might be fulfilled
> which was spoken of the Lord by the prophet, saying,
> 23 Behold, a virgin shall be with child . . .
>
> *(MATTHEW 1)*

Indeed, the prophet Isaiah did say that. (Isaiah 7:14) For Matthew is helping write the second part of a Sacred Book, a Book moreover possessed by a forward-moving and linear sense of time: by an arrow pointing from Creation to Apocalypse. As Walter J. Ong has repeatedly asserted, much literary time follows Greek time in being circular, on the model of a Year renewed each spring. "The world's Great Age begins anew, The Golden Years return." Or they *may* return, or may return diminished, or we may *hope* for their return. But Scriptural (hence Jewish) time is going some-where. True, there's more than a hint of circularity in the Old Testament, the needle stuck in that jagged, nagging groove of exile, over and over exile, if not from our land then from God's favor (since I the Lord thy God am a jealous God, and by gum you'll slip and I'll by gum take suitable action). Yet, "No lion," says Isaiah, "shall be there, nor any ravenous beast shall go up thereon"; that's a future dominated by hopefulness. Moreover it's not something to be returned to; not a long-ago past, no, a forward neon novelty. When the lion and the fatling at last lie down together—that fatling, so often misremembered as a lamb—then *progress* is what Isaiah is saying we'll behold. And progress means a replacement of the past, a discarding of some of its trammels.

It's the forward movement that ensures the Bible's great symmetry, Genesis at last repeated and enhanced by Revelation. (And the Book is symmetrical as Experience is not, Revelation's symmetrizing events having, as of today, not happened save on the page.) "Behold, he cometh with clouds" (Revelation 1:7): that's a text asking for multiple inscription. Those clouds obscure our perception as long as He hasn't yet come. (Jewish time moves forward too, as much as Christian; it differs only in not assuming the Messiah has come. It still asserts there *will be* a Messiah.)

I've had no need to return to the Bible, because I've not been parted from it, ever. So I can't illustrate any then-and-now illumination. I can affirm, though, that my long life as a writer about the innovative literature of our century has been enabled at every step by familiarity with the Bible. The writers I've dealt with, from the generation of Joyce and Pound, born in the 1880s, to that of Bunting and Beckett, born in the 1900s, had all of them one thing in common: thorough familiarity with a Christian tradition, whether they regarded themselves as part of it or not. Something already underway in the 1880s was the slow shifting of the Bible from fact to metaphor, or even just to "literature," as the *Origin of Species* supplanted Genesis, and Archbishop Ussher's chronology, which assigned Creation to 4004 B.C., was crumpled by the prospect of geologic aeons. Accordingly, writers brought up Christian—Joyce, Pound, Eliot—tended to think of a masterwork as some encyclopedic Sacred Book, hence *Ulysses* and the *Cantos*.

Hence too a poetic *oeuvre;* for the Bible is the supreme instance of a totality assembled over many years. So W. B. Yeats, who would talk explicitly of a Sacred Book of the Arts, designed his poetic works to culminate in an Apocalypse amid which we hear him speaking from beyond the grave. And Joyce, though he rejected the Bible's linear time for a circular version (Bloom reenacts the career of Ulysses, and *Finnegans Wake* begins in mid-sentence because in mid-cycle), saw in Israelite exile a prototype of Irish experience, and made *Ulysses* seem to have been written by numerous hands, something scholarship had come to suspect was true of "Homer," as it has been always manifestly true of the Bible.

That I didn't have the usual troubles with Pound's *Cantos* is one boon I attribute to biblical experience. The usual troubles? Well, it's a wild mixture (isn't it?) of genres, a miscellany, a ragbag—revery, narrative, didacticism, denunciation. . . . As, for that matter, is the Old Testament on which it's partly modeled. You can't miss, surely, the sudden voice of a King James Version prophet as one of the pivotal Cantos, XLV, opens:

> With usura hath no man a house of good stone
> each block cut smooth and well fitting
> that design might cover their face, . . .
> with usura, sin against nature,
> is thy bread ever more of stale rags
> is thy bread dry as paper, . . .

For Pound grew up in a Bible-centered Protestant world. And (he once told me) in the Detention Camp in Pisa, 1946, he'd found a Gideon Bible and, for the first time, read it straight through, the only person, he guessed, to have done that *after* having read Confucius. (For Confucius was made known to the West thanks to Jesuits who'd read the Bible first and tended to judge him a tad naive.)

So in the first Pisan Canto, XLIV, a bare one-line reference sends us to First Thessalonians 4:11, where we find "And that ye study to be quiet, and to do your own business, and to work with your own hands . . ." That's not only Confucian, it's to be correlated with the small-scale economy so many of Pound's fiscal concerns postulate. I could multiply such instances. The habits of study Comp Lit professors impressed on him just after the turn of the century were derived from biblical study. It was from the Bible that a whole tradition of scholarship learned how to examine remote and difficult texts, such as the *Divina Commedia,* the *Odyssey,* the crabbed manuscripts left by scribes who'd listened to troubadours. And a pupil of such scholars was responsible for the *Cantos.*

And another Bible-centered American was the man responsible for *The Waste Land* (". . . I will show you fear in a handful of dust"). Eliot's route, from proper Unitarianism through a kind of smug detachment that saw a hippopotamus washed in Blood of the Lamb "While the True Church remains below / Wrapt in the old miasmal mist," to the fervid orthodoxy of *Ash Wednesday* and *Little Gidding,* has often been traced, and often by readers who wish he'd kept his 1920 distance from the True Church. Insofar as such a wish alienates them from the man they'd expound, I'm glad not to share it. And I'll gladly point out a model for the 1935 *Collected Poems,* namely the Bible.

The Yeatsian Sacred Book tradition, first of all; though Yeats claimed revelatory splendors Eliot would have eschewed. But Eliot saw his *Collected Poems* structured by poem answering to poem, in particular Anglican poem responding to pre-Anglican, "A Song for Simeon" to "Gerontion," *Ash Wednesday* to *The Hollow Men.* And the model is not far to seek; we need only look to St. Matthew, where again and again an A.D. event "fulfills" one from B.C. Eliot makes this kind of relationship especially plain in a passage from "Journey of the Magi":

> Then at dawn we came down to a temperate valley,
> Wet, below the snow line, smelling of vegetation,
> With a running stream and a water-mill beating the
> darkness
> And three trees on the low sky,
> And an old white horse galloped away in the
> meadow.
> Then we came to a tavern with vine-leaves over the
> lintel,
> Six hands at an open door dicing for pieces of
> silver,
> And feet kicking the empty wine-skins. . . .

A time will come when the "three trees" will be crosses, the "vine-leaves" will point to John 15:1 ("I am the true vine"), the dicing hands to Matthew 27:35 ("they . . . parted his garments, casting lots," which in turn remembers Psalm 22:18, "They part my garments among them, and cast lots upon my vesture"), the pieces of silver of course to Matthew 27, where Judas is paid thirty of them and hangs himself. In the time of the Magi, though, these are all neutral signifiers, only later to accrete weight. Eliot modeled the relationship of late poems to early on a similar pattern. Prufrock will one day grow into the "I" of *Four Quartets*.

I grew up a Presbyterian / Methodist Protestant. I have been for thirty years a Catholic convert. Catholicism's emphasis on the Bible is less—the Book is deemed indispensible but auxiliary testimony—and its tolerance for the King James Version is rather slight. I can't guess how often I've been warned away from that, by mentors who've possibly never looked at it. They're likely repeating a seminary cliché. I even wonder too how many priests have done something I once did: read the Bible clear through in *any* version. Current Catholic liturgy prescribes a three-year cycle of readings, which even so offers but a fraction of the Book. No, we don't need to hear at Sunday Mass about those names of Israeli cities, "Kinah, and Dimonah, and Adadah . . ." But what I do miss, as we progress through the liturgical year, is any sense of that vast time-scheme, Creation to Re-creation (Apocalypse). What gets read is structured by the liturgical calendar, gospel glimpses of the life of Jesus from Advent (December) to Resurrection (April), with, each Mass, a cognate fragment from one epistle and one prophecy. (And from April through to December? A long stretch of teachings and reflections.)

Missing something—yes—I now simply read the Bible more widely, more remotely. A discovery, some years back, was the Ronald A. Knox translation. The Right Reverend Monsignor Knox (1888–1957) had commenced in 1939 to translate the Book single-handed from the (Catholic-authorized) Latin Vulgate into clean English. Like me, he was a Catholic convert; his father had been Anglican bishop of Manchester. Unlike me, he had siblings, diverse and talented; a brother, E. V. Knox, had even been editor of *Punch* back when *Punch* spoke, if obliquely, for, ah, civilization. He was accustomed to bringing ingenuity to bear. A key anecdote has Ronald Knox, in a train, staring at a crossword puzzle—a British one, than which none more fiendish—till another passenger offered him a pencil. No thank you, was his response, I've just finished it.

Is it a paraphrase, asked Ronald Knox, when you translate *"Comment vous portez-vous?"* by "How are you?" Yet if God had authorized *"Comment vous portez-vous?"* literalists were not lacking who would have thundered at anything less than "How do you carry yourself?" Yes, there are strange things indeed in the King James Bible. A favorite example of Knox's was Amos 4:3. "And ye shall go out at the breeches, every cow at that which is before her; and ye shall cast them into the palace, saith the Lord." Knox's version was "Leave the city walls you must, the Lord says, one by this breach, one by that, and be cast away in Armon." That's close to what we find in St. Jerome's Vulgate *("Et per aperturas exibitis altera contra alteram, et proicemini in Armon, dicit Dominus")*. So at what Hebrew was St. Jerome looking, as *(ut pinxit Carpaccio)* his fluffy dog grinned on the rug? And what on earth was the text the King James committee had been wrestling with?

Versions: manuscripts: chaos. Life is short. It's understandable that Catholicism has simply endorsed the Douay's English and its Vulgate (Latin) original, quite as Anglicanism endorsed the Authorized Version, "Translated out of the Original Tongues," moreover "Appointed to be Read in Churches." Why the Knox version (published 1955) was never endorsed by his bishops is a theme in Ecclesiastical Politics. (It was approved "for private use.") Evelyn Waugh's 1959 biography sets forth many pertinent facts, notably that a large segment of the R.C. hierarchy didn't want a retranslation from scratch: no, simply what they were used to, albeit retouched gently. Some of them kicked and screamed. When he was working on the New Testament, 1939–ff., a six-man review committee almost brought him to a halt till its most recalcitrant member, a Jesuit named Father Martindale, got trapped in Denmark by the German invasion and was held incommunicado for the rest of the war. "Without him," remarks Waugh, "the committee worked smoothly. It seldom met."

So here's the King James version of a dialogue that boded no good for Job:

6 Now there was a day when the sons of God came to present themselves before the Lord, and Satan came also among them.

7 And the Lord said unto Satan, Whence comest thou? Then Satan answered the Lord, and said, From going to and fro in the earth, and from walking up and down in it.

(JOB 1:6—7)

Yes, yes, Appointed to be Read in Churches, notably churches plagued by a heavy echo. That Satan? He's but one more of those read-aloud voices. But here is Knox, with a truly Byronic Satan:

One day, when the heavenly powers stood waiting upon the Lord's presence, and among them, man's Enemy, the Lord asked him, where he had been? Roaming about the earth, said he, to and fro about the earth.

That's even almost word-for-word close to the Vulgate: *"Circuivi terram et perambulavi eam."* Though a Cicero would have arranged the Latin more tightly, and Knox improves on it, repeating *"terram"* rather than plugging in a pronoun. Knox also captures a certain rakish air of disregard, hinted at by the Vulgate's elegant variation, *"Circuivi," "perambulavi."* Yes, to and fro about the earth, ho hum, and it's not, to my mind, worth the forethought its inhabitants expend. A Dark Angel, I can knock it askew in one minute. Yes, yes, "To and fro about the earth." And just watch what I'll be doing to this Job of yours.

Some talents are distributed to siblings, and it's worth remembering that Ronald Knox's brother the *Punch* editor, on discarding a shaving brush wrote it a commemorative ode in the idiom of Swinburne, the whole addressed to the Badger with whose hair he had long lathered his jowls:

> And now the thing moults; I must buy another.
> Yet for the sake of many a happy morn
> I praise the dumb friend out of whom 'twas torn,
> Nor aught of what wild kisses went to smother
> Th' unprofitable harvest of the night
> Shall fade from my remembrance. . . .

Ronald Arbuthnot Knox could be similarly resourceful, in the narrow place where he worked to replace the limp Douay, a committee of bishops watching and often clucking. His Jonah (Jonas) is a testy pukka sahib in his garden complaining to a Lord who's not spared his ivy plant, whereto the Lord slyly responds, "And may I not spare Nineve?"

Discoveries, those continue to await. Did you know, by the way, that the Cretan Liar beloved of logicians ("All Cretans are liars, said the man from Crete") is ensconced in St. Paul's Epistle to Titus?

> 12 One of themselves, even a prophet of their own, said, The Cretans are always liars, evil beasts, slow bellies.
>
> (*TITUS 1*)

Some sources call that an allusion to the sage Epimenides (sixth century B.C.); other sources are tactfully silent, maybe wondering how St. Paul, formerly a fierce bureaucrat named Saul, might have heard of Epimenides. Did he maybe just hear, in the way of bureaucrats, that a Cretan said

Cretans lied? On the other hand there's learned speculation as to whether, in Tarsus, he might have had something like "Hellenic culture up to the level of a man of liberal education." A deskman? A Yaleman? Me, on this point, at present, I'm agnostic.

Notes

1. In the March 1984 *Harper's*, reprinted in my 1989 collection *Mazes* as "The Wherefores of How-To."

2. First, Wilkins had to wrestle with the meaning of "cubit." The *Aegyptian Geometrical cubit* of 9 feet, proposed by Origen and Augustine to ensure a capacious Ark, must be rejected because elsewhere in the Bible (I Samuel 17) it would specify a 54-foot Goliath with a head "too heavy for *David* to carry." So, okay, we're meant to make do with a smaller cubit, hence a smaller Ark.

Author Biographies

BRADFORD MORROW's novels include *Trinity Fields* (Viking, 1995) and *The Almanac Branch* (Penguin, 1996). *The Almanac Branch* won the PEN/Faulkner Award for Fiction. Morrow is the editor of *Conjunctions,* the literary journal, and lives in New York City.

JAYNE ANNE PHILLIPS's most recent novel is *Shelter* (Houghton Mifflin, 1994). Among her other books are *Black Tickets* (1979) and *Machine Dreams* (1984). She lives in Newton, Massachusetts.

VALERIE SAYERS's novels include *Due East* (1987), *How I Got Him Back* (1989), *Who Do You Love* (1991), and her most recent novel, *The Distance Between Us* (1994), all of which were published by Doubleday. She lives in South Bend, Indiana.

Author Biographies

JAMES CARROLL's many novels include *Mortal Friends* (1978), *Fault Lines* (1980), *Prince of Peace* (1984), *Memorial Bridge* (1991), and *The City Below* (Houghton Mifflin, 1994). He lives in Boston.

JOHN BARTH's eleven volumes of fiction include the National Book Award–winning novella series, *Chimera*. Barth has also published two collections of essays among his other works of nonfiction, including *The Friday Book* and *Further Fridays*. He lives in Baltimore.

CATHERINE TEXIER is the author of *Love Is Strange* (Norton, 1993), a book of stories, and *Love Me Tender* and *Panic Blood* (Viking/Penguin, 1990), both novels. She recently completed her fourth novel, *The Ritual*. She is co-editor of the fiction anthology *Between C & D* (Penguin, 1988), and has lived in New York City since 1981.

BHARATI MUKHERJEE's fiction includes the novel *Jasmine* (Grove Weidenfeld, 1989), and *The Middleman and Other Stories,* which won the National Book Critics Circle Award in 1988. She is the coauthor, with her husband, Clark Blaise, of *The Sorrow and the Terror* (1988). She resides in Berkeley, California, and Iowa City.

CLARK BLAISE's novels include *Resident Aliens* (Viking, 1986). His nonfiction includes *Days and Nights in Calcutta* (1977), a memoir in collaboration with his wife, Bharati Mukherjee. He resides in Iowa City.

MARY GAITSKILL's books include *Bad Behavior* (Vintage, 1989), a book of stories, and *Two Girls, Fat and Thin* (Bantam, 1992), a novel. She lives in San Francisco.

JAMES McCOURT's books include the novel *Time Remaining* (Knopf, 1993) and the book of stories *Avenged* (Penguin, 1985). He lives in New York City.

MARILYNNE ROBINSON's novels and books of stories include *Housekeeping* and *Mother Country*. She lives in Iowa City.

RICHARD BAUSCH is the author of *Rare and Endangered Species* (stories, Vintage, 1995). In 1994 Vintage reprinted two of his novels, *The Last Good Time* and *Rebel Powers*. His books of stories include *The Fireman's Wife* (Simon & Schuster, 1990) and *Spirits* (Penguin, 1988). Among other novels is *Mr. Field's Daughter* (Simon & Schuster, 1989). He lives in Broad Run, Virginia.

LAURA FURMAN's novels include *The Shadow Line* and *Tuxedo Park*. She has published books of stories that include *The Glass House* and *Watch Time Fly*, both from Vintage. *American Short Fiction* is a literary magazine she founded and edits. She lives in Austin, Texas.

MAUREEN HOWARD's many books of short fiction and novels include *Before My Time* (1974), *Facts of Life* (1978), *Grace Abounding* (1982), *Expensive Habits* (1986), and *Natural History* (Norton, 1992). She lives in New York City.

ROBERT FLYNN's novels include *In the House of the Lord, North to Yesterday*, and *The Sounds of Rescue*—all from Knopf. His most recent book is *The Last Klick* (Baskerville, 1994). He directs the Writing Program at Trinity University in San Antonio.

LES STANDIFORD's novels include *Done Deal* and its sequels *Raw Deal* and *Deal to Die For*, among other books of fiction—all are published by

HarperCollins. His novel *Spill* is being made into a movie by Twentieth Century Fox. He lives in Miami.

DAVID BRADLEY's novel *The Chaneysville Incident* (Dutton, 1981) won the PEN/Faulkner Award for Best Novel. *South Street* was his first novel. He lives in Philadelphia and La Jolla, California.

JOYCE CAROL OATES is most recently the author of the novel *Zombie* (Dutton). Among her many novels and books of stories are *Black Water* and *What I Lived For*. She lives in Princeton, New Jersey, with her husband, Raymond Smith, editor of *The Ontario Review*.

ROBERT COLES's books include the Children of Crisis series and The Inner Lives of Children series, including *The Spiritual Life of Children*. He has written biographies and literary studies as well, including a biography of the poet William Carlos Williams and a biography of the psychoanalyst Anna Freud. He lives in Cambridge, Massachusetts.

KATHLEEN NORRIS is the author of *Dakota: A Spiritual Geography* (Houghton Mifflin, 1993) and two books of poems. She lives in Lemmon, South Dakota.

PETER SCHJELDAHL's selected essays are in *The Hydrogen Jukebox* (University of California Press, 1993). His books of poems include *An Adventure of the Thought Police*. He is the art and cultural critic for *The Village Voice,* and is the former art and film critic of *The New York Times*. He lives in New York City.

ELIZABETH HARDWICK was born in Lexington, Kentucky. Among her three novels is *Sleepless Nights*, and among several volumes of literary criticism is *Seduction and Betrayal* (Random House, 1990). She was a founder of *The New York Review of Books* and lives in New York City.

SCOTT RUSSELL SANDERS is author of *The Paradise of Bombs* and *Staying Put* (Beacon, 1993), prize-winning books of essays, and *Writing from the Center* (University of Indiana, 1995). He has also published several works of fiction. He lives in Bloomington, Indiana.

MICHAEL DORRIS's books of fiction include *A Yellow Raft in Blue Water, Working Men,* and, with his wife Louise Erdrich, *The Crown of Columbus* (HarperCollins). His nonfiction includes *The Broken Cord* and *Paper Trail.* He lives in New Hampshire.

TERRY TEMPEST WILLIAMS is the author of the memoir *Refuge* (Pantheon, 1992) and *An Unspoken Hunger: Stories from the Field* (Vintage, 1995). She is writer-in-residence at the Utah Museum of Natural History in Salt Lake City.

BILL McKIBBEN's most recent book is *Hope, Human and Wild: True Stories of Living Lightly on the Earth* (Little, Brown, 1995). He is also the author of *The End of Nature* (Anchor, 1990). He lives in the Adirondack Mountains with his wife, the writer Sue Halpern.

HELEN VENDLER is a leading critic of poetry in English, and has recently completed a commentary on Shakespeare's *Sonnets.* She is the author of books on Yeats, Stevens, Herbert, and Keats, and several volumes of essays, including *Part of Nature, Part of Us, The Music of What Happens,* and, most recently, *Soul Says*—all from Harvard University Press. She has edited anthologies of poetry in the twentieth century and writes for *The New Yorker* and the *New York Review of Books,* among other journals. She lives in Cambridge, Massachusetts.

ALFRED CORN's most recent of six books of poems is *Autobiographies* (Viking/Penguin, 1992). He has also published a volume of essays, *The Metamorphoses of Metaphor,* and is the editor of *Incarnation: Contemporary Writers on the New Testament.* He lives in New York City.

JOY HARJO's books of poetry include *Secrets from the Center of the World* and *The Woman Who Fell from the Sky* (Norton, 1994). She is the editor of *Reinventing the Enemy's Language,* an anthology of Native American women's writing, as well as a memoir, *A Love Supreme.* She has recorded with her band, Poetic Justice, in Albuquerque.

TOM CLARK's books of poetry include *Stones* (Harper) and *When Things Get Tough on Easy Street, Paradise Resisted,* and *Disordered Ideas*—all from Black Sparrow Press. He has written biographies of Celine, Damon Runyon, and *Charles Olson: The Allegory of a Poet's Life* (Norton, 1991). The former poetry editor of *The Paris Review,* he lives in Berkeley, California.

ANN LAUTERBACH is a MacArthur Prize Fellow. Her books of poetry include *And for Example* (1994), *Clamor,* and *Before Recollection*—all from Viking/Penguin. She lives in New York City.

LAWRENCE JOSEPH's books of poetry include *Curriculum Vitae* and *Before Our Eyes* (Farrar, Straus & Giroux, 1993). His critical essays appear in *Paris Review, The Nation,* and *The Village Voice.* He is the first professor of law inducted into the American Academy of Poets. He lives in New York City.

DENISE LEVERTOV's most recent book is the memoir *Tessarae* (New Directions, 1995). A new book of poems, to appear in 1996, follows the many volumes that include *With Eyes at the Back of Our Heads* and *Jacob's Ladder.* She lives in Seattle.

ROBERT POLITO is most recently the author of *Savage Art: A Biography of Jim Thompson* (Knopf, 1995) and of the book of poems *Doubles* (University of Chicago Press, 1995). He is director of the writing program at New York's New School for Social Research.

LORENZO THOMAS's books of poetry include *Chances Are Few* (Blue Wind, 1979) and *The Bathers* (Reed & Cannon, 1981). He is a noted authority on African cultures and the history of blues music. He lives in Houston.

HUGH KENNER's books include *The Pound Era* (1971), *Joyce's Voices* (1978), *A Reader's Guide to Samuel Beckett* (1973), *A Homemade World: The American Modernist Writers* (1974), *A Sinking Island: The Modern English Writers* (1987), and two recently reprinted volumes of essays, *Mazes* (Knopf) and *Historical Fictions*. One of the major literary critics of the century, he also writes a column on computer frontiers for several magazines. He lives in Athens, Georgia.

About the Editor

David Rosenberg is a writer, poet, translator, and scholar whose work has been universally praised. Winner of the 1992 PEN/Book-of-the-Month Club Prize for *A Poet's Bible,* and coauthor of the bestselling *The Book of J* (with Harold Bloom), he has recently completed *The Book of S: Companion to J.* He has also edited a number of well-received serious literary collections. His first collection, *Congregation: Contemporary Writers Read the Jewish Bible,* has been in print for nearly ten years and is a classic in its field. He and his wife, the writer Rhonda Rosenberg, divide their time between New York City and Miami.